Regionalism and Human Protection

Regionalism and Human Protection

Reflections from Southeast Asia and Africa

Edited by

Charles T. Hunt
Noel M. Morada

BRILL
NIJHOFF

LEIDEN | BOSTON

Originally published, in part, as Volume 8, No. 2-3 (2016) of Brill's journal *Global Responsibility to Protect.*

Cover illustrations: Top: Ghanaian police officer Mary Sebastian of the African Union-United Nations Hybrid Operation in Darfur (UNAMID) with school children at the El Sereif camp for internally displaced persons (IDPs), located west of Nyala, South Darfur. 28 May 2014 - Nyala, Sudan. (Photo credits: UN Photo/ Albert González Farran). Bottom: Security Council Members Visit Rohingya Refugee Camp in Bangladesh 29 April 2018 - Cox's Bazar, Bangladesh (Photo Credits: UN Photo/Caroline Gluck).

Library of Congress Control Number: 2018962052

Typeface for the Latin, Greek, and Cyrillic scripts: "Brill". See and download: brill.com/brill-typeface.

ISBN 978-90-04-36320-5 (paperback)
ISBN 978-90-04-36321-2 (e-book)

This book is printed on acid-free paper and produced in a sustainable manner.

Contents

Acknowledgements

The editors would like to thank the Australian Government, Department of Foreign Affairs and Trade, for supporting the Southeast Asia-Africa dialogue in Bangkok in 2014 as part of the activities of the *Asia Pacific Centre for the Responsibility to Protect* [DFAT Agreement 71895]. We are also grateful to all those who participated in the event and the authors of the contributions to this volume. We would like to extend special thanks to Dr Pranee Thiparat of the Department of International Relations, Chulalongkorn University, and Thai country program coordinator of the *Asia Pacific Centre for the Responsibility to Protect*, for her assistance in ensuring the success of the workshop in Bangkok. Thanks are also due to the editorial team at Brill including Anna Schmitt Nagelbach and Geli Mademli.

Notes on Contributors

Alex J. Bellamy
is Professor of Peace and Conflict Studies and Director of the Asia Pacific Centre for the Responsibility to Protect at The University of Queensland, Australia. He is also Fellow of the Academy of Social Sciences in Australia and non-resident Senior Advisor at the International Peace Institute, New York.

Chukwuemeka Eze
is the Executive Director of the West Africa Network for Peacebuilding. He is the lead interface between WANEP and ECOWAS through an MOU for the implementation of the ECOWAS Early Warning Mechanism. Between November 2016 and May 2017, he served as Senior Adviser on Mediation and Political Dialogue to the Special Representative of the UN Secretary General in Guinea Bissau. Eze has 20 years' experience in peacebuilding, political dialogue, early warning and conflict assessment.

Charles T. Hunt
is Vice-Chancellor's Senior Research Fellow and ARC DECRA Fellow at the Social & Global Studies Centre in the School of Global, Urban and Social Studies at RMIT University, Melbourne, and an Honorary Research Fellow at the Asia Pacific Centre for the Responsibility to Protect, University of Queensland, Brisbane, Australia. He is author or editor of five books on issues of peace, conflict and human protection, including: *UN Peace Operations and International Policing* (Routledge, 2015).

Obinna Franklin Ifediora
is a PhD student at the Asia Pacific Centre for the Responsibility to Protect (AP R2P), School of Political Science and International Studies, University of Queensland. His research focuses on the bases of implementing the Responsibility to Protect in Africa. His earlier publications on the Responsibility to Protect includes 'The Structural Bases of Implementing the Responsibility to Protect in Africa: Towards Advancing the African Governance Architecture', *African Conflict and Peacebuilding Review* (University of Indiana Press).

Noel M. Morada
is Director for Regional Diplomacy and Capacity Building at the Asia Pacific Centre for the Responsibility to Protect, School of Political Science and International Studies, The University of Queensland St. Lucia, Brisbane, Australia. His research and publications focus on human security issues in Southeast Asia and ASEAN regionalism.

Tim Murithi
is Extraordinary Professor of African Studies, Centre for African Studies, University of the Free State, South Africa and editor of *Routledge Handbook of Africa's International Relations*.

Phil Orchard
is an Associate Professor of International Relations at the University of Wollongong and a Senior Research Fellow at the Asia-Pacific Centre for the Responsibility to Protect. His research focuses on international efforts to provide legal and institutional protections to forced migrants and war-affected civilians. He is the author of *A Right to Flee: Refugees, States, and the Construction of International Cooperation* (Cambridge University Press, 2014), which won the 2016 International Studies Association Ethnicity, Nationalism, and Migration Studies Section Distinguished Book Award, and the forthcoming book *Protecting the Internally Displaced: Rhetoric and Reality* (Routledge, 2018). He is also the co-editor, with Alexander Betts, of *Implementation in World Politics: How Norms Change Practice* (Oxford University Press, 2014).

Sriprapha Petcharamesree
is currently a full time faculty member at the Institute of Human Rights and Peace Studies, Mahidol University, Thailand. She was appointed by the Thai Government as the Thai Representative to the asean Inter Governmental Commission on Human Rights (AICHR) from October 2009 till December 2012 when she decided not to continue for the second term. Also as a human rights advocate, she has been engaging with civil society groups in the region to push for the setting up of the effective asean human rights mechanisms. She is co-chairing the Working Group for an ASEAN Human Rights Mechanism since 2013.

Maria Tanyag
is a Postdoctoral Research Fellow at the Monash University's Centre for Gender, Peace and Security, Australia.

Ma. Lourdes Veneracion-Rallonza
is an Assistant Professor at the Department of Political Science, Ateneo de Manila University, Philippines.

Introduction

Regionalism and Human Protection: Reflections from Southeast Asia and Africa

Charles T. Hunt and Noel M. Morada

Regional arrangements, programs and capacities are critical to addressing human protection challenges in the current global order.[1] The regions of Southeast Asia and Africa have both experienced mass atrocity crimes in recent times.[2] In response, both regions have developed innovative societal and institutional capacities aimed at preventing and responding to the commission of mass atrocity crimes and other large-scale human rights abuses.[3] Region-to-region exchange between Southeast Asia and Africa has continued since the Bandung conference of 1955,[4] and this type of south-south cooperation is resurgent in global politics.[5] Dialogue between regions of the global south offers an important avenue for sharing experiences and creating opportunities for learning from other contexts that have significant similarities as well as differences.[6]

This volume is the product of a Southeast Asia-Africa Dialogue held in Bangkok organized by the Asia Pacific Centre for the Responsibility to Protect and the Department of International Relations at Chulalongkorn University. The dialogue was part of the Centre's initiative on South-South exchange among scholars, practitioners and civil society advocates from the two regions.

---

1 Amitav Acharya, 'The Emerging Regional Architecture of World Politics', *World Politics*, 59/4: 629–652 (2007).

2 Deborah Mayersen and Annie Pohlman. *Genocide and Mass Atrocities in Asia: Legacies and Prevention* (Abingdon: Routledge, 2013); Timothy J. Stapleton, *A History of Genocide in Africa* (Santa Barbara, CA: Praeger, 2017)

3 Dan Kuwali and Frans Viljoen, eds. *Africa and the Responsibility to Protect: Article 4(h) of the African Union Constitutive Act.* (Oxford: Routledge, 2013); Alex J. Bellamy, *East Asia's Other Miracle: Explaining the Decline of Mass Atrocities* (Oxford University Press, 2017): 142–160.

4 Andrew Phillips, 'Beyond Bandung: the 1955 Asian-African Conference and its legacies for international order', *Australian Journal of International Affairs*, 70/4: 329–341 (2016); Amitav Acharya, 'Studying the Bandung conference from a Global IR perspective', *Australian Journal of International Affairs* 70/4: 342–357 (2016).

5 Branislav Gosovic, 'The resurgence of South–South cooperation', *Third World Quarterly*, 37/4: 733–743 (2016).

6 Kevin Gray and Barry K. Gills, 'South–South cooperation and the rise of the Global South', *Third World Quarterly*, 37/4: 557–574 (2016).

 | DOI:10.1163/9789004363212_002

The book has three main objectives. The first is to create a space for dialogue and exchange of ideas among scholars, civil society representatives, and practitioners on the current state, dynamics, and challenges in norm promotion and capacity building in human rights, mass atrocities prevention, and civilian protection in Southeast Asia and Africa. The second is to identify the challenges and opportunities confronting regional institutions or frameworks such as the Association of Southeast Asian Nations (ASEAN) and the African Union (AU) or sub-regional arrangements in implementing human protection norms. Third, the pages of this book are intended to highlight the roles played by various stakeholders in building the capacity of states and regional arrangements in these regions to prevent and respond to human protection issues.

The contributors to this volume are from academe and civil society, some of whom have been or continue to be engaged in norm promotion and capacity building in Southeast Asia and Africa. Chapters provide a detailed examination of how norms concerning human rights, civilian protection and prevention of mass atrocities have fared, investigating their expression in regional organisations and thematic policy agendas as well as the role of civil society. The insights and analyses of the challenges and opportunities faced by states and societies in the two regions on human protection contribute to building knowledge and nuanced understanding of the dynamics of translating principles and norms on human rights protection and the Responsibility to Protect (R2P), for example, into practice.

The first set of chapters in this book focus on Southeast Asia. Noel M. Morada's overview of ASEAN regionalism examines the evolution and milestones of the regional organisation. He looks into efforts by ASEAN to transform itself from a primarily state-centric inter-governmental body to one that is more open to people-oriented principles and participatory regionalism. The Asian financial crisis in 1997 that led to democratic transitions in some ASEAN member states such as Indonesia and Thailand was a critical factor that forced ASEAN to examine its traditional norms on sovereignty and non-interference, which eventually ushered in the idea of building an ASEAN Community based on the principles of democracy, human rights and good governance. The adoption of the ASEAN Charter in 2008 subsequently brought about the creation of ASEAN mechanisms for promoting human rights protection (AICHR), protection of women and children (ACWC), as well as peace and reconciliation (AIPR). His chapter argues that although ASEAN has not formally adopted the language of the R2P in its relevant documents, there are certain elements of the principle that have been incorporated by ASEAN in its norm promotion such as comprehensive security and human security, human rights protection, peacebuilding, protection of women and children, among others. Morada contends that the main challenge for ASEAN in advancing human protection in the region is the willingness and commitment of its member states to implementing these norms at home. The inter-governmental nature of ASEAN regionalism and the continuing tension among member states with regard to upholding universal and relativist principles on human rights, for example, are major challenges to advancing human protection in ASEAN.

Sriprapha Petcharamesree's chapter examines the ASEAN human rights regime and the challenges and prospects of mainstreaming the R2P in the region by examining the roles and performance of the AICHR. She argues that it will take some time for ASEAN to adopt the R2P given that most its members still adhere to traditional norms of sovereignty and non-interference, as well as consensus-decision making. For her, a paradigm shift is necessary in order for ASEAN to effectively care for people, which can be anchored on the ASEAN Human Rights Declaration and employing the "ASEAN minus X" decision-making formula to prevent and respond to systematic human rights violations that could amount to the four crimes covered by the R2P. It is also necessary for ASEAN members to start engaging in national and regional dialogues on the principle as well as encouraging ASEAN to learn from the efforts of other regional bodies in promoting human rights and mass atrocities prevention.

Lourdes Veneracion-Rallonza's chapter examines the link between women, peace and security (WPS) as a global agenda and ASEAN's regional agenda on human protection and atrocities prevention. Specifically, she explores how WPS has been incorporated by ASEAN members by mapping out the discourse and institutional entry points both at the domestic and regional levels. She then examines how some ASEAN members—Cambodia, Indonesia, Myanmar, and the Philippines—have integrated the WPS framework into various policy actions and programs in their respective efforts in addressing violence against women. Her chapter argues that these ASEAN members have the potential to be "vertical norm entrepreneurs" based on their existing national action plans on WPS. The Philippines for example is the most advance among the ASEAN members in that it has already in place a government inter-agency mechanisms and it continues to engage civil society in promoting WPS. The potential for "horizontal norm entrepreneurship" is also present in ASEAN as it adopted a common position in the WPS Open Debates, as well as opportunities for inclusion of WPS in the agenda of both the AICHR and the ACWC.

Maria Tanyag's chapter situates the growing academic and policy interest in advancing international normative frameworks of the Responsibility to Protect (R2P) and Women, Peace, and Security (WPS) in ASEAN within broader feminist critiques of the 'protection gap' that results from the 'siloing' of international security and peace agendas. It attempts to build on recent works that suggest a rethinking of ASEAN as constituted by three distinct community pillars (political-security, economic, and socio-cultural) for fully addressing human security and development in the region. Using the ASEAN Regional Plan for Action (RPA) of the 2013 Declaration on the Elimination of Violence Against Women (EVAW), which covers a ten-year period (2016–2025), her chapter makes a case for how the RPA can serve as a critical vector for broadening the significance of R2P and WPS in the region to address sexual and gender-based violence as occurring both in crisis situations and 'everyday life'.

Noel Morada's chapter on ASEAN and human protection in Myanmar examines ASEAN's diplomacy in dealing with Myanmar's human rights protection issues. He argues that although in practice ASEAN has put aside its non-interference principle in response to human protection problems within Myanmar including the crisis in Rakhine, the organisation's collective efforts have been rebuffed by the previous military junta and the current civilian government who also invoked the same principle in protecting its sovereignty. While there are increasing calls from some ASEAN members and other non-state actors in the region to consider relaxing the non-interference principle when it comes to humanitarian crisis issues affecting the region, it appears that reaching a consensus on this within the group would be extremely difficult given the strong resistance of some members to the idea. Even so, ASEAN's role in influencing the situation in Rakhine would most likely be limited to providing humanitarian assistance for affected communities and capacity building for Myanmar's security sector in order to prevent future atrocities from happening in the area.

Alex J. Bellamy's chapter examines the extent to which the broader Asia Pacific region has translated the R2P from commitment to practice. Specifically, he identifies a number of key challenges that remain—both ideational and institutional—in ensuring that the R2P and mass atrocities prevention become a lived reality despite the dramatic decline of atrocity crimes in East Asia. He also identifies a set of recommendations on how to build national architectures for atrocities prevention as well as acting on Track 2 recommendations for developing regional early warning system, strengthening ASEAN mechanisms for peace and human rights protection, and assisting member states in building their national capacities for atrocities prevention.

The second set of chapters in the book focus on Africa. Charles T. Hunt's overview of regionalism in Africa examines the extent to which human protection norms have diffused in the continent's regional organisations and communities. The chapter provides an overview of competing concepts of regionalism in the African context and identifies the factors that have affected African regionalization. Hunt examines how perspectives and institutional expressions at the regional level(s) have been influenced by – and in turn influenced – the uptake and development of norms that promote human protection. He argues that the regions of Africa have been at once norm makers, shapers and takers, as well as major recipients of intervention and assistance under the rubric of human protection. The chapter poses a number of questions that must be answered if human protection norms are to become a mainstay of regional institutional architectures as well as the actions they enable and undertake on the African continent.

Chukwuemeka B. Eze's contribution is focused on role of Civil Society Organisations (CSOs) in promoting human protection norms in the west African sub-region. His chapter assesses the contributions of CSOs towards the promotion of human rights protection, mass atrocities prevention and civilian protection in conflict-affected areas in West Africa with particular attention given to the work of the West Africa Network for Peacebuilding (WANEP). Eze argues that while the responsibility of peace, security and ensuring human protection resides with governments, CSOs such as WANEP have played important roles that have complemented the work of government actors and state-based organisations. Furthermore, he shows how in the case of the Economic Community of West African States (ECOWAS), political leadership has begun to acknowledge the critical functions CSOs perform in, for instance, conflict and atrocities early warning systems. In particular, the chapter highlights the comparative advantages of CSOs in contributing to the prevention and resolution of conflicts due of their in-depth knowledge of the local context and expertise in working closely with communities. Eze therefore argues for a deepening engagement by (inter)governmental entities with CSOs in order to enable their continued involvement in pursuit of human protection.

Tim Murithi's chapter evaluates the role of the AU as a norm entrepreneur and examines how the AU approach to promoting pan-African norms relating to sovereignty and non-interference, human protection and mass atrocities prevention has evolved over time. He discusses the major turning points in Africa's normative frameworks and mechanisms addressing human protection and identifies the key factors that have shaped the corollary debates. The chapter also traces the emergence of the good governance and development agendas at the AU that have accompanied the rise of protection norms and reflects on the influence of the relationship between the AU and other international organisations such as the United Nations (UN) in determining the outcomes experienced by people on the continent. Murithi argues that although there is evidence of significant norm entrepreneurship on the part of the AU, its success in safeguarding human protection and preventing mass atrocities has been limited overall. The chapter identifies some of the outstanding challenges facing the continental body as it faces down a range of human protection emergencies and attempts to address their root causes through wide-ranging security and development agendas at the regional level. Murithi's contribution concludes by proposing some recommendations for enhancing human protection in Africa through the AU.

Obinna Ifediora's chapter explores the potential for regional organisations to meet an enhanced 'regional responsibility to protect'. Highlighting the difficulties faced in arriving at consensus in the UN's Security Council, Ifediora argues that regional bodies such as the AU, acting in accordance with Chapter VIII of the UN Charter, can provide critical upstream preventive support that harnesses their comparative advantage and local knowledge. The chapter emphasises how efforts to operationalize the African Standby Force have been rendered ineffectual when most needed. It is therefore argued that 'pacific' solutions influenced by African approaches to conflict resolution should focus more on 'greater mediation' of what he describes as conflicts of governance. Ifediora argues that such an approach will offer a more fruitful avenue for mitigating the risks of atrocity crimes. The chapter further argues that this realisation should give rise to a transformation in the nature and direction of capacity-development provided by the international community and development partners to African regional organisations and proffers the concept of 'preventive arbitration' as one potential mechanism that could be supported in this regard.

The chapter by Phil Orchard takes a comparative perspective and contrasts experiences in Africa with those in Southeast Asia. His contribution looks into how the two regions have responded to the issue of protection of internally displaced persons (IDPs). According to him, forcible displacement can constitute a mass atrocity crime, which is well considered within the non-binding Guiding Principles on Internal Displacement. In Africa, the Kampala Convention of the AU has brought the Guiding Principles and protections against mass atrocities targeting IDPs into hard law, which includes robust implementation and enforcement mechanisms. He stresses however that these mechanisms thus far remain anticipatory, far from effective, and that international assistance is necessary to entrench the rights provided by the Convention. In contrast to Africa, Orchard highlights that ASEAN provides no overt protections for IDPs in the Southeast Asia context. However, he contends that the ASEAN Human Rights Declaration and the group's response to the Rohingya crisis in Myanmar that has spilled over into neighbouring member states may indicate that policy-focused change is happening, albeit incrementally.

The book's conclusion draws together the major lessons identified in the respective regions, reflects on the opportunities for inter-regional learning, and closes with a discussion of the aspects of south-south dialogue and exchange on human protection that warrant further research.

Southeast Asian Regionalism, Norm Promotion and Capacity Building for Human Protection: An Overview

Noel M. Morada
University of Queensland
n.morada@uq.edu.au

Abstract

This chapter provides an overview of how the Association of Southeast Asian Nations (ASEAN) has responded to human protection issues such as human rights, mass atrocities prevention, and civilian protection in armed conflicts. It examines the evolution and dynamics of ASEAN's regionalism and the factors that shaped and transformed its norms. While ASEAN has adopted the language of human security and human protection, traditional norms of sovereignty and non-interference remain sticky. The pluralist nature of ASEAN also limits the organization from responding effectively to crisis situations within member states such as identity-based conflicts. However, there are also opportunities for continuing engagement on human protection issues with various stakeholders at the regional and domestic levels. Some ASEAN member states are more open to mainstreaming the principle of Responsibility to Protect in the agenda of ASEAN and recognize the importance of building the capacity of member states in preventing mass atrocities.

Keywords

ASEAN Community – human rights – ASEAN Way – Myanmar

A number of endogenous and exogenous factors have influenced the development of Southeast Asian regionalism, including those that relate to the promotion of norms and capacity building for human protection. This chapter provides an overview of how the Association of Southeast Asian Nations (ASEAN), a regional organization created in 1967, has responded to human protection issues such as human rights, mass atrocities prevention, and civilian protection in armed conflicts. Specifically, it examines the evolution and dynamics of ASEAN's regionalism since its foundation, the factors that shaped

 | DOI:10.1163/9789004363212_003

and transformed its norms, and the extent to which non-state actors, globalization, and universal norms have influenced the debate on human protection issues in Southeast Asia. The chapter argues that although ASEAN's brand of regionalism has adopted the language of human security and human protection in its ASEAN Community project, traditional norms of sovereignty and non-interference remain sticky in the way that the organization has responded to human rights protection issues in the region. The pluralist nature of ASEAN essentially limits the capacity of the organization to respond effectively to crisis situations within member states that stem from political or identity-based conflicts. At the same time, however, there are opportunities for advancing human protection norms in the region through continuing engagement with state and non-state actors and stakeholders at the regional and domestic levels. In particular, there are ASEAN member states that are more open to mainstreaming the principle of Responsibility to Protect in the agenda of ASEAN and recognize also the importance of building the capacity of member states in preventing mass atrocities. Indeed, there is growing recognition among scholars and thinkers in the region that an incremental approach to mainstreaming RtoP in the region may be enhanced by: 1) anchoring it on its compatibility with ASEAN human protection norms;[1] 2) taking advantage of "entry points" in ASEAN human rights protection mechanisms;[2] 3) increasing awareness in the region about the need to address human security issues in the context of internal conflicts;[3] and 4) recognizing the role of civil society groups in exerting pressure on member states to take seriously their primary responsibility to protect vulnerable populations at home.[4]

The next section of this chapter provides a discussion of the concept of regionalism and the various approaches used by some scholars in understanding the nature and dynamics of ASEAN's brand of regionalism. Thereafter, the last section discusses the important milestones and their significance to ASEAN's human protection norms and capacity.

---

1 See Rizal Sukma, 'The ASEAN political security community (APSC): opportunities and constraints for R2P in Southeast Asia,' 25/1 (2012), pp. 135–152.

2 See Herman J. Kraft, 'RtoP by increments: the AICHR and localizing the Responsibility to Protect in Southeast Asia,' *The Pacific Review* 25/1 (2012), pp. 27–49.

3 See Mely Caballero-Anthony, 'The Responsibility to Protect: opening up spaces for advancing human security,' *The Pacific Review* 25/1 (2012), pp. 113–124.

4 See Lina Alexandra, 'Indonesia and the Responsibility to Protect,' *The Pacific Review* 25/1 (2012), pp. 51–74.

Regionalism

Regionalism and regionalization are concepts that entered the recent debate in the study of comparative regional integration. According to Soderbaum, regionalism refers to 'the policy and project of cooperation between state and non-state actors in a given region or a form of world order', which is often associated with a formal agenda or programme and one that is expected to lead to institution building. The latter, on the other hand, is 'a process of cooperation, integration, cohesion, and identity creating a regional space (issue-specific or general)'.[5] In particular, according to Fawcett, regionalization is 'no more than a concentration activity—of trade, peoples, ideas, even conflict—at the regional level…[which] may give rise to the formation of regions, and in turn to the emergence of regional actors, networks, and organizations'.[6] In contrast to the early debate on comparative regional integration, which focused on classical approaches to European integration, the recent debate focused on both the exogenous (interaction between regionalization and globalization) and endogenous (where a large number of actors within the region shape the process of regionalization) perspectives.[7]

Some scholars have adopted various approaches in explaining the development of ASEAN regionalism. For example, Michael Liefer, a well-known expert on the international relations of Southeast Asia who has written mainly from a realist perspective, had examined the vulnerability of states and their attempts to manage 'the insecurity of their region'.[8] Indeed, in the context of the Cold War era, the creation of ASEAN primarily aimed at promoting regional stability to enhance national resilience among its members. In particular, the organization's *raison d'etre* at the time was to prevent the expansion of

5 Fredrik Soderbaum, 'Comparative Regional Integration and Regionalism', in Todd Landman and Neill Robinson (eds), *The Sage Handbook of Comparative Politics* (London: SAGE Publications Ltd, 2009), p. 6.

6 Louise Fawcett, 'Regionalism from a historical perspective', in M. Farrell et al (eds.) *Global Politics of Regionalism: Theory and* Practice (London: Pluto Press, 2005) as quoted in Soderbaum, 'Comparative Regional Integration and Regionalism', pp. 6–7.

7 Soderbaum, 'Comparative Regional Integration and Regionalism', p. 11.

8 Donald K. Emmerson, 'What do the blind-sided see? Reapproaching regionalism in Southeast Asia', *The Pacific Review*, 18/1 (2005), p. 2. According to Emmerson, Leifer also wrote about other themes, such as identity, interests, institutions, and ideas in his analysis of Southeast Asian regionalism, which also 'animate, respectively, the perspectives of realism, culturalism, rationalism, liberalism, and constructivism' particularly in the context of understanding the role of external variables in shaping ASEAN's evolution.

communism, which for member states was the primary external and internal threat in Southeast Asia following the fall of South Vietnam in 1975 and subsequent communist victories in Cambodia and Laos. However, in the aftermath of the end of the Cold War and as ASEAN expanded its membership to include other states in the region, scholarship on Southeast Asian regionalism began to examine issues related to identity formation, democracy, and economic integration using other approaches, such as liberalism, constructivism and rationalism. Some scholarly works, for example, examined the impact of external factors—such as the rise of China as an economic and military power, the Asian financial crisis, and the Global War on Terror—on ASEAN regionalism. Other works have looked at the impact of democratic transitions in some member states (for example, Indonesia, the Philippines and Thailand) on ASEAN's traditional norms, including the promotion of human rights protection and democratic values in the region, as well as the development of what has been termed as 'participatory regionalism'.[9]

Apart from the concept of regionalism and regionalization, it is also useful to consider the pluralist and solidarist conceptions of international society in understanding Southeast Asian regionalism. Specifically, these concepts explain the fundamental differences in the way that states define the basis of cooperation amongst themselves based on acceptable reciprocal norms and moral values. In the English School of international relations, international society is defined as:

> a group of states, conscious of certain common interests and common values, form a society in the sense that they conceive themselves to be bound by a common set of rules in their relations with one another, and share in the working of common institutions.[10]

Hedley Bull characterized English School debates on international society as a dialogue between two competing conceptions: pluralism and solidarism.

---

9 See for example Emmerson's examination of the impact of the Asian financial crisis and the Global War on Terror on various approaches to understanding Southeast Asian regionalism. Amitav Acharya and Lee Jones examined the impact of democratic transitions on ASEAN regionalism. See Amitav Acharya, 'Democratisation and the Prospects of Participatory Regionalism in Southeast Asia', *Third World Quarterly* 24/2 (2003), pp. 375–390 and Lee Jones, 'Democratization and foreign policy in Southeast Asia: the case of the ASEAN Inter-Parliamentary Myanmar Caucus', *Cambridge Review of International Affairs*, 22/3 (2009), pp. 387–406.

10 Hedley Bull, *The Anarchical Society: An Study of Order and International Politics* (Houndmills: McMillan, 1977), p. 13.

While they agree that the international society of states 'includes commonly agreed values, rules, and institutions', the two camps, however, differ about the 'normative content' of this society.[11] For pluralists, the normative content of an international society is 'limited to a mutual interest in the continued existence of the units comprising the society… manifested in the reciprocal recognition of state sovereignty and the norm of non-intervention.' Pluralists also argue that an agreement among states about issues like human rights and redistributive justice is not possible even as they believe that 'moral and political codes' are rooted in specific cultural contexts and cannot be universal.[12] Solidarists, on the other hand, consider states in an international society as having agreement or solidarity 'in developing and enforcing international law and where the use of force is considered legitimate in order to enforce the law…and the upholding of the society's moral purpose'.[13] Solidarists point to the emergence of international human rights regimes, for example, as evidence for their argument that diverse communities are able to reach agreement on moral norms, which must be upheld by members of the society.[14]

It can be argued that ASEAN is a pluralist international society given its traditional norms that underscore reciprocal recognition of sovereignty and non-intervention. It is the anchor of ASEAN's intersubjective systemic structure and the basis of its collective identity. From a solidarist perspective, the European Union (EU) is a more developed international society that has established common policies, institutions, and legal frameworks from which its identity stems. To some extent, the English School debate between the solidarist and pluralist perspectives about the international society of states may be a useful framework in examining how Southeast Asian regionalism has evolved, particularly in the context of the ASEAN's efforts in promoting norms and capacity building for human protection. In this paper, human protection covers human rights, mass atrocities and protection of civilians in armed conflicts.

---

11 Alex J. Bellamy, 'Introduction: International Society and the English School' in Alex J. Bellamy (ed.) *International Society and Its Critiques* (New York, New York: Oxford University Press, 2005), pp. 9–10.

12 *ibid.*, p. 10.

13 *ibid.*

14 *ibid.*, pp. 10–11. This section of the paper is adopted from Noel M. Morada, 'Europe and Southeast Asia: ASEAN-EU Interregionalism between Pluralist and Solidarist Societies', *Review of European Studies*, 4/3 (July 2012), p. 89.

The next section of this chapter looks in more detail the salient turning points in ASEAN's evolution and their significance to Southeast Asian regionalism. Specifically, it identifies key events that contributed to norm promotion and institution building in ASEAN.

Evolution of Southeast Asian Regionalism

Southeast Asian regionalism has evolved in different phases since initial attempts were made in the early 1960s by various states in responding to both the challenges of nation-state building and securing their territorial integrity against external threats. In particular, its formative stages may be divided into two periods: the Cold War (1961–1991) and the post-Cold War expanded regionalism (1991–1999). Early attempts at regional cooperation saw the formation of the Association of Southeast Asia (ASA) in 1961 and later the MAPHILINDO (for Malaysia, Philippines, and Indonesia) in 1963. However, territorial disputes among the founding members scuttled the Malay Federation as both Indonesia and the Philippines refused to recognize the inclusion of Sabah and Sarawak in the newly independent Malay state.[15]

The ASEAN—formed on 8 August 1967 by Malaysia, Indonesia, the Philippines, Singapore and Thailand—was the successor to the ASA. The Bangkok Declaration spelled out its basic framework for regional cooperation, which included the organization's traditional norms and principles of non-interference and respect for territorial integrity of member states. Following the unification of Vietnam in 1975 and the subsequent victories of the Khmer Rouge in Cambodia and the Pathet Lao in Laos, the region fell into two camps: the non-communist states of ASEAN and the three Indochinese states led by Vietnam. Tension between the two blocs was further aggravated in 1979 by the Vietnamese invasion of Cambodia that ousted the Khmer Rouge and subsequent occupation. While Vietnam and the pro-Hanoi installed government of Heng Samrin in Phnom

15 For an in-depth discussion of early and contemporary approaches to understanding Southeast Asian on regionalism, see Vincent K. Pollard, 'ASA and ASEAN, 1961–1967: Southeast Asian Regionalism', *Asian Survey* 10/30 (1970), pp. 244–255; Amitav Acharya, 'How Ideas Spread: Whose Norms Matter? Norm Localization and Institutional Change in Asian Regionalism', *International Organization* 58/2 (2004), pp. 239–275; and Noel M. Morada, 'ASEAN at 40: Prospects for Community Building in Southeast Asia', *Asia Pacific Review* 15/1 (2008), 36–55.

Penh justified the humanitarian intervention in order to save the country from the mass atrocities committed by Pol Pot, the members of ASEAN saw the Vietnamese invasion as a violation of international law, specifically the national sovereignty and territorial integrity of Cambodia. ASEAN then supported the anti-Vietnamese coalition government-in-exile in the UN and successfully campaigned in denying international recognition to the pro-Hanoi government in Cambodia. It also provided support to the non-communist factions of the Cambodian resistance forces along the Thai-Cambodian border, while China continued to support the Khmer Rouge faction in the coalition. ASEAN's preoccupation with the Cambodian conflict from 1979 to 1989 stemmed from the belief that regional stability necessitated that members fully stood behind Thailand, which is the frontline state in the conflict. This position therefore became the anchor of ASEAN's cohesion during this period.

Overall, regionalism within the framework of ASEAN during the Cold War period enabled its members to undertake regional cooperation based on the following fundamentals: 1) ensuring national resilience amidst internal and external threats; 2) promoting inter-governmental cooperation; and 3) protecting state-centered traditional norms such as non-interference and respect for territorial integrity of states. It was also during this period that the organization's diplomatic culture developed—called the 'ASEAN Way'—which is a decision-making code based on consultation and consensus among its members. Given the political, economic, and social-cultural diversity of its member states, the 'ASEAN Way' served as an important mechanism for handling differences and enabled them to negotiate and arrive at a common position on issues, even if based only on the least common denominator.

In the post-Cold War period, ASEAN engaged in expanded regionalism as a strategy in managing the uncertainties of the security environment in this part of the world. A number of factors shaped ASEAN's conscious efforts in dealing with regional security concerns, including: 1) the withdrawal of American military bases in the Philippines; 2) the rise of China as an economic and military power; and 3) the unresolved maritime disputes in the South China Sea. Although the withdrawal of Vietnamese forces from Cambodia in 1989 and the collapse of the former Soviet Union in 1991 contributed to the diplomatic resolution of the Cambodian conflict, ASEAN still had to deal with the aforementioned emerging security challenges in the region. Specifically, the organization adopted a twin strategy in managing the regional security environment. Firstly, by expanding its membership to include Vietnam (in 1994), Laos, Myanmar (both in 1997), and Cambodia (in 1999). Secondly, by promoting its norms and diplomatic culture beyond the region through the creation of the ASEAN Regional

Forum (ARF) in order to engage not only its dialogue partners (e.g., the US, Japan, and other Western countries) but also emerging powers (e.g., China, Russia, India) and other actors (e.g., North Korea, Pakistan). With expanded membership that covers all countries of the region at the time, ASEAN was attempting to realize its vision of 'One Southeast Asia', which was also aimed at countering the growing influence of China particularly in Myanmar and Cambodia. At the same time, by creating the ARF, the organization was also opening the process of dialogue and engagement with China, with a view towards socializing it into ASEAN's norms and diplomatic culture. Through the mechanism of 'ASEAN+1', for example, the hope was that engaging with China would contribute to confidence building and peaceful management of maritime disputes in the South China Sea. This became even more important in the context of China's occupation of the Mischief Reef in 1995, which the Philippines also claimed.

ASEAN's expanded regionalism in the post-Cold War context thus was clearly an attempt to manage the uncertainties of the external security environment. It remained primarily a state-centric regionalism and still valued the traditional norms of ASEAN that upheld state sovereignty and non-interference. However, this expanded regionalism based on ASEAN's traditional norms soon had to face the challenges brought about by the Asian Financial Crisis (AFC) in 1997 and the subsequent democratic transitions in Indonesia and Thailand. The next section of this chapter provides a discussion of ASEAN's norm-building phase and the significance of this period to ASEAN regionalism.

ASEAN Norm-Building Phase (1997–2007)

The AFC in 1997 forced ASEAN member states to re-examine the organization's raison d'etre following the political and economic instability that resulted from the crisis. Specifically, the importance of norm building became a central theme in ASEAN's push for transforming itself into a more people-centered and people-oriented organization. This was a consequence of significant democratic transitions in Indonesia and Thailand, as well as the push for 'reformasi' in Malaysia in the aftermath of the AFC. For example, the end of Suharto's New Order in Indonesia in 1998 ushered in a democratic order anchored on good governance, rule of law, and protection of human rights. These principles were subsequently articulated by Indonesia in its initiative to form an ASEAN Security Community (which was later modified into Political Security Community) as part of its efforts in promoting norm-building in the region. As chair of ASEAN in 2003, Indonesia incorporated these principles in the Bali Concord II as emerging values that are relevant to promoting the political security pillar of the ASEAN Community. There is no question that these aspirational values resonated well in the region especially in light of democratization efforts in Indonesia, the struggle for democratic reform in Malaysia in 1998, the push for independence of East

Timor in 2002, and the violent clampdown by the military junta in Myanmar in 2007 against protests led by Buddhist monks in the country. These key events also contributed to efforts by Indonesia and other democratic member states to mainstream democracy, human rights protection, and rule of law as part of ASEAN's people-oriented principles, which subsequently were included during the drafting of the ASEAN Charter between 2006 and 2007.

The significance of ASEAN's norm building phase in the context of regionalism during this period was two-fold. First, it saw the efforts of ASEAN to find a balance between state-centered (e.g., sovereignty, non-interference, and territorial integrity) and people-centered values (e.g., human security, human rights, and human development). Whereas the older and more democratic members of ASEAN were open to incorporating the latter set of principles in its ASEAN Charter, newer members were more reluctant to accept them as this may also undermine the traditional state-centered norms of ASEAN. This was clearly the case, for example in 2006, when members of the High Level Task Force (HLTF) that drafted the ASEAN Charter had disagreements on incorporating a provision for creating a regional human rights body. The impasse over the issue was resolved when members agreed to include such provision on the condition that the Terms of Reference be subject to negotiations after the adoption and ratification of ASEAN Charter. Second, participatory regionalism is slowly evolving in Southeast Asia. This is so given that ASEAN appears to have been more open to greater participation of non-state actors or stakeholders in the process of shaping and sharing of norms in the region. Although consensus decision-making remains the norm among members in ASEAN, there are now more opportunities for engaging with non-state stakeholders especially through consultations and informal meetings. For example, Malaysia as chair of ASEAN in 2005 initiated the first ASEAN Civil Society meeting that paved the way for interface between civil society groups and ASEAN leaders as part of the regular summit activity. As well, the HLTF on the ASEAN Charter conducted a series of consultations in national capitals with various stakeholders to gather their inputs on the charter. Also, ASEAN has recognized and engaged with a number of non-government and sectoral organizations in the region on a range of issues and mutual concerns, including human rights protection, social and economic development, and narrowing the development gaps among and within member states.

ASEAN Community Building Phase (2008–2015)

Following the adoption of its Charter in 2008, ASEAN embarked on a self-conscious community-building phase as a regional organization. The ASEAN Community consists of three related pillars, namely, the ASEAN Political Security Community (APSC), the ASEAN Economic Community (AEC), and the ASEAN Social Cultural Community (ASCC). The adoption of the respective blueprints of these pillars in 2009 coincided with the launching of the ASEAN Inter-Governmental Commission on Human Rights (AICHR). This was followed by the creation of the ASEAN Commission on the Protection of Women and Children (ACWC) in 2010, the adoption of the ASEAN Human Rights Declaration in 2012, and the creation of the ASEAN Institute for Peace and Reconciliation in 2012.

The adoption of the language of protection in the documents of the ASEAN Community pillars, particularly in the APSC and ASCC, as well as in the mandates of the AICHR, ACWC and the AIPR was a significant milestone in ASEAN's community building phase. In the APSC blueprint, for example, the protection of human rights were mentioned five times, along with other relevant terms such as 'peace-oriented values' (4), 'peace, conflict management and resolution' (6), and 'promotion of inter-communal understanding' (2). Table 1 below summarizes the key terms associated with protection principles and concerns within ASEAN, and the number of times these terms cited in relevant ASEAN documents. Figure 1 below is from the same data and presented in chart format.

TABLE 1 *ASEAN Documents and Key Terms Related to Protection Principles and Issues*

Key Terms	ASEAN Charter	APSC	ASCC	AICHR TOR	ACWC TOR	AIPR TOR	Total mention
Rule of law/rules-based community	3	6		1			10
Good governance	3	4		1			8
Democracy/democratic values/respect for fundamental freedoms	3	3		3	1		10
Human rights protection	4	5	4	4	1		18
Respect for rights of women and children/ protection of women and children		1	3		3		7
Adherence to international laws/norms/international humanitarian law/ principles on human rights protection/protection of women and children	1	1	1	2	1		6

Key Terms	ASEAN Charter	APSC	ASCC	AICHR TOR	ACWC TOR	AIPR TOR	Total mention
Promote awareness of and capacity building human rights protection/peace, reconciliation and conflict prevention	1	1	1	2	1	2	8
Social protection			2				2
People-oriented ASEAN	2	1	2				5
Comprehensive security/ human security/human development	1	2	1				4
Rights and responsibilities of Member States/shared responsibilities	2	1	1	1	1	1	7
Culture of peace/ peace-oriented values	1	4					5
Peace, conflict management/resolution	1	6			1	8	16
Peacebuilding/peace process		3				2	5
Peace and stability	2	4					6
Tolerance/respect for diversity/inter-communal understanding/non-discrimination/inter-faith dialogue	1	2	1	1	1	1	7
Gender mainstreaming/ elimination of violence against women		1	3			1	5
Humanitarian assistance/ refugees/displaced persons		6					6
Protection of migrant workers/protection against human trafficking/people smuggling		3	1				4

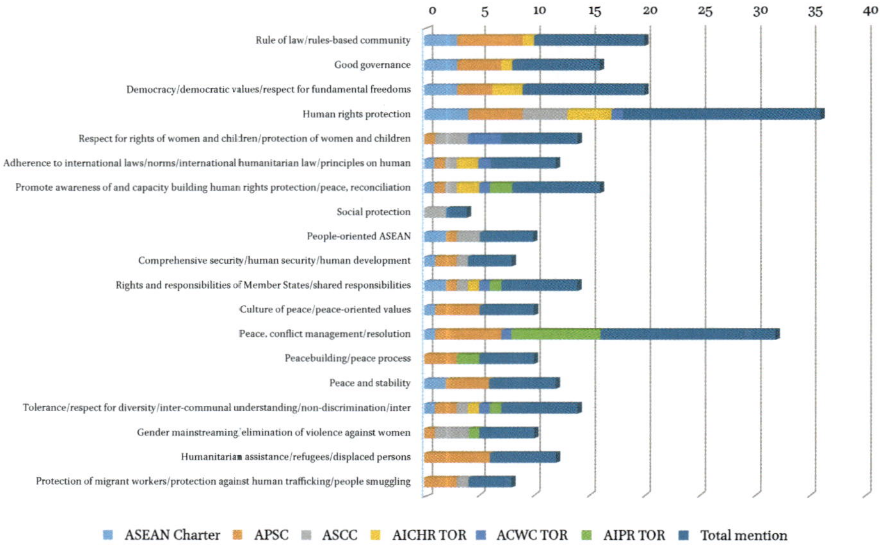

FIGURE 1 *ASEAN Human Protection Principles and Issues*

It is clear from the table above that: 1) human rights protection was a key component of ASEAN's vision of itself as a community; 2) both the rights and *responsibilities* of member states were acknowledged; and 3) special emphasis was placed on the values of tolerance and respect for diversity. Promoting awareness and building capacity in human rights protection, peace and reconciliation, and protection of women and children are not only affirmed in these documents but are also considered important priorities in the mandate of existing ASEAN mechanisms such as the AICHR, ACWC and AIPR. In terms of the total number of mentions across these documents, human rights protection scored the highest (18), followed by peace, conflict management and conflict resolution (16), and rule of law, democracy, and democratic values (each with 10 mentions).

It is also significant to note that with regard to the ASEAN Charter, the APSC and the ASCC blueprints, these documents highlighted the primary responsibility of member states in implementing the above principles. This even as they also uphold state sovereignty, along with values such as people-oriented ASEAN, tolerance for diversity, and adherence to international norms such as international humanitarian law and protection of human rights, as well as protection of women and children. Thus, one can argue that the concept of state responsibility in relation to promotion of human protection, respect for diversity, and adherence to international norms are not alien to ASEAN.[16] It has been part of the community-building efforts of the organization and in promoting ASEAN regionalism.

The adoption of these principles in key ASEAN documents could not have come at a more auspicious time, as the region faced a number of human protection challenges and concerns. This include the humanitarian crisis in Myanmar in 2008 following Cyclone Nargis and the impact of the global economic crisis in the same year on human security and human development in ASEAN. As well, the continuing identity-based internal conflicts in some member states—southern Thailand and Mindanao in the Philippines—highlighted the importance of promoting peace and reconciliation. Meanwhile, the outbreak of communal violence in Myanmar's Rakhine state in 2012 between Buddhist majority and Muslim minority groups, specifically targeting the stateless Rohingyas,[17] along with the protection of religious minorities in Indonesia, underscored the need to promote tolerance and respect for diversity within ASEAN member states. In particular, Myanmar was in the spotlight in 2014 when it assumed the role of ASEAN Chair, given that it failed to demonstrate willingness to address the plight of the Rohingyas and contain attacks against the Muslim minority by Buddhist extremists in the country. Specifically, it remained adamant in resisting international pressure including those from ASEAN for the Myanmar government to address the root causes of the conflict in Rakhine and to allow for unimpeded international humanitarian assistance to the Rohingyas.

The communal conflict in Myanmar underscored further the spillover effects of the Rohingya crisis in the region in May 2015 following the discovery of mass graves in Thailand and Malaysia allegedly used by human traffickers that victimized desperate Rohingya refugees fleeing Rakhine and Bangladesh. A number of ASEAN government leaders, human rights advocates, and parliamentarians in the region have called for re-examination of ASEAN's non-interference principle to enable ASEAN to respond to the plight of the Rohingyas and hold Myanmar accountable for failing to take its primary responsibility to protect them. Former Malaysian Prime Minister Mahathir Mohammad called for the expulsion of Myanmar from ASEAN as he alleged that the government has failed to put a stop to the slow genocide against Rohingyas.[18]

---

16 The High Level Advisory Panel's (HLAP) also underscored this point in its Report on 'Mainstreaming Responsibility to Protect in Southeast Asia: Pathway Towards a Caring ASEAN Community', 9 September 2014, pp. 2–3.

17 Rohingya is an unacceptable term for the Myanmar government who refer to them as Bengalis instead.

18 Other efforts from ASEAN members to exert pressure on the Myanmar government include a formal letter signed by the former ASEAN Secretary General Dr. Surin Pitsuwan,

Overall, ASEAN's regionalism since 2008 focused on community building amidst pluralism within ASEAN. While there were incorporation of norms and principles related to human rights protection, democracy, good governance, and rule of law in key ASEAN documents, they effectively remain aspirations rather than necessarily shared values strictly adhered to by member states. In fact, there is a continuing ideological divide within ASEAN on the issue of human rights protection as clearly reflected in the ASEAN Human Rights Declaration (AHRD) adopted in 2012. Specifically, some member states like Cambodia, Laos, Myanmar, Singapore and Vietnam, adhere to a relativist view of human rights that gives more importance to diversity of political values and unique cultural and historical experiences of countries in the region. Although the ASEAN leaders affirmed their support for the Universal Declaration of Human Rights following the adoption of the AHRD in their summit meeting in Phnom Penh in 2012, this was primarily to stave off criticisms from civil society groups in the region who believed that the Declaration fell short of adhering to international standards in human rights protection. Table 2 below provides a summary of the key terms and principles incorporated in the AHRD that reflects both universal and relativist views of human rights. Although the Declaration affirmed the Universal Declaration of Human Rights at least three times in the entire document, along with the UN Charter and the Vienna Declaration and Programme of Action, a number of universal human rights principles were qualified or restricted in accordance with national laws of member states. Both the general and specific principles of the AHRD pertaining to civil and political rights as well as economic, social, and cultural rights underscore the importance of acknowledging national and regional contexts and nuances in promoting human rights protection.

---

former Malaysian Prime Minister Ahmad Badawi, former Malaysian Foreign Minister Syed Hamid Albar, and former Thai Foreign Minister Kasit Promiya in April 2015 asking the ASEAN Chair to address the plight of the Rohingyas. See Humaniti, 'Former ASEAN Leaders Issue Letter on Myanmar Intolerance,' 22 April 2015, http://www.burmapartnership.org/2015/04/former-asean-leaders-issue-letter-on-myanmar-intolerance/, accessed on 15 December 2015. Parliamentarians in the region also called for ASEAN to relax the non-interference principle and to ask the Myanmar government to address the root causes of the plight of the Rohingyas and the communal conflict in the country between Buddhists and Muslim communities. See Laignee Baron, 'Regional MPs warn of Rohingya "crisis"'ahead of ASEAN meeting', *Myanmar Times*, 23 April 2015, http://www.mmtimes.com/index.php/national-news/14085-regional-mps-warn-of-rohingya-crisis-ahead-of-asean-meeting.html, accessed 15 December 2015.

TABLE 2 *The ASEAN Human Rights Declaration: Universal vs. Relative Principles*

Universal	*Relative*
'1. All persons are born free and equal in dignity and rights. They are endowed with reason and conscience and should act towards one another in a spirit of humanity.' '2. Every person is entitled to the rights and freedoms set forth herein without distinction of any kind, such as race, gender, age, language, religion, political or other opinion, national or social origin, economic status, birth, disability, or other status.'	'6. The enjoyment of human rights and fundamental freedoms must be balanced with the performance of corresponding duties as every person has responsibilities to all other individuals, the community and the society where one lives. It is ultimately the primary responsibility of all ASEAN Member States to promote and protect all human rights and fundamental freedoms.'
'7. All human rights are universal, indivisible, interdependent, and interrelated….'	'7…At the same time, the realization of human rights must be considered in the regional and national context bearing in mind different political, economic, legal, social, cultural, historical, and religious backgrounds.'
'8. The human rights and fundamental freedoms of every person shall be exercised with due regard to the human rights and fundamental freedoms of others….'	'8…The exercise of rights and fundamental freedoms shall be subject only to such limitations as are determined by law solely for the purpose of securing due recognition for human rights and fundamental freedoms of others, and to meet the just requirements of national security, public order, public health, public safety, public morality, as well as the general welfare of the peoples in a democratic society.'
'11. Every person has inherent right to life which shall be protected by law…'	'11…No person shall be deprived of life save in accordance with law.'
'16. Every person has the right to seek and receive asylum in another States…'	'16…. in accordance with laws of such State and applicable international agreements.'

TABLE 2 *The ASEAN Human Rights Declaration: Universal vs. Relative Principles* (cont.)

Universal	*Relative*
'18. Every person has the right to a nationality…'	'18…as prescribed by law.'
'26. ASEAN Member States affirm all the economic, social and cultural rights in the Universal Declaration of Human Rights.'	'34. ASEAN Member States may determine the extent to which they should guarantee the economic and social rights found in this Declaration to non-nationals, with due regard to human rights and organization and resources of their respective national economies.'

Source: ASEAN Human Rights Declaration 2012. Numbers correspond to numbered paragraphs in the AHRD.

Apart from the cognitive divide within ASEAN on human rights norms, it is also significant to point out that only five member states currently have national human rights institutions. To some extent, this reflects the importance that each member state attaches to implementing human rights protection at the national level. For those that already have national human rights institutions, there is also significant variation in their adherence to the Paris Principles, which underscores the importance of autonomy or independence of these institutions. As well, only five members of ASEAN have alternately taken seats as elected members of the UN Human Rights Council since its creation in 2006, namely, Indonesia, Malaysia, the Philippines, Thailand, and Vietnam (which does not even have its own national human rights institution). Although Myanmar has opened itself for scrutiny of its human rights record through the Universal Periodic Review (UPR) process of the UNHRC, it has not accepted many of the recommendations for improving human rights protection in the country. Clearly, these realities serve as major constraints to implementing ASEAN's norms and principles in promoting human rights protection in particular and human protection in general at both the national and regional levels. This therefore raises the issue of whether ASEAN norms on human rights and human protection are shared values to which member states are strongly committed or they are just simply aspirations for now.

ASEAN Regionalism and Human Protection: Challenges and Opportunities

The gap between the articulation and implementation of norms for human protection at the national and regional levels stems mainly from the intergovernmental nature of ASEAN, which is influenced by a number of institutional factors, such as: 1) consensus decision-making; 2) revolving chairmanship; 3) limited powers of the Secretary-General; and 4) constraints in financial resources. The 'ASEAN Way' of doing things refers to consultation and consensus decision-making—and also implies the use of veto by member states—especially on issues that tread into their domestic affairs or national sovereignty, such as human rights, civilian protection, and atrocities prevention. Even in cases where the formula of 'ASEAN Minus X' principle can be applied, Article 21 of the ASEAN Charter is clear that this is only in the implementation of economic commitments and still requires consensus. As discussed by Sriprapha Petcharamesree in this volume, there is apparently a de facto 'minority hegemony' in ASEAN when it comes to discussions related to human rights protection. Some member states are more sensitive to this issue as they consider it an interference in their internal affairs and a violation of ASEAN's traditional norms. The practice of revolving chair in ASEAN is another factor that limits the capacity of the organization to discuss issues, as well as to monitor and implement agreements. Each member state is free to pursue its own agenda during its term as ASEAN Chair, and in the case of Myanmar's turn in 2014, it made sure that the issue of the Rohingya was off the agenda. However, some member states—such as Indonesia, Malaysia, and Singapore—during their respective terms as ASEAN Chair raised issues related to human rights, internal conflict, or political violence in other member states. This include violence in Timor Leste in the 1990s, southern Thailand in 2005, Myanmar in 2007, and the communal violence in Rakhine state in 2012, despite some opposition from concerned member states.

The ASEAN Secretary General's limited mandate and authority is another constraining factor in ASEAN's capacity to promote and implement norms on human protection. Specifically, the Secretary-General heads the ASEAN Secretariat, implements decisions made in the ASEAN ministerial meetings and the Summit of Leaders, as well as coordinates with the United Nations and other ASEAN dialogue partners on a range of projects. While there were proposals to enhance the role of the Secretary-General, there has been no significant progress in this area for quite some time. In fact, since the adoption of the ASEAN Charter in 2008, the role has been limited to being the 'chief administrative officer' of the organization and manager of the Secretariat. Even so, the effectiveness of the ASEAN Secretary-General is also a function of the personalities appointed to the position. For example, former Thai foreign minister Surin Pitsuwan, who served as ASEAN Secretary-General between 2008 and 2012, was a strong advocate of human security and played a significant role in convincing Myanmar's military junta to allow international humanitarian assistance to the country in the aftermath of Cyclone Nargis in 2008. He is also an advocate of 'positive interference' and relaxation of ASEAN's non-interference principle if internal problems of a member state begin to spill over into other member states.

As chief administrative officer of ASEAN, the Secretary-General is constrained by a limited budget with which the Secretariat has to operate, as annual contributions of each member-state is only about US$1.8 million annually. In fact, ASEAN relies heavily on the support of dialogue partners for its projects, which includes, among others, capacity building in human rights education, addressing social development gaps in the region, disaster risk management, and combatting human trafficking and other transnational crimes. Support for these projects are donor-driven and must align with the funding priorities of donor countries, apart from the fact that member states must give their consent in undertaking them under the name of ASEAN.

As an intergovernmental regional organization, decisions in ASEAN are essentially executive agreements among the respective governments of member states. Unlike its counterpart in Europe and Africa, ASEAN has neither a regional legislative assembly nor a regional court that could pass legally binding laws or promulgate judicial decisions, respectively, which could compel member states to comply with and implement agreements at home. Thus, ASEAN can only rely on national legislatures and courts within member states to implement or comply with norms, agreements, or action plans at the domestic level. Given the differences in the political systems of member states, the implementation of regional agreements would therefore be subject to domestic constraints and the political dynamics of competing interests at home. As it is, the current institutional design of ASEAN has limited openings for participatory regionalism that would meaningfully engage parliamentarians, civil society groups, and other non-government stakeholders in Southeast Asia. As well, current mechanisms for their involvement in ASEAN decision-making is mainly through a 'consultative process' that is determined by consensus among member states. There is no question that despite the creation of regional mechanisms such as the AICHR, ACWC, and AIPR, the space for engaging civil society groups within ASEAN needs further opening in order to advance and deepen the commitment of states to human protection norms.

Notwithstanding the foregoing challenges, there are also opportunities for sustaining the engagement in the region on norm promotion and capacity building for human protection. For one, existing mechanisms can be enhanced through creative interactions between ASEAN officials and non-state actors. For example, civil society groups, academia and think thank groups can create their own network at home and engage more pro-actively with their representatives to the AICHR, ACWC, and AIPR on mainstreaming human protection norms. They could also organise regular consultations and national dialogues on human rights protection and atrocities prevention with relevant government agencies with a view towards developing national and regional capacities for human protection. For example, in the process of consultations for the review the Terms of Reference of AICHR and the ASEAN Charter, these groups could provide inputs and practical recommendations for strengthening regional and national mechanisms. Specifically, they could identify gaps and propose steps to enhance further ASEAN's capacity in advancing human rights protection, civilian protection, and atrocities prevention. Encouraging ASEAN member states to pursue deeper partnership with the UN and meaningful engagement with other regional organisations, particularly in the context of South-South dialogues, could also contribute to enhancing ASEAN's capacity for human protection. As well, building regional networks of various stakeholders (e.g., parliamentarians, NGOs, and academe/think tank institutions) for protection of human rights, peace and conflict prevention, as well as women, peace and security could also contribute to promoting norms and capacity building in ASEAN on human protection.

At the domestic level, each ASEAN member state could focus on Pillars I and II of the R2P in implementing the norm at home. It is significant to note that for many ASEAN members who have participated in the annual interactive dialogue on R2P at the UN General Assembly, the goals and objectives of the principle are acceptable and not disputed. They have consistently reaffirmed the primary responsibility of states to protect their populations from atrocity crimes and have recognized the importance of capacity building for atrocities prevention, which were reiterated in the annual R2P report of the Secretary General since 2009. An important priority to pursue is the development of home-grown knowledge system that is appropriate for ASEAN member states, bearing in mind the various atrocity risk factors that they each face such as history of past atrocities, ethnic conflicts, weak institutions for human protection, economic and social inequality, and lack of access to basic services.[19] Understanding these risk factors in the context of each society in the region can contribute to building mechanisms and frameworks for

19 See Framework of Analysis For Atrocity Crimes: A Tool for Prevention (New York: United Nations 2014).

preventing atrocities as well as in developing early warning systems that could help states respond accordingly to situations that could potentially escalate to crisis levels. It is in this regard that academic institutions and think tanks could play a vital role, specifically in undertaking policy-relevant research related to human protection norms and capacity building, specifically through seminars and public education.

The promotion of human rights protection at home is another priority that must be pursued by ASEAN member states, even for those that already have national human rights institutions in place. The autonomy and independence of these national institutions are crucial to enhance their effectiveness in dealing with human rights violations that have been committed in the past or in the present times. A number of enabling factors could exert pressure on governments in the region to give more attention to human rights protection. For one, the network of civil society groups in ASEAN working on human protection issues have grown significantly over the last decade, with a number of them willing and able to provide inputs to ASEAN member states through interactive dialogue with various representatives appointed to AICHR, ACWC, and AIPR, for example. They are also engaged in lobbying efforts with ASEAN dialogue partners such as the EU, US, Australia, and Japan on human rights and human security concerns, even as they also receive assistance from these countries for their advocacy work on these issues at the domestic level. Australia and Japan are also at the forefront of providing capacity building assistance to ASEAN members that enable non-government and government stakeholders to work together in partnership in dealing with human protection-related issues, such as transitional justice, security sector reform, and human security in the Philippines, Indonesia, and Myanmar. The Universal Periodic Review (UPR) mechanism of the UN Human Rights Council is also an important mechanism that non-government stakeholders could use to monitor and exert pressure on ASEAN members to comply with universal norms on human rights protection. A number of ASEAN member states, including Myanmar and Vietnam, have submitted themselves to the UPR process and encouraging them to continue doing so could, even incrementally, contribute to improving human rights protection at the domestic level. More importantly in the case of Myanmar, the work of the UN Special Rapporteur in that country should continue even under the new National League for Democracy (NLD)-led government in order to encourage it to deepen further the democratic transition process and give priority to peace talks with ethnic minority groups in conflict-areas. The network of ASEAN parliamentarians who are advocating for human rights protection across the region could also play a significant role in pushing ASEAN members to re-examine traditional norms of non-interference and sovereignty, especially in light of growing concerns over the plight of ethnic minorities and the stateless Rohingyas in Myanmar. Specifically, the ASEAN Parliamentarians for Human Rights could encourage their members to monitor and hold their respective governments accountable in parliament on human rights violations at home as part of their formal legislative functions.

For a number of countries in the region, addressing past atrocities remain a sensitive political issue but nonetheless must be pursued seriously by states and non-state stakeholders at home as part of national healing and reconciliation. For example, past atrocities under Suharto's 'new order' recently surfaced once again in public discourse in Indonesia following the release of Joshua Oppenheimer's documentary film 'The Act of Killing', which involved a cast of former soldiers and militias narrating their involvement in committing atrocities against civilians suspected of being communist sympathizers in the 1960s. Consequently, human rights advocates in Indonesia have been exerting pressure on President Widodo to start addressing the past atrocities of the military in light of certain information revealed in the documentary. Meanwhile, in Cambodia, the Extraordinary Chamber of the Courts of Cambodia (ECCC) in 2014 convicted top Khmer Rouge leaders—Nuon Chhea and Ieng Sary—for crimes against humanity in 2014 and are still to be put on trial for genocide. However, Prime Minister Hun Sen has been exerting efforts to limit the scope of the work of the ECCC and to end its mandate as soon as possible without putting on trial other perpetrators to atrocity crimes committed by the Khmer Rouge. The Cambodian ruling-party's main justification for this is to promote 'peace and stability' in the country over justice and accountability of former Khmer Rouge cadre and supporters. Myanmar will also face the same issue of balancing between justice and peace following the victory of Aung San Suu Kyi's party in the November 2015 elections. Indeed, transitional justice is a very difficult problem that post-conflict societies in the region are confronted with as they attempt to rebuild and promote stability and development in the long run.

Conducting national dialogue would be a useful starting point in addressing grievances of victims of atrocities and also in holding accountable those who committed such crimes. It could even serve as a useful avenue for generating important lessons learned and practical knowledge for enhancing the rule of law and access to justice, promoting security sector reform, as well as implementing judicial reform and transitional justice programs especially in conflict and post-conflict areas.

As discussed above and in other contributions to this volume, armed rebellion against the state, which are rooted in ethnic and other identify-based conflicts in Southeast Asia, continue to pose a major challenge to nation-state building in the region. By addressing the root causes of armed rebellion at home, states could then help mitigate the risk factors for atrocity crimes and in the long-term help enhance the legitimacy of the state. It is in this regard that R2P should be perceived as a friend rather than an enemy of state sovereignty, especially if it is linked to good governance, rule of law, and human protection.

Conclusion

From the foregoing discussion, it is clear that ASEAN has achieved significant milestones in its evolution as a regional organization since its creation in 1967. Following the end of the Cold War and faced with a number of non-traditional security problems, ASEAN has acknowledged the importance of promoting a more comprehensive view of security that should also include the protection of peoples' welfare and individual rights and freedoms. Since 2003, and following the launch of the ASEAN Community project, ASEAN's brand of regionalism has adopted the language of human security and human protection in its formal documents and agreements. However, traditional norms of sovereignty and non-interference remain sticky in the way that the organization has responded to human rights protection issues in the region. Some member states remain jealous in guarding their sovereignty and are reluctant to accept and implement universal norms on human rights protection. The pluralist nature of ASEAN essentially limits the capacity of the organization to respond effectively to crisis situations within member states that stem from identity-based conflicts, for example. Notwithstanding these constraints, however, there are also opportunities for advancing human protection norms in the region through continuing engagement with state and non-state actors and stakeholders at the regional and domestic levels. In particular, there are ASEAN member states that are more open to mainstreaming the principle of Responsibility to Protect in the agenda of ASEAN even as they also recognize the importance of building the capacity of member states in preventing mass atrocities. At the domestic level, civil society groups together with those from the academe/think tanks play a critical role in building public awareness about human protection norms and in encouraging national governments to take seriously their primary responsibilities in protecting human rights and in protecting vulnerable populations from atrocity crimes.

ASEAN Human Rights Regime and Mainstreaming the Responsibility to Protect: Challenges and Prospects

Sriprapha Petcharamesree
Mahidol University
sripraphapet@gmail.com

Abstract

This chapter explores the challenges and prospects of mainstreaming RtoP in the Association of Southeast Asian Nations (ASEAN) through the analysis of the roles and performance of the ASEAN human rights bodies, in particular the ASEAN Intergovernmental Commission on Human Rights (AICHR). The author argues that although ASEAN has made some progress in institutionalizing the promotion and protection of human rights and fundamental freedoms, it will take more time for ASEAN to mark substantial shift in intra-ASEAN relations and suggests that, in Southeast Asia where sovereignty is still jealously guarded, norms and ideas such as RtoP cannot yet have a decisive impact in practice. Specifically, mainstreaming RtoP in ASEAN is constrained by the principles of non-interference and consensus decision-making, which unfortunately remains the norm. In order for ASEAN to effectively care for people, a paradigm shift is necessary. Such shift can be anchored in the ASEAN Human Rights Declaration (AHDR) as well as employing the 'ASEAN minus X' decision-making formula, activating the Troika, and dispatching of special envoys. These options, which are not new to ASEAN and have historically helped in its engagement with human rights, could also enable ASEAN to prevent and respond to systematic human rights violations and other issues which may amount to war crimes. As well, promoting national and regional dialogues on RtoP could influence ASEAN member states, especially those who are not yet comfortable with the principle. Different workshops and seminars that the AICHR has been organizing already provide the body opportunities for sharing and learning from other regions.

Keywords

Responsibility to Protect – ASEAN – human rights – AICHR

In the report presented to the UN General Assembly in September 2014 entitled 'Mainstreaming the Responsibility to Protect in Southeast Asia' prepared

 | DOI:10.1163/9789004363212_004

by the High Level Advisory Panel (HLAP) on RtoP in Southeast Asia led by Dr. Surin Pitsuwan, former Minister of Foreign Affairs of Thailand and ASEAN Secretary General, the panel argued that 'the commitment of ASEAN member states to R2P' is a 'logical extension of the commitments that they have made to each other within the ASEAN framework.'[1] Four arguments in support of mainstreaming responsibility to protect (RtoP) in Southeast Asia were advanced, one of which was that:

> ASEAN already has important mechanisms and instruments that are particularly relevant to the implementation of the R2P such as the ASEAN Intergovernmental Commission on Human Rights, its Commission on the Promotion and Protection of the Rights of Women and Children, the ASEAN Treaty of Amity and Cooperation, and the Treaty on the Southeast Asia Nuclear Weapon-Free Zone.[2]

Writing on humanitarian intervention in Southeast Asia, Pruitt-Hamm argued along the same line. Specifically, he pointed out that:

> to maximize the recognition of and compliance with human rights norms in Southeast Asia… governments should form a regional human rights regime similar to those found in Africa, Europe and the Americas. At the same time, human rights activists should encourage the development and acceptance of non-military forms of intervention.[3]

Both Bruce and Surin had high hopes for ASEAN's regional human rights regime to play a role in making "humanitarian intervention and/or responsibility to protect", an important aspect of building an ASEAN caring community that promotes the protection of human rights of ASEAN people and one that can become part of the norms of the region. To some extent, the ASEAN Charter has created certain expectations along this line as it declares that among the

1 Cited in Alex J. Bellamy, 'To Build Regional Community, Southeast Asian Leaders Advocate for "Responsibility to Protect"', 5 September 2014, http://theglobalobservatory.org/2014/09/southeast-asia-responsibility-to-protect-r2p/ accessed 20 February 2015.

2 For details see High Level Advisory Panel on the Responsibility to Protect in Southeast Asia, 'Mainstreaming the Responsibility to Protect in Southeast Asia: Pathway Towards a Caring ASEAN community', 9 September 2014, http://r2psoutheasasia.org/report/, accessed 20 February 2015.

3 Bruce Pruitt-Hamm, 'Humanitarian Intervention in Southeast Asia in the Post Cold War World: Dilemmas in the Definition and Design of International Law', *Pacific Rim Law & Policy Journal*, 3/1 (1994), p. 186.

purposes of the organization are 'strengthening democracy, enhancing good governance and the rule of law, and promoting the protection of human rights and fundamental freedoms.'[4] The same principles appear in the ASEAN Charter. The document also upholds the United Nations Charter and international law, including international humanitarian law, subscribed by ASEAN Member States.'[5]

Some developments in ASEAN—such as the inclusion of promotion and protection of human rights and fundamental freedoms in the ASEAN Charter, the establishment of the regional human rights bodies, and the adoption of ASEAN Human Rights Declaration (AHRD)—may make us believe that RtoP "is a logical extension" of the normative commitments of ASEAN member states. However, the reality suggests otherwise. ASEAN still strictly adheres to its working principles stated in the ASEAN Charter, which apply to all its members and in the conduct of their international relations. Specifically, Article 2 of the Charter prescribes:

> [n]on-interference in the internal affairs of ASEAN Member States; respect for the right of every [m]ember [s]tate to lead its national existence free from external interference, subversion and coercion; and enhanced consultations on matters seriously affecting the common interest of ASEAN.[6]

Although the non interference principle is recognized and applied to all in the conduct of international relations, its application by ASEAN and within ASEAN has been extremely strict and has presented one of the major obstacles for the ASEAN human rights bodies to interpret their mandates and perform their functions effectively since their inception.

This chapter examines the challenges and prospects of mainstreaming RtoP in ASEAN through the analysis of the roles and performance of the ASEAN human rights bodies, in particular the ASEAN Intergovernmental Commission on Human Rights (AICHR). The author argues that although ASEAN has made some progress in institutionalizing the promotion and protection of human rights and fundamental freedoms, it will take more time for ASEAN to make a substantial shift in intra-ASEAN relations and suggests that, in Southeast Asia where sovereignty is still jealously guarded, norms and ideas such as RtoP cannot yet have a decisive impact in practice. Specifically, mainstreaming RtoP

4 The Association of Southeast Asian Nations, 'The ASEAN Charter', Article 1 para. 7.

5 *ibid.*

6 ASEAN, 'The ASEAN Charter', Article 2.

in ASEAN is constrained by the principles of non-interference and consensus decision-making, which unfortunately remains the norm. It will first analyse how the concepts of RtoP and state sovereignty are perceived by ASEAN and its member states. Then it looks into the development of the ASEAN human rights regime after 1993 when the organization made a commitment to establishing an appropriate regional human rights mechanism and framework. It will also look into how the AICHR has been dealing with serious human rights violations by focusing on the plight of the Rohingyas. Finally, it identifies a set of recommendations pertaining to enhancing the role of AICHR in promoting human rights protection in the region as well as prospects for introducing some elements of RtoP into the AICHR and ASEAN community building.

Perceptions of RtoP and State Sovereignty in ASEAN

ASEAN Member States and Concept of Sovereignty and RtoP

According to Drummond:

> [t]here is an ostensible tension between the normative entrenchment of non-interference in Southeast Asia and the potential for RtoP to legitimate actions that may constitute "interference". Such views are prefaced on the assumption that RtoP and non-interference are antithetical because of the perceived tension between individual human rights that RtoP seeks to uphold, and the primacy of state sovereignty that non-interference operates to preserve.[7]

Indeed, the analysis quoted is accurate in the sense that in Southeast Asia, state sovereignty cannot be compromised and interference is not accepted. This section analyses the perceptions (and misperceptions) of state sovereignty and RtoP particularly by member states of ASEAN. It shows that the principles of state sovereignty and non-interference in internal affairs of member states are strictly upheld and opportunities for relaxing this principle are very limited, especially when it comes to protection of rights of individuals in the region.

---

7 Catherine Drummond, 'Non-interference and the Responsibility to Protect: Canvassing the Relationship between Sovereignty and Humanity in Southeast Asia', no date, p. 1, http://www.polsis.uq.edu.au/dialogue/articledrummond2.pdf, accessed 20 February 2015.

The concept of state sovereignty is clearly recognized in international law including the UN Charter. Non-intervention and non-interference is the norm, and intervention even for humanitarian purposes is an exception to the rule. The main thrust of most arguments against intervention lies in both legal and moral grounds: that is, intervention violates the sovereignty of states in their internal affairs.

Attempts to redefine the concepts of sovereignty and intervention have been made by many scholars and diplomats. This includes the work of the International Commission on Intervention and State Sovereignty (ICISS). The ICISS introduced an innovative concept of sovereignty, which emphasizes the responsibility of sovereign states to protect populations from serious harm and if the state in question 'is unwilling or unable to halt or avert it, the principle of non intervention yields to the international responsibility to protect.'[8] In this way, sovereignty is 'conditional upon how a state treats its citizens, based on the belief that the state's authority arises ultimately from sovereign individuals.'[9]

However, many of the ASEAN Member States do not agree with this new concept as discussed below. While all ten ASEAN Member States (AMS) were present at the World Summit and agreed to adopt the principle, 'ASEAN has not officially incorporated the principle into its official norms'.[10] In fact, the RtoP remains a controversial issue in ASEAN. Different ASEAN member states view RtoP in different ways as exemplified in their interventions at the different UN forums on RtoP. During the Informal Interactive Dialogue on the Report of the Secretary-General on 'Fulfilling our collective responsibility: international assistance and the responsibility to protect' held in New York on 8 September 2014, at least six ASEAN countries expressed their views and reservations. Under the direction of the then Minister of Foreign Affairs, Marty Natalegawa, Indonesia stated that it 'fully and firmly subscribes to the finest purposes and objectives of the concept of Responsibility to Protect'.[11] Indonesia affirmed that 'we were an enthusiastic participant at the World Summit in 2005, where

8 Thomas Weiss, *Humanitarian Intervention*, (Cambridge : Polity Press, Second Edition, 2013), p. 109.

9 Andrew Heywood, *Global Politics*, (Palgrave Macmillan, 2011), p. 326.

10 Rizal Sukma, The ASEAN political and security community (APSC): opportunities and constraints for the R2P in Southeast Asia, *The Pacific Review*, 25/1 (2012), p. 136.

11 Statement by the Deputy Permanent Representative of the Republic of Indonesia to the United Nations at the Informal Interactive Dialogue on the Report of the Secretary-General on 'Fulfilling our collective responsibility: international assistance and the responsibility to protect', New York, 8 September 2014.

the question of Responsibility to Protect first entered the mainstream of international discourse'.[12] Furthermore:

> Indonesia has always supported the three pillars of the responsibility to protect, and committed itself to active participation and deliberation on implementing them. It is our unwavering position that the Responsibility to Protect is, and must be, a universal principle.[13]

Whilst Indonesia's delegation supported all three pillars of RtoP, other countries, though accepting the pillar I regarding responsibility of state to protect its own people and, to a certain extent, accepting the needs for capacity building, seemed to reject the third pillar arguing for the respect of state sovereignty and non-interference in internal affairs. The Philippines, one of the few most open and progressive countries in ASEAN is one of them. While affirming that a state's ' fundamental duty to protect their own people from atrocity crimes' and 'agreeing that assistance and capacity building … should be based on a clear understanding of the nature of atrocity crimes',[14] the Philippines pointed out that responsibility to prevent atrocity crimes:

> does not invite ways and means that are outside the ambit of the Charter of the United Nations' even as it upheld the principle of state sovereignty as 'sacrosanct' as it is 'the building block of international law and the conducts of international relations.[15]

Although it recognized that 'assistance and capacity building' are important, it also argued that there is 'no one-size-fits-all.'[16] The Philippines essentially echoed the Singapore delegation's statement, which quoted the Secretary-General's report a year earlier saying that 'there is no one size-fits-all approach to atrocity prevention. Every country's national circumstances differ.'[17]

12 *ibid.*

13 *ibid.*

14 Philippines Statement, UN General Assembly Informal Interactive Dialogue on the Responsibility to Protect: "Fulfilling our collective responsibility: International assistance and the responsibility to protect," 6th annual informal, interactive dialogue on the Responsibility to Protect, New York City, 8 September 2014.

15 *ibid.*

16 *ibid.*

17 Statement by Ambassador Karen Tan, Permanent Representative of Singapore to the United Nations, at the Informal Interactive Dialogue of the General Assembly on Responsibility to Protect, New York, 11 September 2013.

Although Myanmar did not reject RtoP outright, it also stressed that in the absence of consensus about the concept and a formula on how it can be implemented at various levels, member states should deliberate its 'careful and cautious consideration.'[18] Myanmar expressed its concerns over the different interpretations and the misuse or abuse of the concept. Meanwhile, Malaysia, though not completely opposed to the second pillar of RtoP on international assistance and capacity building, cautioned that it 'upholds the sovereignty of states and consent should remain paramount above all else when considering international assistance…and should be premised on a case-by-case basis.'[19] It also pointed out that Malaysia does not object to RtoP but that the principle 'requires comprehensive and in-depth discussions so as to enable international community to clearly define its understandings, applications, implementations, and effects on states on both international and internal dimensions.'[20] Thailand although emphasized the importance of national capacity building, specifically, pointed out that regional mechanisms 'can contribute significantly to capacity building for states.' But cautioned that 'national ownership is key to success.'[21] It joined Malaysia, Singapore, Myanmar and the Philippines that 'international assistance and capacity building for states should be based on constructive engagement and consent of the host government' and that '[i]t should not be an imposition of values or pretext for interference into a State's internal affairs'.[22]

Based on the foregoing interventions in the UN General Assembly on RtoP, it appears that most ASEAN member states agree in general that sovereign states have obligations to protect their own people against the four crimes and therefore are not opposed to Pillar I of RtoP. However, Pillar II, which is about international responsibility to assist and encouraging states to fulfill their Pillar I obligations, is viewed as subject to consent of state concerned. However, most

---

18 Intervention by H.E. Mr. Kyaw Tin, Permanent Representative of the Republic of the Union of Myanmar to the United Nations at the General Assembly Informal Interactive Dialogue on the Report of the Secretary-General on the Responsibility to Protect, New York, 8 September 2014.

19 Statement by H.E. Ambassador Hussein Haniff, Permanent Representative of Malaysia to United Nations on 'Fulfilling our responsibility: international assistance and the responsibility to protect' New York, 8 September 2014.

20 *ibid.*

21 Statement by H.E. Mr. Norachit Sinhaseni, Ambassador and Permanent Representative of Thailand to the United Nations, Intervention of Thailand at the UNGA informal interactive dialogue on the report of the Secretary General on R2P, 'Fulfilling our collective responsibility: International assistance and the R2P', New York, 8 September 2014.

22 *ibid.*

states in ASEAN except Indonesia are not quite comfortable to embrace the concept of international responsibility to undertake non-coercive and possibly even coercive measures under Pillar III to protect people from the four crimes if all else fails. Although calls for further discussions about RtoP were made, the perceptions of ASEAN member states on how it relates international responsibility to state sovereignty have not changed much since 2005. It is purely about traditional sovereignty of state which guards against possible interventions.

ASEAN and the Role of Regional Organizations in Implementing RtoP

Paragraph 139 of the World Summit Outcome Document recognized the important role of regional organizations in preventing and responding to mass atrocities. However, actualizing RtoP differs from one region to another. By far, Africa seems to be ahead even of the United Nations in this regard as the African Union (AU) claims to be pioneering the idea of international responsibility to intervene if states fail to protect their populations from mass atrocity crimes. Specifically, the AU under Article 4(h) of its Constitutive Act, incorporated the organization's right to intervene in a member state, 'pursuant to a decision of the Assembly in respect of grave circumstances, namely war crimes, genocide and crimes against humanity'.[23] The AU also adopted the Ezulwini Consensus in 2005, which welcomed RtoP as a tool for the prevention of mass atrocities.[24]

In Europe, the European Union (EU) considers the RtoP as an emerging norm to which it has reaffirmed its commitment in 2013 by adopting an inter institutional 'Consensus on R2P', including a common understanding of the implications of the principle to its external policies 'in dealing with situations of concern.'[25] In promoting the universality of the principle at the UN, the EU views RtoP as an essential part of the UN's collective security model and in the strengthening of the ICC as part of 'the responsibility to fight impunity.'[26] It also supported the Brazilian initiative called 'Responsibility while Protecting' that called for the most efficient and least harmful application of the RtoP principle and to ensure the development of a criteria in implementing Pillar III of the principle at the UNSC.[27] As well, the EU is also at the forefront of encouraging the five permanent members of the UN Security Council to adopt

23 African Union, 'The common African position on the proposed reform of the United Nations: The Ezulwini Consensus', Executive Council 7th Extraordinary Session, March 7,8, 2005, Addis Ababa, Ethiopia, Ext/EX.CL/2 (VII).

24 *ibid.*

25 European Parliament recommendation to the Council of 18 April 2013 on the UN principle of the 'Responsibility to Protect', 18 April 2013, http://www.europarl.europa.eu/sides/getDoc.do?type=TA&reference=P7-TA-2013-0180&language=EN, accessed 1 March 2015.

26 *ibid.*

27 *ibid.*

a voluntary code of conduct that limits the use of the Permanant-Five's right of veto in mass atrocity crime situations.[28]

ASEAN member states apparently differ from their African and European counterparts who are more receptive to the principle. Despite the recognition of the Pillar I of the RtoP, debates on RtoP within Southeast Asia have been rather minimal. According to Drummond: 'This recognition is illustrative of a normative shift away from the traditional understanding of state sovereignty and towards an acceptance of sovereignty as responsibility, which is the underlying premise of the Responsibility to Protect (R2P).'[29]

As discussed earlier, state sovereignty as a concept and in practice, among ASEAN member states, remains rather absolute. Any 'meaningful embrace of R2P necessitates reorienting the traditional national security paradigm to prioritise the needs of individuals'.[30] Since the advent of the ASEAN charter, we witness some changes. An 'emerging flexibility on non-interference has allowed the protection of individual human rights to grow in leaps and bounds in comparison to where the Association was a decade ago.'[31] Indeed, various platforms from which ASEAN could move towards a greater acceptance of RtoP have been gradually established in the region as pointed by in the Report of the High-Level Advisory Panel on the Responsibility to Protect in Southeast Asia, chaired by Surin. This author argues, however, that although ASEAN has made some progress in institutionalizing human rights and fundamental freedoms, it will take some time for the organization to mark a substantial shift in intra-ASEAN relations and suggests that in Southeast Asia, where sovereignty is still jealously guarded, norms and ideas such as RtoP cannot yet have a decisive impact in practice.

In February 2015, Prime Minister Hun Sen affirmed Cambodia's commitment to the RtoP principle and further elaborated that:

> while the UN Charter basically affirms the sovereignty of Member States as a key principle in the promotion of international peace and security, it is also important to acknowledge that the exercise of sovereign rights of states carries with it certain obligations or responsibilities... with the primary responsibility to protect their people against genocide, war crime, crimes against humanity and ethnics cleansing.[32]

28 *ibid.*

29 Drummond, 'Non-interference and the Responsibility to Protect', p, 1.

30 *ibid., p. 1.*

31 *ibid., p. 1.*

32 Address at the International Conference on Responsibility to Protect: Progress, Challenges and Opportunities in the Asia-Pacific: Cambodia Takes Leading Role in the Prevention

He proposed that Cambodia could play a leading role in implementing RtoP principle in the context of ASEAN by mainstreaming the norm in various ASEAN mechanisms that are already in place such as the AICHR, the ASEAN Commission on the Promotion and the Protection of the Rights of Women and Children (ACWC), and the ASEAN Institute for Peace and Reconciliation (AIPR).[33] Hun Sen also pointed out that although the RtoP has not been adopted formally in the language of ASEAN, some elements of the principle are included in certain ASEAN declarations and statements.[34] He emphasized that the RtoP principle was supported by all ASEAN members at the UN in 2005 and stated that Cambodia, together with Indonesia, supports the concept of RtoP and offers to facilitate the mainstreaming of the concept in the region especially through its existing mechanisms. This may be considered as a prospective project.

Notwithstanding the strong support for RtoP by a few ASEAN members, there are still some skeptics in the region. As Kasim and Putra have pointed out, 'it is early days yet for the doctrine of R2P. It has a long way to go before it becomes as entrenched as the Westphalian principle of inviolable state sovereignty.'[35] They found the tensions between the two principles—state sovereignty and the responsibility of the international community to protect human lives in situations of failing states—difficult to reconcile in the context of ASEAN.[36] For them, the 'deep-seated attachment to the sanctified idea of sovereignty is still too strong for a warm embrace of R2P: the fear of foreign interference in domestic affairs is overpowering.'[37] In ASEAN, even humanitarian assistance can also be controversial as was demonstrated in the case of the immediate humanitarian assistance to victims of Cyclone Nargis in Myanmar in 2008. In addition, there seems to be some misperceptions among ASEAN member states about RtoP, to wit: 1) it might lead to '21st century colonialism' and a tool by the West against weak Asian states; 2) it is synonymous with military intervention and the use of coercive force; and 3) it does not apply in the

---

of Genocide in ASEAN, 26 February 2015, http://cnv.org.kh/address-at-the-international-conference-on-the-responsibility-to-protect-progress-challenges-and-opportunity-in-asia-pacific-cambodia-takes-the-leading-role-in-the-prevention-of-genocide-i/ accessed 1 April 2015.

33 *ibid.*

34 *ibid.*

35 Yang Razali Kassim and Nur Azha Putra, 'Responsibility to Protect: How Should Southeast Asia Respond?', RSIS Commentaries, 25 April 2010, http://www.rsis.edu.sg/rsis-publication/nts/1333-responsibility-to-protect-how/#.VS96tfApo2E, accessed 1 April 2015.

36 *ibid.*

37 *ibid.*

region because crimes against humanity like those in Africa would not happen in Southeast Asia.[38] Although the writing was a bit dated and since then ASEAN member states have been participating in different forums, as discussed in the earlier section which examined statements made by various ASEAN countries, the author contends that the 'misperceptions' still remain. This view was confirmed by Surin Pitsuwan.[39]

Some ASEAN leaders however seem to forget the Cambodian genocide in the 1970s as well as the massacre in 1991 in East Timor that happened in the region. Sovereignty remains at the heart of the discourse and language of ASEAN, which has been formalized and legally recognized in most of its documents especially the ASEAN Charter. This despite the recognition of other concepts including 'strengthening democracy, enhance good governance and the rule of law, and to promote and protect human rights and fundamental freedoms' as well as 'upholding the United Nations Charter and international law, including international humanitarian law, subscribed to by ASEAN Member States.'[40] It should be reiterated that under the ASEAN Charter, ASEAN Members shall act accordingly based on certain principles, which include, among others, respect for sovereignty and territorial integrity of member states, non-interference in their internal affairs, and respect for the right of member states to lead their national existence.[41]

Although the working principles stated in Article 2 of the ASEAN Charter are the same norms in the United Nations Charter and all other regional/sub-regional organizations, adherence by ASEAN Member States to these principles is strictly observed even in times of serious and systematic human rights violations that could lead to genocide, crimes against humanity, and humanitarian crisis. Historically, ASEAN has not openly intervened in serious human rights violations and humanitarian crisis in the region, except in two cases: 1) in Myanmar during Cyclone Nargis but with the government's consent and for humanitarian reasons; and 2) in East Timor to support UN operations but with consent of Indonesia after 1999. The Santa Cruz massacre in East Timor in 1991 was not discussed in ASEAN until the late 1990s after the organization was criticised by the international community for its silence on the issue. Even so, ASEAN argued then that 'the East Timor case was an international problem and therefore only the UN had the legitimacy and capacity to undertake peace

---

38 *ibid.*

39 Surin Pitsuwan, Talk given to participants of Track II Dialogue on Force Migration in the Asia Pacific, 28 February 2016, Bangkok.

40 ASEAN, The ASEAN Charter, Article 1, para. 7.

41 *ibid.*, Article 2.

keeping operations and mobilize the necessary massive resources for it.'[42] Singapore's then Prime Minister Goh Chok Tong pointed out that 'East Timor was not a problem created by ASEAN... [it] is an international problem... [and] remains an issue with the United Nations.'[43] However, some ASEAN members participated in the UN Peace Keeping operations. ASEAN's participation in the UN peacekeeping in East Timor created differences between old and new members of ASEAN. The five founding members—Thailand, Philippines, Malaysia, Singapore and Brunei—contributed either military or humanitarian assistance, while the new members—Myanmar, Cambodia, Laos, and Vietnam—did not contribute because such action might set a precedent for intervention in the region.[44] In particular, the Myanmar military junta stated that 'the decision of some ASEAN countries to be involved in peace-keeping operations in East Timor is not a coordinated ASEAN position'.[45] Even with Indonesia's consent, ASEAN failed to reach a consensus to take collective action because of the concern over violating the principle of non- interference. Vietnam's position on East Timor is also interesting to look at. In 1975, it supported UN General Assembly Resolution 3845 against the occupation of East Timor by Indonesia. After its admission into ASEAN in 1995, Vietnam strictly adhered to the principle of non-interference. Not only did it not support the participation of ASEAN in the UN Peacekeeping operations, but it also did not allow Thai transport planes, en route to East Timor, to fly over the country at night. Some important observations can be made here with regard to ASEAN's response to the crisis in East Timor. First, it was not a collective ASEAN initiative but one that was made by individual member states. Second, the principle of state sovereignty and non-interference in domestic affairs of a member state (Indonesia) was fully respected as consent was given. Third, ASEAN member states did not reach a consensus to respond collectively, instead, had a consensus to act individually on the case of Timor. Fourth, some member states of ASEAN having joined the UN peace operations wanted to ensure that no single Western country such as Australia played a dominant role in the operations. As then Malaysian Prime Minister Mahathir Mohamad pointed out, 'people in the region felt threatened by too much participation on the part of big Western countries'.[46]

---

42 Cited in Sunsanee Sutthisunsanee, *Response of ASEAN to Human Rights Violations in Southeast Asia: Cass studies of Cambodia and East Timor*, Unpublished MA Thesis for the fulfillment of MA in Human Rights, Mahidol University, October 2006, p. 49.

43 *ibid.*

44 *ibid.*

45 *ibid.*

46 *ibid, p. 60.*

It can also be argued that ASEAN has not been very consistent in its practice of 'intervention' in the region. In 1997, in the aftermath of a coup staged by Hun Sen against Prince Ranarridh, ASEAN took a collective response to the political crisis in Cambodia even without the consent of its government. In particular, it decided to postpone Cambodia's admission into ASEAN and insisted that Prince Ranarridh will continue to be recognized as the first prime minister of Cambodia.[47] Sorpong Peou pointed out that 'while it was clear that ASEAN had a real interest to responding actively to Cambodia's political problem, this meant breaking precedent with its hallowed principle of 'non-interference'[48] and for the first time the idea of a more 'constructive intervention' in Cambodia's affairs involving diplomatic mediation was openly advocated.[49] It must be noted however that ASEAN's intervention in Cambodia was made when the latter was not yet member of the Association.

Notwithstanding ASEAN's intervention in internal conflicts of non-member states like East Timor and Cambodia, there were also occasions when ASEAN decided as a group to exert pressure on member states where human rights violations have occurred. This is true in the case of Myanmar after it was admitted as full member of ASEAN in 1997. As Yun Sun pointed out, Myanmar's domestic politics and human rights record have complicated its status as a member of ASEAN. Specifically, it was forced to forfeit its chairmanship in 2005 after pressure from the West and which was viewed as a national humiliation by many in Myanmar. As well, the military's violent crackdown in 2007 against the Buddhist-led protests drew strong condemnation from ASEAN foreign ministers, who 'expressed their revulsion to Myanmar Foreign Minister Nyan Win' even as they also urged the government 'to exercise restraint and seek a political solution.'[50]

ASEAN's reservations about Myanmar did not subside until the country embarked on political and economic reforms in 2011. However, this was overshadowed again by a series of communal violence in Rakhine that started in June 2012, which put ASEAN and some of its member states in a rather difficult position. The response to the crisis from the region was done mainly through bilateral engagement with the Myanmar government. For example,

---

47 Sorpong Peou, 'Diplomatic Pragmatism: ASEAN's response to the July 1997 Coup' in Dylan Hendrickson (ed.) *Safeguarding peace: Cambodias constitutional challenge*, Accord No. 5 (1998), p. 32.

48 *ibid.*

49 *ibid.*

50 Yun Sun, 'Myanmar's ASEAN Chairmanship: An Early Assessment', 23 September 2014, http://www.isn.ethz.ch/Digital-Library/Articles/Detail/?lng=en&id=183736, accessed 1 August 2015.

in August 2012, Indonesian President Susilo Bambang Yudhoyono requested his Myanmar counterpart to allow observers to travel to the crisis-affected areas, while Indonesian Foreign Minister Marty Natalegawa in February 2013 announced a US$1 million humanitarian assistance to Rakhine prior to his trip to the area at the invitation of the Myanmar government. For its part, the Malaysian government, which has been involved in discussions with Nay Pi Taw on the Rohingya issue for some years, supported some Malaysian relief organizations in response to the crisis in Rakhine.[51]

From the foregoing, it can be argued that ASEAN and its members tend to be more comfortable with interventions in other states outside ASEAN. However, selectively, ASEAN was able to relax the principle of non-interference and applied constructive engagement such as sending the ASEAN Troika to offer good office soon after the 1997 Cambodian political conflict. The regional pressure on Myanmar not to chair ASEAN in 2005 and interventions in the crisis of Rakhine state by Indonesia and Malaysia show that despite the constraints in its capacity to properly intervene, ASEAN and individual member states could decide to intervene if the crisis starts to attract international attention and cause some spillover effects into other member states.

The next section examines whether the perceptions and behavior of ASEAN and its members have changed after the establishment of regional mechanisms on human rights and the adoption of the ASEAN Human Rights Declaration. Specifically, it provides an overview of the ASEAN human rights bodies and the standards adhered to by ASEAN based on international commitment and obligations. Thereafter, an examination of how ASEAN has been dealing with the plight of Rohingya is presented.

The ASEAN Human Rights Regime and R2P

Regional Mechanisms and Framework on Human Rights Protection

For many human rights advocates in the region, the establishment of the AICHR in October 2009 and the ACWC in April 2010 presented great promise for the protection and promotion of human rights and the rights of women and children in the region. Unfortunately, more and more people criticize their ineffectiveness in carrying out their respective mandates. The inclusion of the

51 Lilianne Fan and Hanna B. Krebs, 'Regional organisations and humanitarian action: the case of ASEAN', September 2014, http://www.odi.org/sites/odi.org.uk/files/odi-assets/publications-opinion-files/9207.pdf, accessed 1 August 2015, p. 10.

creation of an ASEAN human rights body in Article 14 of the ASEAN Charter was not a miracle but a necessity.

The AICHR is a Charter-based body whose mandate includes the promotion and protection of human rights of all ASEAN peoples. It does not have its own secretariat and all representatives of member states are appointed by their respective governments. Except for Indonesia and Thailand, all representatives are chosen by the government without a participatory and transparent selection process. Representatives in AICHR perceive themselves as 'representative' of the appointing government. Among the major criticisms of the AICHR is that the body does not have an explicit mandate to perform a protection duty. Although the criticisms rest on some facts, AICHR could interpret their mandates and functions expansively and creatively. For example, the AICHR could influence ASEAN Member States (AMS) to consider acceding to and ratifying international human rights instruments (Article 4.5 of its Terms of Reference); seek to obtain information from AMS' on the protection and promotion of human rights (Article 4.10); and conduct thematic studies relating to human rights in ASEAN (Article 4.12) including looking into certain systematic human rights violations in the region. However, activities organised by the AICHR so far focus mainly on human rights promotion and awareness-raising, which is easier to reach a consensus on among its representatives.[52] Except for two human rights dialogues organised by the Indonesian and Thai Representatives to discuss certain human rights issues in their respective countries,[53] no concrete actions are yet to be taken to address any particular serious human rights violations in the region. The AICHR is not equipped with monitoring and/or investigative powers and cannot effectively reconcile the principle of non-interference with the protection of human rights. It does not work with an accusatory approach, or naming and shaming of erring members, but rather upholds ASEAN traditional principles emphasizing the importance of the different histories and circumstances of member states.

Another human rights body established by ASEAN is the ACWC, which is a specialised body dealing specifically with the rights of women and children. Although the Terms of Reference (TOR) of the ACWC that have been developed and implemented are seen as a bit more advanced than the one of AICHR, they both carry more or less the same characteristics in terms of structure, memberships, and appointment as well as mandates and functions. For both bodies,

52 Each representative desiring to organise any activities such as workshop, trainings, youth debates, etc, is required by the AICHR's rules of procedures to present a concept note for the AICHR approval.

53 Not all representatives of AICHR are required to participate.

their protection mandates are also hindered by the core ASEAN principle of non-interference in internal affairs of AMS and by the principles of consultation and consensus.

The adoption in November 2012 of the ASEAN Human Rights Declaration (AHRD) is another milestone for ASEAN. Although some provisions of the AHRD are below international standards, many of its provisions could still be applied for the proper promotion and protection of human rights in the region. It also reflects the dominant perceptions in ASEAN about human rights including the section covering civil and political rights, which took the AICHR quite some time to agree on. Specifically, the Indonesian and Thai initiatives to include protection of people from enforced disappearances was rejected because the concept was new or non-existent in some member countries. The right to freedom of association, although included in the version submitted to the ASEAN foreign ministers, was removed at the last minute before its adoption because one country was not comfortable with it. This recognizes the different political contexts of member states and perceptions about human rights of their respective governments. As well, respect for national sovereignty was underscored throughout the text through references to national laws, the inclusion of limitation clauses, the emphasis on responsibilities of the individual vis-à-vis society and the state and the direct reference, and reaffirmation of the principle of non-interference in internal affairs. Although ASEAN to some extent shows some political commitment towards the development of human rights regime in ASEAN through the adoption of the AHRD, further steps towards effective human rights mechanisms and adherence to stronger human rights standards in the region will take a long time.

Even with the establishment of the ASEAN human rights mechanisms and framework, there has been little change to the perceptions of many ASEAN member states on human rights. It must be pointed out here that in studying ASEAN perceptions of human rights[54] is important to understand how ASEAN leaders view human rights. According to Tommy Koh "[there was no] issue that took up more of our time, [and no issue] as controversial and which divided the ASEAN family so deeply as human rights."[55] Others have also argued that

54 The following paragraphs of the chapter are modified from Sriprapha Petcharamesree, 'The Human Rights Body: A Test for Democracy Building of ASEAN', (IDEA, 2009), http://www.idea.int/resources/analysis/upload/Sriprapha_low_2.pdf.

55 Prof. Tommy Koh is Ambassador-at-Large and Director of the Institute of Policy Studies, Ministry of Foreign Affairs, Singapore. This quotation is drawn from a talk he gave at the Seventh Workshop on an ASEAN Human Rights Mechanism, 12–13 June 2008 in Singapore.

ASEAN's credibility was built on the region's stability, as well as the economic success and cohesion of its members.[56] These achievements by ASEAN's are anchored in two important pillars: the norm of non-interference and the principle of consensus decision-making, which are stated in the 1976 Treaty of Amity and Cooperation in South East Asia and reaffirmed in the 2008 ASEAN Charter.

The inclusion of human rights clauses in the ASEAN Charter does not help ASEAN to develop a human rights discourse or change its perception of human rights. The norm of non-interference in internal affairs was repeated in not only in the ASEAN Charter but also in the TORs of the AICHR and the AHRD.

The working principles of ASEAN have been based on non-intervention and freedom from external interference. These principles have been reaffirmed throughout the history of ASEAN. There were some attempts to test the adherence to the principle of non interference of ASEAN. Former Thai Foreign Minister and later ASEAN Secretary General Surin Pitsuwan, and former Malaysian Deputy Prime Minister Anwar Ibrahim, have proposed the concepts of constructive engagement and flexible engagement, respectively. Surin said in 1998 that:

> it is time that ASEAN's cherished principle of non-intervention is modified to allow it to play a constructive role in preventing or resolving domestic issues with regional implications. . . when a matter of domestic concern poses a threat to regional stability, a dose of peer pressure or friendly advice at the right time can be helpful'.[57]

There has been little observable change in stance in the period since 1999. Prime Minister Hun Sen affirmed the non-interference principle by saying that '[m]any Asian countries advocate state sovereignty and non-interference in internal affairs. No state can dictate and make judgments on others about human rights. Foreign policies should not be linked to human rights'.[58] In the most recent meeting with the current Chair of AICHR, the ASEAN working principles were reiterated.[59] Despite a few exceptions where ASEAN and some

---

56 Simon SC Tay and Jesus Estanislao, 'The Relevance of ASEAN : Crisis and Change' in Simon SC Tay, Jesus Estanislao and Hadi Soesastro (eds.), *A New ASEAN in a New Millennium*, (Jakarta, CSIS, 2000), p. 14.

57 Quoted in Sutthisunsanee, *Response of ASEAN to Human Rights Violations in Southeast Asia*, p. 26.

58 Kassim and Putra, 'Responsibility to Protect: How Should Southeast Asia Respond?'.

59 Meeting with the Chair of AICHR, 3 March 2016, Vientiane, Loa PDR.

member states did intervene in some cases as already elaborated in previous section, long term reconciliation between the principle of human rights and that of non-interference is not foreseeable in the near future. The Rohingya issue, which will be discussed below, is an interesting dilemma for ASEAN as it attempts to adhere to the principle of non-interference and at the same time being pressured to also recognize the need to protect the Rohingyas.

ASEAN and International Human Rights Protection Obligations

As part of international community, one could say that with varying degrees of engagement, Member States of ASEAN have been active in participating in the UN's existing human rights regime. The ratifications of international human rights treaties vary from one country to another ranging from so-called human rights ratifying 'champions' such as Cambodia and the Philippines to very limited ratifications as evident in the cases of Brunei Darussalam, Malaysia, Myanmar and Singapore. Only Cambodia and the Philippines are party to the Rome Statute that established the International Criminal Court.[60] Seven out of 10 ASEAN member states have ratified or acceded to the Convention on the Prevention and Punishment of the Crime of Genocide.[61] It is interesting to note that the ratification of the Genocide Convention of some countries was made before their independence, such as Cambodia and Lao PDR.

It may be argued that the behavior of ASEAN Member States with regard to the ratification of international human rights conventions is not only a reflection of their commitments to international human rights norms but also of their perceptions about human rights and their level of comfort. Only two Conventions, namely the Convention on the Rights of the Child (CRC) and the Convention on the Elimination of All Forms of Discrimination Against Women (CEDAW), were ratified by all ASEAN member states.[62] The Convention on the Rights of Person with Disabilities is another example that may be universally ratified by the ASEAN member states in the near future.[63] All these conventions deal with vulnerable groups of people who need of protection. One could also

60 The States Parties to the Rome Statute can be found at: http://www.icc-cpi.int/en_menus/asp/states%20parties/Pages/the%20states%20parties%20to%20the%20rome%20statute.aspx, accessed 13 April 2015.

61 The seven countries include Cambodia (1950), Laos (1950), Malaysia (1994), Myanmar (1956), Philippines (1950), Singapore (1995), and Vietnam (1981). See details at https://treaties.un.org/Pages/ViewDetails.aspx?src=TREATY&mtdsg_no=IV-1&chapter=4&lang=e, accessed 13 April 2015.

62 Some countries such as Brunei, Singapore, Malaysia made a 'blanket reservation'.

63 Only Brunei did not ratify the International Convention on the Rights of Person with disabilities (CRPD) yet. As of August 2015, the process of submitting the instrument of ratification to the UN is ongoing.

add that these groups of people are not perceived as politically sensitive in the eyes of many ASEAN governments.

The commitment of ASEAN member states to international human rights norms is rather remarkable in terms of ratification and participation in the UN activities. Many have become significantly invested in the Universal Periodic Review (UPR) process. Some members, such as Indonesia, Malaysia, Philippines, Thailand and Vietnam, have taken turns to run for seats in the UN Human Rights Council. However, the acceptance of human rights as a universal concept is still problematic both in theory and practice. As mentioned earlier, the debates on the universality of human rights and ASEAN values were revived and became quite heated during the drafting process of the AHRD. Some ASEAN members were able to incorporate the concept of ASEAN values into the Declaration as reflected in the General Principles No.7, which states that 'All human rights are universal, indivisible, interdependent and interrelated... the realization of human rights in the regional and national context bearing in mind different political, economic, legal, social, cultural, historical and religious backgrounds'.[64] The formulation is different from the universally accepted document – the 1993 Vienna Declaration and Program of Action (VDPA) – which was adopted by all ten members of ASEAN.[65] Many attempts by majority of representatives of AICHR for the AHRD to literally use the VDPA failed because one country openly objected to it throughout the drafting process. The 'minority hegemony'—through the use of veto in the context of consultation and consensus principle in ASEAN—seems to go against the universal and international norms. Therefore, the ratification of an international normative framework on human rights of ASEAN member states does not necessarily translate into applying such norms at the regional or national levels. The ASEAN way, which includes non-interference in internal affairs, consultation and consensus, as well as cooperation and non confrontation have been inhibiting ASEAN in responding more strongly to serious and systematic human rights violations such as the case of Rohingyas.

The Plight of the Rohingya – Dilemma for ASEAN Human Rights Protection

As a regional organization, ASEAN has been hesitant to deal with the Rohingya issue in Myanmar, which has been one of the most pressing human rights problems in the region since the 1990s. The UNHCR sees the plight of the

64 'ASEAN Human Rights Declaration', http://www.asean.org/news/asean-statement-communiques/item/asean-human-rights-declaration, accessed 20 April 2015.

65 Vienna Declaration and Plan of Action, para. 5, http://www.ohchr.org/EN/ProfessionalInterest/Pages/Vienna.aspx, accessed 13 April 2015.

Rohingyas as the biggest humanitarian challenge in Southeast Asia today. Indeed, some ASEAN members together with the rest of the international community have expressed serious concerns regarding the issue. For example, former Indonesian Foreign Minister Marty Natalegawa raised the issue at an emergency meeting of the Organization of Islamic Cooperation (OIC) in Mecca in August 2012, referred to their persecution as a crime against humanity, which is 'not in line with its recent efforts towards democracy' and that '[a]ny act of discrimination on the basis of religion or ethnicity is unacceptable.'[66] Human Rights Watch in 2013 called the situation as a 'crime against humanity and ethnic cleansing'[67] and explained that the deportation, forced population transfers, and other abuses against Rohingyas have long been acknowledged by the United Nations as constituting international crimes, which referred to these abuses as 'widespread', 'systematic', and resulting from 'state policy.'[68]

Many NGOs and academic institutions in the region as well as international bodies have called on ASEAN to respond to the humanitarian crisis affecting the Rohingyas. During his term as ASEAN Secretary General, Surin Pisuwan, with the support of former Foreign Minister of Indonesia Marty Natalegawa, had proposed that ASEAN foreign ministers should once again offer humanitarian assistance similar to the aftermath of Cyclone Nargis in Myanmar in 2008 even as individual ASEAN states also offered assistance to the Rohingyas.[69] Surin warned that failure on the part of ASEAN and the rest of the international community to respond to the crisis could lead to the Rohingyas '[becoming] radicalised and the entire region could be destabilized.'[70] Thus far, the only thing that ASEAN foreign ministers have done was to issue a statement in August 2012 where they said that they were following closely developments since the outbreak of violence and were ready to lend humanitarian assistance 'upon the request of the Government of Myanmar.' However, Myanmar rejected the offer on the ground that the conflict in Rakhine is an internal affair. It also kept the issue of Rohingyas off the ASEAN's agenda during its

---

66 S. Rajaratnam School of International Studies, 'Plight of the Rohingya: ASEAN Credibility Again at Stake', 19 November 2012, http://www.fairobserver.com/region/central_south_asia/plight-rohingya-asean-credibility-again-stake/, accessed 25 April 2015.

67 See details in Human Rights Watch, 'All you can do is pray: Crimes against Humanity and Ethnic cleansing of Rohingya Muslims in Burma's Arakan State', 2013, https://www.hrw.org/report/2013/04/22/all-you-can-do-pray/crimes-against-humanity-and-ethnic-cleansing-rohingya-muslims, p. 11.

68 *ibid.*

69 S. Rajaratnam School of International Studies, 'Plight of the Rohingya: ASEAN Credibility Again at Stake'.

70 *ibid.*

chairmanship in 2014 and invoked the ASEAN Charter in upholding the principle of 'non-interference in other member countries' internal affairs.'[71] While the United Nations and the United States have both increased the pressure on the government in Nay Pyi Taw to take steps to address the problem, including pushing for a full resumption of humanitarian aid in the state, ASEAN as a regional organization remained largely silent.[72]

However, the discovery of mass graves in the southern provinces of Thailand and across the Malaysian border, along with boatloads of Rohingyas (and Bangladeshis) fleeing Myanmar and Bangladesh, prompted Malaysian Foreign Minister Datuk Seri Anifah Aman to call for collective ASEAN response to the refugee crisis. Specifically, he stressed that 'the problem should be resolved within ASEAN'[73] even as he pointed out that since the problem has spilled over into other ASEAN states, the issue is no longer just Myanmar's internal issue. While respecting the sovereignty of member states, he stressed ASEAN should address the issue through engagement with Myanmar and for it to 'look for the best way possible so that the issue will not be internationalized.'[74] Even so, attempts by the ASEAN Secretary General to include the Rohingya issue into ASEAN's agenda and efforts within the AICHR to discuss the matter have both failed. Together with some ASEAN members, Myanmar opposed these attempts by invoking the principle of non-interference in internal affairs and the need for consensus in taking up the issue.

Despite the adoption of the AHRD, it is clear that the principle of non-interference has been used by some ASEAN members as a shield from accountability for human rights violations and impunity. Thus, the AICHR and the AHRD have failed to effectively enable ASEAN as an organization to respond to atrocities being committed against Rohingyas in Myanmar. Although ASEAN as a group has failed to respond collectively to the Rohingya problem, the three affected members—Malaysia, Indonesia, and Thailand—have nevertheless initiated regional discussions on the issue. On 20 May 2015, the three foreign ministers from these countries met in Putrajaya to 'discuss the issue of irregular movement of people' into Indonesia, Malaysia and Thailand in an effort to find

71 Tim Mclaughlin and Nyan Lynn Aung, 'Govt succeeds in keeping Rohingya off ASEAN Summit agenda', *The Myanmar Times*, 12 May 2014, http://www.mmtimes.com/index.php/national-news/nay-pyi-taw/10324-govt-succeeds-in-keeping-rohingya-off-asean-summit-agenda.html, accessed 30 April 2015.

72 *ibid.*

73 'Rohingya refugee issue now for Asean to solve, says Anifah', *The Star Online*, 25 April 2015, http://www.thestar.com.my/News/Nation/2015/04/25/Rohingya-refugee-issue-now-for-Asean-to-solve-says-Anifah/, accessed 5May 2015.

74 *ibid.*

'a solution to the crisis…and its serious impact on the national security of the affected countries.'[75] Among other things, they: 1) expressed deep concern over the plight of the irregular migrants; 2) emphasized that necessary measures were taken by the three countries on humanitarian grounds; 3) stressed that the issue cannot be addressed solely by the three countries; 4) acknowledged the need for comprehensive and durable solution to the crisis by engaging relevant stakeholders and through the various existing international mechanisms; and 5) agreed to implement interim measures by addressing the root causes and the role of affected countries in fulfilling their obligations under international and domestic laws, 'including the provision of humanitarian assistance to the irregular migrants.'[76] In particular, Indonesia and Malaysia agreed to continue extending humanitarian assistance to irregular migrants still at sea and offering them temporary shelter, provided that the resettlement and repatriation process will be done in one year by the international community. They also invited other countries in the region 'to join in this endeavor.'[77] Meanwhile, the Thai government organised a special meeting in Bangkok on Irregular Migration in the Indian Ocean on 29 May 2015,[78] which aimed at generating a regional response to 'the alarming rise in the irregular movement of persons in the Indian Ocean.' The meeting adopted a number of ad hoc measures and agreed to share responsibilities, including engaging in further discussions and bilateral consultations in accordance with existing regional mechanisms and frameworks.

Although the statement made after the 1st Special Meeting held on 29 May 2015 called for 'addressing root causes and improving livelihood in at risk communities'[79] but the fact that the term Rohingyas was not mentioned and that the two meetings put the issue into the larger framework of irregular movement at sea and human trafficking, it makes it difficult to properly deal with the issue. By framing and conflating issues into irregular movement

75 Joint Statement: ministerial Meeting on Irregular Movement of People in Southeast Asia, Asia Pacific Centre for the Responsibility to Protect (R2P), 20 May 2015, https://www.facebook.com/r2papuq/posts/1119504018063472, accessed 1 August 2015.

76 *ibid.*

77 *ibid.*

78 Ministry of Foreign affairs of the Kingdom of Thailand, 'Summary of Special Meeting on Irregular Migration in the Indian Ocean, 29 May 2015, http://www.mfa.go.th/main/en/media-center/14/56880-Summary-Special-Meeting-on-Irregular-Migration-in.html, accessed 1 August 2015.

79 'Press Release: Special Meeting on Irregular Migration in the Indian Ocean', http://www.europarl.europa.eu/meetdocs/2014_2019/documents/dase/dv/dase0610_4_pressrelease1_/dase0610_4_pressrelease1_en.pdf, accessed 20 February 2016.

and trafficking, this approach fails to address the root causes of migration at sea and the plight of Rohingyas in the region. As well, these initiatives came from individual states affected by 'irregular movements' and not by ASEAN as a regional entity. More importantly, these meetings also framed the Rohingya problem as a humanitarian and not as a human rights issue, and the actions to be taken seem to be based mainly on humanitarian grounds instead of the RtoP framework to prevent atrocity crimes.

From the foregoing, it is evident that ASEAN as a regional organization, and AICHR as a regional human rights institution, have been constrained from taking an active stance in responding to human rights violations in the region. There is no question that the Rohingya issue requires a certain level of coordinated regional response, which may or may not be pursued within the framework of RtoP. Failure to respond means that ASEAN would continue to face reputational costs as the issue sends a strong message to the international community that the organization is incapable of addressing serious human rights violations, which are clearly manifestations of atrocity crimes.

Conclusions and Recommendations

This chapter demonstrates quite clearly that even with the setting up of the ASEAN human rights regime, it is unlikely that it can effectively contribute to mainstreaming the RtoP in the region. This stems primarily from the tension between, on the one hand, the protection of human rights—which to some extent, requires a certain type of intervention—and, on the other hand, the non-interference principle that remains an important pillar of ASEAN diplomacy in the region. Without a more democratic decision making process and a system of accountability in enforcing its principles, ASEAN as an organization is constrained from engaging in interventions, much less raising serious concerns about human rights violations in the region.

The current institutional design of ASEAN and its human rights regime are also less accommodating to a holistic understanding and application of RtoP in the region. Specifically, the ASEAN Charter neither allows for a more flexible interpretation of state sovereignty nor provides for any exception to the rule of non- interference. Although ASEAN members recognize the importance of the principle of RtoP the behavior of ASEAN and its member states is more telling. For many ASEAN members, instead of stressing the human rights and democratic aspects of the regional grouping, they tend to emphasise the implementation of long-term reforms in the economic, social and education sectors, and the pursuit of a broad, inclusive but non-political dialogue with all stakeholders. Accordingly, this approach can foster regional cooperation, as it is easier to achieve consensus on a non-political matter. The promotion of democratic values, including human rights protection and RtoP, is considered too politically sensitive.

The establishment of ASEAN human rights mechanisms shows that ASEAN's stance on human rights has evolved over time, but trying to forge a regional position on human rights to eventually protect the rights of all peoples would require a significant shift in the so-called 'ASEAN Way' of decision-making. The fact that ASEAN members have diverse political systems also serves as another problem for the AICHR, given that there is low level of democratization in several ASEAN member states. In fact, for some of them, promoting democracy and human rights protection pose a threat to national sovereignty. Clearly, self-serving interpretations of the principle of non-interference in the internal affairs of states, as well as abuse and misuse of the principle of consensus will continue to hinder the mainstreaming RtoP in the region.

Thus far, ASEAN continues to insist on its traditional norms despite advocating for a more people-oriented and people-centred organization or community. In fact, many ASEAN members still hesitate to engage with civil society and remain suspicious of the exercise of freedoms and political rights by the people. The recognition of human rights protection in ASEAN has not effectively translated into better protection of human rights of people in the region. Evidently, most ASEAN members are not yet comfortable with redefining sovereignty as responsibility and would therefore resist any attempts to employ RtoP as part of the human rights discourse in the region.

However, in order for ASEAN to open a little room for RtoP, there is a need for strengthen existing regional mechanisms for the protection and promotion of human rights and a broader meaning and application of the principle of non-interference in the internal affairs of one another. A more balanced pursuit of state and human security can create an environment favourable for each other's mutual reinforcement and advancement and the fundamental changes in the political structures and mindsets at the national level.[80] Indeed, a paradigm shift is required if ASEAN is to effectively care for the peoples of the region. While the AHRD does not include the capacity to apply legal sanctions against erring member states, it can still be a useful framework in finding some common position in the form of joint statements by the AICHR. Additionally, some formula which are not new to ASEAN—such as 'ASEAN

80 Abad, M.C. Jr., 'The Challenge of Balancing State Security with Human Security', Paper presented at the 9th Harvard Project for Asian and International Affairs Conference, Beijing, 27–30 August 2000, para. 41–42.

minus X', the ASEAN Troika, and dispatching of special envoys—which have historically shaped ASEAN's engagement may be useful in dealing with human rights violations in the region or issues related to the four crimes under the RtoP principle. Promoting national and regional dialogues on RtoP could influence ASEAN member states, especially those who are not yet comfortable with the principle. Different workshops and seminars that the AICHR has been organizing already provide the body opportunities for sharing and learning from other regions. In a number of meetings, some representatives of AICHR have openly suggested the discussions on ASEAN principles including non-interference and consensus. This may contribute to a better understanding and incorporation of Pillars I and II of the RtoP. Finally, the post-2015 visioning of ASEAN and review of the AICHR's Terms of Reference are opportunities for realizing the goal of making ASEAN a truly people-oriented and people-centered community. It is now time for ASEAN and AICHR to demonstrate that they could accommodate people's concerns and be mindful that failing the Declaration is worse than passing a document which was criticized as not up to international standard.

Building the Women, Peace and Security Agenda in the ASEAN through Multi-Focal Norm Entrepreneurship

Ma. Lourdes Veneracion-Rallonza
Ateneo de Manila University
mrallonza@ateneo.edu

Abstract

Women, Peace and Security (WPS) as a global agenda has gained traction since it was institutionalized in the United Nations Security Council (UNSCR) fifteen years ago. By December 2014, 46 out of 193 Member States of the United Nations have adopted their National Action Plans to systematically implement their respective country commitments to WPS. To date, 24 of the countries with National Action Plans (NAP) are in Europe while 13 are in Africa; the Asia Pacific Region has 6 and the Americas have 3. In Southeast Asia, only the Philippines has developed a NAP within the framework of the WPS while other countries integrated it in the existing broad policy and programmatic frames such as addressing violence against women. At the level of the Association of Southeast Asian Nations (ASEAN), taking on the agenda of WPS has yet to move beyond communicative rhetoric. This paper is an attempt to explore how WPS can be made part of the regional agenda on human protection and mass atrocities prevention, by mapping out discursive and institutional entry points within several ASEAN Member States and within ASEAN itself through the idea of multi-focal norm entrepreneurship.

Keywords

women – peace and security – norm entrepreneurship – multi-focal norm entrepreneurship

Advocacy for the protection of vulnerable groups has been embedded in various normative discourses institutionalized through policy frames and agenda. Some of these discourses might compete while others build on or complement each other. In the case of the responsibility to protect (R2P)—or the normative frame obligating states to protect of populations against mass

 | DOI:10.1163/9789004363212_005

atrocity crimes such as genocide, war crimes, crimes against humanity, and ethnic cleansing—there have been attempts to include the gender perspective in its preventive goals and actions.[1] Fairly recently, for example, United Nations Security Council Resolution (UNSCR) 2171 on conflict prevention acknowledged sexual and gender-based violence (SGBV) as grave violations of international humanitarian and international human rights law and can be seen as an indicator of further commission of mass atrocity crimes. To address this problem, UNSCR 2171 reiterates the need to promote gender equality as part of the comprehensive approach to prevent conflict and sustain peace.[2] Furthermore, it reaffirms 'the important role of women in the prevention and resolution of conflicts and in peacebuilding' and reiterates:

> its call to increase the equal, full and meaningful, participation, representation and involvement of women in conflict prevention and mediation efforts in a mutually reinforcing manner in line with resolutions 1325 (2000), 1820 (2008), 1888 (2009), 1889 (2009), 1960 (2010), 2106 (2013) and 2122 (2013)...[3]

These aforementioned resolutions comprise the UN Security Council's (UNSC) women, peace and security (WPS) agenda, consciously integrated into the discourse of R2P. Taken together, they manifest the application of a gender perspective in mass atrocity prevention.

Preventing mass atrocity crimes — namely, war crimes, crimes against humanity, genocide, and ethnic cleansing — must take gender as seriously. In the case of the commission of violence against civilian populations, gender plays a role in how women and men experience them. For example, men are generally killed since they are perceived to be protectors of their communities; women are usually raped, forcibly impregnated, and subjected to numerous forms of

1 See for example, Sarah Teitt, 'Women's Empowerment and Atrocities Prevention', 2014, http://www.e-ir.info/2014/11/11/womens-empowerment-and-atrocities-prevention/, accessed 21 June 2015; Eli Stamnes, 'The Responsibility to Protect: Integrating Gender Perspectives in Policies and Practices', *Global Responsibility to Protect* 4/2: 172–197 (2012); Sara Davies and Sarah Teitt, 'Engendering the Responsibility to Protect: Women and the Prevention of Mass Atrocities', *Global Responsibility to Protect* 4/2:198–222 (2012); and Sara Davies, Zim Nwokora, Eli Stamnes and Sara Teitt (eds), *Responsibility to Protect and Women, Peace and Security: Aligning the Protection Agendas* (Leiden: Martinus Nijhoff, 2013).

2 United Nations Security Council, S/Res/2171 2014, Preambular Clause 9, http://www.un.org/ga/search/view_doc.asp?symbol=S/RES/2171(2014), accessed 23 June 2015.

3 *ibid.*, Preambular Clause 21.

sexual violence because they are generally perceived to be bearers of their collective's honor and culture[4] — to kill the men means killing the defenders; to sexually violate women means the humiliation and demoralization of their communities. In both cases, the collective is weakened and thus, defeated. To advance justice in this setting or in post-conflict situations intended to prevent the recurrence of atrocities also need awareness on gender — how both women and men deal with their trauma and victimization and how they can participate in the rehabilitation of themselves and their communities. In other words, preventing mass atrocity crimes — a central idea in the discourse and practice of R2P — thus find complementarity with WPS in light of the application of the gender perspective in preventative interventions. In the context of war and armed conflict the most gravely affected are civilian populations and vulnerable groups. Through the use of gender lens, the differential impact of war and armed conflict on women and girls, as well as the acknowledgement of the varied roles they play during these conflict situations and post-conflict transitions, are accounted for more significantly. Thus, the protection of women and the prevention of violence against them as well as women's empowerment are discursive pillars that must be taken into in policy frames — and WPS provides such a roadmap.

From a historical perspective, WPS resonates well in Southeast Asia. Seven out of ten members of the Association of Southeast Asian Nations (ASEAN) have history of armed conflict including those involving the United States of America and the former Soviet Union in Vietnam, Laos, and Cambodia during the Cold War period until 1975, Vietnam's invasion of Cambodia in 1979 that ousted the Khmer Rouge four years later, as well as internal armed conflicts in Myanmar, Indonesia, the Philippines, and southern Thailand. Some of these countries have already transitioned from the Cold War that allowed them to focus on post-conflict reconstruction and rehabilitation. In the case of Indonesia, the end of Soeharto's regime in 1998 let loose ethnic and religious sentiments that fueled identity conflict clashes between collectives such as those that took place in Poso (1998–2000), Ambon (1999–2001), West Kalimantan (1997, 1999–2001),

4 See, for example, Miranda Alison, 'Wartime Sexual Violence: Women's Human Rights and Questions of Masculinity' *Review of International Studies*, 33:75–90 (2007); Susan Brownmiller, *Against Our Will: Men, Women and Rape* (New York: Fawcett Columbine, 1975); Radhika Coomaraswamy, 'Of Kali Born: Violence and the Law in Sri Lanka' in Margaret Schuler (ed.), *Freedom from Violence: Women's Strategies from Around the World*, (New York: Widbooks, 1992); Todd Salzman. 'Rape Camps as a Means of Ethnic Cleansing: Religious, Cultural and Ethical Responses To Rape Victims in Former Yugoslavia', *Human Right Quarterly* 20:348–78 (1998); Mary Ann Tetreault, 'Justice for All: Wartime Rape and Women's Human Rights', *Global Governance* 3/2:197–212 (1997); and Nira Yuval-Davis, *Gender and Nation* (London: Sage Publications, 1997).

North Maluku (1999–2001), and Central Kalimantan (2001) (Smith 2010). Ethno-nationalist struggles against the state, on the other hand, transpired in Aceh in the 1970s led by the Free Aceh Independence Movement or *Gerakan Aceh Merdeka* (GAM) and in West Papua in 1969 by the Free Papua Movement or *Organisasi Papua Merdeka* (OPM). Peace negotiations and eventual peace settlement with GAM came after the devastation of the tsunami in 2004; the armed struggle in West Papua continues to date. In Myanmar (Burma), armed political struggles for autonomy and ethnicity raged in the Kachin, Karenni (Kayah), Kayin, Rakhine, and Shan States since the 1960s and continues to date in some areas. Efforts by the central government Myanmar to end these insurgencies through peace negotiations have been explored since 2004, with the most recent one under the framework of the National Ceasefire Agreement in April 2015 involving several armed ethnic groups. In October 2015, prior to the general elections, the Myanmar government signed a nationwide ceasefire agreement with eight rebel groups. In the Philippines, the government has engaged in peace talks with armed groups since the end of the 1986 following the ouster of Marcos. A peace agreement with the Moro National Liberation Front (MNLF) was signed in 1996, and with the Moro Islamic Liberation Front (MILF) in 2014. Peace negotiations with the Communist Party of the Philippines-New People's Army-National Democratic Front (CPP-NPA-NDF) has been stalled since 2012 while the so called 'closure agreement' with the Cordillera *Bodong* Administration- Cordillera Peoples Liberation Army- (CPLA-CBA) and the *Rebolusyonaryong Partidong Manggagawang Pilipino*-Revolutionary Proletariat Army-Alex Boncayao Brigade-Tabara-Paduano Group (RPMP-RPA-ABB-TPG) continued to be implemented.

This paper examines the possibility of developing a WPS agenda at the regional level, particularly through the ASEAN. First, it identifies existing discursive policy frames within several ASEAN member states as regards the protection and empowerment of women in light of the Convention on the Elimination of All Forms of Discrimination Against Women (CEDAW) and UNSCR 1325. It then looks at incipient institutional initiatives at the ASEAN as well as relevant sectoral bodies and investigates whether they can serve as strategic openings for WPS. Lastly, it explores the possibility of a mutli-focal norm entrepreneurship for the grounding of WPS in the ASEAN.

Evolution of WPS in the Global Stage

The year 2015 marks the fifteenth year of the adoption of UNCSR 1325 on WPS and on the occasion of its anniversary, the *Global Study on the Implementation of UNSCR 1325* was launched. At the onset, UNSCR 1325 was seen as a significant political milestone because it signified the recognition of women's issues in armed conflict and post-conflict situations as international peace and security concerns. It was also the first time that the UNSC placed women in the international peace and security global agenda.

Prior to UNSCR 1325 , previous UN initiatives that recognised the unique situation of women in armed conflict situations took place in other so called non-'high politics' fora. First of which was the efforts of the Committee on the Status of Women's (CSW) for the recognition of the special needs of women and children during armed conflict in 1969 that they brought to the attention of the Economic and Social Council (ECOSOC). The ECOSOC, for its part, recommended the issue to be taken on by the UN General Assembly (UNGA) and subsequently, the *Declaration on the Protection of Women and Children in Emergency and Armed Conflict* was adopted in 1974. The following year, women's participation in peacebuilding became part of the agenda of the UN Women's Conference in Mexico. And in the UN International Decade for Women (1976–85) that followed, women's agency in the context of peacebuilding was one of its main themes to advance the human rights of women globally.

In 1991, the UN Compensation Commission sought for the reparation for victims (including those who suffered sexual violence) of the Iraqi invasion of Kuwait and in 1992, General Recommendation 19 under the *Convention on the Elimination of all forms of Discrimination against Women* (CEDAW) on violence against women (VAW) took note of trafficking and prostitution in the context of armed conflict, war, and occupation. The following year, the 1992 UN World Conference on Human Rights in Vienna recognized conflict-related VAW as violation of both international human rights law and international humanitarian law. During the 1995 UN World Conference on Women in Beijing and its resulting *Beijing Platform for Action* (BPFA) specifically listed 'women in armed conflict' as one of the critical areas of concern facing women. By 1996, the Special Rapporteur on Violence against Women, Including Its Causes and Consequences under the Commission on Human Rights came out with its report that included the situation of women in armed conflict; the same issue area was likewise included in its 1998 and 2000 reports When the Rome Statute of the International Criminal Court (ICC) was signed in 1998, rape and sexual violence was explicitly included under war crimes, crimes against humanity, and a crime constitutive of genocide. During the same year, the CSW picked up on issue on women in armed conflict. This came to the attention of the Representative of Bangladesh in the UNSC and during his term as UNSC President, Ambassador Anwarul Chowdhury, led the initiative in placing WPS in the agenda of the Council.

According to the recollection of Ambassador Chowdhury, when he was President of the UNSC that month that he tabled the WPS initiative at the UNSC, disinterest and indifference prevailed, with some state representatives even expressing that he 'was diluting the Council's mandate by trying to bring a 'soft issue' onto its agenda.'[5] Despite this rather cold reception of the issue, Ambassador Chowdhury still saw the need to advance the first international security policy that would finally recognize the gender dimensions of armed conflict and peace in the context of women's equality agenda. His idea was 'not making war safe for women, but to structure the peace in a way that there is no recurrence of war and conflict.'[6] On 31 October 2000, the UNSC adopted Resolution 1325:

> In a nutshell, within the framework of Article 25 of the UN Charter, UNSCR 1325 obligates states to protect and respect the human rights of women and girls, open opportunities and guarantee the participation of women in all levels of decision-making; and provide for gender perspectives in peace processes.[7]

To a large extent, the adoption of UNSCR 1325 was made possible through norm entrepreneurship of actors who advance the existence of a particular shared concern and explore collective solutions.[8] According to Ikenberry and Kupchan, norm entrepreneurs influence international political life through their capacity to push their ideas in international negotiation fora;[9] in the same vein, Sikkink argues that norm entrepreneurs play a critical role in a way that they are able push state actors to accept international agreements that may have not been originally part of their interests.[10] In light of these descriptions, a norm entrepreneurship role was taken on by Ambassador Chowdhury during his term as President of the UNSC. He, along with the assistance and advocacy

5 Anwarul Chowdhury, 'Women and Conflict: A Frontline Issue?', *NATO Review* (2010), http://www.nato.int/docu/Review/2010/Women-Security/Women-resolution-1325/EN/index.htm, accessed 2 June 2015.

6 *ibid.*

7 Ma. Lourdes Veneracion-Rallonza, 'Grounding the International Norm on Women, Peace and Security: The Role of Domestic Norm Entrepreneurs and the Challenges Ahead', *Femina Politica* 22/2: 67–85 (2013), p. 70.

8 *ibid.*, p. 67.

9 John Ikenberry and Charles Kupchan., 'Socialization and Hegemonic Power', *International Organization* 44:3 (1990).

10 Kathryn Sikkink, 'Human Rights, Principled-Issue Networks and Sovereignty in Latin America', *International Organization* 47:3 (1993).

of the NGO Working Group on Women and International Peace and Security[11] as well as the support of the subsequent President of the UNSC from Namibia, helped bring WPS in the agenda of the Council and thus catapulting it in the stage of 'high politics.'

Nine years later, the UNSC adopted Resolution 1889 that affirmed UNSCR 1325 and called for various actors to ensure the inclusion of women in initiatives towards addressing sexual violence during armed conflict. Most recently, UNSCR 2122 was adopted in 2013 that made stronger calls for women's participation and leadership in resolving conflicts and building peace and recognized the need for an integrated approach to sustainable peace that takes into account 'coherence between political, security, development, human rights, including gender equality, and the rule of law and justice activities'. Additionally, in October 2013, the Committee on the Convention on the Elimination of Discrimination against Women (CEDAW Committee) adopted General Recommendation 30 on women in conflict prevention, conflict and post-conflict situations that explicitly linked CEDAW to the specific context of armed conflict and peace building. Most recently, in October 2015, UNSCR 2242 — that seeks to further look into the changing dynamics of conflict and violence — was adopted.

Specifically regarding the issue of sexual violence in armed conflict, the UNSC likewise adopted Resolution 1820 in 2008 followed by supporting Resolutions 1888 (2009), 1960 (2010) and 2106 (2013). Foremost, the discursive substance of these resolutions has been the formal recognition of rape and sexual violence as a weapon or tactic of war and the call to address this concern through various mechanisms and interventions.

WPS-related/Specific Initiatives in Several ASEAN Member States: The Relevance of National Action Plans

From 2005, 51 countries launched their National Action Plans (NAP) on WPS (refer to Table 1 below). NAPS serve as (1) framework for translation of international norms to national situation; (2) instrument for the concrete articulation

11 The Hague Appeal for Peace, International Alert, International Women's Tribune Center, the Women's Caucus for Gender Justice, the Women's Commission for Women Refugees and Children, and the Women's International Peace and Freedom comprised the NGO Working Group on Women and International Peace and Security. For a fuller discussion on civil society involvement in the crafting of UNSCR 1325, refer to Felicity Hill, Mikele Aboitiz and Sara Poehlman-Doumbouya, 'Nongovernmental Organizations' Role in the Build-up and Implementation of Security Council Resolution 1325', *Signs* 28/4 (2003).

TABLE 1 *National Action Plans on Women, Peace and Security*

Year of Launch	Countries
2005	Denmark
2006	Norway, Sweden, United Kingdom
2007	Austria, Cote D'Ivoire, Netherlands, Spain, Switzerland
2008	Finland, Iceland, Uganda
2009	Belgium, Chile, Guinea, Liberia, Portugal
2010	Bosnia Herzegovina, Canada, Democratic Republic of Congo, Estonia, France, Italy, Philippines, Rwanda, Sierra Leone
2011	Burundi, Croatia, Georgia, Guinea-Bissau, Ireland, Lithuania, Nepal, Senegal, Serbia, Slovenia, United States of America
2012	Australia, Germany, Ghana
2013	Kyrgyztan/Kyrgyz Republic, Macedonia, Nigeria
2014	Gambia, Iraq, Republic of Korea
2015	Afghanistan, Japan, New Zealand, Palestine, and Paraguay

http://www.peacewomen.org/naps/

of government priorities and the coordination of implementation at the national level; (3) document that serve as guide to policy implementation; and (4) guide that identifies various relevant agencies, actors and stakeholders in the implementation.

Since 2010, some of the country-NAPs underwent revisions such as that of Denmark (2010), Sweden (2009), Switzerland (2010), Netherlands (2011), Norway (2011), United Kingdom (2012), Austria (2012), Finland (2012), Iceland (2013), and the Philippines (2014). To date, most of the countries with NAPs are in Europe (24) and Africa (13) — 6 countries are from the Asia Pacific region, and 3 in the Americas. Interestingly, countries with NAPs can be categorized as those donor and receiving countries as well as countries that have recently experienced armed conflict in their contemporary history or are experiencing cycles or recurring conflicts and those that have not. Some NAPs are internally-oriented as they focus on security sector reform while others are more oriented towards external assistance in the form of funding and capacity development of bilateral partners. At the end of 2015, additional countries that launched their respective NAPs were Afghanistan, Japan, New Zealand, Palestine, and Paraguay.

Given the armed conflict historical landscape in the South East Asian region — be they past or on-going — it is interesting to note that, as will be shown below in the cases of Cambodia, Indonesia, Myanmar and Philippines, women have been largely absent in the reconstruction of conflict narratives in these countries. Most of the documented cases on the impact of armed conflict on women and their role in peacebuilding have been done by civil society and international organizations. Relatedly, in light of all ten ASEAN member states being State Parties to CEDAW, a very useful source of information as regards women in armed conflict is that of the CEDAW Committee's Concluding Comments/Observations. According to Ciorciari, 'international instruments provide useful starting points for protecting the human rights of some of the region's most vulnerable people'[12] and taking off from this notion, CEDAW can provide the space for surfacing WPS.

In reviewing the combined 4th and 5th Periodic Reports of Cambodia in 2013, the CEDAW Committee framed their Concluding Observations along the lines of legal aid and access to justice as raised in its concern 'that the Extraordinary Chambers in the Courts of Cambodia have not adequately addressed cases of gender-based violence, in particular sexual violence, against women committed under the Khmer Rouge regime' and that the Cambodian government has yet to provide other mechanisms 'including non-judicial programmes, to provide effective redress to victims of other forms of gender-based violence' committed during this period; additionally, the Committee also expressed concern on Cambodia's failure to 'incorporate effectively the provisions of the Convention and of Security Council Resolution 1325 into its post-conflict programmes'.[13]

In December 2014, the Cambodian Council of Ministers approved the *National Action Plan to Prevent Violence against Women* (NAP VAW) for 2014–2018. This document explicitly cited that Cambodia 'is bound by all decisions of the Security Council of the UN, especially decisions relating to women, peace, and security.'[14] However, despite this pronouncement, mention of UNSCR 1325 only appeared twice in the document: first, under the item of expected output under Strategic Area 3 (Formulating and Implementing Policies and Laws)

---

12 John Ciorciari, 'Institutionalizing Human Rights in Southeast Asia', *Human Rights Quarterly* 34:3 (2012), p. 716.

13 CEDAW, 'Concluding Observations on the Fourth and Fifth Periodic Report of Cambodia' adopted by the Committee at its fifty-sixth session (30 September-18 October 2013), http://docstore.ohchr.org/SelfServices/FilesHandler.ashx?enc=6QkG1d%2fPPRiCAqhKb7yhsglff%2fiazrVw%2bcyfdY9GxZ62YXIcKp9qTzonRzgoWWfPCWuduIoAQDgIdC71U7lPYiIf fLoiBHKqR9Sh2V03nWax969tKGbDUkflPsXeZyF8sAhoDtowkyo5T8krCgqvhQ%3d%3d, accessed 30 November 2014.

14 Ministry of Women Affairs, *National Action Plan to Prevent Violence against Women*, December 2014, Unofficial English translation.

pertaining to 'compliance to internationally agreed upon commitments to address violence against women particularly within the framework of UNSCR 1325'; and second, under Strategic Area 4 (Capacity Building) on the activity of increasing the 'capacity of the Cambodian National Police to Implement the Village Safety Policy in a gender-sensitive way and in line with UNSCR 1325'. The NAP was silent on addressing the issue of sexual violence committed during the Khmer Rouge regime. In fact, according to an NGO source, although forced marriage had been recognized by the ECCC as a crime during this period, they have yet to do the same for rape and sexual violence.

In the case of Indonesia, the CEDAW Committee, in its 2012 review of the Combined 6th and 7th Periodic Reports, took note of the issue on VAW in armed conflict, particularly, rape and sexual violence during:

> the events of 1965, the 1974–1999 conflict in the then East Timor Province, the May 1998 riots, the conflict in Aceh Province, the deployment of security and defence forces in Maluku Province and Poso (Central Sulawesi Province) and the conflicts in East Java and Papua Provinces.[15]

The foremost concern of the Committee had been that of impunity and the lack of retributive and restorative justice for victims as well as the growing incidence of intercommunal conflict and number of internally displaced people (IDPs) due to this situation. Thus, the Committee's recommendations were for policy formulation and legislation, and participation of women in post-conflict reconstruction and peacebuilding.

More recently, Indonesia, through Presidential Decree Number 182014 recognizes the need for 'the protection of women and children during armed conflict, the protection of women and girls' rights and mechanisms of handling social conflict and violence, including the treatment for victims and survivors of violent conflict' and seeks women's empowerment by 'referring to efforts for strengthening human rights, improving the quality of life of women and girls affected by conflict and increasing the participation of women and girls in peacebuilding efforts.'[16] During the first quarter of 2015, Indonesia launched

---

15 CEDAW, 'Concluding Observations on the Combined Sixth and Seventh Period Reports of Indonesia', adopted by the Committee during its 52nd Session, 9–27 July 2012, available at http://daccess-dds-ny.un.org/doc/UNDOC/GEN/N12/455/72/PDF/N1245572.pdf?OpenElement, accessed 30 November 2014.

16 Dwi Rubiyanti Kholifa, 'Indonesian Implementation of UNCSR 1325: Adapting to the National Context', 8 April 2014, https://www.womenpeacemakersprogram.org/news/indonesian-implementation-of-unscr-1325-adapting-to-the-national-context/, accessed 13 November 2014.

its NAP on the *Empowerment and Protection of Women and Children in Social Conflicts* anchored on CEDAW, the ASEAN Human Rights Declaration (AHRD), Law No. 7 on the management of social conflict, and Presidential Decree No. 8 on the protection of women in social conflict. Interestingly, according to some members of civil society who participated in the consultations of drafting the NAP, a concern was raised as regards the documents definition of 'conflict' being confined only to social or communal (or ethnic and religious) conflict and not including conflict brought about by separatist/independence struggles such as those in Aceh, Papua, and Maluka. Thus, although related to WPS, the critique was that the very definition of 'conflict' limited its scope. Nonetheless, there were still efforts at specifically using the WPS frame. One example of this was the development of a gender policy in the provincial government of Aceh framed along the principles of UNSCR 1325 of 'allocating reconstruction funding, increasing women's participation in peace processes, and addressing needs and capacities of female ex-combatants.'[17] This project involved UN Women as a provider of technical assistance.

As regards Myanmar, sexual violence in armed conflict was raised by the CEDAW Committee in its review of the country's combined 2nd and 3rd Periodic Reports in 2008. According to the Committee's Concluding Observation, there is a 'deep concern at the high prevalence of sexual and other forms of violence, including rape, perpetrated by members of the armed forces against rural ethnic women, including Shan, Mon, Karen, Palaung and Chin women.'[18] Although the Committee recognized efforts at persecuting perpetrators, they still raised concern about the limited number of cases and the inadequacy of mechanisms to address the pervasiveness of impunity. The Committee thus recommended the strengthening of efforts to combat impunity and access to justice of victims, improved provisions for capacity development of state security forces, monitoring of women's situation in conflict-affected areas, and the drafting of policy that would integrate UNSCRs 1325 and 1820.

Four years ago, the *National Plan for Action on the Advancement of Women (2011–2015)* was drafted. To a large extent, the language of the document followed the critical areas of concern identified in the BPFA. It is interesting to

17 UN Women, 'Indonesia Fact Sheet', http://www.unwomen-eseasia.org/docs/factsheets/03%20INDONESIA%20factsheet.pdf, accessed 13 November 2014.

18 CEDAW, 'Concluding Observations on the Combined Second and Third Periodic Reports of Myanmar', adopted by the CEDAW Committee during its 42nd Session, 20 October to 7 November 2008, http://docstore.ohchr.org/SelfServices/FilesHandler.ashx?enc=6QkG1d%2fPPRiCAqhKb7yhsgOTxO5cLIZ0CwAvhyns%2byL9Qo GtuFexI9MoVz2%2fFKXwVzM4d2OZv%2faAMUIZuUKiiPEK9lebyTJrbNMftwlO48K6MgdfRBGdCKaMKazTC%2fOP, accessed 30 November 2014.

note, however, that the BPFA critical issue on 'women in armed conflict' was restated as 'women in emergencies' and was framed more along the lines of women affected by natural disasters.[19] Nonetheless, an explicit effort to place WPS in the agenda came in 2013 during the commemoration of the adoption of UNSCR 1325 where an unprecedented gathering of various stakeholders was convened in the capital, Nay Pyi Taw, during the Open Day on WPS to discuss the gendered dimensions of armed conflict and the role of women in peace processes. The activity was organized by the Ministry of Social Welfare, Relief and Resettlement, Myanmar Women's Affairs Federation and the UN system in Myanmar.

As for the Philippines, after reviewing the country's Combined 5th and 6th Periodic Reports in 2006, the CEDAW Committee raised the concern about 'the precarious situation of rural and indigenous women, as well as the Muslim women in the autonomous region of Muslim Mindanao, who lack access to adequate health services, education, clean water and sanitation services and credit facilities' as well as 'women's limited access to justice in cases of violence, especially in the conflict zones, and the lack of sanctions against the perpetrators of such violence.'[20] As such, the Committee recommended to respond to these issues in light of developing programs and services.

In the first quarter of 2010, then President Gloria Macapagal-Arroyo signed EO 865 that created the National Steering Committee on Women, Peace and Security (NSC WPS), which also occurred towards the end of the consultation and re-validation process of the civil society-led draft NAP on UNSCRs 1325 and 1820.[21] The NSC WPS is an institutional mechanism co-chaired by the Office of the Presidential Adviser on the Peace Process (OPAPP) and the Philippine

19 Draft National Plan of Action for the Advancement of Women, 2011–2015, http://www.burmalibrary.org/docs09/UNCT_UNCountryTeam_Annex2-Plan%20of%20Action_eng.pdf, accessed 15 June 2015.

20 CEDAW, 'Concluding Observations on the Combined Fifth and Sixth Periodic Reports of the Philippines', adopted by the CEDAW Committee during its 36th session, 7–25 August 2006, http://docstore.ohchr.org/SelfServices/FilesHandler.ashx?enc=6QkG1d%2fPPRiCAqhKb7yhss1YTnoqfX85YJz37paIgUBv4vlgYcYCxopgO%2fMtF1URo4inWo8Kmt7ON5Vqrd1zgkBFouIs1Z%2fIb51RmktHrSGwqkd7QdsDpcuWrDnFMuNh, accessed 30 November 2014.

21 For the narrative on the civil society-led process of drafting the 2010 NAP, see Ma. Lourdes Veneracion-Rallonza, 'Grounding the International Norm on Women, Peace and Security'. Also refer to Ma. Lourdes Veneracion-Rallonza and Miguel Niccolo Rallonza, 'Women Count: Security Council Resolution 1325– Civil Society Monitoring Report, Philippines', WE Act 1325 and GNWP report, 9 January 2015, http://weact1325.org/wp-content/uploads/2012/04/Women-Count-2014_Phil-Report_COMPLETE-VERSION.02.13.15.pdf, accessed 30 May 2015.

Commission on Women (PCW), and includes cabinet secretaries from defense, social welfare, interior and local government, justice, foreign affairs, the National Commission on Indigenous Peoples (NCIP), and the National Commission on Muslim Filipinos (NCMF). In the same year, the *Philippine National Action Plan on UNSCRs 1325 and 1820* was launched — the first ever NAP on UNSCR 1325 in Asia and the 26th in the world. The Philippine NAP contained four pillars, namely, protection and prevention, empowerment and participation, promotion and mainstreaming, and capacity development and monitoring/reporting. Four years later, after rounds of consultation with NSC WPS, *Payapa at Masaganang Pamayanan* (PAMANA)[22] implementing agencies, and CSO members of Women Engaged in Action on UNSCR 1325 (WE Act 1325) as well as review and approval of the Executive Committee of the NSC WPS, the 2014 Amended Philippine NAP was launched.

The second generation Philippine NAP streamlined the action points originally listed in 2010, specifically, aligning action points to relevant government agencies' mandates, and measurable indicators to track attainment of targets. Additionally, this updated version was also crafted in the 'language' of government and was vetted to each of the agencies involved in its implementation. This was a significant development upon the 2010 NAP, which was civil society-led and thus came from a perspective that may have not explicitly highlighted how government works in terms of policy and programmatic dynamics.

In contrast to Indonesia, the Philippines' 2014 NAP is a formal document that refers to international instruments including CEDAW, the Rome Statute of the ICC, and UNSCRs on WPS, and a national law, the *Magna Carta of Women*. This updated version benefitted from the experiences of NAP implementation since 2010, primarily by engaging government agencies mandated to operationalize WPS in the country. For example, in the area of capacity development, relevant partner agencies were trained on NAP orientation, planning and budgeting. Others, such as the Department of Foreign Affairs (DFA) and the Philippine Army underwent more focused, agency-adapted WPS training programs. The Philippine Army in the first quarter of 2014 strategically

22 PAMANA is the complementary track to the peace process of the Philippine Government that aims to 'increase livelihood and job opportunities in conflict-affected and vulnerable communities; strengthen capacity of local government units (LGUs) to pursue local peace and development plans and programs; ensure transparency and accountability; and enable greater community participation in pursuing peace and development'. Objectives of PAMANA available at http://www.pamana.net/pamana, accessed 17 September 2014.

conducted an Army-wide WPS training of ground officers and personnel through their Gender and Development (GAD) program to craft an evidence-informed policy based on ground realities. Additionally, the Army also conducted a WPS executive course for ranking Army officers and decision makers. By the end of 2014, the Office of the Army Gender and Development (OAGAD) was activated— the first and the only institutional infrastructure, thus far, in the Philippine security sector that distinctively integrates WPS. Part of their strategic NAP objectives are strengthening and sustaining NAP-WPS mechanisms and the inclusion of NAP-WPS imperatives in the Army Transformation Roadmap (ATR). As regards policy, OPAPP and PCW, Chair and Vice Chair of the NSC WPS respectively, launched a specific NAP policy in the form of Joint Memorandum Circular (JMC) 2014–01 on the *Integration of Women, Peace and Security Programs, Activities and Projects* (*PAPs*) *in the Annual Gender and Development* (*GAD*) *Plans and Budgets* (*GPBs*) *and Gender and Development Accomplishment Reports* (*GAD ARs*). This JMC serves as the clear policy mandate for NAP WPS in the country.

On the occasion of the fifteen year anniversary of UNSCR 1325 in October 2015, OPAPP Secretary Teresita Quintos-Deles, succinctly summarized the evolution of the Philippine NAP WPS implementation in the last five years during the High-Level Review on UNSCR 1325 on Women, Peace and Security held in New York:

> Implementation of the Philippine NAP is a painstaking process because we want to cover all bases: policy, planning, implementation and monitoring mechanisms, and budget. Modest initial results are now being reported. Among the outcomes already being gleaned are the strengthened presence of women in peace negotiations and the implementation of peace accords; the establishment of 'women-friendly spaces' to ensure the needed measure of private and safe space for internally displaced women and girls in evacuation centers; the adoption of explicit gender equality policies and mechanisms as an integral part of the governance of the Armed Forces of the Philippines; culture-sensitive trauma healing programs for Muslim women; the inclusion of WPS issues in the training of our foreign service officers; the plan to establish a dedicated team of public prosecutors for cases of sexual and gender-based violence in situations of armed conflict.[23]

23 Philippine Country Statement by Secretary Teresita Quintos Deles during the High-Level Review on the United Nations Security Council Resolution (UNSCR) 1325 on Women,

In the last decade, of the 10 members of the ASEAN, Cambodia, Indonesia, Myanmar, and the Philippines were the ASEAN member states that received explicit recommendations on women in armed conflict from the CEDAW Committee. In the case of Cambodia, the CEDAW Committee recommended actions relating to legal aid and access to justice;[24] Indonesia received recommendations on the issue of violence against women in armed conflict;[25] while Myanmar was recommended to take action on the use of sexual violence in the context of armed conflict;[26] and the CEDAW Committee recommended that the Philippines look into the situation of women in conflict-affected areas.[27]

Unfortunately, the respective policy and/or activity-centred interventions of some of the AMS may not necessarily respond to the Committee's recommendations. In fact, of the four member states, only the NAPs of Indonesia and the Philippines cited CEDAW as one of their normative bases apart from specific national law/policy as reference. As regards reference to the UNSCRs on WPS, only Cambodia and the Philippines did so. Myanmar was unique in the sense that it referred to BPFA but couched the language in terms of 'women in emergencies.'

These four countries – just as the other six ASEAN Member States — have existing institutional infrastructures that can carry out the implementation of policy interventions with regard to the protection of women. Cambodia and Indonesia have ministry level institutions — the Ministry of Women's Affairs

---

Peace and Security, http://opapp.gov.ph/news/philippine-country-statement-secretary-teresita-quintos-deles-during-high-level-review-united.

24 CEDAW, 'Concluding Observations on the Fourth and Fifth Periodic Report of Cambodia', adopted by the Committee at its fifty-sixth session (30 September-18 October 2013), http://docstore.ohchr.org/SelfServices/FilesHandler.ashx?enc=6QkG1d%2fPPRiCAqhKb7yhs-glff%2fiazrVw%2bcyfdY9GxZ62YXIcKp9qTzonRzgoWWfPCWuduIoAQDgIdC71U7lPYiIff LoiBHKqR9Sh2V03nWax969tKGbDUkflPsXeZyF8sAhoDtowkyo5T8krCgqvhQ%3d%3d.

25 CEDAW, 'Concluding Observations on the Combined Sixth and Seventh Period Reports of Indonesia', adopted by the Committee during its 52nd Session, 9–27 July 2012, http://daccess-dds-ny.un.org/doc/UNDOC/GEN/N12/455/72/PDF/N1245572.pdf?OpenElement.

26 CEDAW, 'Concluding Observations on the Combined Second and Third Periodic Reports of Myanmar', adopted by the CEDAW Committee during its 42nd Session, 20 October to 7 November 2008, http://docstore.ohchr.org/SelfServices/FilesHandler.ashx?enc=6QkG1d%2fPPRiCAqhKb7yhsgOTxO5cLIZoCwAvhyns%2byL9QoGtuFexI9MoVz2%2fFKXwVzM4d2OZv%2faAMUIZuUK1iPEK9lebyTJrbNMftwlO48K6MgdfRBGdCKaMKazTC%2fOP.

27 CEDAW, 'Concluding Observations on the Combined Fifth and Sixth Periodic Reports of the Philippines', adopted by the CEDAW Committee during its 36th session, 7–25 August 2006, http://docstore.ohchr.org/SelfServices/FilesHandler.ashx?enc=6QkG1d%2fPPRiCAqhKb7yhss1YTnoqfX85YJz37paIgUBv4vlgYcYCxopgO%2fMtF1URo4inWo8Kmt7ON5Vqrd1zgkBFouIs1Z%2fIb51RmktHrSGwqkd7QdsDpcuWrDnFMuNh.

for the former and Ministry of Women's Empowerment and Child Protection for the latter. In the case of Myanmar, it has an institutional body, namely, the Myanmar National Committee for Women's Affairs, under the Ministry of Social Welfare, Relief and Resettlement. The Philippines, on the other hand, has PCW as a specialized body for women's concerns.

However, when it comes to explicit WPS concerns, it seems that only the Philippines has a specific NAP on WPS as well as an inter-agency institutional infrastructure to implement it. At the same time, coming out with the NAP WPS in the country also showcased 'collaborative politics' between these government institutions and civil society organizations.[28] This practice has been a great enabler for the Philippines to institutionalize and sustain WPS in comparison with Cambodia, Indonesia, and Myanmar. Furthermore, the Philippines is the only country in the region that has a NAP explicitly on WPS in the context of armed conflict and peacebuilding and not just integrated in the discursive policy frame of VAW. Given these elements, Philippines is well placed to serve as a lead country-WPS norm entrepreneur with support and insight from Indonesia, Cambodia, and Myanmar — together, they can be viable actors for vertical WPS norm entrepreneurship.

The idea of vertical norm entrepreneurship builds on Finnemore and Sikkink's two-level norm game taking place between international and national fronts where both levels tend to shape each other — international affecting the national and vice versa.[29] On the one hand, the situation of women and girls in armed conflict situations in various countries has driven international institutions to take action; on the other hand, the presence of country NAPS on WPS is a concrete manifestation of the international shaping the policy discourse and practice on women in armed conflict at the national level. The question now is on how countries can take their NAPS beyond their national territories to the so called 'middle space' represented by the regions to which they belong.

ASEAN and WPS: Discursive and Institutional Entry Points

Responding to the WPS agenda also comes in the form of regional and sub-regional collaboration particularly in contexts of cross-border conflict

28 Veneracion-Rallonza, 'Grounding the International Norm on Women, Peace and Security', p. 68.

29 Martha Finnemore and Kathryn Sikkink, 'International Norm Dynamics and Political Change', *International Organization* 46/1 (1998), p. 893.

situations. In this regard, it is worthy to note that several Regional Action Plans (RAPs) have been crafted. Examples of which are the European Union's (EU) 2008 *Comprehensive Approach to the EU's Implementation of UNSCR 1325 on Women, Peace and Security* and *Implementation of UNSCR 1325 as Reinforced by UNSCR 1820 in the Context of European Security and Defense Policy*, its 2010 *Indicators for the Comprehensive Approach to the EU Implementation of the UNSCRs 1325 and 1820 on Women, Peace and Security*; the African Union's (AU) 2009 regional gender policy that includes UNSCR 1325; League of Arab States' *2012 Strategy on the Protection of Arab Women, Peace and Security*; Economic Community of West African States' (ECOWAS) 2010 *Dakar Declaration on UNSCR 1325*; and the 2012 *Pacific Regional Action Plan on WPS*.

In ASEAN, seven of its members–Cambodia, Indonesia, Malaysia, Singapore, Thailand, Vietnam, and the Philippines—were among the first among 113 countries that supported the 2013 UN *Declaration of Commitment to End Sexual Violence in Conflict* which seeks to build and/or further strengthen institutional protective mechanisms for women in conflict and other humanitarian crisis situations. Myanmar became the eighth ASEAN Member and 150th UN Member State to support this Declaration in June 2014. In the same month, Indonesia, Malaysia, Myanmar, and the Philippines sent High-level government delegations to attend *the Global Summit to End Sexual Violence* organized and hosted by the government of the United Kingdom.

For the first time, in 2013, in a speech delivered on behalf of ASEAN member states during the UNSC Open Debate on WPS, H.E. Ambassador Le Hoai Trung, Permanent Representative of the Socialist Republic of Viet Nam, discussed the issue of sexual violence in armed conflict. He stressed 'ASEAN readiness and commitment to join efforts with the international community to ensure the elimination of sexual violence in armed conflict, and implement effective measures of accountability and redress in the field of women and peace and security.'[30] During the 2014 UNSC Open Debate on WPS, ASEAN, through Ms Nguyen Phuong Nga of Viet Nam, supported the call to respond to the situation of women displaced by armed conflict:

> The role of women and issues related to women, including sexual and gender-based violence, gender equality and social exclusion, have been increasingly integrated in relevant mechanisms and regimes. Women's

30 Statement by H.E. Ambassador Le Hoai Trung Permanent Representative of the Socialist Republic of Viet Nam on behalf of Member States of the Association of Southeast Asian Nations at the Security Council Open Debate on Women, Peace and Security, 17 April 2013, http://www.vietnam-un.org/en/vnun.php?id=243&cid=20, 30 May 2015.

> participation in peace and security issues has been growing across the spectrum…ASEAN is deeply concerned about the increasing number of refugees, internally displaced persons (IDPs) and stateless people…When basic institutions are in tatters, one cannot hope for better basic services for women and girls, let alone ways to address their specific health care needs. Of further concern is the fact that immediate security needs and chaos may force the normative framework and efforts for the protection of women and girls to be neglected and relegated to obscurity.[31]

In this regard, identifiable focused areas of the ASEAN were articulated in the statement, namely, (1) addressing the root cause/s of conflict; (2) women's participation; and (3) integration of women, peace and security in regional mechanisms such as the ASEAN Intergovernmental Commission on Human Rights (AICHR) and the ASEAN Commission on the Promotion and Protection of the Rights of Women and Children (ACWC).

As set forth in the General Principles of the ADHR, the rights of women (as well as other vulnerable and marginalized groups), are an 'inalienable, integral and indivisible part of human rights and fundamental freedoms.'[32] Within the ASEAN institutional infrastructure, AICHR is the body that is mandated to advance the promotion and protection of human rights and fundamental freedoms of peoples in the South East Asian region. It has the functional mandate to 'draft regional declarations, hold consultations, and issue general reports about general human rights conditions.'[33] To a large extent, AICHR encompasses the broad field of human rights implementation. Additionally, it was born out of the ASEAN Political and Security Community (APSC) as a mechanism to promote and protect human rights.[34] On the other hand, ACWC's mandate is specific to advancing the human rights of children and women.[35] It was envisioned to 'promote implementation of relevant laws, propose policies

31 Statement of by Ms. Nguyen Phuong Nga, Permanent Mission of Viet Nam to the UN, October 2014, http://peacewomen.org/sites/default/files/scwps2014_statement_vietnam_0.pdf, accessed 5 June 2015.

32 ASEAN Declaration on Human Rights, General Principle Number 4.

33 Ciorciari, 'Institutionalizing Human Rights in Southeast Asia', p. 716.

34 See ASEAN, 'ASEAN Political and Security Community Blueprint', 2009, http://www.asean.org/archive/5187-18.pdf, accessed 24 April 2015.

35 Refer to the Terms of Reference of the ASEAN Commission on the Protection of WomenandChildren,http://www1.umn.edu/humanrts/research/Philippines/ASEAN%20TOR%20on%20the%20%20Rights%20of%20Women%20and%20Children.pdf, accessed 13 November 2014.

and programs to protect the rights of women and children.'[36] ACWC was an institutional body conceived under the ASEAN Social and Cultural Community (ASCC) as a commitment to promote social justice and mainstreaming rights of 'vulnerable groups' 'into its policies and all spheres of life.'[37]

In theory, based on their respective mandates, AICHR and ACWC can serve as institutional entry points to advance WPS (whether individually or cooperatively). For example, drawing from AICHR and ACWC's mandates to 'develop strategies for the promotion and protection of human rights and fundamental freedoms' and to 'develop policies, programs and innovative strategies to promote and protect the rights of women and children' respectively, can be used to explore specific initiatives to address WPS areas such as protection/prevention and empowerment and participation. In terms of a regional mechanism, both can draw from the *Declaration on the Elimination of Violence against Women and Elimination of Violence against Children (DEVAWC) in ASEAN* that cited the 'UNSCRs 1325 (2000), 1820 (2008), 1888 (2009), and 1889 (2009) on WPS' as bases to explicitly include WPS in the ASEAN agenda. Furthermore, both AICHR and ACWC can likewise refer to the following international and national instruments in recommending actions to various bodies within the ASEAN: CEDAW and General Recommendations 8 (on representation), 23 (on political and public life), and 30 (on conflict prevention, conflict and post-conflict situations); *Declaration of the Advancement of Women in the ASEAN Region*, specifically, Operative Clause 1 (on women's participation in all fields and at various levels); and *Ha Noi Declaration*, particularly, Operative Clause 2 (on protection in armed conflict situations), 4 (on institutional mechanisms), 10 (on building capacities of government actors), and 13 (on women's empowerment and participation). In April 2014, AICHR held a consultation meeting with ACWC where both bodies identified four priority areas of cooperation: (1) education; (2) disability; (3) trafficking in persons, particularly, women and children; and (4) gender, peace and security.[38]

Taking all these together, there are several points worth noting as regards the possibility for horizontal norm entrepreneurship. First, several ASEAN member states — namely, Cambodia, Indonesia, Malaysia, Myanmar, Singapore, the Philippines, Thailand, and Viet Nam — already indicated their commitment to end sexual violence in conflict through the 2013 UNGA Declaration —which

36 Ciorciari, 'Institutionalizing Human Rights in Southeast Asia', p. 724.

37 See ASEAN, 'ASEAN Social and Cultural Community Blueprint'.

38 ASEAN Secretariat, 'The AICHR and ACWC Consultation Meeting', 25 April 2014, http://aichr.org/press-release/joint-press-release-the-aichr-and-acwc-consultation-meeting/, accessed 16 June 2015.

in turn refers to the broader WPS agenda. Furthermore, Viet Nam, as representative of ASEAN in UNSC Open Debates on WPS, officially and publicly articulated the position of the regional institution on WPS in the international security forum. Thus, at least in as far as political rhetoric will go, these ASEAN member states can be seen as advancing WPS individually and collectively on the world stage. Secondly, within the institutional human rights infrastructure of the ASEAN, both AICHR and ACWC have the mandate to operationalize international instruments (such as CEDAW) and regional consensus documents (DEVAWC, *Declaration on the Advancement of Women*, and *Ha Noi Declaration*) within which human rights of women in the context of conflict and peace are institutionalized. Horizontal norm entrepreneurship can thus come in the form of engaging all the ASEAN community pillars to address both protection and empowerment of women in conflict and post-conflict situations.

Concluding Insights: Prospects for Building WPS in South East Asia through Multi-focal Norm Entrepreneurship

The idea of multi-focal norm entrepreneurship is an exploration into the potential of vertical, horizontal, and even intersectional norm entrepreneurs. In the case of the former, they can be states that could bring a normative agenda up to regional and international levels; as regards the latter, they can be states within an institutional infrastructure and/or institutional bodies within an organization that could advance a specific norm. Moreover, linking both vertical and horizontal opportunities can likewise yield an intersectional potential for norm entrepreneurship.

As this paper tried to show, Cambodia, Myanmar, Indonesia, and the Philippines have the potential of being *vertical* norm entrepreneurs by virtue of existing NAPS related to WPS. At the same time, these ASEAN member states also individually supported the issue of ending sexual violence in conflict, a central WPS concern. However, between the four of them, the Philippines seem to be more advanced in the way that its NAP is specific and explicit to WPS and it has the inter-agency mechanism to implement it; additionally, it also has been actively engaged with civil society with regard promoting the NAP through advocacy, policy review, and capacity development.

The potential for *horizontal* norm entrepreneurship — that is, states working together within an institution on a common cause — is also present in the ASEAN. This was indicated, at the very least, with the ASEAN position delivered by Viet Nam during two WPS Open Debates. Within the ASEAN, there is still room to expand the work of AICHR and ACWC that could draw attention to

WPS — AICHR is already trying to do this through the activities they have lined up for 2016; ACWC, on the other hand, could include WPS in their next four-year work plan. CEDAW General Recommendation 30 offers the clearest and most nuanced guide for operationalizing the protection of women's human rights in conflict and post-conflict situations. AICHR and ACWC can strategically use CEDAW General Recommendation 30 framework in drafting declarations, recommending policies, crafting regional work plans, documentation, among others. At the same time, they can draw from existing ASEAN declarations to further contextualize WPS in accordance with the realities in the region.

Within ASEAN, the Philippines has been the strongest advocate for women's human rights — an agenda that the country carries in Summit meetings. At the same time, within AICHR, the Philippines has also been consistently bringing to light the human rights of women. In fact, it has taken on the thematic study women in natural disasters and conflict as one of its committed activities in AICHR. In December 2013, the Working Group for an ASEAN Human Rights Mechanism, in cooperation with UN Women, convened a workshop on WPS in the ASEAN; two years later, the Philippines hosted the ASEAN Institute for Peace and Reconciliation (AIPR) conference on WPS. The potential for the Philippines, therefore, to serve as an *intersectional* WPS norm entrepreneur is viable should it choose to serve as one.

Women affected by armed conflict in South East Asia need protection, particularly, in light of conflict-related displacement, migration, and trafficking — all of which are concerns shared by ASEAN member states. But beyond the victim/vulnerability discourse, women's agency — their role in peacebuilding and conflict transformation — must also be recognized. WPS is the normative framework that captures these realities. As regards ASEAN, getting WPS as part of the agenda would need the strategy of multi-focal norm entrepreneurship where the roadmap would towards institutionalization. Foremost, it has to move beyond the socio-cultural front of the ASEAN and must be taken as a serious agenda in the politico-front. AICHR can be instrumental in pushing for this since it has been born out of the political and security pillar of the ASEAN. In moving forward, an ASEAN Regional Action Plan can likewise be considered — one that would advance both women's victimization in armed conflict and their agency in post-conflict situations:

> What ASEAN should work towards is establishing a regional action plan that is unique in the way it embraces the WPS agenda. It needs a plan that recognises all forms of 'violence' against women including economic insecurities and disadvantages in the labour force. The plan needs to recognise the role of women in areas of conflict prevention both in

> governance and in relief and recovery. It needs to identify women other than just being part of the 'vulnerable populations' and see women as resilient and resourceful individuals.[39]

Preventing the commission of mass atrocity crimes — particularly grave gendered crimes — need a discursive roadmap, a policy frame, an institutional infrastructure which can be provided by a WPS agenda. In the ASEAN, state actors, international and regional institutional mechanisms and instruments have been identified to do this. The basic question at this point in time is why they would not have an ASEAN Regional Action Plan (RAP) on WPS. However, they may, nonetheless, have one in the future.[40]

39 Tamara Nair, 'Women, Peace and Security in the ASEAN: Need for a Distinct Action Plan', RSIS Commentary, 23 December 2015, http://www.rsis.edu.sg/wpcontent/uploads/2015/12/CO15278.pdf?utm_source=getresponse&utm_medium=email&utm_campaign=rsis_publications&utm_content=RSIS+Commentary+278%2F2015+Women%2C+Peace+and+Security+in+ASEAN%3A+Need+For+Distinct+Action+Plan+by+Tamara+Nair+.

40 A recent development in this direction is the adoption of a JOINT STATEMENT ON PROMOTING WOMEN, PEACE AND SECURITY IN ASEAN released in November 2017 during the ASEAN Chairship of the Philippines. The statement is available online at https://asean.org/storage/2017/11/8.-ADOPTION_Joint-Statement-on-Promoting-Women-Peace-and-Security-in-ASEANACWC-Endorsed_rev2.pdf.

Bridging the Protection Gap: Rethinking the 'Three Pillars' to Eliminate Sexual and Gender-Based Violence in ASEAN

Maria Tanyag[1]
Monash University
Maria.Tanyag@monash.edu

Abstract

This chapter situates the growing academic and policy interest in advancing international normative frameworks namely the Responsibility to Protect (R2P) and Women, Peace, and Security (WPS) in ASEAN within broader feminist critiques of the 'protection gap' that results from the 'siloing' of international security and peace agendas. It builds on recent works that suggest a rethinking of ASEAN as constituted by three distinct community pillars (political-security, economic, and socio-cultural) for fully addressing human security and development in the region. Using the ASEAN Regional Plan for Action (RPA) of the 2013 Declaration on the Elimination of Violence Against Women (EVAW), which covers a ten-year period (2016–2025), this chapter makes a case for how the RPA can serve as a critical vector for broadening the significance of R2P and WPS in the region to address sexual and gender-based violence as occurring both in crisis situations and 'everyday life'.

Keywords

ASEAN – Women, Peace, and Security agenda – Responsibility to Protect – VAW – SGBV – gender

---

1 This chapter has been developed from an initial think piece for the Asia-Pacific Centre for the Responsibility to Protect's *Asia Pacific Outlook*. The author is grateful to the Centre for enlisting her as a representative to attend the civil society consultations on the Regional Plans of Action (RPAs) on the Elimination of Violence against Women and Children (EVAWC) convened by the ASEAN Commission on the Promotion and Protection of the Rights of Women and Children (ACWC) on 29–30 March 2016 in Bangkok, Thailand.

 | DOI:10.1163/9789004363212_006

Perhaps you have never imagined what it would feel like if you were a woman fleeing your home with your young children, escaping a violent conflict between government troops and rebel soldiers, crossing a national border, pitching a tent in a muddy refugee camp, and then being treated by aid staff workers as though you and the children you are supporting were indistinguishable, "womenandchildren."

CYNTHIA ENLOE[2]

Introduction

Despite the noted decline of mass atrocities in the Asia Pacific region, feminist perspectives that render visible the 'continuum of violence' argue that this does not automatically mean a decline of violence per se.[3] By contrast, they draw our attention to what forms of violence remain invisible, 'under the radar' or excluded from global peace and security agendas. In the case of Southeast Asia, a growing body of academic and policy research have sought to investigate and build knowledge around regional norm promotion of R2P and WPS. Building on critical research on how these two international peace and security frameworks are advanced through ASEAN, this chapter considers how both are relevant and constitute urgent concerns in light of the region's designation as among the top areas where a large number of people are frequently exposed to multiple natural hazards and internal displacement.[4] Indeed, recalling the historical roots of the R2P doctrine, the conceptual reframing of sovereignty as responsibility emerged from the development of national and international

2 Cynthia Enloe, *Bananas, Beaches and Bases: Making Feminist Sense of International Politics* (Berkeley, CA; London: University of California Press, 2014/1989 p. 1).

3 Jacqui True, 'Winning the Battle but Losing the War on Violence,' *International Feminist Journal of Politics*, 17/4 (2015), pp. 554–572; Sara Davies, Jacqui True and Maria Tanyag, 'How women's silence secures the peace: analysing sexual and gender-based violence in a low-intensity conflict,' 24/3 (2016), (pp. 459–473). See for further discussion of the so-called 'East Asian Peace' Alex Bellamy, 'Atrocity Prevention: From Promise to Practice in the Asia Pacific,' *Global Responsibility to Protect* 8 (2016), pp. 180–199.

4 Internal Displacement Monitoring Centre (IDMC), *Disaster-related Displacement Risk: Measuring the Risk and Addressing the Drivers* (Geneva: Internal Displacement Monitoring Centre and the Norwegian Refugee Council, 2015), p. 8.

principles for the protection of internally displaced persons (IDPs).[5] Moreover, the regional promotion and implementation of WPS is equally imperative for ASEAN to address the cross-border needs and gender-specific vulnerabilities of women and girls who represent half of the displaced populations in the Asia Pacific region.

This chapter is divided into three main parts. First, I provide a critical review of the existing scholarship around the potential alignments of WPS and R2P as key international normative frameworks for addressing the distinct vulnerability of women and girls to different forms of sexual and gender-based violence (SGBV) in crisis situations. Second, I build on feminist critiques of the 'siloing' that results from a 'pillars approach' for what should be an interconnected peace and security agenda. This means that gender equality which includes the elimination of SGBV is considered as cutting across political, economic and socio-cultural dimensions rather than compartmentalised as a socio-cultural concern only. However, I argue that ASEAN itself is structured according to 'three community pillars' thus replicating some of these global challenges at the regional level. Finally, I use the RPA on EVAW to suggest a potential pathway for bridging the protection gap resulting from the siloing of ASEAN's three community pillars. The RPA primarily discusses violence against women with contextual references to how they occur in crisis situations of armed conflicts and natural disasters, as well as in 'everyday life'. The RPA therefore can serve as a crucial vector for linking conflict-related SGBV and substantive gender equality reforms as a way to deepen the advancement of R2P and WPS in ASEAN. By doing so, the RPA can instigate the strengthening of the institutional integration of ASEAN's three community pillars in eliminating gendered violence and inequalities.

Gender Alignments of WPS and R2P

The R2P doctrine and WPS agenda constitute key international normative frameworks on civilian protection and prevention of mass atrocities in

5 Lucy Hall and Laura J. Shepherd, 'WPS and R2P: Theorising Responsibility and Protection' in Davies et al., *Responsibility to Protect and Women, Peace and Security* (Leiden: BRILL, 2013), p. 54. See also Francis M. Deng and Roberta Cohen, *Masses in Flight* (Washington, DC: Brookings Institution Press, 1998); Roberta Cohen, "Reconciling R2P with IDP Protection," in Sara E. Davies and Luke Glanville (eds.), *Protecting the Displaced: Deepening the Responsibility to Protect* (Leiden: Martinus Nijhoff Publishers, 2010), pp. 35–58.

armed conflict.[6] A growing body of research have started to map out how and where the two separate frameworks intersect. Largely due to its historical development, R2P has been commonly associated with militarised humanitarian interventions.[7] It emerged as a galvanizing principle in response to the inaction of the international community in the face of mass atrocities perpetrated in countries such as Rwanda and Bosnia in the 1990s. Under the R2P doctrine, state sovereignty is reconceptualised as a duty to protect civilian populations from genocide, war crimes, ethnic cleansing and crimes against humanity. Moreover, when a state has demonstrated its inability to uphold this duty and as a last resort, the international community has an obligation to intervene in a timely and decisive manner. It is also, as various scholars point out, 'gender-blind' in that it does not explicitly acknowledge the multitude and distinct experiences of women and girls in armed conflict.[8] And yet, as Davies, Nwokora, Stamnes and Teitt argue, 'the responsibility to protect those at risk of sexual and gender based violence is not just part of a wider protection agenda—it is a fundamental sovereign obligation.'[9]

WPS rectifies R2P's relative neglect of gendered inequalities by drawing attention to the disproportionate consequences of wars and conflicts on women and girls, and the important roles they play for achieving sustainable peace and security.[10] The WPS agenda is built on UN Security Council Resolution 1325 and several subsequent resolutions. It identifies three priority areas which broadly align with R2P: the meaningful *participation* of women in peace and security governance; the *protection* of women's rights and bodies in conflict and post-conflict situations; and lastly, *prevention* of systematic and widespread SGBV.[11]

---

6 Sarah Hewitt, 'Overcoming the Gender Gap: The Possibilities of Alignment between the Responsibility to Protect and the Women, Peace and Security Agenda,' *Global Responsibility to Protect* 8 (2016), pp. 3–28; Jacqui True, 'Explaining the global diffusion of the Women, Peace and Security agenda,' *International Political Science Review* 37/3 (2016), pp. 307–323.

7 Sara Davies, Sarah Teitt, and Zim Nwokora, 'Bridging the Gap: Early Warning, Gender, and the Responsibility to Protect', *Cooperation and Conflict*, 50/2 (2015), pp. 228–249.

8 Davies, Teitt and Nwokora, 'Bridging the Gap: Early Warning, Gender, and the Responsibility to Protect'; Sara Davies, Zim Nwokora, Eli Stamnes, and Sara Teitt (eds.), *Responsibility to Protect and Women, Peace and Security: Aligning the Protection Agendas* (Leiden: Martinus Nijhoff Publishers, 2013), pp. 1–6; Hall and Shepherd, 'WPS and R2P'.

9 Davies et al., *Responsibility to Protect and Women, Peace and Security: Aligning the Protection Agendas*, p. 1.

10 UN Women, *Peace and Security: In Brief*, 2013, http://www.unwomen.org/en/what-we-do/peace-and-security accessed 31 August 2016.

11 Laura Shepherd, 'Advancing the Women, Peace and Security agenda: 2015 and beyond,' *Norwegian Peacebuilding Resource Centre Expert Analysis*, 28 August 2014, http://www

Thus, WPS and R2P not only share the same goals in terms of protecting civilian populations—half of which consist of women and girls—and preventing mass atrocities in conflict situations including SGBV. Both are also regarded as capable of mutually reinforcing one another to effectively advance a more comprehensive approach to peace and security.[12] However, despite their shared goals, the two remain disjointed. Failure to link WPS with R2P undermines the importance of engaging 'all actors and early warning mechanisms throughout the UN system' which is necessary for fulfilling both protection mandates.[13]

Davies, Teitt and Nwokora argue that one potential avenue for linking WPS and R2P is through the development and explicit inclusion of gender-specific indicators for early warning frameworks that predict countries at risk of, and therefore help prevent mass atrocities.[14] For instance, studies have empirically demonstrated the causal relationships between the occurrence of mass SGBV, and pre-existing gender hierarchies that influence the distribution of resources and access to political and economic decision-making in a given society.[15] These studies indicate that normalized and systemic gender discrimination as root causes of violence help us determine where mass atrocities including SGBV are likely to occur. They also reveal which groups of women and girls are most likely to be targeted due to their societal exclusions including lack of access to justice and state protection mechanisms.[16] Therefore, incorporating gender-specific indicators in early warning frameworks addresses the three shared goals of WPS and R2P on prevention, protection and participation by underscoring how these goals are in fact interconnected and mutually reinforcing. As I discuss further below, drawing from feminist perspectives wherein violence is reconceptualised as a continuum is necessary for bridging the protection gaps between forms of violence that occur in 'everyday life' and in securitised settings of armed conflict.

.peacebuilding.no/Themes/Inclusivity-and-gender/Publications/Advancing-the-Women-Peace-and-Security-agenda-2015-and-beyond; Laura J. Shepherd and Jacqui True, 'The Women, Peace and Security Agenda and Australian Leadership in the World: From Rhetoric to Commitment?' *Australian Journal of International Affairs*, 68/3 (2014), 257–284.

12 Hewitt, "Overcoming the Gender Gap'.

13 Davies, Teitt and Nwokora, 'Bridging the Gap: Early Warning, Gender, and the Responsibility to Protect,' p. 229.

14 Ibid.

15 Jennifer Bond and Laurel Sherret, 'Mapping Gender and the Responsibility to Protect: Seeking Intersections, Finding Parallels,' *Global Responsibility to Protect* 4/2 (2012), pp. 133–153; Sara Davies and Jacqui True, 'Reframing conflict-related sexual and gender-based violence: Bringing gender analysis back in,' *Security Dialogue* 46/6 (2015), pp. 495–512;

16 Davies and True, 'Reframing conflict-related sexual and gender-based violence'; Davies, True and Tanyag, 'How women's silence secures the peace: analysing sexual and gender-based violence in a low-intensity conflict'.

Mainstreaming WPS into R2P implementation frameworks, however, warrants some caution. As several scholars point out, integrating the two might undermine or limit the much broader agenda of WPS given the current remit of R2P.[17] First, both WPS and R2P emphasise securitised settings of armed conflicts which risk obscuring how the causes and consequences of particular forms of mass atrocities are rooted in pre-existing or deeply-embedded gendered inequalities that must be equally addressed. This is manifested in that WPS and, to a certain extent, R2P due to its gender-blindness, have a tendency to privilege protection over prevention. SGBV in conflict is prevalently assumed as inevitable through a disproportionate focus on victims and perpetrators.[18] As True and Tanyag point out, securitisation of sexual violence in conflict particularly through WPS has 'either detracted from, or served to depoliticize, comprehensive gender equality goals and outcomes.'[19] Although WPS reflects a broader understanding of the causal role played by gender before and after conflicts particularly through an explicit aim for stronger women's participation in peace processes, women's experiences in conflict are often reduced in practice as single-issue concerns that can be readily crossed out of checklists rather than constitute substantive gender equality goals.[20] Preventing SGBV in conflict therefore must involve the integrated implementation of WPS alongside the sustainable development goals and the Convention on the Elimination of All Forms of Discrimination Against Women (CEDAW).[21]

Second, integrating the two might come at the cost of reducing women's identities and experiences in conflict settings to that of victimhood thereby denying them of political agency. For example, Hall and Shepherd in theorising the discursive links between WPS and the R2P doctrine, demonstrate that the concept of protection itself is gendered such that protection is 'afforded *to* women *by* men, and, in return for the security provided by the protective

17 See for examples Katrina Lee-Koo, 'Translating UNSCR 1325 into Practice: Lessons Learned and Obstacles Ahead', in Davies et al., *Responsibility to Protect and Women, Peace and Security*, pp. 35–52; Hall and Shepherd, 'WPS and R2P'.

18 Inger Skjelsbæk, 'Responsibility to Protect or Prevent? Victims and Perpetrators of Sexual Violence Crimes in Armed Conflict', in Davies et al., *Responsibility to Protect and Women, Peace and Security*, pp. 81–100.

19 Jacqui True and Maria Tanyag "Global Violence and Security from a Gendered Perspective," in Anthony Burke and Rita Parker (eds.), *Global Insecurity: Futures of Global Chaos and Governance* (Palgrave, 2017), pp. 43–63.

20 Ibid.

21 Shepherd, 'Advancing the Women, Peace and Security agenda;' UN Women, *Preventing Conflict, Transforming Justice, Securing the Peace: A Global Study on the Implementation of United Nations Security Council Resolution 1325*, 2015, http://wps.unwomen.org/en accessed 31 August 2016.

services, women accept the authority of their male protectors.'[22] This logic, they argue, is reproduced through R2P wherein the protector identity is vested upon the sovereign state and the international community – both remaining male-dominated arenas.[23] Consequently, a masculine construction of the protector 'produces a feminised infantilized subject in need of protection.'[24] This occurs as many feminist scholars also note when women are treated as essentially weak, vulnerable and passive victims usually conflated with children and the elderly.[25] While WPS is similarly informed by such 'protection stereotypes', it nevertheless provides a broader understanding of and has gradually encompassed women's agency and not just experiences of victimhood. Still, references to women's political agency in peace and security agendas such as WPS are often hinged on essentialist constructions of women as *innate* peacebuilders due to 'feminine qualities such as nurturing, empathy, cooperation, non-violence with a focus on community well-being rather individual interests.'[26]

Treating women as either helpless victims or essentially pacifists is problematic in that both produce women as a homogenous group. This means that their inclusion within international security and development agendas is predicated on fitting them within these stereotypes. Such an approach, which fails to encompass the range of gender and sexual identities, can create and exacerbate the insecurities experienced by broader groups of women and girls as well as men and boys.[27] Feminist research has long argued that gender is not a synonym for women.[28] To establish the gender alignments between WPS and R2P as Stamnes argues, 'it is not enough simply to add the perspective and participation of women. Social structures and institutions, and their particular hierarchies of femininities and masculinities, must be the subject of investigation and change.'[29] From a feminist perspective, integrating R2P and WPS

22 Hall and Shepherd, 'WPS and R2P,' p. 63

23 See also Hilary Charlesworth, 'Feminist Reflections on the Responsibility to Protect', *Global Responsibility to Protect,* 2/3 (2010), pp. 232–249.

24 Hall and Shepherd, 'WPS and R2P,' p. 70; Marion I. Young, "The Logic of Masculinist Protection: Reflections on the Current Security State," *Signs* 29/1(2003), pp. 1–25.

25 Charlesworth, 'Feminist Reflections on the Responsibility to Protect'.

26 True and Tanyag, 'Global Violence and Security from a Gendered Perspective'; Jean Bethke Elshtain, *Women and War* (Chicago, IL: University of Chicago Press, 1995); Charlesworth, 'Feminist Reflections on the Responsibility to Protect'.

27 True and Tanyag, 'Global Violence and Security from a Gendered Perspective'; Charlesworth, 'Feminist Reflections on the Responsibility to Protect'.

28 Hall and Shepherd, 'WPS and R2P,' p. 74; True and Tanyag, 'Global Violence and Security from a Gendered Perspective'.

29 Eli Stamnes, 'The Responsibility to Protect: Integrating Gender Perspectives into Policies and Practices,' *Global Responsibility to Protect,* 4/2 (2012), p. 190.

therefore is not about making wars safer for women but rather fundamentally rethinking how we understand international peace and security as occurring in a continuum across various socio-cultural, political and economic dimensions, across household, state and global levels, as well as during times of crisis and in everyday life.[30]

Feminist Continuum of Violence

Feminist theorising of global violence recognises that violence occurs in a continuum, and thus mutually shaped by material and ideological or cultural factors.[31] First, this entails examining how violence occurring in crisis contexts such as armed conflicts is structurally connected to the violence experienced in 'everyday life'.[32] Indeed, as feminist scholars argue, security from the perspective of women is not simply the absence of war or conflict. It also means addressing the various gendered inequalities they contend with post-conflict especially in terms of the economic devaluing of the unpaid care and domestic work they perform in society.[33] Second, violence is manifested in different but interconnected forms across physical, structural and symbolic insecurities.[34] That is, violence does not only consist of direct harms inflicted upon an individual body, it also constitutes discrimination and marginalisation from accessing material resources and political decision-making which in turn are rendered normal by cultural or religious narratives and representations. Lastly, violence from a feminist perspective challenges the artificial separation between so-called public and private realms. For instance, as Charlesworth argue,

> The lives of women appear peripheral to the development of the responsibility to protect principle, except for occasional references to the need to protect women from mass rape. The principle focuses on the public realm of the state and the government as the source of injury, but for most women, danger comes from the 'private' realm of the family or

30 Jacqui True, *The Political Economy of Violence Against Women* (New York: Oxford University Press, 2012); True and Tanyag, 'Global Violence and Security from a Gendered Perspective'.

31 True, *The Political Economy of Violence Against Women*; True and Tanyag, 'Global Violence and Security from a Gendered Perspective'.

32 True and Tanyag 'Global Violence and Security from a Gendered Perspective'; Juanita Elias and Shirin Rai, 'The Everyday Gendered Political Economy of Violence,' *Politics & Gender* 11/2 (2015), pp. 424–429.

33 Ibid.

34 Johan Galtung, 'Violence, Peace, and Peace Research," *Journal of Peace Research* 6/3 (1969), pp. 167–191.

> community as much as from the state… Discrimination against women in areas such as inheritance and family law is justified by custom or religion.[35]

The political violence experienced by women in the public sphere is intimately related to the more 'invisible' forms of violence they experience in the private sphere of the family, clan and/or ethnic community where many women and girls are typically denied bodily autonomy.[36] As Yuval-Davis emphasises, women's bodies serve as symbolic carriers of group identity and are therefore at the heart of political contestations on how society and the roles and relationships within it ought to be.[37] Indeed, studies have shown that various conflict-related SGBV are perpetrated with impunity against women and girls precisely because they embody the ethnic, religious, or indigenous minority groups they belong to.[38]

Moreover, 'private sphere' violence against women and girls is co-constitutive of public forms of political violence including armed conflicts. Cockburn, for example, argues that

> [P]atriarchal gender relations predispose our societies to war. They are a driving force perpetuating war. They are among the causes of war. This is not, of course, to say that gender is the only dimension of power implicated in war. It is not to diminish the commonly understood importance of economic factors (particularly an ever-expansive capitalism) and antagonisms between ethnic communities, states and blocs (particularly the institution of the nation-state) as causes of war.[39]

---

35 Charlesworth, 'Feminist Reflections on the Responsibility to Protect', p. 242.

36 True, 'Winning the Battle but Losing the War on Violence,' p. 555; Davies and True, 'Reframing conflict-related sexual and gender-based violence'; Davies, True and Tanyag, 'How women's silence secures the peace'; Maria Tanyag, 'Peace, Sex and Violence in Mindanao,' 15 August 2016, http://www.internationalaffairs.org.au/australian_outlook/peace-sex-and-violence-in-mindanao/ accessed 31 August 2016.

37 Nira Yuval-Davis, *Gender and Nation* (London: Sage, 1997); Maria Eriksson Baaz and Maria Stern, 'Why Do Soldiers Rape? Masculinity, Violence, and Sexuality in the Armed Forces in the Congo (DRC)', *International Studies Quarterly*, 53/2 (2009), pp. 495–518.

38 Davies and True, 'Reframing conflict-related sexual and gender-based violence'; Baaz and Stern, 'Why Do Soldiers Rape?

39 Cynthia Cockburn, 'Gender Relations as Causal in Militarization and War,' *International Feminist Journal of Politics* 12/2 (2010), p. 140.

When we recognise violence as encompassing multidimensional threats we become attentive to the ways by which binary logics distinguishing conflict / peace time, private/public, household/the state actually undermine the core goals of both WPS and R2P.

I argue that both WPS and R2P need to be more strongly tethered to the feminist notion of a continuum of violence. Instead, what is actually prevalent is a siloed approach that *separates* rather than *connects* the immediate political-military pillar and long-term socio-economic development pillar of international peace and security.[40] For example, as True points out, 'most UN peacebuilding missions have given primacy to re-establishing law and order (the military/political security pillar) rather than restoring women and men's livelihoods (the economic security pillar) after conflict.'[41] That is, post-conflict economic reforms underpinned by principles of gender equality and women's empowerment typically receive less political attention and resources compared to re-establishing law and order.[42]

Obscuring the equal importance of political-military and socio-economic concerns is detrimental to women and girls because the absence of inter and intra-state armed conflicts does not automatically mean a cessation of SGBV perpetrated against women and girls at the household and community levels. Moreover, this does not help us identify and consequently address the various structural and symbolic barriers that prevent broader groups of women and girls from fully participating in political and economic decision-making which is one of the core goals of WPS.

WPS and ASEAN's Three Community Pillars

In this section, I now turn to the case of ASEAN to further illustrate how the siloing of political-military and socio-economic development pillars of

40 True and Tanyag, 'Global Violence and Security from a Gendered Perspective'; Shepherd, 'Advancing the Women, Peace and Security agenda'; Jacqui True, 'The Political Economy of Gender in UN Peacekeeping,' in Dianne Otto and Gina Heathcote (eds), *Rethinking Peacekeeping, Gender Equality and Collective Security* (Palgrave Macmillan, 2014), pp. 243–262.

41 True, 'The Political Economy of Gender in UN Peacekeeping,' p. 245.

42 See for example Jacqui True, 'Post-conflict economic reform is a Women, Peace and Security Issue,' 31 July 2016, http://wilpf.org/post-conflict-economic-reform-is-a-women-peace-and-security-issue/ accessed 31 August 2016.

international peace and security agenda is reinforced at the regional level. Specifically, I build on current debates around the norm promotion for human protection and atrocities prevention within ASEAN through institutional engagements with the WPS agenda primarily and R2P secondarily. ASEAN provides an interesting case in that its conceptualisation of regional peace and security is also built on three community pillars namely *political-security, economic,* and *socio-cultural* communities. I argue that the 'community pillars' approach in ASEAN replicates some of the global challenges I discussed above in terms of comprehensively advancing the participation, protection, and prevention goals of WPS. Thus, ASEAN can potentially promote a regional WPS and R2P agenda that is informed by a feminist continuum of violence. This effort also serves to instigate a rethinking of the separation of the three community pillars in policy and practice. Importantly, advancing WPS and R2P in such a manner is consistent with the calls from CSOs in the region for improved coordination among the three ASEAN communities for the elimination of violence against women.[43]

TABLE 1 *2017 Global Climate Risk Index (CRI) and Southeast Asia (annual averages)*[44]

Rank	Country	Deaths per 100 000 Inhabitants	Total losses in million US$ PPP	Losses per unit GDP in %	Number of events (total 1996–2015)
2	Myanmar	14.71	1 300.74	0.737	41
5	Philippines	1.00	2 761.53	0.628	283
8	Vietnam	0.41	2 119.37	0.621	206
10	Thailand	0.22	7 574.62	1.004	136

43 See Maria Tanyag, 'Sexual & Gender based violence: Regional Consultation of the ASEAN Commission on Women and Children with Civil Society Organisations on the Implementation of Regional Plans of Actions on the Elimination of Violence against Women and Children,' *Asia Pacific Outlook*, April 2016, Issue 2 (Asia-Pacific Centre for the Responsibility to Protect).

44 Sönke Kreft, David Eckstein and Inga Melchior, *Global Climate Risk Index 2017* (Bonn; Berlin: Germanwatch, 2016), 6.

The promotion of WPS and R2P within ASEAN is highly relevant and indeed auspicious amidst growing evidence-based claims that Southeast Asia is among the most crisis-prone regions in the world.[45] The occurrence of multiple and overlapping insecurities brought about by protracted internal conflicts and devastating natural disasters such as typhoons and earthquakes has caused immense death and displacement in the region. In particular, UNHCR notes that one third of the total global refugees are in the Asia Pacific at an estimated 3.5 million people. This is in addition to the 1.9 million internally displaced and 1.4 million stateless people.[46] Moreover, Germanwatch's 2017 Global Climate Risk Index (CRI) identifies four ASEAN countries in the top ten countries most affected by climate-related disasters globally from 1996 to 2015 (see Table 1).[47] Lastly, Southeast Asia also consists of fragile states. The Fund for Peace Fragile States Index (FSI) offers an early warning for states on the brink of failure in terms of the inability to provide reasonable public services, the loss of legitimate authority and physical control over its territory among other indicators.[48] According to this index, all ASEAN member states except Singapore are characterised by varying levels of fragility and political instability (see Table 2). What these findings underscore albeit less explicitly is the need for further research and policy development to simultaneously address the conflict-specific and routine vulnerability of women and girls in this region which makes WPS an ASEAN regional governance priority.[49] Importantly, the diverse political and economic conditions affecting fragility among ASEAN member states and their different levels of capacity to address increasing precarity point to the importance of regional level cooperation.

---

45 Tamara Nair, 'Women, Peace and Security in the ASEAN: Need for a Distinct Action Plan,' RSIS Commentary, 23 December 2015, https://www.rsis.edu.sg/wp-content/uploads/2016/03/Women-Peace-and-Security-in-the-Asia-Pacific.pdf accessed 31 August 2016. See also UNFPA, *Shelter from the Storm: State of the World Population 2015* (New York: UNFPA, 2015); IDMC, *Disaster-related Displacement Risk.*

46 UNHCR, 'Asia and the Pacific' in *Global Reports 2013*, 2014–2015, http://www.unhcr.org/asia-and-the-pacific.html accessed 31 August 2016.

47 This index quantifies the impacts of extreme weather events in terms of direct fatalities and indirect or long-term socio-economic losses sustained as a result of a disaster. For further information regarding the methodology used see https://germanwatch.org/en/download/16411.pdf, accessed 6 April 2017.

48 For further information regarding the methodology used see http://fsi.fundforpeace.org/methodology. See also OECD, *States of Fragility 2015: Meeting Post-2015 Ambitions*, 2015, http://www.oecd.org/dac/governance-peace/publications/documentuploads/SOF2015.pdf; UNFPA, *Shelter from the Storm.*

49 Sara E. Davies, Kimberly Nackers and Sarah Teitt, 'Women, Peace and Security as an ASEAN priority,' *Australian Journal of International Affairs* 68/3 (2014), pp. 333–355.

TABLE 2 *2016 Fragile States Index and ASEAN member states*

Rating	Country	Rank
Alert	Myanmar	26
High Warning	Cambodia	46
	Philippines	54
	Laos	55
Elevated Warning	Thailand	74
	Indonesia	86
	Vietnam	106
Warning	Malaysia	115
	Brunei	123
Very Stable	Singapore	161

ASEAN as a regional organisation has made significant strides in adopting a normative commitment to human security and protection, including the advancement of women, peace and security concerns. ASEAN's community building phase from 2008–2015 was marked by efforts to embed ASEAN regionalism within frameworks that adhere to international norms including state sovereignty as responsibility, and the protection of women and children.[50] This period began in 15 December 2008 when the ASEAN Charter was adopted which formally codified a new set of values, commitments and targets to achieve enhanced regional cooperation and integration.[51] The Charter specifically established ASEAN as a community comprising three pillars: ASEAN Political-Security Community (APSC), the ASEAN Economic Community (AEC), and the ASEAN Social Cultural Community (ASCC). Under Article 14, the Charter also created the ASEAN Intergovernmental Commission on Human Rights (AICHR) which is intended to serve as an 'overarching body with a cross-cutting mandate that handles matters related to human rights cooperation with other ASEAN bodies, external partners and stakeholders.'[52] This was

50 Noel M. Morada, 'Southeast Asian Regionalism, Norm Promotion and Capacity Building for Human Protection: An Overview,' *Global Responsibility to Protect* 8 (2016), pp. 111–132.

51 See 'Charter of the Association of Southeast Asian Nations,'http://asean.org/asean/asean-charter/charter-of-the-association-of-southeast-asian-nations/ accessed 31 August 2016.

52 See 'Overview,' http://asean.org/asean-political-security-community/asean-intergovernmental-commission-on-human-rights-aichr/overview/ accessed 31 August 2016.

followed by the momentous adoption of the ASEAN Human Rights Declaration and the creation of ASEAN Institute for Peace and Reconciliation (AIPR) in 2012.

As part of ASEAN's community building phase, the region has also developed an institutionally complex approach to the promotion of gender equality and women's rights.[53] Among the several institutions and mechanisms dedicated to advancing 'women-specific' concerns are through the ASEAN Ministerial Meeting on Women (AMMW) and within it is the ASEAN Committee on Women (ACW). Another example is the ASEAN Ministerial Meeting on Social Welfare and Development (AMMSWD) which then houses the ASEAN Commission on the Promotion and Protection of the Rights of Women and Children (ACWC).[54] The ACWC, as various scholars point out, is a pivotal ASEAN regional human rights mechanism because it is specifically mandated 'to promote and protect the human rights and fundamental freedoms of women and children in ASEAN, based principally on the Convention on the Elimination of All Forms of Discrimination against Women (CEDAW) and the Convention on the Rights of the Child (CRC).'[55] Tellingly, however, the ACWC and the various specific mechanisms for promoting women's rights while increasingly complex, remain institutionally compartmentalised under the ASEAN socio-cultural pillar.

For example, Morada in mapping the adoption of a protection language across the documents of the ASEAN community pillars makes a strong case for the extensive normative scaffolding upon which potential engagements with WPS and R2P can be deepened. He identifies the frequency by which textual references on human protection were made in the ASEAN charter, blueprints for APSC and ASCC, and under the terms of reference (TOR) of AICHR, ACWC and AIPR. He finds that across all these documents, references to 'human rights protection scored the highest (18), followed by peace, conflict management and conflict resolution (16), and rule of law, democracy, and democratic values (each with 10 mentions).'[56] However, while the community building phase which has created the 'three pillars' approach has paved the way for establishing

53 Mathew Davies, 'Women and Development, Not Gender and Politics: Explaining ASEAN's Failure to Engage with the Women, Peace and Security Agenda,' *Contemporary Southeast Asia* 38/1 (2016), pp. 106–127.

54 Davies, 'Women and Development, Not Gender and Politics,' p. 110.

55 Davies, 'Women and Development, Not Gender and Politics'; Ma. Lourdes Veneracion-Rallonza, 'Building the Women, Peace and Security Agenda in the ASEAN through Multi-Focal Norm Entrepreneurship,' *Global Responsibility to Protect* 8 (2016), pp. 158–179.

56 Morada, 'Southeast Asian Regionalism, Norm Promotion and Capacity Building for Human Protection,' p. 122.

the language of human protection within ASEAN, it has paradoxically also served to create 'silos' in the prevention of SGBV and promotion of gender-equality more broadly. This is evident in that references to 'respect for rights of women and children/ protection of women and children'; and 'gender mainstreaming/ elimination of violence against women' are almost exclusively only made under ACWC and the socio-cultural pillar. 'Adherence to international laws/norms/international humanitarian law/ principles on human rights protection/protection of women and children' only had a total of 6 mentions with one for each of the political-security and socio-cultural pillars. Meanwhile, references to 'peace process', 'peacebuilding', and 'conflict management/resolution' are all concentrated in the political-security pillar. 'Humanitarian assistance/ refugees/displaced persons' is only ever referenced as a political-security issue with no mentions under ASCC, AICHR, and AIPR.[57] From a feminist perspective, this compartmentalisation of gender equality out of the political-security pillar embodies how gender biases consciously or unconsciously feed into institutional design.[58] Consequently, it serves to symbolically embed political and security decision-making as primarily masculine arenas.

Three Community Pillars and Protection Gaps

Building on the feminist critiques already raised regarding the challenges to deepening the advancement of WPS and R2P globally, I argue that the ASEAN structure defined by three community pillars serves as a main impediment to meaningfully incorporating gender within regional peace and security frameworks. Indeed as Nair points out, 'there is [a] failure to engage women in peace and security issues across the socio-cultural, political-security and economic pillars upon which the ASEAN Community vision rests... The protection of women's (human) rights have essentially been confined to the socio-cultural areas and this is addressed separately from political and security concerns.'[59] First, As Davies, Nackers and Teitt argue, 'in the ASEAN Political-Security Community pillar, women are presented as benefitting from peace and security, but, crucially, not presented as being essential and conducive to its realisation.'[60] They further point out that references to women under the ACWC TOR primarily discursively represent women as victims in need of protection.[61] Moreover,

57 Ibid.

58 See for example Diane Elson (ed), *Male bias in the Development Process,* 2nd ed (Manchester; New York: Manchester University Press, 1995).

59 Nair, 'Women, Peace and Security in the ASEAN,' p. 2.

60 Davies, Nackers and Teitt, 'Women, Peace and Security as an ASEAN priority'.

61 Ibid, p. 342.

Davies argues that ASEAN primarily through its political elites holds a conservative and limited notion of gender which denies women of political agency while at the same time recognising their socio-cultural and economic contributions for regional growth.[62] What these critiques highlight is the regional reproduction of similar dichotomies between masculine protectors in this case ASEAN and its member states, and the collectively feminised and infantilised subjects of 'women and children' in ASEAN. Keeping women only under the rubric of socio-cultural and economic pillars implicitly promotes a deeply paternalistic and hierarchical relationship wherein protection is only ever afforded *to* women rather than them occupying key roles in promoting peace and security.

Second, while there have been an increasing push to shift ASEAN security discussions to incorporate 'non-traditional' security issues such as human rights, health and climate change, these remain severed from the masculinised political-security community pillar.[63] This siloing serves to deny ASEAN women a space in discussions of peace and conflict at national and regional levels – a clear undermining of core WPS goals. It also serves to reinforce a militarised notion of security rather than it encompassing all spheres of political, economic and socio-cultural activities. Importantly, as Pisanò rightly points out, 'there are no references to human rights or, specifically, to women's and children's rights in the ASEAN Economic Community Blueprint.'[64] This is an astonishing omission which highlights the imperative for employing a feminist political economy perspective that draws our attention to the continuum of violence. That the economic community pillar has remained impervious to gender as well as human rights mainstreaming is very telling of the detrimental impact of the siloing that occurs in peace and security agendas. CSOs have lobbied against the continued severance of ASEAN's three pillars as a crucial barrier to addressing the various root causes of violence against women which includes the lingering threat of intensifying ASEAN women's economic marginalisation in the face of greater economic integration among member states.[65] More to the point, the economic insecurities enforced and exacerbated through ASEAN regionalisation remain neglected from discussions of collective security. And

62 Davies, 'Women and Development, Not Gender and Politics'.

63 Davies, Nackers and Teitt, 'Women, Peace and Security as an ASEAN priority,' p. 342.

64 Attilio Pisanò, 'Towards an ASEAN human rights mechanism: the ASEAN Commission on the Promotion and Protection of the Rights of Women and Children,' The International Journal of Human Rights, 20/3 (2016), p. 327.

65 Tanyag, 'Sexual & Gender based violence'.

yet, they constitute the vast forms of violence including poverty and exploitation sustained in 'everyday life'.

Advancing a broader understanding of gender and violence – beyond the current paternalistic, or conservative view in ASEAN – is contingent on reconceptualising the recent albeit foundational ideas of ASEAN as constituted by three distinct community pillars. This is certainly a daunting but not an impossible task for ASEAN. Veneracion-Rallonza, for instance, identifies the institutional entry points for advancing WPS in ASEAN. First, this can occur via AICHR and ACWC given their shared mandate '"to develop strategies for the promotion and protection of human rights and fundamental freedoms" and to "develop policies, programs and innovative strategies to promote and protect the rights of women and children" respectively.'[66] Second, through 'horizontal and vertical norm entrepreneurship' key member states such as the Philippines can instigate norm adoption and implementation among member states, as well as across the range of ASEAN institutions and mechanisms. Indeed, she further highlights how seven ASEAN member states namely Cambodia, Indonesia, Malaysia, Singapore, Thailand, Vietnam, and the Philippines have already expressed their support for the 2013 UN Declaration of Commitment to End Sexual Violence in Conflict.[67] This commitment, she notes, included sending High-level government delegations to attend the Global Summit to End Sexual Violence in the UK.[68]

Given this recent progress, I argue that ASEAN's limited engagement with WPS is perhaps increasingly less a function of 'inherent' conservatism as others have argued, and more reflective of globally prevalent institutional constraints that sever the political-military from the socio-economic, and as well as of the gendered ideologies that shape or justify this separation. In particular, it is the siloing of the ASEAN community pillars that prevents from comprehensively advancing a feminist continuum of violence perspective which is a requisite for sustainable peace. This distinction is important in order to acknowledge the ways by which ASEAN bodies such as the ACWC have actively attempted to create spaces for CSOs to redefine ASEAN's collective security.[69] Moreover, it is precisely through the siloing of ASEAN's community pillars that the

66 Veneracion-Rallonza, 'Building the Women, Peace and Security Agenda in the ASEAN through Multi-Focal Norm Entrepreneurship,' p. 176

67 Ibid, p. 174.

68 Ibid.

69 Tanyag, 'Sexual & Gender based violence'; see also Veneracion-Rallonza 'Building the Women, Peace and Security Agenda in the ASEAN through Multi-Focal Norm Entrepreneurship.'

so-called 'ASEAN Way' – or the privileging of non-interference and consensus building – continues to be regarded as fundamental to regional peace and security thereby potentially undermining broader advancement in WPS-R2P norm promotion.[70] So long as 'women's concerns' and gender remain institutionally severed or neglected from the political-security pillar – as in women are primarily referred to under the ACWC and the socio-cultural pillar, then we cannot likely expect to see broader groups of women participating in peace, conflict and human rights decision-making in ASEAN. Relatedly, we are also less likely to achieve any fundamental rethinking on regional peace and security that recognises the political agency of broader groups of women and girls in ASEAN. Building on this critique, I now examine the RPA on EVAW which I identify as another pathway for promoting a gender-sensitive agenda on human protection and atrocities prevention. In the next section, I briefly outline how the RPA can serve as a vector not only for advancing WPS and R2P in the region, but also for rethinking the three-pillars to comprehensively end SGBV and promote gender equality as a cross-cutting issue that all ASEAN communities must address.

Regional Plan of Action on EVAW as a Vector for WPS and R2P

On 9 October 2013, ASEAN member states adopted the Declaration on the elimination of Violence against Women and Elimination of Violence against Children.[71] The ASEAN Declaration on the elimination of Violence against Women and Elimination of Violence against Children is significant because it explicitly references UNSC Resolutions 1325, 1820, 1888, and 1889 that collectively comprise the framework for the global WPS agenda. At the same time, it reaffirms ASEAN member states' commitments to other gender equality instruments such as CEDAW, the Declaration on the elimination of Violence against Women (Vienna Declaration), the Beijing Platform for Action (BPfA) and succeeding outcome documents as well as the now concluded Millennium Development Goals. The declaration in this regard is thus moored, although not explicitly, to an understanding that violence against women occurs in securitised settings of armed conflict which falls within the ambit of WPS agenda; and is also part of a wider issue of gender equality as addressed extensively by the other gender equality instruments such as CEDAW. Furthermore, the declaration states that

70 Davies, Nackers and Teitt, 'Women, Peace and Security as an ASEAN priority,' p. 343.

71 I note that the one declaration actually 'lumps together' Violence against Women and Violence against Children. A distinct RPA has been developed however for each one.

> violence against women and violence against children occur irrespective of the stages of the life cycle, whether at home, in school, in the workplace, in public or private spaces (including cyber space) as a result of gender bias, discriminatory and harmful traditional practices and must be eliminated as they impair human rights and fundamental freedoms of women and children.

It goes on to also identify specific groups of women such as: 'women and children particularly for those who are in vulnerable situations', 'women and children in disasters, women and children in armed conflict, women and children in refugee camps, women and children on the move, stateless women and children, migrant women and children, women and children belonging to ethnic and/or indigenous groups.' Finally, through the declaration, ASEAN member states commit to 'strengthen *a holistic, multi-disciplinary approach* to promote the rights of women and children and adopt a gender responsive, child sensitive, and age-responsive approach to eliminate violence against women and violence against children in the region.'[72] This includes creating 'an enabling environment for the participation of women and children, including victims/survivors, in the prevention and elimination of violence against women and violence against children.'

The yoking together of women and children in the declaration draws on narratives of vulnerability and protection stereotypes that may contradict efforts to promote the political agency of broader groups of women and girls in ASEAN. Nevertheless, the declaration at least in principle already aligns with the core goals of WPS and R2P in terms of prevention, protection and participation. It can therefore serve as an important normative starting point for discussing peace and security in ASEAN which views violence as occurring in a continuum. That is, experiences of violence are not just 'contained' in crisis settings where the R2P and WPS are salient but also as interconnected with broader issues of gender equality and human rights before, during and after crises where CEDAW, BPfA and the current Sustainable Development Goals (SDGs) are applicable frameworks. In terms of ASEAN's structure, this means prevention of SGBV and the promotion of women's political and economic rights are equal concerns for the political-security and economic pillars, and not just that of the socio-cultural pillar and the ACWC specifically. Thus, even as ASEAN currently lacks a 'specialised' regional action plan on WPS, the recently developed RPA on EVAW can potentially serve as a vector towards building a

---

72 Emphasis mine.

more inclusive and lasting peace in the region. Indeed, the RPA on EVAW is important because while the Philippines is the only country thus far that has created a WPS national action plan, all ASEAN member states have signed and ratified CEDAW.[73] More to the point, what the RPA on EVAW actually presents is an opportunity to overcome ongoing regional and national level challenges around the promotion of WPS by a recourse to the shared regional commitment of all ASEAN member states to uphold gender equality.

The RPA covers a ten-year period coinciding with the ASEAN Community Blueprint for 2016–2025.[74] It is intended to provide concrete strategies for the effective implementation of the declaration at regional and national levels. Under *Section VII. Policy Statement and Ultimate Goal*, it stipulates that 'ASEAN has a policy of zero tolerance for all forms of VAW. Recognizing VAW as a violation of human rights, ASEAN is determined to eliminate all forms of VAW as a matter of priority.' The ACWC and ACW – although both subsumed within the socio-cultural pillar of ASEAN – jointly developed the plan in close partnership with regional and national-level CSOs. The RPA to this end explicitly sets out the key role of CSOs as partners and collaborators in ending all forms of violence against women and children in ASEAN. Crucially, the RPA has opened opportunities for promoting women's political participation that is consistent with WPS goals. For instance, Action 2, paragraph 18 as well as other reinforcing sections in the RPA, call upon member states to 'incorporate the prevention of and response to all forms of VAW into the planning and delivery of disaster risk reduction programs and protocols as well as in all humanitarian responses following natural disasters, conflict situations, or other emergencies (national and regional levels).'

The RPA presents an opportunity to potentially bridge the protection gap engendered by a 'pillars approach' in ASEAN. For example, the first of the two listed objectives of the RPA is 'for ASEAN to institutionalise EVAW policies and sustained support across pillars and sectors.' Similarly, under *Section V. Guiding Principles for Development and Implementation of the ASEAN RPA on EVAW*, it expressly stipulates that 'the impact of VAW cuts across all the three pillars of ASEAN economic, political-security and socio-cultural, and all three pillars are similarly committed to ending such violence.' In addition, under Action 7,

73 See ACWC TOR, http://www.asean.org/storage/images/archive/documents/TOR-ACWC.pdf accessed 31 August 2016.

74 ASEAN Regional Plan of Action on the Elimination of Violence against Women (ASEAN RPA on EVAW) (Jakarta: ASEAN Secretariat, February 2016), http://www.asean.org/wp-content/uploads/2012/05/Final-ASEAN-RPA-on-EVAW-IJP-11.02.2016-as-input-ASEC.pdf accessed 31 August 2016.

paragraph 59, it lists the need to 'establish and/or strengthen coordination strategies between the three ASEAN pillars to end VAW, and support the effective delivery of a multi-sectoral prevention and response to VAW across all sectors (national and regional levels).' These provisions are pivotal as they specifically name the ASEAN community pillars as a point of engagement which can be re-interpreted to address the continuum between everyday gendered inequalities and violence, and conflict-related SGBV. This is pertinent again in the case of Southeast Asia where for instance as Davies, True and Tanyag point out, 'SGBV is an effective form of political and economic violence that exacerbates gender and other material inequalities and grievances.'[75] It is precisely the varying levels of state fragility in Southeast Asia that renders multiply-marginalised women and girls in the region as primary targets of egregious violence which often also go unreported and therefore perpetrated with impunity.[76]

Conclusion

For norm promotion on human protection and atrocities prevention to fully integrate and benefit broader groups of women and girls in ASEAN, it must be underpinned by the introspective scrutiny of the current silos that define ASEAN's three community pillars. Critical feminist research have demonstrated the strong gender alignments between WPS and R2P in terms of their shared goals on prevention, protection and participation. However, integrating the two must not detract from attaining comprehensive gender equality goals such as those embodied in CEDAW, BPfA and SDGs. This means pre-existing gendered inequalities must be equally addressed with conflict-related SGBV. Attaining 'immediate' political and military goals to protect civilians and prevent mass atrocities are equally important and mutually reinforcing with establishing long-term socio-cultural and economic reforms post-crisis. Thus, deepening ASEAN's engagement with WPS and R2P must be anchored upon a feminist continuum of violence which renders visible the connections between physical, structural and symbolic forms; across political, economic and socio-cultural dimensions; and the gender dynamics within families and kinship or ethnic networks, at level of the state, in ASEAN's 'three pillars', and globally.

75 Davies, True and Tanyag, 'How women's silence secures the peace: analysing sexual and gender-based violence in a low-intensity conflict', p. 461.

76 Ibid.

Concretising the RPA on EVAW entails an explicit avoidance of the pitfalls associated with taking violence in securitised settings as separate from culturally-embedded and emergent forms of violence as ASEAN deals with continued crises such as internal conflicts and disasters. This is achieved by progressively narrowing the institutional divides and policy gaps across the political-security, economic and socio-cultural community pillars. It is therefore integral for various stakeholders to engage the RPA on EVAW in this direction. As I have argued here, a clear starting point is in the progressive inclusion of gender under the political-security and economic pillars. Crucially, the goals envisioned under the RPA on EVAW are consistent with the ASEAN Community's Post-2015 Vision whereby member states reaffirmed their commitment "to identifying the best approaches to address emerging challenges, and respond effectively to the shifting regional geo-economics and geo-politics, especially in relation to peace, stability, security and prosperity in the region and beyond."[77]

77 Chairman's Statement of the 25th ASEAN Summit: "Moving Forward in Unity to a Peaceful and Prosperous Community", Nay Pyi Taw, 12 November 2014, http://www.asean.org/wp-content/uploads/images/pdf/2014_upload/Chairman%20Statement%20of%20the%2025th%20ASEAN%20Summit.pdf, accessed 6 April 2017.

ASEAN and Human Protection in Myanmar: From Non-Interference to Non-Indifference?

Noel M. Morada
University of Queensland
n.morada@uq.edu.au

Abstract

Since the adoption of the ASEAN Charter in 2008, the friction between the group's traditional norms of sovereignty and non-interference and its people-oriented principles upholding universal norms such as human rights has become more pronounced in the case of Myanmar. This chapter examines ASEAN's diplomacy in dealing with Myanmar's human rights protection issues. It argues that although in practice ASEAN has put aside its non-interference principle in response to human protection problems within Myanmar including the crisis in Rakhine, the organisation's collective efforts have been rebuffed by the previous military junta and the current civilian government which also invoked the same principle in protecting its sovereignty. While there are increasing calls from some ASEAN members and other non-state actors in the region to consider relaxing the non-interference principle when it comes to humanitarian crisis issues affecting the region, it appears that reaching a consensus on this within the group would be extremely difficult given the strong resistance of some members to the idea.

Keywords

ASEAN Charter – non-interference – human rights – Rakhine – humanitarian crisis

Introduction

The ratification of the ASEAN Charter in 2008 is a significant milestone in the evolution of Southeast Asian regionalism. While it reaffirmed the traditional norms of ASEAN, it also upheld various universal principles such as human rights protection, respect for diversity, and protection of minority groups among others. To some extent, upholding these traditional norms and people-centred principles in the Charter at the same time proved to be more difficult especially in dealing with internal conflicts faced by a member state that spill

 | DOI:10.1163/9789004363212_007

over into neighbouring countries. Nowhere is this more clearly demonstrated than in the case of Myanmar which has faced pressures from ASEAN and the international community for over 20 years due to various human rights violations before and after the military junta ruled the country. In fact, even after Aung San Suu Kyi's National League for Democracy (NLD) took over the government in March 2016, Myanmar remains a problem for ASEAN especially with regard to the continuing communal conflict in Rakhine state where the stateless Rohingya people are still discriminated and persecuted. This chapter examines ASEAN's diplomacy in dealing with Myanmar's human rights protection issues. It argues that although in practice ASEAN has put aside its non-interference principle in response to human protection problems within Myanmar including the crisis in Rakhine, the organisation's collective efforts have been rebuffed by the previous military junta and the current civilian government that also invoked the same principle in protecting its sovereignty. While there are increasing calls from some ASEAN members and other non-state actors in the region to consider relaxing the non-interference principle when it comes to humanitarian crisis issues affecting the region, it appears that reaching a consensus on this within the group would be extremely difficult given the strong resistance of some members to the idea. Even so, ASEAN's role in influencing the situation in Rakhine would most likely be limited to providing humanitarian assistance for affected communities and capacity building for Myanmar's security sector in order to prevent future atrocities from happening in the area.

The next section of this chapter provides an overview of Myanmar's membership in ASEAN, followed by a discussion of significant human protection issues that have affected its relations with the regional organisation. The last section of this chapter then focuses on the crisis in Rakhine state and the Rohingya issue with which ASEAN's non-interference principle has been put the test even as some members invoke the non-indifference principle in exerting pressure on the Myanmar government to uphold its primary responsibility to protect vulnerable populations within its borders, including the stateless Rohingyas.

Myanmar in ASEAN: An Overview

ASEAN admitted Myanmar as a member in 1997, along with Laos. While there were some concerns by the international community, especially the bloc's Western dialogue partners, about its admission into the group without significant improvement in the human rights situation in the country, ASEAN members at the time were of the view that ending Myanmar's isolation as a pariah state would serve the long-term strategic interest of the organisation. Specifically, by promoting the idea of "One Southeast Asia" wherein all states in the region were part of ASEAN, the founding ASEAN-5 members[1] thought that this would not only contain the potential for any growing influence of China in other non-member states like Myanmar but, more importantly, strengthen the regional organisation's bargaining position vis-à-vis major powers in the region.[2] This effort was also undertaken by ASEAN-5 in the context of the uncertain post-Cold War regional security environment following the withdrawal of US bases in the Philippines in 1992 and the rise of China as an economic and military power. At the time, "constructive engagement" with non-likeminded states (e.g., China, North Korea, Russia, and non-ASEAN members in Southeast Asia) served as the guiding principle in ASEAN's attempts at navigating and constructing a security framework in the region and beyond.

Specifically with regard to Myanmar, constructive engagement was espoused by Thailand, Malaysia, and Singapore in an effort to socialize the military junta into adopting a market economy, which could then open investment opportunities for its ASEAN neighbors and lessen its economic dependence on China. As well, with improvement in the economy of Myanmar using ASEAN investments, this would also stimulate economic growth in Thailand and the rest of the region, and also contain drug flows[3] and Burmese migration. Former Malaysian Prime Minister Mahathir Mohamad, a strong advocate of Myanmar's admission into ASEAN, argued that membership in the organization would have a positive effect on the country overall through the process of socialization. Specifically, he argued that it would encourage the military junta to "put the house in order" after Myanmar becomes an ASEAN member and would make it "less afraid of the democratic process."[4] After the country's admission as a member in 1997 until 2000, ASEAN's engagement policy with the military junta continued with the aim of fostering political change in Myanmar but was faced with some constraints. This includes the Asian financial crisis, which has weakened ASEAN's standing and internal cohesion due to political and/or economic instabilities in Malaysia, Indonesia, and Thailand.

1 The founding members of ASEAN are Indonesia, Malaysia, The Philippines, Singapore, and Thailand. Brunei Darussalam was admitted as member in 1984 after its independence from Great Britain. Vietnam was admitted in 1995, followed by Laos and Myanmar in 1997, and Cambodia in 1999.

2 See Jose T Almonte, "ASEAN 10: Implications for the Asia-Pacific", 11th Asia Pacific Roundtable, ASEAN-ISIS, Istana Hotel, Kuala Lumpur, Malaysia, 7 June 1997.

3 Lee Jones, "ASEAN's Albatross: ASEAN's Burma Policy from Critical Engagement to Critical Disengagement," Asian Security, 4 (3), p. 274.

4 Ibid.

The financial crisis also discredited the "Asian values" argument being promoted by more authoritarian states in ASEAN that served as a useful "shield" against interference in the domestic affairs of countries in the region, including Myanmar, to advance human rights protection and Western-style democratization.[5] With increasing frustrations especially from its Western dialogue partners about the lack of significant change in Myanmar after its admission as a member, ASEAN pleaded for patience and increased international assistance to enable the country to comply with international demands for improvement in human rights conditions.[6]

Meanwhile, ASEAN members were determined to continue with their backdoor diplomacy through a flurry of diplomatic missions in Myanmar aimed at breaking the stalemate between the military junta and the National League for Democracy (NLD) led by Aung San Suu Kyi. Specifically, Malaysia, the Philippines, and Thailand participated in a conference in Seoul in 2000 and urged the UNHCR and UNDP to extend assistance and for the UN to appoint a new special envoy to Myanmar. Razali Ismail, who was a close associate of former Malaysian Prime Minister Mahathir Mohamad, was appointed as the new UN special envoy and who facilitated the resumption of reconciliation talks between the military junta and NLD in September 2000.[7] In early 2001, Mahathir visited Yangon in an effort to push for political progress in the country and was able to secure promise from the junta for a "blueprint" that included the holding of elections in the near future.[8] In a reciprocal visit by General Than Shwe in Kuala Lumpur in September 2001, the junta leader reaffirmed Myanmar's commitment to push forward democratic reforms and reconciliation in the country.[9] Mahathir visited Yangon again in August 2002 but he and his foreign minister Syed Hamid Albar were not allowed by the military junta to meet with Suu Kyi.[10] During his trip, he pointed out that democratic reform in Myanmar would be "a slow and gradual process" even as he warned that rapid change "could lead to anarchy."[11] In general, ASEAN painstakingly highlighted

5 Ibid., p. 276.

6 Ibid., p. 277.

7 Ibid., pp. 277–278.

8 Ibid., p. 278.

9 Agence France Press, "Malaysia hails Myanmar's move to push ahead with democracy," 25 September 2001, Burma Related News, from http://www.burmalibrary.org/TinKyi/archives/2001-09/msg00020.html, accessed on 6 February 2017.

10 "Burmese junta vetoed plans for meeting with Suu Kyi," 21 August 2002, Malaysiakini.com, from http://www.malaysiakini.com/news/12648, accessed on 6 February 2017.

11 "Mahathir warns rapid Burma reforms would risk sparking anarchy," 19 August 2002, Malaysiakini.com, from http://www.malaysiakini.com/news/12626, accessed on 6 February 2017.

the "progress" in the process of democratization being made in Myanmar even as it also campaigned vigorously in the UN against passing harsh resolutions against the junta that could undermine the process national reconciliation in the country.[12] Among other things, the constructive engagement with Myanmar resulted in the release of political prisoners, including Suu Kyi from house arrest in 2002, which were welcomed by ASEAN's Western dialogue partners.

However, in May 2003, the political situation in Myanmar deteriorated following an attack in Depayin against the NLD by a group of USDP supporters that led to the death of four bodyguards of Suu Kyi. The military junta once again put Suu Kyi into "protective custody", which greatly upset members of ASEAN—especially Malaysia—and its Western dialogue partners. Mahathir even went to the extent of suggesting the expulsion of Myanmar from ASEAN if it remained intransigent and continues to undermine the credibility of the regional organization.[13] Although Thailand did not support the idea, it tried to convince the military junta that international pressure would be eased if the Myanmar government moved in the right direction. Specifically, Bangkok even drafted a roadmap for the country's democratic transition but which was not accepted by the junta. Instead, Myanmar drafted its own 7-point roadmap to democracy, which was announced by former Prime Minister General Khin Nyunt on 30 August 2003 and which includes, among other things, promised the drafting of a new constitution and holding of free and fair elections in the country.[14] Even so, the military junta refused to release Suu Kyi from house arrest despite continued appeals from ASEAN and pressures from Western countries. This political stalemate between the military

12 Lee Jones, ibid., p. 278.

13 Ibid., p. 279–280.

14 See H.E. U Khin Maung Win, Deputy Minister for Foreign Affairs of the Union of Myanmar, "Myanmar Roadmap to Democracy: The Way Forward," Seminar on Understanding Myanmar, 27–28 January 2004, MICT Park, Yangon, Myanmar Institute of Strategic and International Studies, from http://www.ibiblio.org/obl/docs/KMWroadmap104.htm, accessed on 6 February 2017. Specifically, the 7-point roadmap to democracy include the following: 1) reconvening of the National Convention that has been adjourned since 1996; 2) after the successful holding of the National Convention, step by step implementation of the process necessary for the emergence of a genuine and disciplined democratic state; 3) drafting of a new constitution in accordance with basic principles and detailed basic principle laid down by the National Convention; 4) adoption of the constitution through national referendum; 5) holding of free and fair elections for Pyithu Hluttaws (Legislative bodies) according to the new constitution; 6) convening of Hluttaws attended by Hluttaw members in accordance with the new constitution; and 7) building a modern, developed and democratic nation by the state leaders elected by the Hluttaw; and the government and other central organs formed by the Hluttaw.

and the NLD increasingly became a serious concern for ASEAN and its Western dialogue partners as Myanmar would soon assume the chairmanship of ASEAN in 2006–2007—a development that could severely undermine the organization's credibility. Specifically, Myanmar's chairmanship posed a major challenge to ASEAN's efforts to build a community based on the Bali Concord II adopted in 2003, which seeks to promote "good governance, rule of law, and democracy" in the region. As well, the issue could also overshadow the process of drafting the ASEAN Charter that began in 2005 which, among other things, envisioned a people-centered community that upholds international norms, including the promotion and protection of human rights. Western dialogue partners of ASEAN also threatened to boycott the latter's meetings if Myanmar becomes chair. Given all these factors, the rest of ASEAN worked so hard to persuade the military junta to agree to pass on the chairmanship of ASEAN to the Philippines to avoid further embarrassment for the organization. There is no question that resolving the chairmanship issue was a major relief for ASEAN, which enabled its members to focus on finalizing the organization's charter under the leadership of the Philippines. The creation of regional human rights body under the ASEAN Charter was a major agenda of the Philippines as chair at the time. However, this was not fully supported by other members—particularly Myanmar and Vietnam.[15] In fact, the inclusion of this provision almost scuttled the ASEAN Charter's endorsement by ASEAN foreign ministers in 2007 if not for a compromise solution proposed by Singapore who was take over from the Philippines as next chair of ASEAN.[16] Specifically, the high level task force that drafted the charter agreed to the creation of a regional human rights body but that its terms of reference will be negotiated later once the ASEAN charter has been ratified by all members.

Notwithstanding ASEAN's initial although quite limited success in overcoming these challenges faced by the organization following Myanmar's admission as a member, human protection issues in the country continued to burden the organization since 2006. The next section focuses on some of these concerns and how they shaped ASEAN's responses to human rights protection issues in the region, beginning with the 2007 protests led by Buddhist monks and Cyclone Nargis in 2008.

15 See Noel M. Morada, "The ASEAN Charter and the Promotion of R2P in Southeast Asia: Challenges and Consttraints," Global Responsibility to Protect, 1 (2009), pp. 198–199. See also John Arendshorst, "The Dilemma of Non-Interference: Myanmar, Human Rights, and the ASEAN Charter," Northwestern Journal of International Human Rights, 8 (1) Fall 2009, p. 113.

16 Noel M. Morada, ibid.

ASEAN and Human Protection in Myanmar

Since 2006, ASEAN's cohesion was severely tested amidst growing international pressure for the organisation to do more in addressing fundamental human rights issues in that country. While ASEAN's engagement with Myanmar initially focused on freeing Suu Kyi and promoting reconciliation between the military and pro-democracy forces in the country, the issue of human rights took on a wider dimension following the violent crackdown against protests led by Buddhist monks in 2007 and the humanitarian crisis that ensued in the aftermath of Cyclone Nargis in 2008. The events raised issues about Myanmar's commitment to universal norms on human rights and international humanitarian law even as they also demonstrated ASEAN's limitations in reining in an erring member amidst mounting international pressures.

2007 Protests led by Buddhist Monks

The Myanmar government's decision to lift subsidies on fuel in August 2007 triggered widespread protests throughout the country against the military junta. Initially, the government attempted to contain the situation by arresting those who participated in the demonstrations against the cut in fuel subsidies. However, following a violent dispersal of a peaceful protest in Pakkoku that injured three monks on 5 September, some young monks retaliated the next day by holding hostage several government officials and set a deadline for the military to apologise for the violent incident. The military, however, refused to apologise and further aggravated the situation. Specifically, more monks participated in the protests even as they also began to withdraw religious services to the military. The demonstrations spread in Yangon (with an estimated 50,000 to 100,000 people participating), Mandalay, Sittwe and more than 20 other cities throughout the country by 24 September. Thousands of monks and over a hundred nuns took part on the sixth day of protests in Yangon even as an alliance of Buddhist monks threatened to continue the protests until the military junta is deposed.[17] About 1,000 protesting monks and NLD supporters also passed by the house of Aung San Suu Kyi, who was under house arrest, and chanted prayers for her.[18] Then former ASEAN Secretary General Ong Keng

---

17 "Nuns in Burma anti-junta rallies," BBC News, 23 September 2007, from http://news.bbc.co.uk/2/hi/asia-pacific/7009005.stm, accessed on 12 February 2017.

18 "Burmese military threatens monks," BBC News, 24 September 2007, from http://news.bbc.co.uk/2/hi/asia-pacific/7010839.stm, accessed on 12 February 2017.

Yong expressed hope that the government would not take strong actions that would lead to a confrontation.[19]

On 26 September, the military began its violent crackdown on protesters by attacking them with batons and tear gas, arresting civilians and Buddhist monks, and sealing off the Shwedagon Pagoda, which is a major site of demonstrations in Yangon. The next day, government troops raided various monasteries across the country and arrested more monks and their sympathisers even as protests continued, which resulted in some fatalities and injuries as soldiers fired at the demonstrators with bullets and insecticides.[20] The total number of casualties in the military crackdown remain contested, with the government claiming only 10–15 killed while the UN special rapporteur said there were at least an additional 16 more people who died during the violent crackdown, with some 74 people missing and up to 1,000 detained in connection with the protests.[21] In an effort to prevent any news and information related to the crackdown directly being sent out of Myanmar by citizens or protesters, the military on 28 September shut down all access to the internet in the country by closing down internet cafes.[22]

The international community led by ASEAN's Western dialogue partners denounced the military junta's violent crackdown against the protesters and announced sanctions against the regime. Specifically, the US froze the bank accounts of some 14 military officials,[23] including General Than Shwe, and

---

19 "Nuns in Burma anti-junta rallies," ibid.

20 "Japan mourns video journalist killed in Yangon," Reuters, 8 October 2007, from http://www.reuters.com/article/us-myanmar-japan-funeral-idUST23546620071009; "Fears of mounting death toll in Burma," Financial Times, 29 September 2007, from http://www.ft.com/cms/s/0/32f71724-6e62-11dc-b818-0000779fd2ac.html?ft_site=falcon&desktop=true; and "UN envoy Gambari in Burma crisis talks," Financial Times, 30 September 2007, from https://www.ft.com/content/0d0623bc-6de4-11dc-b8ab-0000779fd2ac, all accessed on 12 February 2017.

21 Warren Hoge, "UN report finds 31 killed in Myanmar crackdown," The New York Times online, 7 December 2007, from http://www.nytimes.com/2007/12/07/world/asia/07iht-07nations.8645448.html, accessed on 12 February 2017.

22 Seth Mydans, "Monks silenced, and for now, the internet is, too," The New York Times online, 4 October 2007, from http://www.nytimes.com/2007/10/04/world/asia/04info.html, accessed on 12 February 2017;

23 Associated Press, "Bush imposes economic sanctions on key officials from Myanmar government," Fox News online, 27 September 2007, from http://www.foxnews.com/story/2007/09/27/bush-imposes-economic-sanctions-on-key-officials-from-myanmar-government.html, accessed on 12 February 2017.

the European Union imposed restrictions on imports from Myanmar such as timber and gems.[24] US citizens were also banned from making business transactions with designated individuals in Myanmar, while the EU also adopted arms and trade embargoes provided these did not harm the general population. Japan also imposed sanctions against Myanmar in response to the death of a Japanese journalist during the crackdown, while Australia announced targeted financial sanctions and visa restrictions against the military junta.[25] ASEAN, however, did not support these sanctions against Myanmar as such policies only exacerbate further the suffering of the ordinary people in the country. Even so, given the intense international pressure, a proposal was made for the inclusion of Myanmar's violent crackdown against protesting civilians in the agenda of the ASEAN Summit in November of the same year, which was chaired by Singapore. Specifically, Singapore invited the UN special envoy Ismail Gambari to give a briefing to the ASEAN leaders about his fact-finding visit to the country in the aftermath of the political crisis. However, Myanmar used its veto power and invoked the non-interference principle to block the inclusion of the country's political crisis in the summit's agenda, which was supported by Laos and Vietnam.[26] The ASEAN Chairman's statement at the end of the summit in Singapore reflects the deep concern of other members regarding the situation in Myanmar, notwithstanding assurances from Prime Minister Thein Sein, to wit:

> "We had an extensive and open discussion on Myanmar. We were given a comprehensive briefing by Myanmar PM Thein Sein, where he emphasised that the situation in Myanmar was a domestic affair, and that Myanmar was fully capable of handling the situation by itself. He reaffirmed that Myanmar had every confidence in managing the good offices of the UN. As ASEAN Chair, Singapore issued a statement to clarify ASEAN's role

24 "EU imposes fresh sanctions on Myanmar," Deustche Welle (DW) online, 19 November 2007, from http://www.dw.com/en/eu-imposes-fresh-sanctions-on-myanmar/a-2934373, accessed on 12 February 2017.

25 Craig Skehan, "PM launches sanctions against junta," The Sydney Morning Herald online, 27 September 2007, from http://www.smh.com.au/news/world/pm-launches-sanctions-against-junta/2007/09/27/1190486462513.html. See also "Overview of Burma sanctions," BBC News online, 18 December 2009, from http://news.bbc.co.uk/2/hi/asia-pacific/8195956.stm, accessed 12 February 2017.

26 Wayne Arnold, "Rift over Myanmar emerges at ASEAN summit," The New York Times online, 19 November 2007, from http://www.nytimes.com/2007/11/19/world/asia/19iht-asean.3.8393052.html, accessed on 12 February 2017.

> and stand. We reiterated that the Myanmar Government should continue to work with the UN in order to open up a meaningful dialogue with Daw Aung San Suu Kyi and the National League for Democracy (NLD); make full use of the good offices of the UN Secretary-General and Professor Gambari in this process; lift restrictions on Daw Aung San Suu Kyi and release all political detainees; work towards a peaceful transition to democracy; and address the economic difficulties faced by the people of Myanmar. We emphasised that we will strive to prevent the Myanmar issue from obstructing ASEAN's integration efforts, especially the ASEAN Charter and the establishment of the ASEAN Community."[27]

It is significant to note that it was also during this meeting that leaders of the ten member states signed the ASEAN Charter, which marked an important milestone in its 40 years existence. Notwithstanding the signing of the charter, however, then Philippine President Gloria Macapagal-Arroyo stated during the summit meeting that the ratification of the ASEAN charter would face some difficulties in her country's legislature if Myanmar failed to release Suu Kyi from house arrest and get back to its promised path to democratization.[28] It was an attempt on the part of the Philippines to persuade other members of ASEAN to seriously examine the implications of the military junta's continuing intransigence for the group's cohesion and credibility vis-à-vis its dialogue partners and the international community at large. Indeed, without provisions in the ASEAN Charter for sanctions against erring members, Myanmar will continue to be a burden to ASEAN's community building efforts and in promoting international norms and principles such as good governance, rule of law, and human rights protection in the region. The time that the ASEAN Charter is being ratified by members could have been a good opportunity for the group to exert concerted pressure on the Myanmar government to abide by these principles and fulfil its primary responsibility to protect the human rights of its people. Such opportunity however was missed as ASEAN remained divided between those who strongly adhere to the non-interference principle and those that

---

27 Chairman's Statement of the 13th ASEAN Summit, "One ASEAN at the Heart of Dynamic Asia" Singapore, 20 November 2007, from http://asean.org/?static_post=chairman-s-statement-of-the-13th-asean-summit-one-asean-at-the-heart-of-dynamic-asia-singapore-20-november-2007, accessed on 13 February 2017.

28 Ibid.

believe in balancing the traditional norms of ASEAN with universal norms and people-centred principles. Certainly, the ASEAN Charter affirms both state-centred (e.g., sovereignty and non-interference) and people-centred (e.g., universal human rights and international humanitarian law) principles. It also recognizes the primary responsibility of states to protect human rights and reaffirms the concept of comprehensive security, which includes human security.

2008 Cyclone Nargis

Less than a year after the widespread protests in September 2007, tropical Cyclone Nargis hit the southern part of Myanmar on 2 May 2008 that resulted in a massive humanitarian crisis in the country. Official figures indicate that there were 84,500 people killed and more than 53,000 were missing after the two-day disaster that devastated the Ayerwaddy Delta region.[29] (The military junta stopped updating the death toll past 138,000 apparently due to fears of a political fallout even as some reports from diplomatic, humanitarian aid, and media sources claimed that the government underestimated the number of people killed in the worst natural disaster that hit the country.) The high death toll and casualties were partly blamed on the government who, despite assertions to the contrary, were blamed by critics for failing to provide early warning and organize evacuation plans to people living in low-lying areas.[30] While the government initially accepted relief assistance from neighbouring countries immediately after the cyclone hit the country, the military junta on 9 May blocked international humanitarian assistance especially from Western countries as it feared that relief operations involving foreign aid workers and some military troops could be a pretext for intervention. This drew strong condemnation from the international community, including some permanent members of the UN Security Council. Specifically, the French ambassador the UN condemned the military junta's refusal to accept international aid to those in need could lead to "a true crime against humanity" even as he denied the Myanmar's UN ambassador's allegation that Paris sent a warship, which he

29 "Myanmar: Cyclone Nargis 2008 Facts and Figures," International Federation of Red Cross and Red Crescent Societies online, 3 May 2011, from http://www.ifrc.org/en/news-and-media/news-stories/asia-pacific/myanmar/myanmar-cyclone-nargis-2008-facts-and-figures/, accessed on 13 February 2017.

30 Associated Press, "Cyclone Nargis embodied the perfect storm," NBCNews.com, 8 May 2008, from http://www.nbcnews.com/id/24526960/ns/world_news-asia_pacific/t/cyclone-nargis-embodied-perfect-storm/#.WKEEtBi1Bw, accessed on 13 February 2017.

asserted was a ship carrying 1,500 tons of food and medicine for survivors.[31] For his part, UK Prime Minister Gordon Brown accused the military junta of negligence by turning a natural disaster into a man-made catastrophe even as he called for holding the regime accountable.[32] Meanwhile, then French Foreign Minister Bernard Kouchner called on the UN to invoke the responsibility to protect as basis for a resolution that would force the military junta to allow international assistance into the country even without the consent of the Myanmar government.[33] Some UN officials however resisted such call even as they expressed hope that the junta would eventually be persuaded to allow international relief assistance and foreign aid workers to come in.[34]

Meanwhile, despite the ongoing humanitarian crisis, the military junta pushed through with the national referendum on the constitution, which was held on 10 May (while referendum in areas affected by Cyclone Nargis was postponed to 24 May). The government claimed on 15 May that the constitution was approved by 92 percent of voters with 99 percent voter turnout in two-thirds of the country's regions that held the vote.[35] The NLD campaigned against the approval of the constitution but not as effectively as the military junta, which conducted the campaign in favour of the constitution as a military operation.[36] As well, the more the military junta faced international pressures to postpone the referendum, the more it insisted on holding it in an effort to show political will and stand up against external interference.[37] While there were questions raised about the credibility of the referendum's results, the people of Myanmar for the most part participated in the exercise and approved the constitution as a matter of realism given that the alternative is continuation of direct military rule.[38]

31 "France angered by Burmese delays," BBC News online, 17 May 2008, from http://news.bbc.co.uk/2/hi/asia-pacific/7405998.stm, accessed on 13 February 2017.

32 Ibid.

33 Seth Mydans, "Myanmar faces pressure to allow major aid effort," New York Times online, 8 May 2008, from http://www.nytimes.com/2008/05/08/world/asia/08myanmar.html, accessed on 13 February 2017.

34 Ibid.

35 "Burma 'approves new constitution'," BBC news online, 15 May 2008, from http://news.bbc.co.uk/2/hi/asia-pacific/7402105.stm, accessed on 20 February 2017.

36 Derek Tonkin, "The 2008 Constitution in the Context of Myanmar Reality," in Li Chenyang and Wilhelm Hofmeister (eds.) *Myanmar: Prospect for Change* (Singapore and Kunming: Select Publishing, Konrad Adenauer Stiftung and Yunnan University, 2009), p. 60.

37 Ibid.

38 Ibid.

Eventually, the impasse over international humanitarian assistance to the country was resolved only after ASEAN used its influence over Myanmar through backdoor diplomacy. Specifically, former ASEAN Secretary General Surin Pitsuwan led a delegation of officials from the region in a visit to Yangon and convinced the military junta to allow international humanitarian assistance to come in using ASEAN as the main conduit. A week after the disaster, the ASEAN-Emergency Rapid Assessment Team (ASEAN-ERAT) was set up and, in coordination with the ASEAN Committee on Disaster Management (ACDM), was dispatched to Myanmar to make an initial assessment of the critical needs in the aftermath of Cyclone Nargis. The ASEAN-ERAT, which was also tasked to complement the work of the UN Disaster Assessment and Coordination (UNDAC) team and those of the Myanmar government, recommended the creation of the "Humanitarian Coalition for the Victims of Cyclone Nargis" that would act as "a coordinating platform for relief and recovery" in the country.[39] In a subsequent special meeting of the ASEAN foreign ministers in Singapore, the ASEAN Humanitarian Task Force for the Victims of Cyclone Nargis (AHTF) was set up as the main mechanism "to facilitate the effective and distribution and facilitation of incoming international assistance", including the deployment of relief workers.[40] Meanwhile, on 25 May, an ASEAN-UN International Pledging Conference was held in Yangon with 51 countries participating and focused on increasing the relief aid to Myanmar and expediting the delivery of humanitarian assistance and operations especially in desperate places around the country. A tripartite core group (TCG) was also set up between ASEAN, the UN and the government of Myanmar to coordinate, facilitate, and monitor the flow of international assistance to the country.[41]

Clearly, ASEAN played a critical role in Myanmar as the main interlocutor between the military junta and the international community at the height of the humanitarian crisis. Specifically, it effectively broke the impasse caused by the military's intransigence as it offered serve as the main conduit for international humanitarian assistance. This opportunity provided a face-saving option for the military junta to relent on its hard line position against external aid. To some extent, ASEAN also served as a shield to an embattled member state who was being condemned by the international community for its apparent callous response to the suffering of its own people. Indeed, it can be argued that without its diplomatic strategy of sustained constructive engagement

39 "A Bridge to Recovery: ASEAN's Response to Cyclone Nargis," Jakarta: ASEAN Secretariat, July 2009, p. 10.

40 Ibid.

41 Ibid., p. 12

with Myanmar's military junta, ASEAN would not have effectively responded to the humanitarian crisis in a member state whose regime is considered a pariah to the international community.

Notwithstanding the positive role that ASEAN played, the regional organization certainly did not put aside Myanmar's political crisis of 2007. Specifically, in the 2009 ASEAN Summit in Thailand, the leaders expressed continuing concerns about the process of national reconciliation between the military junta and the democratic supporters of Suu Kyi, which were reflected in the formal statement issued at the end of the meeting, to wit:

> "We had open discussions on Myanmar. We were briefed by H.E. Prime Minister Thein Sein on recent political development and the progress made in the implementation of the 7-step Roadmap to Democracy. We encouraged the Myanmar Government to facilitate the national reconciliation process to be more inclusive so as to strengthen national unity, thereby contributing to peace and prosperity in Myanmar. In this connection, the release of political detainees and the inclusion of all political parties in the political process leading to the general elections in 2010 will contribute significantly to the national reconciliation process. We underscored the necessity for and welcomed Myanmar Government's willingness to engage in active cooperation actively with the UN Secretary-General's Special Envoy as well as the UN Special Rapporteur on Human Rights in order to address the international community's concern about the situation in Myanmar."[42]

From the statement, it is quite clear that ASEAN remained steadfast in pushing for the implementation of the roadmap for democracy in Myanmar, which will culminate in the 2010 elections. The group's call for the release of political detainees and for participation of all political parties in the elections also indicate that it puts premium on the credibility of the first political exercise since the 1990 elections in which the NLD won by a landslide. Indeed, ASEAN sent a delegation of observers in the 2010 general elections, which brought the military-backed Union Solidarity and Development Party (USDP) into power. The NLD staged a boycott of the 2010 elections but it participated in

42 Chairman's Statement of the 14th ASEAN Summit, "ASEAN Charter for ASEAN Peoples", Cha-am, 28 February – 1 March 2009, from http://asean.org/chairman-s-statement-of-the-14th-asean-summit-asean-charter-for-asean-peoples-cha-am-28-february-1-march-2009/, accessed on 14 February 2017.

the 2012-by elections that saw Suu Kyi and her party winning 48 seats in parliament that was still dominated by the military.

The next section examines the Rohingya issue in Myanmar and how it has played out in the regional dynamics of promoting human protection norms and ASEAN's traditional non-interference principle.

ASEAN and the Rohingya Issue: Time to Relax the Non-Interference Principle?

Prior to 2012, the Rohingya issue in Myanmar was not a major concern for ASEAN except for their outflow as "Illegal migrants" in the Indian Ocean. In 2009, Thailand as chair of the 14th ASEAN Summit, called for "cooperation among countries of origin, transit, and destination" even as it also underscored the importance of addressing the issue "in a larger context, such as the contact group of affected countries" and through the Bali process. The ASEAN Secretary General was also tasked to coordinate with the Myanmar government "obtain relevant statistics" related to the illegal immigrants in the Indian Ocean.[43] Since 2007, Thailand has been criticized by various human rights groups for failing to protect the Rohingyas who were fleeing from Bangladesh and Myanmar, some of whom were allegedly abused and detained as illegal migrants by military authorities after their boats landed in Thai territory and were towed back to sea, adrift for several days with barely enough food and water.[44] The increased outflow of Rohingya refugees in 2009 was precipitated by a crackdown in Bangladesh against undocumented asylum seekers in effort to stem the exodus of more than 8,000 Rohingyas before the Myanmar elections in 2010. It was also brought about by panic among undocumented Rohingyas when it was reported in the Bangladesh media that Myanmar has agreed to repatriate some 9,000 refugees in late December 2009 following a meeting between the Bangladesh foreign minister and his Myanmar counterpart.[45]

However, ASEAN was forced to respond to this humanitarian crisis in Myanmar following the eruption of communal violence in Rakhine in May and June

43 Ibid.

44 Ian MacKinnon and James Sturcke, "After 20 days adrift, Burmese boat people land with tales of abuse and starvation," The Guardian online, 4 February 2009, from https://www.theguardian.com/world/2009/feb/04/burmese-boat-survivors, accessed on 20 March 2017.

45 Chris Lewa, "Unregistered Rohingya Refugees in Bangladesh: Crackdown, Forced Displacement, and Hunger," The Arakan Project, 11 February 2010, pp. 3–4.

2012 between Muslim and Buddhist communities, which further aggravated the outflow of Rohingya refugees. Specifically, former ASEAN Secretary General Surin Pitsuwan expressed that he has taken a "personal interest" regarding the situation of the Rohingyas in Rakhine during the annual ASEAN ministerial meeting in Phnom Penh in July that year and sought the cooperation of both Myanmar and Bangladesh during his meeting with their respective foreign ministers.[46] In their special meeting in August 2012, ASEAN foreign ministers issued a statement that expressed continuing concerns about the situation in Rakhine. On the one hand, they encouraged the government of Myanmar to continue and enhance the steps it has taken with the help of UN agencies and non-government organisations in responding to the humanitarian crisis and expressed readiness to assist Myanmar in addressing the crisis in Rakhine, with the consent of the government. On the other hand, however, the ministers also underscored that "the promotion of national solidarity and harmony among various communities in Myanmar constitute an integral part of [the country's] democratisation and reform process", even as they also expressed the expectation that it will "continue to remain consistent with its commitment on the irreversibility of democratization and reform process in the country."[47]

It is significant to note that ASEAN's statement did not use the term "Rohingya" upon the insistence of the Myanmar government. This issue will continue as a bone of contention in promoting the protection of the stateless Muslim community in Rakhine not just among ASEAN members and non-government organizations in the region but also with the UN and other international humanitarian organisations. In fact, when Myanmar assumed the chairmanship of ASEAN in 2014, it refused to include the humanitarian crisis in Rakhine in the agenda of ASEAN meetings and even insisted that this issue not be discussed in the ASEAN Civil Society Conference/ASEAN People's Forum when it hosted these meetings.[48] It was also during Myanmar's chairmanship that another communal conflict between Muslim and Buddhist communities erupted in July 2014, this time in Mandalay and other parts of the country outside

46 "Rohingya raised at ASEAN meeting," Radio Free Asia.com, 13 July 2012, from http://www.rfa.org/english/news/myanmar/rohingya-07132012163418.html, accessed on 23 March 2017.

47 "Statement of ASEAN Foreign Ministers on the Recent Developments in the Rakhine State, Myanmar"Phnom Penh, Cambodia, 17 August 2012, from http://www.asean.org/wp-content/uploads/images/archive/documents/Statement%20of%20ASEAN%20FM%20on%20Recent%20Developments%20in%20the%20Rakhine%20State.pdf, accessed on 23 March 2017.

48 This is based on interview with a human rights activist in Jakarta in August 2016 who participated in the ACSC/APF meeting in Yangon in 2014.

Rakhine. It stemmed from the hate speech and attacks instigated by Buddhist nationalists led by Wirathu against Muslim minorities in the country. However, ASEAN failed to issue any statement about these incidents while Myanmar was chair, which is clearly in stark contrast to the previous years. For example, from 2005 up to 2012, ASEAN has consistently included a section on Myanmar (under regional and international developments) in its joint communiques and chairman's statements, which contained the collective sentiments of the rest of the ASEAN members on the political situation in the country. Since Brunei's chairmanship in 2013 followed by Myanmar in 2014, Malaysia in 2015, and Laos in 2016, there were no formal statements issued by ASEAN following the annual ministerial and summit meetings hosted by these member states. The maritime conflict in the South China Sea became the main issue that preoccupied ASEAN during this period, which was reflected in the formal statements issued in the ASEAN foreign ministers and leaders' summit meetings.

Notwithstanding the foregoing developments, the Buddhist-Muslim communal conflict in Rakhine and elsewhere in Myanmar remained a major concern for ASEAN. In the run up to the November 2015 general elections, the persecution of the Rohingyas in Rakhine increased further following the passage of four laws on race and religion aimed at the Muslim community in Myanmar. This resulted in increased refugee outflow especially in April and May 2015 that also led to deaths by hundreds of Rohingyas who fled on boats in the Indian Ocean. Some of these refugees fell victim to human traffickers, which became all the more evident following the discovery of mass graves at the border of Malaysia and Thailand in May 2015.[49] Responding to this tragedy, the foreign ministers of Indonesia, Malaysia, and Thailand met in Putrajaya on 20 May and issued a statement condemning the smuggling and trafficking of irregular migrants and urged the concerned parties to address the root causes and other contributory factors to the influx of the refugees.[50] As well, Indonesia and Malaysia agreed to provide temporary shelter to the stranded Rohingya

49 Ben Li Yih, "Malaysia migrant mass graves: police reveal 139 sites, some with multiple corpses." The Guardian.com, 25 May 2015, from https://www.theguardian.com/world/2015/may/25/malaysia-migrant-mass-graves-police-reveal-139-sites-some-with-multiple-corpses, accessed on 23 March 2017. See also "Thailand mass graves found in Rohingya trafficking camp," Human Rights Watch, 1 May 2015, from https://www.hrw.org/news/2015/05/01/thailand-mass-graves-rohingya-found-trafficking-camp, accessed on 23 March 2017.

50 See "Joint statement: Ministerial meeting on irregular movement of people in Southeast Asia," Reliefweb, 21 May 2015, from http://reliefweb.int/report/myanmar/joint-statement-ministerial-meeting-irregular-movement-people-southeast-asia, accessed on 24 March 2017.

refugees until they can be resettled to a third country. This was a reversal of their previous policy of towing away the migrants' boats in the Indian Ocean away from their shores.[51] It is significant to note that the Putrajaya statement neither used the term "Rohingya" in referring to refugees nor identified Myanmar and Bangladesh as the parties that must address the root causes of the problem. Subsequently, on 29 May, Thailand convened a special meeting of ASEAN, the UN, and other concerned states to respond to the humanitarian crisis and human trafficking of the Rohingyas from Myanmar and Bangladesh. Initially, Myanmar refused to participate in the meeting because of the use of the term "Rohingya" but it later on relented.[52] At the end of the meeting, a statement was issued that, among others, called for addressing the root causes and living conditions of at-risk communities in the areas of origin (i.e., Myanmar and Bangladesh), which includes "capacity building of local communities, providing economic incentives that create more jobs, promoting trade and investment and development assistance to the at-risk areas, providing skills training, infrastructure development, enhancing a sense of security and belonging, promoting full respect for human rights and adequate access of people to basic rights and services such as housing, education and healthcare, with involvement of the private sector and relevant stakeholders, and in this regard, took note with appreciation humanitarian and development assistance offered by countries both inside and outside the region towards at-risk areas."[53] The statement also did not use the term "Rohingya" and did not identify Myanmar and Bangladesh as the countries of origin of the "at-risk communities."

The plight of the Rohingyas and its impact on the region have raised the issue of whether ASEAN should begin to consider relaxing its non-interference principle for it to effectively respond to humanitarian crisis situations in the region. Some former ASEAN officials and parliamentarians in the region have

51 Joe Cochrane, "Indonesia and Malaysia agree to care for stranded migrants," The New York Times online, 20 May 2015, from https://www.nytimes.com/2015/05/21/world/asia/indonesia-malaysia-rohingya-bangladeshi-migrants-agreement.html?action=click&contentCollection=Asia%20Pacific&module=RelatedCoverage&region=Marginalia&pgtype=article, accessed on 24 March 2017.

52 Joe Cochrane, "In reversal, Myanmar agrees to attend meeting on migrant crisis," The New York Times online, 21 May 2015, from https://www.nytimes.com/2015/05/22/world/asia/myanmar-rohingya-migrant-crisis-malaysia-thailand-indonesia.html?_r=0, accessed on 24 March 2017.

53 See "Summary: Special Meeting on Irregular Migration in the Indian Ocean, 29 May 2015, Bangkok, Thailand," Reliefweb, 29 May 2015, from http://reliefweb.int/report/myanmar/summary-special-meeting-irregular-migration-indian-ocean-29-may-2015-bangkok-thailand, accessed on 24 March 2017.

pointed out that indeed it is about time to re-examine the application of the said doctrine, which to some extent has constrained the regional organisation from responding more effectively to internal problems that spill over to other member states. For example, in April 2015, former Malaysian foreign minister Syed Hamid Albar called for a review of the non-interference principle during his speech at the ASEAN Civil Society Conference in Kuala Lumpur. Accordingly, this is imperative if ASEAN is "to build a tolerant society and address human rights abuses and regional security" even as the region cannot be "bogged down with problems that are prolonged or intensified by the blanket application of non-interference."[54] Albar, together with former Malaysian Prime Minister Ahmad Badawi, former ASEAN Secretary General Surin Pitsuwan, and former Thai Foreign Minister Kasit Promiya, also sent a letter to the ASEAN Chair in April 2015 during the summit in Malaysia calling for stepped up engagement to address the issue of intolerance in Myanmar, including discriminatory laws. Specifically, they pointed out that "the rising intolerance against religious and ethnic minorities in Myanmar will undermine the country's reform process, and may affect regional community-building, including ASEAN economic integration."[55] For its part, the ASEAN Parliamentarians for Human Rights (APHR) called on the leaders of ASEAN to urgently respond to the escalating humanitarian crisis and the growing atrocities risks affecting the Rohingyas and other vulnerable minorities in Myanmar. For them, the problem which represent a "direct threat to ASEAN nations" as it poses security risks and economic strains to the region even as it undermines the shared commitment of member states to "protecting all people from persecution and violence."[56]

The NLD and the Rakhine Crisis

More than a year since Suu Kyi's National League for Democracy took over the government in Myanmar, the crisis in Rakhine is far from having been resolved. In fact, the problem has taken a new and more violent turn following the

54 "ASEAN's non-interference policy must be reviewed: Former Malaysian minister," Channel News Asia, 24 April 2015, from http://www.channelnewsasia.com/news/business/asean-s-non-interference/1804054.html, accessed on 24 March 2017.

55 Humaniti, "Former ASEAN Leaders Issue Letter on Myanmar Intolerance," Burma Partnership online, 22 April 2015, from http://www.burmapartnership.org/2015/04/former-asean-leaders-issue-letter-on-myanmar-intolerance/, accessed on 24 March 2017.

56 "Parliamentarians call on ASEAN leaders to address the Rohingya crisis and the growing risk of atrocity crimes in Myanmar," ASEAN Parliamentarians for Human Rights (APHR) online, 22 April 2015, from http://aseanmp.org/2015/04/22/parliamentarians-call-on-asean-leaders-to-address-the-rohingya-crisis-and-the-escalating-risk-of-atrocity-crimes-in-myanmar/, accessed on 17 April 2017.

attacks by more than 200 militants on 9 October 2016 against border policemen in Maungdaw and Bittadaung townships. This resulted in more Rohingya people fleeing to Bangladesh as the Myanmar military conducted clearing operations in these border areas. Allegations were made by international human rights advocates that the military committed atrocities against the Rohingya community, including the rape of women, during the month-long security operations in Rakhine. A commission set up by the government to investigate the allegations issued a statement in January 2017 that it found no evidence that support either claims of genocide against the Rohingyas or widespread rape allegations committed by security forces. However, it softened its position following a report released the following month from the UN Office of the Human Rights Commissioner that alleged sexual violence against some Rohingya women. For her part, Suu Kyi assured the UN High Commissioner for Human Rights that her government will take appropriate measures if indeed there is clear evidence of abuses or violations committed by security forces.

Meanwhile, ASEAN's response to the renewed crisis in Rakhine was undoubtedly strong, especially from Malaysia and Indonesia. Specifically, Malaysian Prime Minister Najib Razak led protests in December 2016 in Kuala Lumpur against the persecution of the Rohingyas, even as demonstrations were also held in Jakarta and Bangkok by groups sympathetic to the plight of the stateless people in Rakhine. Amidst mounting pressures from its neighbours and the international community, Suu Kyi convened a special meeting of the ASEAN foreign ministers in Yangon, which focused on renewing humanitarian assistance to affected communities in Rakhine. However, the Malaysian foreign minister expressed strong concerns for the Rohingyas during the meeting and proposed that ASEAN set up an independent body of experts and eminent persons to validate official accounts by the Myanmar government on the situation in Rakhine.[57] The suggestion apparently was not accepted by Myanmar and other ASEAN members. In January 2017, as host of the Organisation of the Islamic Cooperation (OIC), Prime Minister Najib Razak called on Naypidaw to put a stop to the atrocities being committed against the Rohingyas even as he accused the Myanmar government of committing genocide.[58] For his part, former Malaysian Foreign Minister and OIC Special Envoy to Myanmar Syed

57 Ye Mon and Shoon Naing, "ASEAN FMs pledge support on Rakhine," Myanmar Times online, 20 December 2016, from http://www.mmtimes.com/index.php/national-news/24298-asean-fms-pledge-support-on-rakhine.html, accessed on 20 December 2016.

58 Simon Roughneen, "Plight of Rohingya strains ASEAN unity," Nikkei Asian Review online, 9 February 2017, from http://asia.nikkei.com/magazine/20170209/On-the-Cover/Plight-of-the-Rohingya-strains-ASEAN-unity, accessed on 9 February 2017.

Hamid Albar called on the UN to stop of the genocide against the Rohingyas.[59] The following month, Malaysia sent a humanitarian aid ship to Yangon and later to Bangladesh to deliver food and emergency supplies to Muslim communities in Rakhine, but Myanmar refused permission for the ship to dock in Rakhine's capital of Sittwe as it insisted that the aid should be equally distributed to both the Buddhist and Muslim communities in the state.[60] Meanwhile, Indonesian President Joko Widodo met with Suu Kyi on the sidelines of the ASEAN Summit in Manila in April 2017 and offered her government capacity building assistance to train the Myanmar police and to facilitate health, education, and livelihood programs.[61]

During her trip to Europe in May 2017, Suu Kyi also faced pressure from the European Union as it publicly supported a resolution passed without a vote in the UN Human Rights Council that called for creating a fact-finding mission to Myanmar to look into human rights violations against the Rohingyas in the aftermath of the October 2016 militant attacks. However, she said that her government is dissociating itself from the resolution as it was not "in keeping with what is actually happening on the ground."[62] Instead, she insisted that her government will only accept recommendations from the advisory commission headed by former UN Secretary General Kofi Annan even as she stressed that any other input would "divide" the communities in Rakhine.[63] In September 2016, the NLD government created the Advisory Commission on Rakhine State headed by Annan, which was tasked to identify a set of recommendations to address the major issues in the communal conflict in Rakhine. In its interim report in March 2017, the Commission recommended that the structural and institutional causes of conflict in the area, including the humanitarian crisis brought about by the October 2016 attacks by militants should be addressed. Specifically, it called on the central and state governments to

---

59 Reuters, "OIC envoy calls for UN intervention in Arakan state," The Irrawady, 18 January 2017, from http://www.irrawaddy.com/news/asia/oic-envoy-calls-for-un-intervention-in-arakan-state.html, accessed on 20 January 2017.

60 Reuters, "Malaysian PM sends off aid ship bound for Burma," The Irrawady Online, 3 February 2017, from http://www.irrawaddy.com/news/burma/malaysian-pm-sends-off-aid-ship-bound-burma.html, accessed on 4 February 2017.

61 "Indonesia ready to help Myanmar achieve political stability," Jakarta Globe online, 29 April 2017, from http://jakartaglobe.id/news/indonesia-ready-help-myanmar-achieve-political-stability-jokowi/, accessed on 1 May 2017.

62 Reuters, "Burma, EU At Odds Over UN Fact-Finding Mission," The Irrawady Online, 3 May 2017, from https://www.irrawaddy.com/news/burma/burma-eu-odds-un-fact-finding-mission.html, accessed on 26 June 2017.

63 Ibid.

allow full and unimpeded humanitarian access to all areas affected by the violence, including adequate assistance to all communities in cooperation with international partners; to allow full, regular, local and foreign media access in Rakhine; and to ensure that the perpetrators of the violence are held accountable based on the conduct of an independent and impartial investigation.[64] As well, the central and state governments should give priority to: 1) addressing socioeconomic development issues in Rakhine; 2) training security forces, including human rights protection and respect for diversity of communities; 3) ensuring freedom of movement of people who are citizens and ensuring that the government establishes a clear strategy and timeline for citizenship verification process; 4) preparing a comprehensive strategy towards the eventual closure of all internally displaced peoples camps in Rakhine; 5) encouraging inter-faith dialogue among communities; 6) ensuring representation and participation in public life especially for the Muslim communities; and 7) for the Myanmar government to continue with its initiative to brief ASEAN members on a regular basis about the broader dimensions and regional implications of the situation in Rakhine, including maintaining a special envoy to engage with its neighbours.[65]

August 2017: ARSA Attacks and Rohingya Exodus

Renewed violence occurred once more in Rakhine a day after the final report of the Kofi Annan Advisory Commission was submitted to Suu Kyi on 24 August 2017. Specifically, following the planned attacks against border policemen by the Arakan Rohingya Salvation Army (ARSA) on 25 August, the Myanmar military responded with lethal force during clearing operations, which resulted in more than 1,000 people killed (including militants and civilians) and over 40,000 internally displaced persons in Rakhine. Since the outbreak of militant attacks in Rakhine, over 600,000 Rohingyas have fled to Bangladesh as of end of November even though the Tatmadaw claimed that it ended its operations against the militants on 5 September. Amidst allegations from human rights advocates and the international community that Myanmar's security forces committed atrocities against the Rohingyas who were fleeing Rakhine, including rape of women and violence against children, the Tatmadaw and the government denied such accusations. Humanitarian organisation Medicins sans Frontiers estimated that at least 6,700 Rohingyas were killed in the in the

64 Interim Recommendations, Advisory Commission on Rakhine State, March 2017, pp. 7–8
65 Ibid., pp. 9–15

first month of the violence in Rakhine state, which includes some 730 children below age five. Some 69 percent died because of gunshot wounds, 9 percent were burned alive inside houses, and 5 percent died of beatings.[66]

UN Secretary General Antonio Guterres on 28 September called on the Myanmar authorities "to end the military operations; to allow unfettered access for humanitarian support; and to ensure the safe, voluntary, dignified and sustainable return of the refugees to their areas of origin."[67] Despite the call of the UN chief for an international response to the Rakhine crisis, the Security Council remained divided, with China and Russia supporting the Myanmar government's position in dealing with the situation. Specifically, China's ambassador to the UN stressed the need for the international community to be patient with the government in Nay Pyi Daw and provide it with the assistance it needs as there is no quick fix to the complex communal conflict in Rakhine. For his part, the Russian ambassador to the UN warned that "excessive pressure" could only exacerbate further the crisis. Meanwhile, many members of the Security Council joined the calls of the US, Britain, and France for an end to violence in Rakhine and a strong response from the 15-member Council.

At the regional level, ASEAN remained divided on the issue despite issuing a statement condemning the ARSA attacks and expressing concern about the humanitarian crisis in Rakhine since the militant attacks. Malaysia in particular dissociated itself from the statement issued by the Philippines as chair of ASEAN as it criticised the statement's failure to even mention the Rohingyas.[68] Nonetheless, in the absence of consensus within ASEAN on the statement, members such as Indonesia and Thailand remained engaged with the government and the military in Myanmar as part of their continuing efforts in assisting the country in managing the conflict in Rakhine through humanitarian assistance and bilateral aid. In particular, during her speech in Washington D.C.

66 Agence France Presse, "6,700 Rohingya killed in first month of Myanmar violence: Doctors Without Borders," Channel News Asia, 14 December 2017, from https://www.channelnewsasia.com/news/asiapacific/6-700-rohingya-killed-in-first-month-of-myanmar-violence-doctors-9498880, accessed on 14 December 2014.

67 "Secretary-General's remarks at open debate of the Security Council on Myanmar [as delivered]", 28 September 2017, from https://www.un.org/sg/en/content/sg/statement/2017-09-28/secretary-generals-remarks-open-debate-security-council-myanmar, accessed on 29 September 2017.

68 Kuala Lumpur's response comes as a surprise to many in the region as it has been the practice in ASEAN not to use the term Rohingya in its statements to accommodate Myanmar. In fact, Malaysia did the same as chair of ASEAN in 2015 when it issued a chairman's statement on the "illegal migrants" in reference to Rohingya refugees coming by boats from Rakhine and Bangladesh.

at the Asia Society, Indonesian Foreign Minister Retno explained that Jakarta is pursuing a "4+1" formula in helping Myanmar deal with the Rakhine crisis: 1) restoration of peace and stability in Rakhine; 2) maximum restraint and end to violence; 3) protection of all civilians regardless of ethnicity or religion; 4) ensure humanitarian access; and 5) implementation of the Kofi Annan report's recommendations. The Thai government for its part has committed to provide shelter for refugees coming from Rakhine even as it also pledged 5 million baht or US$150,000 of humanitarian assistance to Rakhine state through the ICRC. Meanwhile, Singapore pledged SGD $100,000 or USD $73,000 humanitarian aid for displaced communities in Rakhine, which will be coursed through the ASEAN Coordinating Centre for Humanitarian Assistance (AHA Centre). The AHA Centre in mid-October dispatched 80 tons of humanitarian relief aid in Sittwe for affected communities in Rakhine.[69]

Overall, the renewed outbreak of violence and humanitarian crisis in Rakhine presents an opening for the UN and ASEAN to work together with the Myanmar government and other stakeholders in crafting an effective regional response. Specifically, there are three priority areas for immediate action, namely: 1) prevent further escalation of violence in Rakhine; 2) respond more substantively to the humanitarian crisis; and 3) contain the threat of extremist militants, which could seriously undermine regional stability.[70] These are not just essential to ensuring the safe return of refugees and internally displaced persons in Rakhine but also key to implementing the Kofi Annan Advisory Commission's recommendations in the long-term. Indeed, these recommendations should serve as a roadmap for the Myanmar government, ASEAN, and the international community to work together to promote long-term peace in Rakhine.

Conclusion

Since Myanmar's admission into ASEAN in 1997, the regional organisation's cohesion has been extremely put to the test by political developments and humanitarian crises in that country. Indeed, given the Tatmadaw's intransigence

69 "AHA Centre Delivers 80 Tons of Relief Materials to Rakhine State, Myanmar," AHACentre.org, 26 October 2017, from http://ahacentre.org/news/aha-centre-delivers-80-tons-of-relief-materials-to-rakhine-state-myanmar/, accessed on 2 November 2017.

70 See Noel M. Morada, "The Rohingya Crisis: High on Outrage, Short on Action," The Global Observatory, 13 October 2017, from https://theglobalobservatory.org/2017/10/rohingya-crisis-high-on-outrage-short-on-action/, accessed on 13 October 2017.

in heeding calls made by ASEAN and the international community to improve the country's human rights condition up until it lost in the general elections in 2015, the country has proven to be a major challenge to ASEAN's resolve in building a community of caring societies where member states adhere to both universal and regional norms on human protection. With Suu Kyi's NLD party taking over the government in 2016, there were high expectations in the region and elsewhere that there would be significant improvements in Myanmar's human rights situation, including those of the stateless Rohingya people in Rakhine. However, more than a year since the NLD has been in power, human rights protection in the country has not improved and the communal conflict in Rakhine has taken on a new dimension following attacks by militants sympathetic to the Rohingya community in October 2016. ASEAN's human protection diplomacy towards Myanmar has remained vigilant over the past 20 years ever since the latter was accepted as a member. Since 2012, however, the organisation appears to have become more openly critical of Myanmar's inability to address the root causes of the communal conflict in Rakhine and in protecting the stateless Rohingya people. Evidently, the non-interference principle has been put aside in practice by ASEAN in dealing with Myanmar on the crisis in Rakhine despite efforts by the previous military junta and the current civilian government to invoke the same in protecting its sovereignty.

Overall, despite the change of government in Myanmar, the crisis in Rakhine continues to impact the region's security and severely puts to the test ASEAN's solidarity and the commitment of its members to implement the group's human protection principles. While there are increasing calls from some ASEAN members and other non-state actors in the region to consider relaxing the non-interference principle when it comes to humanitarian crisis issues affecting the region, it appears that reaching a consensus on this within the group would be extremely difficult given the strong resistance of some members to the idea. Even so, ASEAN's role in influencing the situation in Rakhine would most likely be limited to providing humanitarian assistance for affected communities and capacity building for Myanmar's security sector in order to prevent future atrocities from happening in the area. In this regard, the consent of the Myanmar government and the cooperation of the military are critical in order for ASEAN's sustained engagement on this issue to be effective and successful in the long-run. At the same time, the NLD government and the military should demonstrate to ASEAN and the international community that they are both committed to improving the situation in Rakhine by taking seriously the primary responsibility of the Myanmar state, including its military, to protect its vulnerable populations from future atrocities.

Atrocity Prevention: From Promise to Practice in the Asia Pacific

Alex J. Bellamy
University of Queensland
a.bellamy@uq.edu.au

Abstract

Drawing upon talks delivered at the Second Global Action Against Mass Atrocity Crimes conference, held in Manila 2016, this paper examines the extent to which the Asia Pacific region has begun to translate its commitment to the Responsibility to Protect (R2P) into practice. It finds that the so-called "East Asian Peace" has transformed the region from one of the world's deadliest to one of the world's most peaceful. But many key challenges remain and there is much to be done to make R2P and atrocity prevention a daily lived reality. This chapter proceeds in three parts. The first briefly describes the dramatic decline of atrocity crimes in East Asia. The second points to some key challenges on the ideational and institutional fronts. The third section turns specifically to the need to develop national architectures for atrocity prevention.

Keywords

Asia Pacific – atrocity crimes – prevention – norm – politics – ASEAN – ASEAN Regional Forum

The Asia Pacific has accomplished much in a short space of time. Most impressively, over the past four decades it has experienced a rapid and dramatic decline in the incidence of atrocity crimes. Over a short time, the so-called "East Asian Peace" has transformed the region from one of the world's deadliest to one of the world's most peaceful. Not only have dozens of armed conflicts come to an end, we have seen countless governments in the region turn their backs on tyranny. Individuals have also played their part – the UN's statistics show that East Asia has some of the lowest homicide rates, globally. But many key challenges remain and there is much to be done to make R2P and atrocity prevention a daily lived reality. To unpack these issues, this chapter proceeds

 | DOI:10.1163/9789004363212_008

in three parts. The first briefly describes the dramatic decline of atrocity crimes in East Asia. The second suggests that although important empirical progress has been made, there remain some key challenges on the ideational and institutional fronts that will need to be overcome if the decline in atrocity crimes is to be sustained in the long term. The third section turns specifically to the need to develop national architectures for atrocity prevention and identifies some ways in which this agenda might be advanced in the region.

The Decline of Atrocity Crimes in East Asia

To identify the trends in the frequency and severity of mass atrocities in East Asia, I pieced together a dataset of every major incidence between 1945 and 2015. For the purposes of this chapter, I defined a 'case' of mass atrocities as any situation where at least 1,000 non-combatants were judged to have been intentionally killed, whether by state or non-state actors. Once that threshold was crossed, subsequent individual massacres by the same perpetrator against the same target group were included. There are two important thresholds here. The first is one of *scale.* It is not enough for an armed group to perpetrate a one-off massacre of a few dozen people. Mass atrocities require a degree of systematicity, even if – as in the case of the Tiananmen massacre in 1989, the killing is temporally and geographically limited. Estimated casualty figures invariably vary widely, for methodological and data-gathering reasons that are well known, and it therefore pays to be conservative.[1] As such, for the purposes of identifying individual cases of mass atrocity, I used the *lowest* common casualty estimate as my guide. Because of the wide variation in casualty estimates in some cases, when it came to estimating the death toll I selected the median figure from a selection of credible estimates. The second threshold is *intention.* For an episode of mass violence to constitute an atrocity crime, non-combatant deaths must be intentionally caused and not the result of incidental collateral damage. This is an especially difficult calculation in conflicts such as counter-insurgencies where there may be high numbers of both intentional and non-intentional killing of civilians and non-combatants. In these cases,

1 For the best accounts of the promise and difficulties of counting civilian casualties see Taylor Seybolt (ed.), *Counting Civilian Casualties: An Introduction to Recording and Estimating Non-Military Deaths in Conflict* (Oxford: Oxford University Press, 2013) and Alex J. Bellamy and Jon Western (eds.), 'The Politics and Practice of Estimating Civilian Casualties', special issue of *Global Responsibility to Protect*, 2017 forthcoming.

I have used the historical literature to distinguish atrocity crimes from the other ways in which civilians and non-combatants are killed.

The first question we need to ask is whether, or not, atrocity crimes have declined in East Asia. There are two ways of answering this question – by considering the *incidence* of mass atrocities (i.e. how many individual cases there are at any given time) and by charting their *scale* (i.e. how many non-combatants or civilians were killed in each individual case). Figure 1 (below) shows the results for the first question. It demonstrates that from a peak around 1974, there has been a consistent and sustained decline in the number of cases of mass atrocities in East Asia. From the picture painted by Figure 1, this decline appears to have occurred in three stages.

The first stage, beginning around 1974 and ending shortly after the end of the Cold War, around 1992, saw consistent decline in the incidence of mass atrocities, approximately halving the regional burden of cases. Key to this decline were developments in China and Indochina. One of the many key points of interest here is that the origins of the decline *preceded* the end of the Cold War by some considerable margin. Moreover, although certainly accelerated by the emergence of the region's 'long peace' in 1979, brought about by the ending of major war between states in the region, the decline in atrocities precedes the long peace and was sustained afterwards.[2] Thus, although the ending of the Cold War and East Asia's 'long peace' certainly contributed to the decline of mass atrocities in the region, they cannot claim sole responsibility for it. The causes go wider than simple *realpolitik* or peace between states, as I will explain later.

During the second stage of decline, running from the early 1990s until around 2010, a much reduced incidence of mass atrocities became the new normal but the rate of decline slowed. During this period, most of the region was atrocity-free but a series of long-standing episodes persisted in Myanmar, and North Korea continued to commit crimes against humanity against its own population. The North Korean regime's ineptitude caused a major famine between 1994 and 1998 in which more than a quarter of a million died. Its preoccupation with regime survival inhibited an effective response.[3] Elsewhere, there were occasional surges of new violence but these were typically short-lived. Indonesia, for example, experienced episodes incidents of inter-communal violence between Christian and Muslim communities and

2 Timo Kivimaki, *The Long Peace of East Asia* (Aldershot: Ashgate Press, 2014).

3 Harrowing first hand accounts of the famine are provided in Barbara Demick, *Nothing to Envy: Real Lives in North Korea* (London: Granta, 2010).

East Timor's vote to separate from Indonesia in 1999 was met by atrocities committed by government-backed militia.

The third phase is quite recent, beginning around 2010, and has seen the almost complete elimination of mass atrocities from East Asia. The single most important driver of decline during this period was the reform process in Myanmar, which gave rise to a series of peace treaties between the government and various armed groups – suspending, if not necessarily terminating, a series of armed conflicts characterized by mass atrocities. Also important, though, was the decline of violence in southern Thailand resulting from the Patani rebellion, the Bangsamoro peace process in The Philippines, and the consolidation of peace in Indonesia.

The picture of decline is similar yet more stark if we consider changes to the *scale* of mass atrocities in East Asia (Figure 2). That is because of the astronomical level of killing of some of the region's major cases – the wars in China and Korea immediately after the Second World War, the various episodes of mass killing in Maoist China, the mass killing of suspected communists in Indonesia, atrocities associated with the various Indochinese wars and the Khmer Rouge genocide. When it comes to the scale of killing, Figure 2 shows three clear peaks. The first might be called the region's 'long Second War World' since the level of mass atrocities continued at more or less Second World War levels until 1953 and mostly involved conflicts that either preceded and underscored the War (as in China) or that emerged as a result of Japan's collapse (as in Korea, Indonesia, Myanmar and elsewhere). The second peak, spanning from 1958 to 1961, was largely a consequence of China's Great Leap Forward.

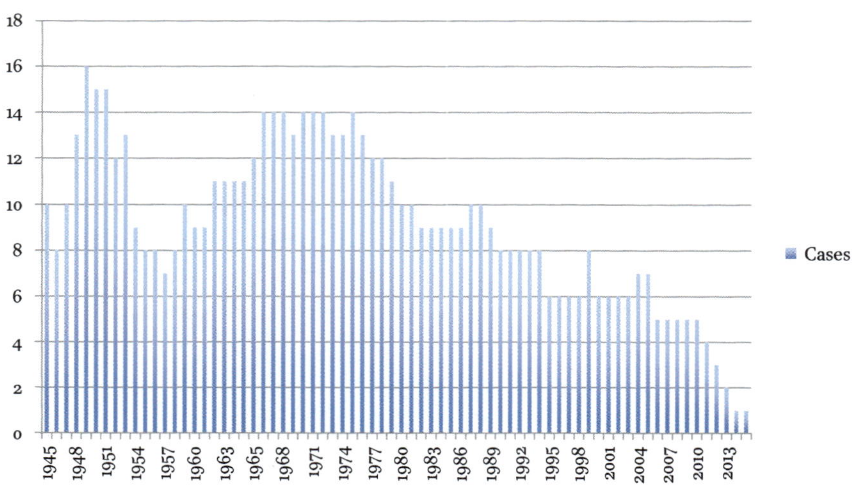

FIGURE 1 *Atrocities in East Asia: Number of Cases per Year (1945–2015)*

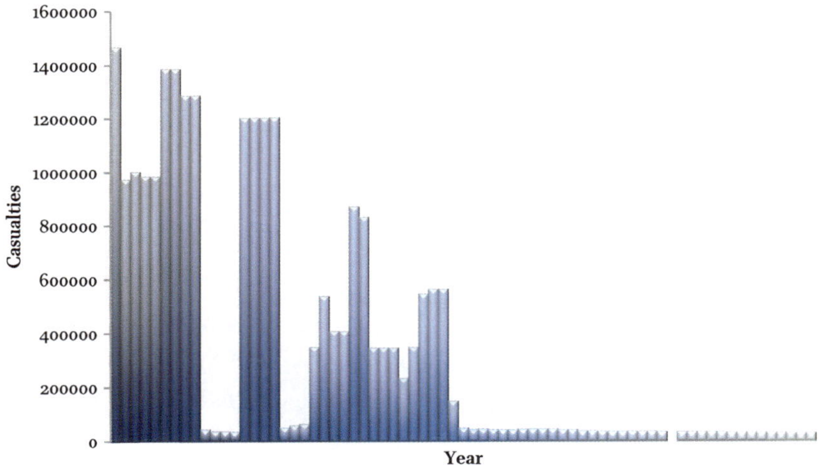

FIGURE 2 *Estimated Civilian Casualties Resulting from Atrocities in East Asia: Number per Year (1945–2015)*

The third peak, began soon after in 1965 with the explosion of anti-communist violence in Indonesia and ended in 1979 with the ousting of the Khmer Rouge regime in Cambodia. During this period, atrocities were widespread across much of the region, but especially in Indochina, China, and Indonesia.

In terms of the troughs in the scale of mass atrocities, two important points distinguish the current decline from past troughs. First, whereas the trough in the mid-1950s lasted just four years and the trough in the early 1960s just three years, the current low has been sustained for three and a half decades. As a result it seems fair to say that these historically low levels of mass atrocities have become the norm, whereas once they were the exception. Second, it is difficult to discern from Figure 2, owing to the distortions to the imagery caused by the 'mega' cases of mass killing, but important to state that after 1992, the contemporary low has been consistently beneath the lowest rates recorded in the 1950s and 1960s. Thus, for a little more than two decades the scale of mass atrocities in East Asia has been consistently lower than that achieved in any single year between 1945 and 1991. Between 1980 and 1992, the scale of killing was consistently below that of the 1960s trough, but a little higher than that achieved briefly in the 1950s. This, of course, lends further weight to the observation earlier that atrocities have continued to decline in East Asia even within the new, much lower, regional norm. Through the course of the last two decades, both the incidence and scale of mass atrocities in East Asia has continued to decline. In other words, the factors that created the new normal in East Asia when it comes to mass atrocities are continuing to exert downwards pressure on them.

We can tell other important things from the data too, which will help guide our explanation of the decline of mass atrocities in East Asia. When we look at which type of actor is committing mass atrocities, we see that states and government backed militia are responsible for 80% (42 of 53 cases) of the individual cases. Moreover, with the exception of Chinese Communist and Khmer Rouge massacres committed before these organisations assumed power, states are responsible for all of the largest scale cases of mass atrocities. However, we can also see a significant shift over time in that respect in that not since crackdowns on protestors in South Korea, Myanmar and China in the late 1980s have states opened *new* campaigns of mass atrocities. Protracted campaigns in North Korea and Myanmar began well before the 1980s. Without exception, since the end of the Cold War only non-state armed groups have launched entirely new campaigns of mass atrocities.

Things are equally unbalanced when we investigate the victims of mass atrocity crimes. In a little more than three-quarters of all the cases, the victims were members of the same population as the perpetrators. Thus, most cases involve a state committing mass atrocities against sections of its own population. The same is also true for non-state armed groups – their principal target has always been other sections of their own community. The remaining quarter is filled with cases where perpetrators targeted populations in other countries, usually in the course of an inter-state war.[4] This only reinforces my view that the ending of inter-state war in East Asia is only one part of the explanation of the decline of mass atrocities in the region. That must be so, since inter-state wars accounted for only a small fraction of the region's mass atrocities.

We might widen our enquiry here to explore the extent to which atrocities and war have been interconnected in East Asia. Studies on the general relationship between war and mass atrocities have demonstrated a strong correlation between them, a tendency that has increased since the late Cold War.[5] Overall, around two-thirds of mass atrocities have occurred in the context of an armed conflict, growing to closer to 90% after the end of the Cold War.[6] In

4 On this type of atrocity see Alexander B. Downes, *Targeting Civilians in War* (Ithaca: Cornell University Press, 2008).

5 See, for instance, Alex J. Bellamy, 'Mass Atrocities and Armed Conflict: Links, Distinctions and Implications for the Responsibility to Protect', Policy Analysis Brief for the Stanley Foundation, February 2011 and Paul Huth and Benjamin Valentino, 'Mass Killing of Civilians in Times of War, 1945–2000' in Hewitt, Wilkenfeld and Gurr (eds.), *Peace and Conflict 2008* (Boulder: Paradigm 2008), pp. 79–92. Some go as far as to posit that war and genocide are causally interlinked. See Martin Shaw, *War and Genocide: Organised Killing in Modern Society* (Cambridge: Polity, 2003).

6 Bellamy, 'Mass Atrocities and Armed Conflict'.

some regions, such as sub-Saharan Africa, the correlation between war and atrocity is said to be even stronger.[7] That is primarily because armed conflict provides an enabling context and rationale for mass atrocities. It is important to recognize, however, that not all armed conflicts give rise to mass atrocities. In fact, most armed groups do not massacre civilians – even when they have the means and opportunity to do so.[8]

Mass atrocities sometimes occur outside the context of armed conflict too. There appear to be four main forms of such 'peacetime' atrocities. First, state-directed suppression. These are atrocities committed by nondemocratic regimes against opponents or marginalized ethnic groups. The most frequent type of 'peacetime' mass atrocity, episodes usually begin soon after an adverse regime change or attempted change (e.g. China, 1949–1953, Indonesia 1965–66).[9] Second, radical transformations of social order imposed by the state. Revolutionary governments often attempt to transform societies rapidly, breaking down traditional norms, customs and social classes and replacing them with wholly new structures. This can often only be achieved through the use of extreme violence to exterminate the vestiges of the old regime, exhort the population to accept the new, and punish transgressions – as in the cases of China's Great Leap and Cultural Revolution and the Khmer Rouge genocide in Cambodia. Third, there is communal violence. These involve atrocities committed by groups not organized by national governments or well-established non-state armed groups. Violence is not entirely spontaneous and is usually incited or orchestrated by local or national political figures, often either state officials, politicians, or local leaders of different varieties (religious, ethnic, clan, etc.). Attacks are often religious or ethnic in nature and can be triggered by a variety of national and local events. The fourth type is post-war retribution. This involves atrocities committed by states and non-state actors in the immediate aftermath of armed conflict as retribution against former enemy groups. Sometimes massacres are intended to avenge specific atrocities committed during the armed conflict, but are also perpetrated for a combination of political reasons not directly connected to the commission of prior atrocities (e.g. pre-emptively eliminating threats/perceived future risk). In East Asia, repressive violence in post-war Vietnam in, and immediately after, 1975 is probably the best example.

7 Scott Straus, *Making and Unmaking Nations: The Origins and Dynamics of Genocide in Contemporary Africa* (Ithaca: Cornell University Press, 2015).

8 Daniel Chirot and Clark McCauley, *Why Not Kill Them All? The Logic and Prevention of Mass Political Murder* (Princeton, NJ: Princeton University Press, 2006).

9 The Political Instability Task Force identified 'transitions' and 'adverse regime changes' as periods of elevated risk. See http://globalpolicy.gmu.edu/pitf.

East Asia's experience has proven somewhat different to the global experience. Whilst, globally speaking, around two-thirds of atrocities since 1945 were committed in a context of armed conflict, growing to close to 90% after the end of the Cold War, in East Asia the influence of armed conflict has been much less pronounced. Overall, just a little over half (28 of 53) of all cases of mass atrocity in East Asia were perpetrated in the context of an armed conflict, meaning that close to half (25 of 53) were perpetrated outside a context of armed conflict. This immediately tells us that in East Asia, the relationship of the state towards its own population is a more important part of the story than it has proven in the rest of the world, indeed almost equally as important as the incidence of armed conflict. What is more, whilst in the rest of the world the relationship between war and atrocities has grown stronger, in East Asia it has grown weaker. Since 1979, a majority of the albeit small number of *new* cases of mass atrocities have occurred outside a context of armed conflict. So, whilst there is a relationship between mass atrocities and war in East Asia, it is not as strong as the relationship is globally.

What is clear is that over the past few decades there has been a dramatic and sustained decline in the incidence and scale of mass atrocities in East Asia. As yet unnoticed, the region has established a new normal in which new cases of mass atrocity are extremely rare and both new and existing cases are less intense that at any point since before the Second World War. This was not simply a function of the end of the Cold War, since the decline preceded the fall of the Berlin Wall by more than a decade. Some scholars suggest that Cold War tensions in East Asia declined after 1979, accounting for the decline in violence. But if we look at what actually happened in 1979, we seen that this argument confuses cause and effect, positing that violence declined because tensions were eased whilst in fact superpower tensions may have eased because violence had declined.[10] 1979 is so significant because it saw the definitive end of Indochina's long wars and the embedding of Deng Xiaoping's reformist regime in China – both of which had the effect of reducing violence in the immediate term and easing tensions in the longer term. The two were tied together in China's short-lived yet bloody invasion of Vietnam, a reprisal for the latter's intervention in Cambodia, early in that year – the last time that two East Asian states have fought each other directly. Nor was the decline in mass atrocities a function of the decline of inter-state conflict and the region's 'long peace' since almost half of all cases of mass atrocities involved violence against sections of the perpetrators' own population.

10 The proposition that Cold War tensions in East Asia eased in 1979, prompting a long peace is found in Muthiah Alagappa (ed.), *Asian Security Order: Instrumental and Normative Features* (Stanford, CA: Stanford University Press, 2003).

Sustaining the Peace

Although East Asia has seen a remarkable decline in the incidence and lethality of mass atrocities, steps need to be taken to ensure that the decline is sustainable. Reflecting on the past decade of practice in the region, and drawing on the insights offered by the other contributors to this volume, we can identify at least five key challenges.

First, there is still a need to raise awareness about R2P and atrocity prevention. By far the foremost challenge, and an issue often raised in dialogues across the region, is the need to build awareness of what R2P *is and is not* and what the principle requires of people and states. Even amongst governing elites, misconceptions remain about R2P – with many still seeing it as a veil for foreign intervention and imperialism – rather than viewing it as an ally of sovereignty. Through the work of the Asia Pacific Centre for the Responsibility to Protect, we have found consistently, that spreading the word about what R2P is, and the UN Secretary-General's strategy for its implementation, is crucial for advancing support for the principle and laying the foundation for its deeper implementation.

Over the past few years there has been a number of regional initiatives aimed at meeting this challenge, including programs designed to help establish nationally led dialogue on R2P and atrocity prevention encompassing government and non-governmental actors, the translation of key documents into national and local languages, the provision of training and training packages that can be delivered in different settings, and the development of networks of partners across the region – most notably the Asia Pacific Partnership for Atrocities Prevention. Through developments such as these, national constituencies of individuals and groups both inside and outside government have begun to emerge and take forward the R2P agenda. This is an inevitably long-term, complex and resource intensive, agenda however, since each country's context, experience and needs are different, requiring approaches that are tailored to each. What is more, individual trajectories are shaped very much by national developments such as changes in government and personnel.

The second challenge is to embed the idea that responsibility is an ally of sovereignty, not its opponent. The underlying logic of R2P is that sovereignty entails a responsibility to protect. The principle's ultimate vision is of a world of responsible sovereigns that protect their own populations from atrocity crimes. This is a vision that resonates well in the Asia Pacific since it was precisely through state consolidation and strengthening – coupled with economic growth and regional cooperation – that the region has achieved its remarkable decline in the incidence of atrocity crimes. Over the past decade, we have seen states in the region increasingly embrace their responsibility to protect as a core part of their sovereignty – a point that a majority of Association of Southeast Asian Nations (ASEAN) member states have now made in the context of the UN General Assembly's annual informal dialogue on the principle. But we have also seen sovereignty stymie progress at times, especially when the ideas of more progressive states in the region are held hostage by the more cautious. This has at times inhibited dialogue on protection issues through the region's new institutions such as the ASEAN Intergovernmental Commission on Human Rights and helped produce a situation whereby ASEAN member states discuss R2P actively in the setting of the UN in New York but have not yet addressed these same issues formally within their own regional institutions. However, it is important to stress that however exasperating sovereignty can be sometimes, there are no short cuts and ASEAN's focus on consensus means that once movement is achieved, any progress will be sustainable and considered legitimate. Ultimately, R2P will succeed or fail based on the extent to which states incorporate protection responsibilities into their own conceptions of sovereignty.

The third challenge is to translate R2P into daily practice. By and large, states in the Asia Pacific region accept the principle that they have a responsibility to protect their populations from atrocity crimes and should work together to protect populations. Some of the region's governments have gone further than this and have committed themselves to taking specific actions aimed at translating R2P from words into deeds. For example, in 2015 Cambodia's Prime Minister, Hun Sen, publicly endorsed R2P and committed his country to furthering implementation of the principle both at home and in the region, including by initiating and facilitating dialogue with ASEAN partners. South Korea has not only appointed an R2P focal point, it also committed to hosting the 2016 meeting of the global R2P focal points network, which comprises representatives from more than one-quarter of the entire UN Membership. In 2015, Japan also appointed an R2P focal point and outlined the ways in which its practical support for human security was also helping to fulfill R2P goals. In these, and other, ways states in the Asia Pacific region have begun to take steps to translate this rhetorical commitment to R2P into daily practice. But these are obviously only early steps. Having won the normative argument about R2P, the challenge we now face is one of how to translate the principle into a daily lived reality across more of the region's states and societies.

To meet this challenge, clarity is needed as to what the expectations are. In other words, what ought states and their societies do in order to implement R2P? To address this question, in 2016 the Asia Pacific Centre for R2P developed a 'Baseline Study' on the implementation of R2P in the Asia Pacific that utilized recommendations made by the UN Secretary-General in his annual reports on the implementation of R2P in order to clarify the steps that states and societies ought to take. These include (but are not limited to):

- Appointing an R2P focal point.
- Signing, ratifying and implementing relevant aspects of international humanitarian law, including the 1951 Refugee Convention and subsequent 1967 Protocol.
- Conducting national assessments of risk and resilience.
- Tackling hate speech and criminalizing incitement.
- Building capacities to manage difference constructively – through a national architecture for atrocity prevention.
- Engaging with regional arrangements to promote implementation of R2P.

Once expectations are established, it will be possible to begin national conversations about how best to make atrocity prevention a lived reality and cross-national and regional conversations about experiences and lessons learned. These conversations can also provide a catalyst for deeper consideration about what the international community can be encouraged to do in order to *support* states in this endeavor. Supporting states and societies in this process of identifying concrete national priorities and taking action to meet the challenge is a long term and complex process that will need tailoring to each specific context. It ought to be a key priority for R2P's second decade.

The fourth challenge involves incorporating R2P into regional deliberations. Over the past decade, impressive progress has been made on Tracks 2 (civil society) and 1.5 (informal government). Indeed, on these tracks the Asia Pacific region has been one of the most active regions in the world in thinking about how to utilise regional arrangements to advance R2P. At this level, there seems to be consensus that the region has the institutions that it needs – in the form of ASEAN for Southeast Asian and the ASEAN Regional Forum (ARF) for the wider region – to help implement R2P and that it is appropriate that these institutions be utilised in this way. The challenge now is to persuade the region's governments to take the first step of introducing R2P and atrocity prevention into their deliberations within these institutional settings.

Five years ago, I had the privilege of co-chairing a Conference for Security Cooperation in the Asia Pacific (CSCAP) Study Group on R2P with delegates from The Philippines, Indonesia and Canada. Overall, the group comprised delegates from seventeen countries, including China, India and Russia. We employed an unusual approach in that group aimed at delivering a consensus final document. The group's final report was negotiated line-by-line, word-by-word to produce a consensus document that, given the diversity of the group, we hoped would reflect a regional consensus. A summary of the report's key findings and recommendations was then adopted by the whole CSCAP membership (CSCAP Memorandum 18, 2011). That report set out a range of modest steps that could be taken to utilize the capacities that the ARF already has in order to advance R2P. This included measures such as:

- Establishing a regional risk reduction centre to assess risk and support preventive action.
- Strengthening capacity for preventive diplomacy and mediation.
- Encouraging member states to provide voluntary background briefings to one another on relevant issues of concern.
- Establishing an inter-sessional process focused on the control of small arms and light weapons.
- Establishing a mechanism to strengthen cooperation with the UN's peacebuilding architecture in order to reinforce atrocity prevention.
- Utilizing the ARF's eminent and expert persons to support the implementation of R2P.
- Establishing practical regional capacities to prevent atrocity crimes and respond to them in a timely and decisive fashion.[11]

The report suggested a careful process for advancing this discussion, starting with an experts level meeting. Although the ARF has yet to consider these recommendations, either formally or informally, CSCAP's work points towards grounds for a regional consensus and its recommendations are a valuable contribution. Over the coming years, state supporters of R2P should consider whether they might want to initiate an experts level meeting to discuss the implementation of R2P in the region as recommended by CSCAP.

More recently, former ASEAN Secretary-General and foreign minister of Thailand, Surin Pitsuwan, convened a High Level Advisory Panel (HLAP) at the request of the UN's Under-Secretary-General for Genocide Prevention, Adama Dieng, to examine and make recommendations on the implementation of R2P in Southeast Asia. After a series of regional consultations, the Panel presented its report at the UN in September 2014. The report made a powerful case that the values of R2P and the ASEAN community were mutually reinforcing and identified a variety of steps that ASEAN member states and the association as a whole could take to strengthen the ASEAN community by implementing R2P. The Panel judged that:

11 CSCAP Study Group on the Responsibility to Protect, Final Report, 2011, p. 22.

> Mainstreaming the Responsibility to Protect in Southeast Asia could make a significant contribution to the establishment of a 'sharing and caring' ASEAN Community, which the Association's Member States aspire to achieve in 2015. The responsibilities of protection stem not just from international law and global commitments made by the region's governments at the United Nations, but also from the commitments that ASEAN Member States have made to each other. The concepts and norms of the Responsibility to Protect converge with ASEAN's vision of a peaceful, just, democratic, people-centered and caring community in Southeast Asia. As such, the Responsibility to Protect provides ASEAN with a major pathway towards realizing its vision of a caring and sharing community in Southeast Asia and supports ASEAN's responsibility to care for the protection of its own people'.[12]

The Panel recommended five specific steps that could be taken to advance the implementation of R2P through ASEAN. First, steps to raise awareness and public knowledge of R2P. Second, the development of regional capacity for early warning and assessment through ASEAN's existing institutions, mechanisms and relevant sectoral bodies. Third, the strengthening of regional consultation and exchange on issues relating to the prevention of atrocity crimes and protection of vulnerable populations. Fourth, steps to incorporate atrocity crimes prevention into the work of the ASEAN Intergovernmental Commission of Human Rights (AICHR). Fifth, the provision of support to civil society efforts to promote human rights and advance atrocities prevention.

As I noted earlier, in 2015 Cambodia's Prime Minister Hun Sen committed his country to leading regional initiatives in this area. Progress is being made in other areas too. For example, informal dialogue has explored whether a thematic study of the AICHR on the implications of implementing R2P in ASEAN member states might be one way of advancing regional dialogue on the question.

The fifth challenge relates to the need to deal with imminent risk. This revolves around the practicalities of protection in the region's most difficult cases – most notably the situation in North Korea and the management of transition in Myanmar. In relation to North Korea, a UN Commission of Inquiry judged that the government was likely committing systematic crimes against

---

12 *Mainstreaming the Responsibility to Protect in Southeast Asia: Pathway Towards a Caring ASEAN Community*, Report of the High Level Advisory Panel on the Responsibility to Protect in Southeast Asia, 9 September 2014, p. 1.

humanity.[13] The Commission's findings were subsequently adopted by the UN General Assembly and referred to the UN Security Council. With the government of North Korea reluctant to engage in any sort of meaningful dialogue on human rights, there are obviously no easy answers on how to advance protection in this case. What is needed, though, is a serious regional conversation on the steps that might be taken to advance the specific recommendations advanced by the Commission of Inquiry and approved by the General Assembly. Myanmar, meanwhile, has made remarkable progress over the past few years but significant challenges remain. Again, as regional conversations move from the norm to practical action, consideration needs to be given about the tangible steps that ought to be taken. There is already evidence, for example, of significantly bilateral engagement on issues such as security sector reform and the Rohingya crisis – with Indonesia, Malaysia and Thailand taking a lead on the latter – but these initiatives will need to be developed if ASEAN is to maintain its commitment to establishing a regional Community. There are other practical challenges too. For instance, guaranteeing non-recurrence in the face of past crimes. As noted earlier, many parts of the region have experienced atrocity crimes, so dealing with the past is a big part of the equation. Furthermore, most states in the region face the challenge of protecting populations from non-state armed groups, and responding effectively to the rise of violent extremism. There are a number of ways in which these challenges might be addressed, but they all require moving from words to deeds in the implementation of R2P.

Strengthening National Architectures for Atrocity Prevention

To put an end to atrocity crimes, we need to forge a world of states capable and committed to protecting their own populations. In the long run, therefore, the success or failure of R2P will be determined not by whether the international community succeeds in responding effectively to major emergencies such as those in Syria and Burundi today – though that is important – but by whether the world's states and societies establish effective national systems for preventing atrocities from occurring in the first place. In this, the long-term vision and underlying logic of R2P are relatively straightforward. The principle envisages a world of responsible and capable sovereign states that protect their own populations from atrocity crimes as a matter of routine (Pillar I). This vision is to

13 *Report of the Commission of Inquiry on Human Rights in the Democratic Peoples' Republic of Korea*, A/HRC/25/63, 7 February 2014.

be achieved through a combination of mutual assistance and collective action: assistance (Pillar II) designed to strengthen the capacity of states to protect their own and collective action (pillar III) aimed at protecting populations and creating the conditions for mutual assistance. The international community's primary underlying goal is to help states in distress to extend their presumably legitimate authority and protection over a country's entire territory.

Ultimately, though they are also concerned with providing immediate relief to populations in need, R2P's second and third pillars are concerned with helping states fulfill their primary responsibility to protect. It is in this sense that R2P is best understood as an *ally of sovereignty* since the principle as a whole is focused on helping states fulfill the responsibilities attached to their sovereignty. What is more, we know that most atrocity crimes that are prevented are done so by national rather than international actors.[14] Getting the national settings right through establishing effective national architectures for atrocity prevention will therefore make a huge positive difference to atrocity prevention overall.

The best way that states can help themselves – and their populations – is by building national architectures to promote atrocity prevention and fostering resilience to the forces that can tear communities apart. National architectures should strive to establish what former Special Adviser to the UN Secretary-General on the prevention of genocide, Francis Deng, described as the 'constructive management of diversity'. Because atrocity crimes are, in effect, extreme forms of identity-related conflict, the cornerstone of atrocity prevention is the building of an inclusive, non-discriminatory form of politics capable of managing diversity constructively. There is much evidence to recommend the constructive management of diversity as a key part of prevention. States and societies imbued with multiple risk factors (diversity, histories of violence, weak institutions, poor economies) that have adopted a constructive approach to managing diversity have tended to avoid atrocity crimes.

For example, post-independence Tanzania was founded on an inclusive ideology supported by strict policies to ensure equality between the country's main religious and ethnic groups especially in the military and public sector. Following decades of military rule, Uruguay established a national human rights institution to address issues of accountability and impunity. All of these countries have thus far escaped atrocities despite having many of the preconditions for them. Similarly positioned countries that embraced exclusionary ideologies have proven less capable of preventing atrocities. For example,

14 Stephen McLoughlin, *The Structural Prevention of Mass Atrocities: Understanding Risk and Resilience* (London: Routledge, 2014).

successive Sudanese governments promoted an exclusionary Islamist ideology, both Tutsi and Hutu-led governments in post-independence Rwanda enacted policies that clearly favored one group over the other, and Cote d'Ivoire's path to civil war and atrocity crimes began with the spread of *Ivoirité* – an ethnic ideology that intentionally marginalised immigrant groups and their descendants. Similar patterns are evident in the Asia Pacific region. States that have embraced diversity typically fare better than those that do not.

At the most abstract, the constructive management of diversity requires state ideologies and constitutions that pay respect to difference and incorporate different identities into the project of the state/society itself. As Scott Straus argues, 'the long-term best asset against the risk of genocide and mass categorical violence is to craft a political vision that incorporates a role for multiple identities as fundamental to the project of the state'. The key to this, Straus argues, is for national leaders to 'articulat[e] a nationalist narrative of pluralism and inclusion [which] provides the greatest source of restraint'.[15]

In practice, the constructive management of diversity requires laws and institutions designed to promote equality between individuals and groups and protect them against discrimination especially. In particular, it requires constitutional and legislative protections for human rights and the rights of groups as the principle bulwarks against discrimination. These protections should be overseen effectively by independent judiciaries and national human rights institutions or ombudsman's offices, with vibrant civil societies capable of holding authorities to account. The establishment of formal institutions and ombudsman's offices demonstrate a state's commitment to protecting diversity and create spaces through which populations can hold authorities accountable. It also involves the prioritisation of equality – including gender equality – across groups in fields such as education, employment (especially public sector), and health. In addition, comprehensive strategies to tackling exclusionary ideologies, combining coercive and persuasive approaches, may be needed.

Finally, there is a need to ensure that potential disputes between groups have a means of peaceful resolution. Recognising that where there are different identities there are likely to be conflicts connected to group loyalties and contending visions of justice, states and societies require means for managing (and ideally resolving) conflicts in a peaceful and constructive fashion. Most obviously, there is a need to prioritise the termination of any armed conflicts and beyond that a need for institutions to facilitate the peaceful management

15 Scott Straus, *Making and Unmaking Nations: War, Leadership and Genocide in Modern Africa* (Ithaca: Cornell University Press, 2015), p. 323.

of disputes. A good example is Ghana's National Peace Council, which promotes and facilitates the non-violent resolution of conflict, conflict prevention and sustainable peace.

This preventive work should ideally be led by national stakeholders. The international community's principal role lies in supporting initiatives designed to enhance the constructive management of difference, via three steps especially. First, by offering diplomatic support for inclusive policies and criticism of exclusionary practices. Second, by supporting institution building and the forging of the capacities needed to manage diversity. Third, by ensuring that aid programs and other forms of assistance do not inadvertently exacerbate inequalities and discrimination.

In 2014, the UN Secretary-General helpfully identified seven specific inhibitors of atrocity crimes.[16] These, in a sense, are the specific building blocks for a national architecture for atrocity prevention.

1. *Professional and accountable security sectors* – security sectors that not only refrain from committing the crimes themselves but which also protect populations, including minority populations, from them and ensure that there is no impunity.
2. *Impartial institutions for overseeing transitions* – political transitions, especially elections, are fraught with dangers. It is imperative that political transitions and elections are overseen by organisations perceived by the whole community as impartial, legitimate and transparent otherwise the results of any process are likely to be disputed, potentially giving rise to violence and atrocities.
3. *Independent judicial and human rights institutions* – independent judiciaries and human rights institutions are fundamental sources of resilience to atrocity crimes and need to be protected and strengthened. The UN Secretary-General has repeatedly asked states to ensure that they have signed, ratified and implemented relevant instruments of international law. In The Philippines, for example, the National Human Rights Commission plays a key role in helping to resolve disputes, protecting vulnerable groups and teaching people their rights. Likewise, after the Maguindanao massacre, the capacity of the judicial system to ensure that there was no impunity helped prevent possible escalation.
4. *Capacity to assess risk and mobilise early response*. It is straightforward – though uncomfortable for governments – to identify general risks, but

16 *Fulfilling our Collective Responsibility: International Assistance and the Responsibility to Protect.* Report of the Secretary-General, A/68/947-S/2014/449, 11 July 2014.

assessing risks with sufficient confidence to mobilise action is much more difficult. The Secretary-General has called for every state to regularly examine its own risk factors, utilizing the UN's own analysis framework for atrocity crimes.[17]

5. *Local capacity to resolve disputes* – disputes are most easily resolved closest to the ground. Thus, local capacities that can help resolve disputes before they escalate into violence are immensely useful. The specific composition will differ from place to place as befits local needs by may include land councils to oversee disputes over land or inter-faith processes designed to foster understanding and resolve disputes between different religious groups.
6. *Media capacity to counteract prejudice and hate speech.* Hate speech can give rise to incitement and lead directly to atrocity crimes. It is therefore important that the national media have the capacity to support the positive management of diversity and counteract acts of prejudice and hate speech that can give rise to incitement and violence. Where hate speech does occur, the media must be sufficiently free, balanced and capable to challenge it and offer alternative narratives.
7. *Capacity for effective and legitimate transitional justice.* Left unaddressed or given impunity, past atrocity crimes can quite often sow the seeds for future crimes. It is imperative that this cycle is broken through effective and legitimate transitional justice. It is imperative that transitional justice also deal properly with sexual and gender based violence.

These sources of resilience might be understood as the core building blocks for a national architecture for atrocity prevention. It would be well worth, therefore, starting a regional conversation about their status in individual national situations and priority areas that require work. From this can be developed action plans to guide concrete initiatives. To begin this process, governments should consider appointing a national R2P focal point and facilitating national dialogues on where the principal sources of risk lay and where resilience can be found and augmented. As mentioned earlier, in the Asia Pacific region, Australia, Japan, New Zealand and South Korea have already have appointed a focal point and Cambodia's prime minister has publicly committed his country to doing the same. Persuading more countries to take this initial step and then facilitating the deepening of national discussion will be difficult, politically, owing to some of the sensitivities mentioned earlier, but it is the crucial next stage in the development of atrocity prevention in the Asia Pacific region.

17 *Framework of Analysis for Atrocity Crimes: A Tool for Prevention*, United Nations, 2014.

ASEAN Norm and Capacity Building for Atrocities Prevention

In all of this, there are number of ways in which the region's institutions might help and this involves acting on some of the Track 2 recommendations described earlier. Three clusters of potential activity stand out. First, strengthening early warning – a point recommended by both CSCAP and the HLAP – and assessing and advising on risks, and risk reduction. Both CSCAP and the HLAP advised the development of a regional capacity for early warning and assessment through the existing institutions, mechanisms and relevant sectoral bodies within ASEAN/ARF. When it comes to effective early response, there is a need to act regionally to overcome challenges at the global level, yet the Asia Pacific region has no early warning capability for genocide, war crimes, ethnic cleansing and crimes against humanity. This makes it more difficult to anticipate crises before they emerge. It is important to foster habits of early warning and of responsiveness to it. There is a need, therefore, to cultivate a regional capacity for early warning and assessment. The work of AICHR, the ASEAN Commission on Women and Children, as well as the work of the ASEAN Institute of Peace and Reconciliation, and other think tanks such as the Bali Institute for Peace and Democracy could provide useful starting points for monitoring emerging issues of concern with a view to addressing and finding early solutions to potential problems.

Second, the AICHR's mandate includes helping states with capacity building. The HLAP also proposed that it consider incorporating the prevention of genocide, war crimes, ethnic cleansing and crimes against humanity into the future agenda of the AICHR. The prevention of these four atrocity crimes is closely related to the promotion of human rights within ASEAN, and is very much a necessary part of promoting a just and caring ASEAN community. One way of opening this dialogue about AICHR and how the region might support individual states would be an AICHR thematic study on the implications of implementing R2P and capacity building for atrocity prevention.

Third, in the wider region, the ARF could also help member states build their national capacities. Beyond the more general recommendations advanced by CSCAP that were described earlier, the Study Group also highlighted ways in which the ARF could support national capacity building such as by facilitating technical assistance in areas such as crisis response, protection, conflict resolution, and elections. Overall, however, these are just small parts of the larger puzzle of establishing a global culture of prevention when it comes to mass atrocities. The central point here, however, is that the sustaining of Asia-Pacific's good recent record in reducing atrocity crimes will depend on the incorporation of atrocity prevention norms into national settings and that, in this endeavor, regional arrangements have important roles to play.

Conclusion

Over the past few decades, the Asia Pacific region has achieved great success in reducing the frequency and scale of atrocity crimes. At the same time, significant normative progress has been made in building a regional consensus around the principle of the Responsibility to Protect. This chapter recognized the progress made but argued that in order to sustain the achievements, it is imperative that steps be taken to translate rhetorical commitments to atrocity prevention into practical realities. This means that the region needs to take steps to address the five key challenges identified earlier and consider practical ways of supporting atrocity prevention. But it also means that individual states need to make good on their commitments by building national architectures for atrocity prevention. Unless states and regional organisations begin to translate their words in support of R2P into deeds, a credibility gap could develop that could undermine not just faith in R2P, but also the perceptions about the legitimacy of regional organisations and governments themselves.

Human Protection in Africa's Regional Arrangements: Regional Perspectives and Institutional Expressions

Charles T. Hunt
RMIT University
charles.hunt@rmit.edu.au

Abstract

Growing international solidarity for protection principles has formed the backdrop for an evolving notion of human protection at the UN in the post-Cold War era. The emergence of the 'Human Rights up Front' initiative, protection of children and Women, Peace and Security policy agendas, and normative frameworks such as the protection of civilians and the Responsibility to Protect are indicative of a tangible human protection agenda at the UN. However, the extent to which human protection norms have diffused in different regions vary in important ways. Africa – one region or many – has been a norm maker, shaper and taker, as well as a major recipient of action in accordance with this nascent normative regime. This chapter provides an overview of regionalism in Africa and examines how perspectives and institutional expressions at the regional level(s) have been influenced by – and in turn influenced – the uptake and development of norms around human protection.

Keywords

Human protection – norms – Africa - regionalism/regionalization - African Union

In the 2011 Cyril Foster Lecture at Oxford University, UN Secretary-General (SG) Ban Ki-moon laid out what he referred to as a 'human protection' agenda.[1] Growing international solidarity for protection principles has formed

1 'Human protection is a subset of the more encompassing concept of human security... Human protection addresses more immediate threats to the survival of individuals and groups.' Ban Ki-moon, 'Human Protection and the 21st Century United Nations', Cyril Foster

 | DOI:10.1163/9789004363212_009

the backdrop for an evolving notion of human protection at the UN in the post-Cold War era and constituted a hallmark of Ban's tenure as SG since 2007. The emergence and mainstreaming of flagship initiatives such as 'Human Rights up Front', policy agendas such as the protection of children and Women, Peace and Security (WPS), and the increasingly prevalent place of normative frameworks such as the protection of civilians in armed conflict and the Responsibility to Protect (RtoP) and the establishment of the International Criminal Court (ICC) are all critical elements of advancing the safeguarding civilians as part of this human protection agenda and demonstrate these trends.

Whilst these trends at the UN seem clear, the extent to which norms associated with this agenda have found resonance, traction and acceptance in the various regions across the world differs in important ways. Africa – one region or many – has been a norm maker, shaper and taker, as well as a major recipient of action in accordance with this nascent normative regime. The aim of this chapter is to provide an overview of regionalism in Africa and examine how perspectives and institutional expressions at the regional level(s) have been influenced by and in turn influenced the uptake and development of norms around human protection.

The chapter proceeds in four parts. The first addresses debates around different concepts of regionalism including the differences between ideas of regionalism and processes of regionalisation. The second section examines African regionalism(s) questioning whether the continent is one region or many, and identifies some of the major organisations associated with these regionalist projects. The third part explores some of the major examples of African regional bodies embedding and realising human protection goals. The fourth section raises a number of questions that warrant further investigation and in-depth case study research to elucidate the current state of regional preparedness as well as the outstanding challenges that remain in promoting and enshrining the protection of human rights and civilian protection at the regional level in Africa. In this chapter, human protection refers to protection of civilians from human rights abuses, within and without armed conflicts, with a particular focus on mass atrocity crimes – genocide, war crimes, crimes against humanity and ethnic cleansing.

Lecture, Oxford University, 2 February 2011. See also: Alex J. Bellamy, 'The humanisation of security? Towards an International Human Protection Regime', *European Journal of International Security* 1/1: 112–133 (2016).

Regionalism: Competing Concepts

The concept of *regionalism* is contested in the study of international relations.[2] In short, exploring the concept of regionalism raises questions regarding who are the relevant actors, what is the nature of the relationships between them and how do the outcomes of interaction result in the formation of regional community and identity? For instance, does it refer primarily to the arrangement and interactions of states? The notion of regional *cultures* or *complexes* has been promoted as a way of depicting a transnational order predicated on the various motivations of states. Some argue that this is best understood to reflect constellations of power and the primary aim of preservation of existential security and sovereignty.[3] However, others point to more cooperative and mutually beneficial pacts between states at this level.[4] The English School branch of international relations theory has promoted ideas around an international society of states grounded in shared interests and values.[5] For them, this is an arena governed by rules, norms and institutions that enable and constrain the conduct of members and in turn shape and influence global politics.[6] In this reading, the pertinent normative frameworks in such an international society can be understood as either solidarist or pluralist in nature.[7]

Despite the popularity of these state-centric imaginaries, the state in Africa rarely reflects a Weberian ideal type where internal order is predicated on the monopoly of legitimate coercion through the machinery of government.[8] Goods such as governance and public security are more accurately understood to emerge from a hybrid political order where a broader set of relationships

2 Andrew Hurrell, 'One World? Many Worlds? The Place of Regions in the Study of International Society', *International Affairs*, 83/1: 127–46 (2007).

3 See, for example: Barry Buzan and Ole Waever, *Regions and Powers: The Structure of International Security* (Cambridge: Cambridge University Press, 2003).

4 Alexander Wendt, *Social Theory and International Politics* (Cambridge: Cambridge University Press, 1999).

5 Hedley Bull, *The Anarchical Society: A Study of Order in World Politics* (New York: Columbia University Press, 1977), pp. 9–13.

6 Ian Clark, *Legitimacy in International Society* (Oxford: Oxford University Press, 2005), p. 6; Tim Dunne, 'The New Agenda' in Alex J. Bellamy (ed.), *International Society and Its Critics* (Oxford: Oxford University Press, 2004), p. 66.

7 Tim Dunne, *Inventing International Society: A History of the English School* (London: Macmillan, 1998). For discussion of solidarist and pluralist conceptions of regionalism, refer to chapter in this volume by Noel Morada.

8 Patrick Chabal and Jean-Pascal Daloz, *Africa Works: Disorder as a political instrument* (Oxford: James Currey, 1999); Mahmood Mamdani, *Citizen and Subject: Contemporary Africa and the Legacy of Late Colonialism* (Princeton University Press, 1996).

between myriad state and non-state providers are what produces political community and social order.[9] Furthermore, the growth of transnational non-state actors as diverse as non-governmental organisations, organised criminal syndicates and even private sector corporations also have agency, resources and influence, and therefore contribute to the creation of regional identity and community. States are not, therefore, necessarily the only relevant unit of analysis when it comes to analyses of African regionalism. What then is the role in formation of regional community of those who do not necessarily represent or act on behalf of governments and international institutions?

A resurgence in the study and importance placed on regionalism in the 1990s led to a distinction being made between 'old' and 'new' regionalism, whereby 'new regionalism' is:

> ...simultaneously linked with domestic factors, sometimes challenging the nation-state while at other times strengthening it. Thus the renewed trend of regionalism is a complex process of change, simultaneously involving state as well as non-state actors, and occurring as a result of global, regional, national and local level forces.[10]

These advances in the study of regionalism also distinguished between two important dimensions – *regionalism* and *regionalisation*. While *Regionalism* connotes an ideology usually associated with a program and strategy and may lead to formal institution-building, *Regionalisation* is rather a process that has specific dynamics and leads to patterns of cooperation, integration, complementarity and convergence within a particular cross-national geographical space – i.e. 'Regioness'.[11] Regionalisation processes can therefore imply more cooperation between heterogeneous entities but can also suggest deeper integration and homogenisation.[12] It is this notion of regionalisation that speaks

9 Volker Boege, Anne Brown and Kevin Clements, 'Hybrid Political Orders, Not Fragile States', *Peace Review*, 21/1: 13–21 (2009); Volker Boege, Anne Brown, Kevin Clements and Anna Nolan, 'On Hybrid Political Orders and Emerging States: State Formation in the Context of 'Fragility'', *Berghof Handbook Dialogue* No. 8 (2008).

10 Björn Hettne and Fredrik Söderbaum, 'Theorising the Rise of Regionness', *New Political Economy*, 5/3: 457–472 (2000), p. 457.

11 Hettne and Söderbaum, 'Theorising the Rise of Regionness', pp. 457–8.

12 Mary Farrell, Björn Hettne and Luk Van Langenhove, *Global Politics of Regionalism: Theory and Practice* (Pluto Press, 2005); Louise L'Estrange Fawcett and Andrew Hurrell, *Regionalism in World Politics: Regional Organization and International Order* (Oxford: Oxford University Press, 1995); Louise Fawcett, 'Exploring Regional Domains: A Comparative History of Regionalism', *International Affairs*, 80/3: 429–46 (2004); Daniel C. Bach,

to the development, localisation and acceptance of normative orders at the regional level. The following section looks at how regionalisation has occurred in the African context.

The Evolution and Contours of African Regionalism: One Region or Many?

The African continent has generated a number of regionalist projects over its long and varied history. The emergence of regional economic, political and security communities has occurred at a range of levels across different historical phases.[13] These have differed in terms of geographically contiguous and territorial parameters as well as the quality and nature of regionalism at play. The unique experiences, identities and agency of local actors has been central to what has been generated.[14] As Taylor has put it, 'constructed "realities" regarding the region and its regionness ... become contested and, indeed, transformed, based on shared notions of community and solidarity.'[15] This has included instances of macro-regionalism, sub-regionalism and even micro-regionalism.[16]

Pan-Africanism / Continentalism

At the macro-regional level, Pan-Africanism is a vital antecedent of contemporary manifestations of African regionalism. Pan-Africanist philosophy traces centuries of history but it played an important role providing intellectual

'Regionalism Versus Regional Integration: The Emergence of a New Paradigm in Africa', in Jean Grugel and Wil Hout (eds.) *Regionalism across the North-South Divide. State Strategies and Globalization* (Oxford: Routledge, 1999), pp. 152–66.

13 Samuel KB Asante and Kingsley Y Amoako, *Regionalism and Africa's Development: Expectations, Reality and Challenges* (Basingstoke: Macmillan, 1997); Robert Sharer, 'Africa, Regionalism and Globalisation', Paper presented at the Regional economic integration and the globalisation process, Report on the proceedings of a Southern African conference (Windhoek, 1998); Daniel C. Bach, *Regionalisation in Africa: Integration & Disintegration* (Indiana University Press, 1999); John Mukum Mbaku, *Africa at the Crossroads: Between Regionalism and Globalization* (Praeger Publishers, 2004).

14 Amitav Acharya, 'The Emerging Regional Architecture of World Politics', *World Politics*, 59/4: 629–652 (2007).

15 Ian Taylor, 'Globalization and Regionalization in Africa: Reactions to Attempts at Neo-Liberal Regionalism', *Review of International Political Economy*, 10/2: 310–330 (2003), p. 327.

16 Fredrik Söderbaum and Ian Taylor, *Afro-Regions: The Dynamics of Cross-Border Micro-Regionalism in Africa* (Nordiska Afrikainstitutet, 2008).

support in the movements emerging around the turn of the 20th century advocating solidarity amongst people of African descent including the diaspora in the struggle against slavery and discrimination in general. It was a major rhetorical device and mobiliser in the fight against colonialism and the demand for political independence for peoples of Africa.

From the earliest post-independence moments there were competing versions of African macro-regionalism producing various visions for unity, ranging from a 'United States of Africa' to a loosely conglomerated interdependent set of regional economic blocs. On the one hand, Ghana's independence leader Kwame Nkrumah and likeminded allies in the Casablanca bloc advocated for full federation of the continent's states.[17] On the other hand, more incremental deepening of economic cooperation and integration was favoured by most Francophone states who found comrades in the Monrovian bloc. Consequently, since the colonial era, there have been multiple organisational expressions of regionalism on the African continent.[18]

Treating the land mass and geographic territory of the continent as the parameters of the region, the Organisation of African Unity (OAU) was created on 25 May 1963 in Addis Ababa, with 32 member governments. The goal of the OAU was to give the principles of Pan-Africanism institutional form, liberate the continent and defend the sovereignty, territorial integrity and independence of African states and bring an end to colonialism as well as white minority rule in Africa.[19] It was therefore built around a firm foundational commitment to the norm of non-interference in the internal affairs of member states. As it assumed institutional form, pan-Africanism became also about promoting independence through 'collective self-reliance'.[20]

The OAU provided effective oversight to the successful decolonisation of the continent, supporting independence of all former colonies by the time South Africa emerged from Apartheid in 1994. However, it was perennially troubled by internal divisions due to Franco-Anglo splits and cold war proxy affiliations to the United States of America or the Soviet Union. It proved incapable of providing the oversight to emancipation of newly liberated states of Africa from dependency on their colonial masters for continued support.[21] Furthermore,

17 See, for further explication: Kwame Nkrumah, *Africa Must Unite* (London: PANAF, 1963).

18 Ralph I. Onwuka and Amadu Sesay, *The Future of Regionalism in Africa* (St. Martin's Press, 1985).

19 C.O.C. Amate, *Inside the OAU: Pan-Africanism in Practice* (London: Macmillan Publishers, 1986).

20 Abdul Karim Bangura, *Toyin Falola and African Epistemologies* (London: Palgrave Macmillan, 2015).

21 Y. El-Ayouty and I. William Zartman *The OAU after Twenty Years* (Praeger, 1984).

the OAU had extremely limited effectiveness or consensus on political and rights-based issues – particularly related to conflict and atrocities committed within sovereign borders (e.g. Idi Amin in Uganda) leading to it being derided as a nothing more than a 'dictator's club'.[22]

Following the end of the Cold War, with burgeoning membership (by then at 53) the OAU underwent an evolution of its aims. A desire to be more influential and effective in addressing the continent's suffering populations led to the creation of the *OAU Mechanism for Conflict Prevention, Management and Resolution* in Cairo in 1993. This, however, did little to resolve ongoing conflicts across the continent – such as those raging in Angola, Sudan, and Somalia – and was unable to prevent or even respond to high profile atrocities in Rwanda in 1994. Ultimately, the OAU proved ineffectual at protecting people from widespread human rights abuses.[23]

From the late 1990s, efforts were put in motion to design a new expression of continental regionalism. This culminated with the transformation of the OUA into the African Union (AU) in 2002.[24] The AU constituted a reinvigoration of pan-Africanism – representing the internationally recognised states of Africa.[25] It reiterated that African states will be better together – a sentiment captured in its motto: 'A United and Strong Africa.' The AU retained a commitment to defending the sovereignty, territorial integrity and independence of Members, under the banner of achieving greater unity and solidarity between the African countries and Africans.[26] However, the globalisation of human security issues was another reason the AU was to be more focused on issues of peace and security than its predecessor.[27]

---

22 R. Murray, *Human Rights in Africa: From the OAU to the African Union* (Cambridge: Cambridge University Press, 2004); G.S. Ndugulile, *The Organization of African Unity (OAU): Its Successes and Failures in the Liberation Struggle* (Centre for Foreign Relations, 1981).

23 Monde Muyangw and Margaret Vogt, *An Assessment of the OAU Mechanism for Conflict Prevention, Management, and Resolution, 1993–2000* (New York: International Peace Academy, 2000), pp. 11–15.

24 Tim Murithi, *The African Union: Pan-Africanism, Peace Building and Development* (Aldershot: Ashgate, 2005).

25 NB: except for Morocco who withdrew from the OUA in 1984 and sits outside the the AU, protesting the membership of western Sahara – whose statehood Morocco contests.

26 Kay Mathews, 'Renaissance of Pan-Africanism: The AU and the New Pan-Africanists', in John Akokpari, Angela Ndinga-Muvumba and Timothy Murithi (eds.), *The African Union and Its Institutions* (Cape Town: Jacana Media, 2008): 25–40.

27 Chrysantus Ayangafac and Jakkie Cilliers, 'African Solutions to African Problems: Assessing the Capacity of African Peace and Security Architecture', in Chester A. Crocker, Fen Osler Hampson and Pamela R Aall (eds.) *Rewiring Regional Security in a Fragmented World* (Washington, DC: US Institute of Peace Press, 2011): 115–48.

One of the major shifts in regional thinking concerned the need to avoid the perceived failings of the OAU and better deal with the costly consequences of spillover effects from conflict and instability on the continent. This meant regional mechanisms that acknowledged shared peace and security challenges at the continental level and addressed proliferation of intra-state conflicts and its associated challenge to absolute sovereign independence.

Another shift was the acknowledged need to focus on economic, social and political rights as well as physical security, broadening the agenda of work in the security domain. Furthermore, increasing trans-nationalisation of processes of organised crime, terrorism and health pandemics created the perception of threats to individuals that transcended the jurisdiction and ability to act of individual states. Providing this security to individuals had come to be viewed as the bedrock for development and long-term peace and prosperity on the continent. The vast majority of these rationales and emerging challenges reflected the human security paradigm that had gained traction in international circles around that time. Human security presented a framework capable of moving beyond the domain of orthodox security thinking that focused primarily on the state and its existential security as the relevant unit of analysis and vehicle for protecting human rights.[28]

Another dimension relates to dealing with the forces and pressures presented by globalisation. Firstly, 'collective self-reliance' as a gathering of political, economic and social resources to balance against the US, Europe, and rising powers, was deemed to be crucial to respond to the shifting tectonics of global political and economic power. In this sense, African regionalism, like elsewhere, has been formed through dual processes from the inside-out as well as the outside-in. By extension, this brought the rationale for growing economic interdependence and integration.[29] For instance, the New Partnership for Africa's Development (NEPAD) – a major building block of the new continental architecture – clearly encapsulates this view in stating:

> Most African countries are small, both in terms of population and per capita incomes. As a consequence of limited markets, they do not offer attractive returns to potential investors, while progress in diversifying production and exports is retarded... These economic conditions point

28 Eboe Hutchful, 'From Military Security to Human Security', in John Akokpari, Angela Ndinga-Muvumba and Timothy Murithi (eds.), *The African Union and Its Institutions* (Cape Town: Jacana Media, 2008), pp. 63–84.

29 Björn Hettne, Andras Inotai and Osvaldo Sunkel, *Globalism and the New Regionalism* (London: Palgrave Macmillan, 1999).

> to the need for African countries to pool their resources and enhance regional development and economic integration.[30]

Scholars such as Taylor have argued that this led to '…reconfiguring parts of Africa as the continent's elites seek to promote economic integration as a means of latching onto what is perceived as the globalisation juggernaut.'[31]

In addition or response to these drivers, the voices of influential leaders on the continent such as former Presidents of South Africa and Nigeria – Thabo Mbeki and Olusegun Obasanjo, respectively – began to promote mantras and manifestos calling for an 'African renaissance' including exhortations for 'African solutions to African problems'.[32] These calls for 'Afro-optimism' were also important catalysts in promoting and chaperoning the creation of regional institutional responses to these issues.

Sub-regionalism

In parallel, significant developments occurred at the sub-regional level. The creation of the *Economic Community of West African States* (ECOWAS) in 1975,[33] was followed by the emergence of the *Southern African Development Cooperation* (SADC) in 1980,[34] and a steady stream of other sub-regional arrangements in the decades that followed.[35] Visions for an African Economic Community articulated in the Lagos Treaty of 1991 with the ultimate aim of

30 African Union, 'New Partnership for Africa's Development', October 2001, http://www.un.org/en/africa/osaa/pdf/nepad/nepad.pdf, p. 19.

31 Ian Taylor, 'Globalization and Regionalization in Africa: Reactions to Attempts at Neo-Liberal Regionalism', *Review of International Political Economy*, 10/2: 310–30 (2003).

32 See, for example: Thabo Mbeki, 'The African Renaissance Statement' (Office of the Executive Deputy President, 13 August 1998) <http://www.anc.org.za/ancdocs/history/mbeki/1998/tm0813.htm>. For more background on this period, see: Washington A.J. Okumu, *The African Renaissance: History, Significance and Strategy* (Trenton, NJ: Africa World Press, 2002), pp. 155–160.

33 Carol Lancaster, 'The Lagos Three: Economic Regionalism in Sub-Saharan Africa' in John Willis Harbeson and Donald S. Rothchild (ed.) *Africa in World Politics: Post-Cold War Challenges* (Boulder: Westview Press Inc., 1995); Samuel KB. Asante, *The Political Economy of Regionalism in Africa: A Decade of the Economic Community of West African States (ECOWAS)* (Praeger New York, 1986); W Alade Fawole, *Crisis of the State and Regionalism in West Africa* (Codesria, 2005).

34 Carolyn Jenkins and Lynne Thomas, 'African Regionalism and the SADC' in Mario Telò (ed.) *European Union and New Regionalism. Regional Actors and Global Governance in a Post-Hegemonic Era.* (Aldershot: Ashgate, 2001).

35 For example, IGAD; COMESA; ECCAS; EAC; ICGLR; CENSAD.

creating a continental economic and monetary union set in motion a process of focused economic integration through these Regional Economic Communities (RECs).[36] This focus on sub-regional building blocs fomented sub-regionalisation and the formation of more coherent sub-regional institutional frameworks a layer beneath the continental level.

Whilst the product of economic motivations and rationale, since the early 1990s these RECs have assumed more of a role and influence in terms of political affairs affecting the sub-region – including security issues. For instance, ECOWAS, SADC and others such as the Intergovernmental Authority on Development (IGAD) in eastern Africa have played a prominent role in attempts to manage and resolve conflict in their near neighbourhoods – an acknowledgement that sub-regions bore the brunt of instability in their vicinity.[37]

Factors that Influenced Evolution of African Regionalisation

The various forms and stages of regional community formation discussed above are the product of different rationales and motivations, but all reflect regional connectivities. When it comes to the changes seen across these arrangements a number of themes stand out. First, the immediate post-Independence era ushered in a period whereby state-centric conceptions of regional order predominated, entrenching and upholding traditional norms (e.g. sovereignty, non-interference, and respect for territorial integrity of states) in response to the nature of international order, distribution of power and geopolitical interests continuing to undermine peace and security. This was seen as critical for adjusting to growing membership and managing the dynamics and uncertainty regarding the global security and economic environment. Regionalisation was a means of consolidating and supporting the resilience of nascent independent states and promoting inter-governmental cooperation at various levels of regionhood.

Second, the turn of the century brought with it the transition from the OAU to the AU – whose architects were striking a balance between state-centric (emphasising non-interference and territorial integrity) and human-centric (human security, human rights, human development) values. Regionalisation in this moment was really a means of: (1) resuscitating pan-Africanism – i.e.

36 Glenn Hook and Ian Kearns (eds.) *Sub Regionalism and World Order* (London: Macmillan, 1999).

37 See, for example: T. Jaye, D. Garuba, and S. Amadi, *ECOWAS and the Dynamics of Conflict and Peace-Building* (African Books Collective, 2011); Laurie Nathan, *Community of Insecurity: SADC's Struggle for Peace and Security in Southern Africa* (Ashgate Publishing Limited, 2013).

renaissance and African solutions to African problems; and (2) giving institutional expression to support for fledgling human security and human development agenda.

Third, in parallel to these developments at the continental level, there was a proliferation and rise in *sub-regional* bodies and importantly an evolution in their nature from their origins as vehicles for economic partnership and integration to become more political entities with increasing agency. These agendas reflect that of the AU to enshrine the protection of human rights as well as protecting traditional norms of non-interference and constitutional transitions of political authority. Indeed, at times, it is sub-regional bodies that have been in the vanguard when it comes to decisions and actions that put human protection at the forefront of their logic and *raison d'etre*.

Fourth, the rise of an international civil society and the emergence of a range of transnational non-state actors – particularly Non-Governmental Organisations (NGOs) – fomented a regionalisation predicated on constituents that extended beyond the nation state – both above and beneath the national level. This saw regionalisation that reflected greater recognition of the importance of state-society relations and the agency of individuals and human-centred conceptions of regional political order.

Ultimately, it is important to note that regionalisation in Africa has not been singular and its institutional expression is not monolithic. Regional identities stretch beyond the continent to reach out to the diaspora but also fall within the continent's geographic bounds to defined sub-regions. The rise in number and centrality of sub-regional political communities across Africa emphasises the importance of disaggregating the notion of region in the African context. Whilst continental projects capture a broad conception of region, the identities associated to sub-regional bodies are strong and their relevance to underwriting human protection has been vital.

In sum, many of the arguments for why regionalisation has occurred in Africa fall into the broad rationale that states and their populations will be stronger together in cooperation and solidarity. This is a notion captured by an oft-cited African proverb, 'If you want to go fast, go alone. If you want to go far, go together with others.'[38] Whatever extent clear regional identities exist, and/or representative organisational embodiment can be identified, these formations – however, 'nascent', 'ascendant', or 'mature'[39] – have had a significant role in shaping the way in which norms to do with human protection have emerged,

38 *Inter alia* used by Jean Ping as AU Commissioner for Peace and Security.

39 Emanuel Adler and Michael Barnett (eds.) *Security Communities* (Cambridge: Cambridge University Press, 1998).

evolved and been mainstreamed in the regional responses to human insecurity on the continent. The following section briefly examines the relationship between African regional identity/organisations and human protection.

African Regionalism and Human Protection Norms

Since the 1990s, Constructivism has been the predominant theoretical framework in international relations for explaining the importance of norms in international society, including the presentation of models that describe norm life-cycles – including ideas of emergence, cascade, contestation, and ultimately internalisation.[40] The literature on the diffusion and acceptance of norms suggests that not all seemingly universal norms take root equally in all parts of the globe. As a consequence, adherence to their content differs depending on the setting. Important here is the idea of norms emanating from the global/transnational level interacting with actors and interpretations at the regional level to alter the meaning of the norm in that context. This is what Acharya calls norm *localisation*,[41] where congruence is built between locally embedded practices and customs and transnationally emergent normative frameworks through feedback, reinterpretation, and modification. For him, it is such localisation, rather than acceptance or outright rejection, which resolves normative contestation at the regional level.

This representation implies that a certain amount of 'norm export' is taking place. In other words, the norms in question emerge elsewhere, are being packaged externally and spread by powerful states or international/transnational society. This discounts the possibility that the genesis of these norms is influenced by the ideas and practices of the global south or that those that are promulgated externally do not have resonance with values and customs intrinsic to systems of social and political order in recipient societies. On the contrary, it is important to recognise that much of the content of norms surrounding human protection is not exclusively external or foisted upon the African context

40 Jeffrey T. Checkel, 'The Constructivist Turn in International Relations Theory', *World Politics* 50/2: 324–48 (1998). See, for example: Martha Finnemore and Kathryn Sikkink, 'International Norm Dynamics and Political Change', *International Organization*, 52/4: 887–917 (1998).

41 See: Amitav Acharya, 'How Ideas Spread: Whose Norms Matter? Norm Localization and Institutional Change in Asian Regionalism', *International Organization*, 58/2: 239–75 (2004); Amitav Acharya, *Whose Ideas Matter? Agency and Power in Asian Regionalism* (Ithaca: Cornell University Press, 2009).

by outsiders.[42] In many ways, human rights discourses have been integral to African regional imaginaries in ways that predate international frameworks such as the Universal Declaration on Human Rights, let alone more recent normative developments at the UN such as the protection of civilians (POC) and the RtoP. For instance, respect for inherent rights of individuals animated resistance to slavery and revolutionary movements for self-determination and decolonisation. Furthermore, it is also argued that the ideas undergirding RtoP find correspondences in the cosmopolitan and communitarian ethics embedded in traditional social orders observable across Africa.[43]

Therefore, as Williams has argued in relation to the RtoP, it is not necessarily accurate to think of the norm localisation process as 'one in which a homogenous set of "local" beliefs are changing some completely "foreign" idea.'[44] Rather there is a continuous feedback process between local and global interpretations of corresponding ideas, leading to localisation that results in normative content with an emplaced flavour. This is similar to what Acharya has more recently promoted as a model of norm *circulation*[45] and reflects a broader understanding of such norms as perpetually unsettled and contested.[46]

There have been few attempts to look at how human protection norms have been interpreted and 'localised' in regions such as Africa.[47] It is therefore helpful to ask to what extent there has been norm diffusion and acceptance.[48] The following section examines some of the ways that these norms have manifested in discourse, institutional expression and action in recent history on the continent – first at the continental level and second at the sub-regional level.[49]

---

42 Charlotte Epstein, 'Stop Telling Us How to Behave: Socialization or Infantilization?', *International Studies Perspectives*, 13/2: 135–45 (2012).

43 Tim Murithi, 'African indigenous and endogenous approaches to peace and conflict resolution' in David J. Francis (ed.), *Peace and Conflict in Africa* (London: Zed, 2008), pp. 16–30.

44 Paul W. Williams, 'The "Responsibility to Protect", Norm Localisation, and African International Society', *Global Responsibility to Protect* 1/3: 392–416 (2009), p. 398.

45 Amitav Acharya, 'The R2P and Norm Diffusion: Towards A Framework of Norm Circulation', *Global Responsibility to Protect*, 5/4: 466–479 (2013).

46 Antje Wiener, *A Theory of Contestation* (Heidelberg: Springer, 2014).

47 Notable exceptions include: Williams, 'The "Responsibility to Protect", Norm Localisation, and African International Society'; Matthias Dembinski and Berenike Schott, 'Converging around Global Norms? Protection of Civilians in African Union and European Union Peacekeeping in Africa', *African Security*, 6/3–4: 276–96 (2013).

48 Jennifer Welsh, 'Norm Contestation and the Responsibility to Protect', *Global Responsibility to Protect*, 5/4: 365–396 (2013). See also: Michael Barnett and Thomas G. Weiss, *Humanitarianism Contested: Where Angels Fear to Tread* (London: Routledge, 2011), pp. 8–34.

49 Hettne, Inotai, and Sunkel, *The New Regionalism and the Future of Security and Development*.

The AU and the APSA

It can be argued that human rights values undergird the principles and norms that accompanied the shift from the OAU to the AU.[50] As is commonly noted, this involved a conceptual departure from an (albeit implicit) policy of non-intervention or *non-interference* to a stance of *non-indifference*.[51] In other words the mantra of the AU was that the suffering of Africans anywhere was a matter of importance for Africans everywhere. In this light, the need for a continental capacity for prevention and intervention became a priority.[52]

The AU Constitutive Act included a range of provisions that evidence this shift. In a clear shift towards rights-centred approach, one of the key objectives of the new body laid out in Article 3 was: 'To promote and protect human and peoples' rights in accordance with the African Charter on Human and Peoples' Rights and other relevant human rights instruments.'[53] Similarly, the principles of the union in Article 4 buttress a commitment to human protection and include the hugely significant 4(h) which enshrines 'the right of the Union to intervene in a Member State pursuant to a decision of the Assembly in respect of grave circumstances, namely: war crimes, genocide and crimes against humanity.'[54]

Pursuant to the AU Constitutive Act, the Peace and Security Council (PSC) Protocol was adopted. This established the basis for what has come to be known as the African Peace and Security Architecture (APSA) providing the institutional framework to assist in implementing the continental peace and security strategy.[55] This is perhaps the strongest expression of human protection

50 Solomon A. Dersso, 'The Role of the African Human Rights System in the Operationalisation of Article 4(H).' in D. Kuwali and F. Viljoen (eds.) *Africa and the Responsibility to Protect: Article 4(H) of the African Union Constitutive Act* (Oxford: Routledge, 2013): 195–206, p. 195.

51 Musifiky Mwanasali, 'From Non-Interference to Non-Indifference: The Emerging Doctrine of Confl Ict Prevention in Africa', in John Akokpari, Angela Ndinga-Muvumba and Timothy Murithi (eds.) *The African Union and Its Institutions* (Cape Town: Jacana Media, 2008), pp. 41–62; Ben Kioko, 'The Right of Intervention under the African Union's Constitutive Act: From Non-Interference to Non-Intervention', *Revue Internationale de la Croix-Rouge/International Review of the Red Cross*, 85/852: 807–26 (2003).

52 Baffour Ankomah, 'African Union: From Non-Interference to Non-Indifference', *New African*, no. 460 (2007), pp. 10–12.

53 AU Constitutive Act, Article 3(h), 2002, http://www.au.int/en/sites/default/files/ConstitutiveAct_EN.pdf

54 AU Constitutive Act, Article 4(h), 2002. For in depth examination, see: Dan Kuwali and Frans Viljoen (eds.) *Africa and the Responsibility to Protect: Article 4(H) of the African Union Constitutive Act* (Oxford: Routledge, 2013).

55 John Akokpari, Angela Ndinga-Muvumba and Timothy Murithi (eds.) *The African Union and Its Institutions* (Cape Town: Jacana Media, 2008).

norms being internalised and informing institutional design. The PSC itself is a collective security arrangement to facilitate timely and efficient response to conflict and crisis situations on the continent. As the peak decision-making body it has become an important site of speech acts and resolution in regard to human protection challenges and humanitarian crises.[56] The *Continental Early Warning System* (CEWS) gathers data and produces timely analyses of political conflict and associated protection crises to inform the work of the rest of the APSA.[57] Grounded in more traditional forms of conflict resolution and dispute settlement, the APSA also contains a *Panel of the Wise* tasked with preventive diplomacy and early intervention to mediate and avert the escalation of conflict.[58]

Another example of human protection norms permeating the APSA was the vision for an *African Standby Force* (ASF). The Protocol establishing the PSC lays out a range of scenarios under which the ASF will undertake missions of peace support and intervention pursuant to Article 4(h) and (j) – many of which see civilian protection as an important, or primary, mission objective. Whilst preparations for the ASF continue to falter, the AU has nevertheless deployed and continues to sustain a number of ad hoc peace support operations – starting with the AU mission in Burundi (AMIB) in 2003, closely followed by the African Union Mission in Sudan-Darfur (AMIS) in 2004 – the first to be given an explicit protection of civilians mandate – that eventually transitioned into the hybrid UN-AU mission (UNAMID). Repeated efforts to stabilise the Comoros were followed by robust interventions in Somalia (AMISOM), Mali (AFISMA), and the Central African Republic (MISCA); all with strong human protection rationales.[59] Recent attempts by some member states to establish

56 Kathryn Sturman and Aïssatou Hayatou, 'The Peace and Security Council of the African Union: From Design to Reality' in Ulf Engel and J. Gomes Porto (eds.) *Africa's New Peace and Security Architecture: Promoting Norms, Institutionalizing Solutions*, Global Security in a Changing World (Ashgate, 2010), pp. 57–76.

57 El-Ghassim Wane, Charles Mwaura, Shewit Hailu, Simone Kopfmüller, Doug Bond, Ulf Engel and João Gomes Porto, 'The Continental Early Warning System: Methodology and Approach' in Ulf Engel and J. Gomes Porto (eds.) *Africa's New Peace and Security Architecture: Promoting Norms, Institutionalizing Solutions*, Global Security in a Changing World (Ashgate, 2010), pp. 91–110.

58 Jamila El Abdellaoui, 'The Panel of the Wise: A Comprehensive Introduction to a Critical Pillar of the African Peace and Security Architecture' *ISS Paper*, no.193 (2009), pp. 2–3; Tim Murithi and Charles Mwaura, 'The Panel of the Wise' in Ulf Engel and J. Gomes Porto (eds.) *Africa's New Peace and Security Architecture: Promoting Norms, Institutionalizing Solutions*, Global Security in a Changing World (Ashgate, 2010), pp. 79–90.

59 APC (2014) 'African-led Peace Support Operations', (African Peace Facility, European Union), http://www.africa-eu-partnership.org/sites/default/files/documents/apf-factsheet

the *African Capacity for Immediate Response to Crises* (ACIRC) – envisaged as a rapid deployment capability for response to political/humanitarian emergencies – is further evidence of moves in the direction of readiness to avert the worst human protection crises.[60]

Beyond the APSA, strictly defined, the African Commission and African Court on Human and Peoples' Rights in Banjul, the Gambia, are another important dimension of the nascent human protection infrastructure within the AU institutional framework. Moves are underway to transform the extant African Court of Justice into a newly mandated African Court of Justice & Human Rights.[61] The development of legal-judicial infrastructure with human rights at the centre is another sign of human protection norms informing and percolating through the regional architecture.[62]

Also at the continental level, a range of other entities have been contributing to raising the profile of human rights protection norms. For instance, the *Economic, Social, and Cultural Council* (ECOSOCC) is responsible for engaging civil society, including those focused on human rights issues, through an institutionally embedded consultative body.[63] Furthermore, the *New Partnership for African Development* (NEPAD) and the supporting *African Peer Review Mechanism* (APRM) are focused on promoting the good governance agenda and emphasising person-to-person links at the elite level that can influence behaviour and adherence to normative commitments.[64] Similarly, the AU

-on-psos.pdf; O. Bachmann, 'The African Standby Force: An Element of Prospective Multilevel Security Governance', *IDS Bulletin* 43/4: 14–19 (2012); Jakkie Cilliers and Johann Pottgieter, 'The African Standby Force' in Ulf Engel and J. Gomes Porto (eds.) *Africa's New Peace and Security Architecture: Promoting Norms, Institutionalizing Solutions*, Global Security in a Changing World (Ashgate, 2010), pp. 111–142.

60 The final element of the APSA is the Peace Fund, envisaged to resource and finance the efforts of the AU's conflict prevention, management and resolution work.

61 Ahmed Motala, 'The African Court on Human and Peoples' Rights: Origins and Prospects', in John Akokpari, Angela Ndinga-Muvumba and Timothy Murithi (eds.) *The African Union and Its Institutions* (Cape Town: Jacana Media, 2008), pp. 271–90.

62 Dersso, 'The Role of the African Human Rights System in the Operationalisation of Article 4(H).' pp. 195–206.

63 Charles Mutasa, 'A Critical Appraisal of the African Union–ECOSOCC Civil Society Interface', in John Akokpari, Angela Ndinga-Muvumba and Timothy Murithi (eds.) *The African Union and Its Institutions* (Cape Town: Jacana Media, 2008), pp. 291–306.

64 For further detail, see: Chris Landsberg, 'The Birth and Evolution of NEPAD', in John Akokpari, Angela Ndinga-Muvumba and Timothy Murithi (eds.) *The African Union and Its Institutions* (Cape Town: Jacana Media, 2008), pp. 207–26; Sheila Bunwaree, 'NEPAD and Its Discontents', in John Akokpari, Angela Ndinga-Muvumba and Timothy Murithi (eds.) *The African Union and Its Institutions* (Cape Town: Jacana Media, 2008), pp. 227–40; Adebayo Adedeji, 'NEPAD's African Peer Review Mechanism: Progress and Prospects', in

'Policy on Post-Conflict Reconstruction and Development' – adopted in July 2006 – is focused on rights-based approaches to peacebuilding including foci on inclusive poverty reduction, transitional justice, etc.[65]

A significant indication of regional posture on human protection came in the arrival at the Ezulwini Consensus in March 2005. In this African position on UN reform, the consensus was also explicit in approving the formulation of the RtoP in the SG Report emerging from the High Level Panel on Threats, Challenges and Change, including the phrase: 'authorization for the use of force by the Security Council should be in line with the conditions and criteria proposed by the Panel, but this condition should not undermine the responsibility of the international community to protect.'[66]

It is apparent that the APSA demonstrates significant progress in terms of institutional embodiment, policy pronouncements on rhetorical and written expressions of commitment to human protection norms. However, its record in responding to need on the continent has been mixed.[67] The major actions taken under its auspices have come primarily as reactive responses to crises rather than proactive efforts to prevent the occurrence or escalation of violent conflict. As Dembinski and Schott argue, the rhetorical commitment to norms of civilian protection as part of peace operations has been at best ineffective when it comes to implementation.[68] This is further emphasised by the fact that the much-lauded Article 4(h) has never been invoked explicitly or acted upon by the Assembly of Heads of State/Government. Similarly, the efforts of the AU to mediate and resolve conflicts on the continent have had a mixed score-card, varying from prompt and effective action in Kenya to redundancy in Libya and Cote d'Ivoire.

Despite clear mandates in the PSC Protocol for these entities in the areas of human rights protection as well as conflict prevention, management and

John Akokpari, Angela Ndinga-Muvumba and Timothy Murithi (eds.) *The African Union and Its Institutions* (Cape Town: Jacana Media, 2008), pp. 241–70.

65 AU, 'AU Policy on Post-Conflict Reconstruction and Development (PCRD)' (Addis Ababa: African Union), pp. 6–8, http://www.peaceau.org/uploads/pcrd-policy-framwowork-eng.pdf

66 Executive Council, 7th Extraordinary Session (7–8 March 2005). The common African position on the proposed reform of the United Nations: 'The Ezulwini Consensus' (Report). African Union.

67 Chrysantus Ayangafac and Jakkie Cilliers, 'African Solutions to African Problems', pp. 126 & 132–4; Tim Murithi, 'The Role of the African Peace and Security Architecture in the Implementation of Article 4(H).', in D. Kuwali and F. Viljoen (eds.) *Africa and the Responsibility to Protect: Article 4(H) of the African Union Constitutive Act* (Oxford: Routledge, 2013): 139–51, pp. 147–149.

68 Dembinski and Schott, 'Converging around Global Norms?' pp. 276–96.

resolution, meeting such great expectations has proven difficult. Similarly, despite some continental consensus on human protection norms when facing outward to the UN, inward looking implementation has been inconsistent and underwhelming. Politics and contestation both within the AU membership and between international actors and the AU continues to threaten the consistency and predictability of the AU when it comes to promoting and protecting human security. Similarly, although the fledgling infrastructure for legal-judicial developments, good governance agendas, and deepening engagement with civil society, point to progress towards human protection aims, these efforts have long time horizons for impact and cannot expect dramatic effects in the short term so show only limited evidence of normative internalisation in practice.[69]

Sub-regional Organisations and Communities

Recognising that intra-regional economic cooperation would be more difficult in the absence of peace and security for populations, a range of sub-regional arrangements within the continent have also built some institutional capacity that have been influenced by and are designed to enshrine and operationalise a commitment to human rights and civilian protection. For instance, the ECOWAS Mechanism on Conflict Prevention, Management, Resolution, Peacekeeping and Security (and the 1999 Protocol on Implementing the Mechanism) constituted significant breakthroughs at the sub-regional level in terms of entrenching human protection norms in institutional design. The protocol reaffirms a general commitment to the principles of the Universal Declaration of Human Rights, as well as to the African Charter on Human and People's Rights, and explicitly reiterates a specific pledge to ensure the 'protection of fundamental human rights and freedoms and the rules of international humanitarian laws.'[70]

In addition to identifying commitments to conflict early warning,[71] humanitarian assistance and peacebuilding, it goes on to outline a number of operational scenarios for ECOWAS forces that are similar to those envisaged by the AU for the ASF. According to Chapter III of the protocol, these are: observation and monitoring; Peace-keeping and restoration of peace; humanitarian intervention in support of humanitarian disaster; enforcement of sanctions,

69 For detailed treatment of the developments relating to socio-economic development governance and the relationship between the AU and civil society, see chapter in this volume by Tim Murithi.

70 (1999) 'Protocol Relating to the Mechanism for Conflict Prevention, Management, Resolution, Peace-Keeping and Security', http://www.comm.ecowas.int/sec/?id=ap101299.

71 For further details, see chapter in this volume by Chukwuemeka B. Eze.

including embargo; preventive deployment; Peace-building, disarmament and demobilisation; Policing activities, including the control of fraud and organised crime; and, any other operations as may be mandated by the Mediation and Security Council.[72] Although less explicit than the ASF policy framework document, the 1999 Protocol does state that the Mechanism shall be applied in event of mass atrocities such as those stipulated in Article 4(h) of the AU Constitutive Act.[73] Given this language and the scope for interpretation of mission groupings such as 'humanitarian intervention in support of humanitarian disaster' and 'any other operations as may be mandated by the Mediation and Security Council', it is fair to say that the ECOWAS leadership envisaged coercive protection operations and the inclusion of protection elements within future missions.

In many respects, ECOWAS has advanced much further than other RECs in developing these frameworks for collective security and particularly so when it comes to placing human protection at the centre. However, SADC and IGAD have also deployed peace support operations in response to the outbreak of political crisis and violent conflict in cases such as Madagascar and Somalia.[74] Likewise, the Economic Community of Central African States (ECCAS) has also taken steps in building the capacities needed to respond to protection crises. For instance, its Multinational Force for Central Africa (FOMAC)[75] was seen in action when it responded in the form of the MICOPAX mission following the eruption of violence in the Central African Republic (CAR).

A range of sub-regional bodies have also established their own equivalences to other elements of the APSA, including early warning capabilities,[76] committees of Elders[77] and other mediation capacities designed to prevent

72 ECOWAS, 1999, Chapter III, Article 22.

73 ECOWAS, 1999, Chapter IV, Article 25.

74 The ASF architecture dictates that it will be entirely dependent on the RECs for force generation and operational capability. This also forms the backdrop for the development of some of this standby capacity in each of the regions. 5 regions have developed (to varying degrees) the five constituent brigades of the ASF.

75 Originally created in 2002. See, for example: Angela Meyer, 'Peace and Security Cooperation in Central Africa: Challenges and Prospects', *Discussion Paper 56* (Uppsala: Nordiska Afrikainstitutet, 2011). See also: http://www.irinnews.org/report/100815/central-african-peacekeeping-force-gears-up-for-action.

76 For example, the SADC Regional Early Warning Centre (REWC), http://www.sadc.int/sadc-secretariat/services-centres/regional-early-warning-centre/.

77 For example, the Committee of Elders established by the Common Market for Eastern and Southern Africa (COMESA) to play a crucial role of preventive diplomacy on issues of peace, security and stability.

conflict-related human suffering.[78] There are also a myriad of efforts underway that could be understood to be *indirectly* contributing to human protection goals. For instance, the integration programs of organisations such as the East African Community (EAC) including a proposed customs union, regional banks, trade links, etc, are envisaged as a means of reducing human insecurity fomented by under-development and bad governance.

Although these developments point to importance being placed on human protection norms in progress with regional architectures for collective security and peace, the litany of violent conflicts across the continent with tragic human consequences suggest that these efforts have proved inadequate in terms of effective prevention or responses that lead to durable protective environments, thus far.

Human Protection Upon Reflection

It is important to be clear that as well as different levels of regionalisation (i.e. as argued above, regionalism in Africa is not monolithic) all (sub-)regional communities can be disaggregated further to the 54 states, arguably even more 'nations', and an abundance of other identity-based communities that are part of socially constructing and refining normative orders in Africa. Therefore, the extent of internalisation of human protection norms in the institutions of African regional organisations only tells part of the story about actual acceptance of such norms and the extent to which they have been contextualised in the social and political values and ideas of the populations of the African continent.

Notwithstanding this caveat, the manifestation of human rights and civilian protection norms within regional arrangements in Africa has been on a significant upward trajectory in recent years, with a particular shift in approach following the inauguration of the AU in 2002. Indeed, some have argued that an African society of states has evolved specifically in relation to norms that govern state behavior regarding human rights and human-centred approaches to security.[79] Compared with some other parts of the world the African continent has been pioneering in this regard. Commitments in policy documents of the AU and a slew of sub-regional arrangements have been both strong and

78 For example, high level mediation teams deployed to resolve conflict in eastern DR Congo by the International Conference of the Great Lakes Region (ICGLR).

79 Paul D. Williams, 'From non-intervention to non-indifference: the origins and development of the African Union's security culture' *African Affairs* 106/423: 253–279 (2007); Williams, 'The "Responsibility to Protect", Norm Localisation, and African International Society', pp. 392–416.

progressive on issues of human rights, preventing and responding to mass atrocity crimes. Furthermore, the same organisations have gone about institutional design and preparations in a way that has factored in and attempted to live up to these lofty aims.

However, despite these emergent architectures for peace, security and human protection, words have not always been translated into tangible and effective deeds. In practice, the rhetorical commitments have resulted in at best inconsistent and at times incompetent responses to humanitarian crisis and need. The report-card reads 'can do better' and 'plenty of room for improvement'.[80] Moreover, despite the elaborate infrastructures under construction, false starts and inconsistency in application means that questions remain about the extent to which human protection norms have truly taken hold in the African context. Whether through diffusion from the global to the regional level, or bottom-up processes of inculcating indigenous beliefs and value-systems, it remains to be seen whether the commitment shown by governments and regional arrangements to human protection norms is anything more than rhetorical. As Williams has argued, whilst the empirics suggest that norms to do with human protection are increasingly visible in the continents institutional frameworks, this may be more for instrumental reasons than genuine efforts to internalise the ideas and practices implied.[81]

In regard to the RtoP, for instance, some influential African states are often said to be 'reluctantly acquiescing' or 'cautiously supporting' these normative developments. This reluctance and caution is perhaps more pertinent in the aftermath of UN–authorised interventions in Libya and Cote d'Ivoire in 2011 leading to regime change in both cases and resulting in suspicion about the potential for abuse by the powerful.

That should not detract from the improvements in this area and advances in this direction. As Krook and True have argued, the content of norms is not static but rather continues to evolve.[82] Indeed, some of the ambiguity around the content of norms is deliberate in order to allow some flexibility and adaptability in the application.[83] Internalisation can also be understood as a

80 Murithi, 'The Role of the African Peace and Security Architecture in the Implementation of Article 4(H).', pp. 147–149.

81 Williams, 'The "Responsibility to Protect", Norm Localisation, and African International Society', p. 398 citing Williams, 'From Non-Intervention to Non-Indifference', pp. 256–262.

82 M. L. Krook and J. True, 'Rethinking the Life Cycles of International Norms: The United Nations and the Global Promotion of Gender Equality', *European Journal of International Relations* 18: 103–27 (2012).

83 W. Sandholtz, 'Dynamics of International Norm Change: Rules against Wartime Plunder', *European Journal of International Relations*, 14: 101–31 (2008).

on-going process with periodic bouts of contestation and continuous circulation. It therefore requires continuous investigation and is important to ask: what are the opportunities and sites of resistance to deepening and enhancing these developments in Africa? The following section identifies some of these in the form of prospects and problems.

The Future of African Regionalism and Human Protection: Prospects and Problems

Issues and challenges to implementation and realisation of these normative goals remain. Some of these questions are raised below as they relate to *normative, political* and *institutional* considerations. Regarding the *normative challenges* it seems important to ask if it is the ideas and values underpinning human protection norms that induce resistance at the regional level? For instance, are attachments to 'traditional' notions of sovereignty always likely to trump sovereignty as responsibility? In other words, is regime security likely to endure as a priority over human security in the crafting of African states' and societies' posture towards regionalisation? If so, to what extent are influential actors such as hegemonic states setting the course for regional bodies in this regard?

Are human rights always a relative concept and does this prevent acceptance of universal norms in this realm? For example, does the fraught relationship with the International Criminal Court – i.e. perceptions of it as a 'Court for Africa(ns)' – create insurmountable barriers to international criminal accountability for mass atrocity crimes? This is particularly salient in cases where the states involved do not have sufficient capacity to prosecute (e.g. Libya) or incumbent governments are unwilling to do so (e.g. accusations of victors justice in Côte d'Ivoire under Ouattara since post-election crisis in 2010/11)?[84] What role have indigenous approaches to conflict resolution and transitional justice played in the region's position on human protection norms? How much does this thinking infuse 'African solutions to African problems' and to what extent can norms at the international level benefit from 'African' input and feedback during the so-called norm localisation/circulation processes?

Regarding *political challenges*, a major question concerns the extent to which a lack of political will and genuine commitment by some African heads of state inhibit a deepening culture of human protection. For instance, does

84 Charles T. Hunt, 'Cote d'Ivoire', in Alex Bellamy and Tim Dunne (eds.) *Oxford Handbook on the Responsibility to Protect* (Oxford: Oxford University Press, 2016), pp. 693–716.

the propensity to default to the norm of non-interference when politically sensitive cases involving powerful stakeholders arise undermine the credibility of emergent human protection norms? For example, in Zimbabwe where until recently, Robert Mugabe was deemed unimpeachable due to his independence heroics or in Cote d'Ivoire in 2011 where efforts were made to protect Gbagbo's sovereign authority despite their respective culpability for bouts of widespread election-related violence. Likewise, in Libya, Ghaddafi's history of largesse and support to the AU may have influenced its decision-making. Is this limiting the progress of human protection on the continent? Furthermore, to what extent are political leaders willing to 'put their money where their mouth is' to resource and support the development of regional capacities in order to overcome a range of technical and bureaucratic capacity issues that inhibit the realisation of human protection across the continent?

Furthermore, what is the role and significance of non-state actors and civil society? To what extent, if at all, are African citizens able to hold their governments and leaders to their commitments and responsibilities under human rights principles, norms, and values? How can civil society organisations across the continent feed into and provide oversight for efforts to contextualise international norms at the (sub-)regional level?[85] What about other influential non-state actors? Where do the many legitimate sources of authority at the local level find a voice and contribute to shaping and ultimately accepting certain political orders that have consequences for the substance and resilience of peace and human security?

Regarding *institutional challenges*, it is necessary to ask if technical issues such as organisational bureaucracy and/or coordination and capacity within the institutional architectures are to blame for tardy or inadequate responses? Do the various components of the APSA or sub-regional frameworks for peace and security have the capacity they need to function effectively? Are the different elements working in mutually reinforcing ways? For instance, do the early warning systems in place feed into and trigger early action? Are the myriad pieces of the architecture sufficiently coordinated and networked such that approaches to human protection are system-wide or are inefficiencies and shortcomings hampering the operationalisation of human protection norms at various regional levels?

85 Paul D. Williams and Jürgen Haacke, 'Regional Approaches to Conflict Management', in Chester A. Crocker, Fen Osler Hampson and Pamela R Aall (eds.) *Rewiring Regional Security in a Fragmented World* (Washington, DC: US Institute of Peace Press, 2011): 49–74, p. 70.

The interplay between different regional groupings and other international governmental and non-governmental organisations appears to be an important element of embedding and institutionalising human protection norms within the region. Therefore, it is important to examine the current state of partnership between the AU and the litany of regional arrangements across Africa. Similarly, what is the condition of Africa-UN relations regarding human protection? How do the peak authorities – e.g. the UN Security Council and the AU Peace and Security Council – work together (or not) in cases of suspected and actual mass atrocities? Likewise, to what extent does cooperation with the European Union or North Atalantic Treaty Organization (NATO) enable human protection and how?[86] What areas can they work together in enhancing human protection in the region? Who needs to do what?

At the other end of the spectrum, to what extent are member states of regional bodies internalising and taking steps to institutionalise such norms? What are the impediments to countries embracing and further entrenching human protection norms in the domestic setting, through the passage of domestic legislation and creation of national instruments on human rights, ratification of international treaties, as well as deeper engagement with civil society and non-state actors?

These questions and speculations comprise some of the opportunities and constraints to contextualising and ultimately seeing the internalisation of universal norms on human rights, the responsibility to protect, and civilian protection in the regional projects, arrangements and institutions of Africa. Many of these issues are taken up in greater detail in the chapters that follow in this volume.

Conclusion

On the African continent, different imaginaries exist at multiple levels of regional analysis. These are tied up with common experiences of oppression (e.g. slavery, (neo-)colonialism, (neo)imperialism), common interests and economic interdependency (e.g. trade, cultural heritage, linguistic groups), and shared visions for supra-national presence in the globalising international

86 Fredrik Söderbaum, 'African Regionalism and EU-African Interregionalism', in M. Teló (ed.) *European Union and New Regionalism: Regional Actors and Global Governance in a Post-Hegemonic Era* (Ashgate, 2007): 269–85.

order. These regional imaginaries have informed the design and construction of organisational forms that display overlaps of membership and identity and have led to some harmonisation in approaches to evolving norms surrounding human protection.

From the pioneering humanitarian interventions of ECOWAS in the 1990s to the progressive moves associated with the transition from the OAU to the AU, the actions and architectures of the regional bodies that constitute the practical incarnation of these notions of 'region' have moved quickly in the direction of promoting human rights and acting in accordance with human protection norms. However, whilst there have been significant advances in this area, the future of regional approaches to norms of human protection remains uncertain and subject to contestation. The African continent, its various regional communities and institutional expressions will have an important role to play in conferring legitimacy to established normative frameworks through acceptance whilst continuing to shape and contribute to on-going evolution of emerging norms (or norm regimes) – particularly those that present tensions and challenge orthodox interpretations of international and regional order.

An objective of this project is to ask: to what extent has regionalism in Africa contributed to the development of human protection norms in the region(s)? In other words, to what extent has feedback – positive and critical – from the African continent informed and re-constituted human protection norms. African regionalisation has been a significant factor in the promotion and development of 'so-called' universal norms related to human rights, protection of civilians, and mass atrocities prevention. Furthermore, regional perceptions and conduct in turn influence the way in which norms are shaped and emerge at the global level as a result of feedback and co-evolutionary processes in the international system.[87] In a dynamical international society where nothing is set in stone, Africa's regional institutions may be able to act as both agents of change (with proposals such as, for instance, the African consensus on RtoP) and a bridge between the global north and south in the effort to sustain and build upon global consensus around human protection norms.

Elaborating on the way in which this is happening in different locales promises a rich opportunity for inter-regional dialogue and learning that may

87 See: Charles T. Hunt, 'Emerging Powers and the Responsibility to Protect: Non-linear Norm Dynamics in Complex International Society', *Cambridge Review of International Affairs* 29/2: 761–781 (2016).

contribute to this process.[88] This is not to overplay the similarities in comparison – different regionalisms and regionalisation processes will be unique and display their own characteristics accordingly. It is nevertheless helpful to investigate how norms influencing and being shaped by regional identities/organisations in one region relate to the experiences others, including other parts of the global south.

---

88 See, for example: Michael Schulz, Fredrik Söderbaum and Joakim Öjendal, 'Key Issues in the New Regionalism: Comparisons from Asia, Africa and the Middle East' in B. Hettne, A. Inotai, O. Sunkel (eds.), *Comparing regionalisms: Implications for global development* (Basingstoke: Palgrave-Macmillan, 2001); Jürgen Haacke and Paul D. Williams, 'Regional arrangements and security challenges: a comparative analysis', *Crisis States Research Centre working papers series*, 2/52 (London, UK: Crisis States Research Centre, London School of Economics and Political Science, 2009).

The African Union as a Norm Entrepreneur: The Limits of Human Protection and Mass Atrocities Prevention

Tim Murithi
University of the Free State
tkmurithi@hotmail.com

Abstract

This chapter will argue that despite its role as a norm entrepreneur the African Union (AU), when analysed through the UN Secretary-General's 3-Pillar framework of responsibility, has only had limited success and faced significant constraints in promoting Pan-African norms relating to sovereignty and non-interference, governance and development in order to achieve human protection and the prevention of mass atrocities. Human protection refers to protection of civilians from human rights abuses with a particular focus on mass atrocity crimes. This chapter will also assess the evolving AU-UN partnership and conclude by assessing the limits of norm building and propose strategies for enhancing human protection in Africa.

Keywords

African Union – human protection – R2P – Pan-Africanism

This chapter will argue that despite its role as a norm entrepreneur, the African Union (AU) has only had limited success in human protection and the prevention of mass atrocities. In this chapter, human protection refers to protection of civilians from human rights abuses, inside and outside of armed conflicts, with a particular focus on mass atrocity crimes – genocide, war crimes, crimes against humanity and ethnic cleansing (see Hunt in this volume). The chapter

1 This paper was presented at the Asia Pacific Centre for the Responsibility to Protect (APR2P) Research Workshop on 'Southeast Asian and African Regionalism: Norm Promotion and Capacity Building in Human Rights, Mass Atrocities Prevention and Civilian Protection', 29 and 30 October 2014, Bangkok, Thailand.

 | DOI:10.1163/9789004363212_010

will utilise the UN Secretary-General's 3-Pillar framework of the responsibility of the state; the requirement of international assistance and the imperative for timely response as a guiding R2P implementation framework for analysing the AU's human protection interventions. This chapter examines how the AU has attempted to promote Pan-African norms relating to sovereignty and non-interference, human protection and mass atrocities prevention, and how these have emerged and evolved over time in Africa. The chapter will also discuss the major turning points in Africa's normative frameworks and mechanisms in dealing with these issues, and the key factors that shaped the debate on human protection (see Morada in this volume) and mass atrocities prevention in conflict areas across the continent. In addition, the chapter will assess the parallel enumeration of governance and development norms, which in their totality contribute towards achieving a broader range of socio-economic human protection provisions and consequently lay the foundation for addressing vulnerable civilians and decrease the prospects for incidents of mass atrocities. In particular, this chapter will argue that despite the emergence and articulation of the norms of Pan-Africanism, mass atrocity prevention, and collective security, the AU's record in human protection remains limited and continues to face several constraints. This chapter will also assess the evolving AU-UN partnership in human protection. This chapter will conclude by assessing the limits of norm building and propose strategies for enhancing human protection in Africa.

The Persistence of Violent Conflict and Civilian Vulnerability

To a large extent efforts to ensure sustainable peace and development in Africa have always been undermined by the dominant international and geopolitical agendas of the day. After colonialism, it was the Cold War. Today after the Cold War the pressures of globalisation are impacting upon Africa's peace and development efforts. However, the continental ability and capacity to promote peace has also been undermined by the lack of political will among African leaders to find ways to address their differences. African leaders have to take responsibility for the lack of peace and security on the continent. Political tension and conflict emerge from a range problems including from political misrule and authoritarianism witnessed today in Zimbabwe and Eritrea for example. Economic mismanagement, kleptocracy and the theft of state resources and their transfer to overseas accounts has also played a role in generating the degree of deprivation that creates conditions that can foment conflict between groups.

The presence of conflict on the continent is also due to poor governance and the lack of respect for the human rights of African citizens and low level of civic education among the majority of Africa's populations. These factors when all added together generate a degree of vulnerability within the civilian population. For example, the poverty that we witness today - with 500 million people or half of the continent's population living on less than US $1.25 per day. The continental average life expectancy is only 54 years; the mortality rate of children under 5 years of age at 140 per 1000 and the illiteracy rate of 41% for those over 15 years old.[2] These conditions are made worse by the public health crises afflicting the continent like ebola, HIV/AIDS, malaria and respiratory problems like tuberculosis.[3]

These conditions add up to a stressful situation for the majority of African people. The tension generated by these conditions is easily exploited by ruthless politicians and self-appointed leaders to unleash and perpetuate conflicts on the continent. Disputes have placed an emotional, mental and psychological strain on the people of the continent from the outbreak of violence in South Sudan and the Central African Republic (CAR), Mali, Somalia, the Democratic Republic of the Congo (DRC), Darfur, Sudan, Libya, northern Nigeria and ongoing political strife in Cabinda region of Angola, the Casamance region of Senegal, and political instability in Zimbabwe, Egypt and Tunisia.

The Rwandan Genocide and the Case for a Revitalised African Normative Framework to Promote Human Protection

Whilst the OAU shepherded states to independence, it was not as effective in monitoring and policing the affairs of its own Member States when it came to issues mentioned earlier such as: human rights abuses, violent conflict, political corruption, economic mismanagement, poor governance, lack of gender equality and poverty eradication. The OAU created a Mechanism for Conflict Prevention, Management and Resolution in Cairo, in 1993. This instrument was ineffective in resolving disputes on the continent. Tragically, the Rwandan genocide which precipitated the worst contemporary case of mass atrocities on the African continent, was initiated in April 1994, and unfolded while the OAU mechanism was operational. Self-evidently the African continent did not have an effective normative framework to mitigate against mass atrocities

2 African Development Bank, 'Addressing Fragility and Building Resilience in Africa: The AfDB Group Strategy 2014–2019', 30 June 2015, p. 1.

3 T. Murithi, 'The African Union at ten: An appraisal', *African Affairs*, 111/445 (2012), p. 663.

and achieve human protection. Simultaneously, it was also during this last decade of the twentieth-century that the conflicts in Somalia led to the collapse of the state and violence in Sierra Leone, Liberia, Angola and the Democratic Republic of the Congo led to the death of millions of Africans. These devastating events illustrated the limitations of the OAU as a normative framework for preventing human rights, mass atrocities and ensuring civilian protection. This was clearly a case of the failure of a state to protect its citizens as well as the failure of timely international assistance. The genocide in Rwanda became a turning point in the development of additional norms to prevent mass atrocities and ensure human protection. Specifically, after the genocide and through some degree of soul searching by both the OAU and UN systems documented in self-critical reports, there was a clamour among Africa's leaders to define and articulate a more robust normative collective security regime.

The African Union and the Advent of a Normative Collective Security Regime

The conflicts that afflicted the African continent from the end of the Cold War to the first decade of the twenty-first century demanded that urgent normative changes be made to the way of doing things. So it became increasingly clear to many leaders on the African continent that it was necessary again to find a way to revive the norms of Pan-Africanism. Subsequently, normative Pan-Africanism was again taken to another level with the launching of the African Union, first as an idea at a Summit of the OAU in Sirte in Libya in 1999. Shortly thereafter, the Constitutive Act of the African Union was signed in Lome, Togo, on 11th July 2000. This led to the official inauguration of the African Union, as the successor to the Organisation of African Unity, in July 2002 in Durban, South Africa. In effect the AU replaced the OAU and took on all its assets and liabilities.

The vision of the AU remained consistent with the norms of Pan-Africanism, which were to promote solidarity and self-help, to end the discrimination and marginalisation of Africa and to ensure its peaceful social, economic and political development. The primary task for the AU was to promote the norms of peace and security, underpinned by a commitment to human protection and the prevention of mass atrocities, so that development could flourish. In addition, the necessity of the AU became evident given the changing context of international relations. Globalisation had become a force to be reckoned with, and individual states would increasingly become more vulnerable in this emerging international landscape. African countries and societies gradually recognised that working individually makes them susceptible to global manipulation and exploitation, which is why the solidarity norm as expressed through the AU resonated with the continent's leadership.

The AU as a Norm Enterpreneur

The evolution of the AU from the OAU was both visionary and timely. The OAU had failed to live up to all of its norms and principles. At the time of the demise of the OAU, Africa was a continent afflicted by the pressures of conflict, poverty and underdevelopment and public health crises. The OAU effectively died of a cancer of inefficiency because it basically could not uphold its original norms of promoting peace, security and development in Africa.

In the thirteen years of its existence, the AU has attempted to play a continental role as a norm entrepreneur. A norm entrepreneur in this instance is understood as a normative leader who encourages others to uphold a range of norms for the improvement of the livelihood of people who are subject to their jurisdiction or authority.[4]

The African Union has the primary responsibility for establishing and operationalising the continent's peace and security architecture. In this regard, it has become the leading norm entrepreneur on issues pertaining to peace and security on the continent. Similarly, on issues relating to governance the AU has sought to establish norms to guide the behaviour of its member states. In particular, the *African Union Charter on Democracy, Elections and Governance* is a seminal document which has been ratified by the required fifteen member states and is subsequently a living document of the Union, which outlines a range of provisions on how countries can improve how they are governed. The challenges with the establishment of these norms is in their rigorous domestication and implementation.[5] The AU has emerged as a home-grown initiative to effectively take the destiny of the continent into the hands of the African people. However, there is a long way to go before the AU's role as a norm entrepreneur is actualised and its vision and mission is realised.

---

4 T. Murithi, 'The African Union at ten: An appraisal', p. 663; see also Cass R Sunstein, 'Social norms and social roles', *Columbia law review* 96/4: 903–968 (1996).

5 Paul Williams, 'The "Responsibility to Protect", Norm Localisation, and African International Society', *Global Responsibility to Protect* 1/3: 392–416 (2009).

The AU's Norms of Human Protection

The AU has sought to promote the norm of collective security. The AU Constitutive Act ascribes to the Union the right to intervene and responsibility to protect in situations of war crimes, crimes against humanity and genocide. In terms of norms and policy this means that African countries have agreed to pool their sovereignty to enable the AU to act as the continental guarantor and protector of the security, rights and well-being of the African people. The African Union Peace and Security Council (PSC) was established as a legal institution of the Union through the *Protocol Relating to the Establishment of the Peace and Security Council of the African Union*, in 2002.[6] The AU PSC is the key institution charged with conducting peace operations on the continent but it is complemented by the Panel of the Wise, the Continental Early Warning System, the African Standby Force (ASF) and a Military Staff Committee (MSC). An AU Peace Fund has been established to secure resources to conduct post-conflict reconstruction efforts. The AU has therefore undoubtedly over the last fifteen years led in promoting the norms of peace and security on the continent. Hunt, elsewhere in this issue, discusses the African Peace Architecture at length, so its analysis will not be duplicated here.

The AU and the Responsibility to Protect

The issue of humanitarian intervention became a key challenge in international relations following the end of the Cold War, as violent conflicts took on a more intra-state, rather than inter-state, dimension fuelled by the crisis of legitimacy affecting nation-states. The International Commission on Intervention and State Sovereignty (ICISS) identified three specific responsibilities, notably the: i) responsibility to prevent; ii) responsibility to react; iii) responsibility to rebuild. Subsequently, the 2009 Report of the UN Secretary-General entitled *Implementing the Responsibility to Protect* proposed a 3-pillar framework focusing on: Pillar One - the protection responsibilities of the State; Pillar Two - international assistance and capacity-building; and Pillar Three - timely and decisive response. Specifically, Pillar One emphasises 'the enduring responsibility of the state to protect its populations, whether nationals or not, from genocide, war crimes, ethnic cleansing and crimes against humanity.'[7] This interpretation of the disaggregated elements of R2P indicate what is

6 African Union, *Protocol Establishing the Peace and Security Council of the African Union*, (Addis Ababa: African Union, 2002).

7 United Nations General Assembly, *Implementing the Responsibility to Protect: Report of the Secretary-General*, A/63/677, 12 January 2009, p. 8.

required to ensure that effective atrocity prevention and human protection interventions.

Is the AU Committed to R2P and Human Protection?

The former Chairperson of the African Union Commission, President Alpha Oumar Konare, advocated for the importance of moving away from the norm of non-intervention to a norm of non-indifference.[8] The AU is learning from the lessons of the OAU and has adopted a much more interventionist stance through its legal frameworks and institutions. The authors of the Constitutive Act of the African Union, of 2000, effectively enshrined a responsibility to protect in the document, and declared that on the African continent regional assistance would be promoted. The AU Peace and Security Council (PSC) was established in 2004 through the Protocol Relating to the Peace and Security Council of 2002.[9] The PSC can assess a potential crisis situation, send fact-finding missions to trouble spots and be in a position to authorise and legitimise the AU's intervention in internal crisis situations. Article 4(h) of the AU Constitutive Act affirms 'the right of the Union to intervene in a Member State pursuant to a decision of the Assembly in respect of grave circumstances, namely: war crimes, genocide and crimes against humanity'.[10] Furthermore, Article 4(j) declares 'the right of Member States to request intervention from the Union in order to restore peace and security'.[11] In particular, Article 7, item (e), of the Protocol on the Peace and Security Council, states that the Council can 'recommend to the Assembly (of Heads of State), intervention, on behalf of the Union, in a Member State in respect of grave circumstances, namely war crimes, genocide and crimes against humanity, as defined in relevant international conventions and instruments'.[12] This is a major qualitative difference between the Charter of the OAU. The AU adopted legal provisions, which for the first time in the history of Africa empowered and mandated the continental organisation to intervene in internal situations that might lead to atrocities

8 Murithi, T, *The African Union: Pan-Africanism, Peacebuilding and Development*. Aldershot: Ashgate, 2005, p. 36.

9 AU, 'Protocol Relating to the Establishment of the Peace and Security Council of the African Union', Addis Ababa, 2002.

10 African Union, 'Constitutive Act of the African Union', 11 July 2000.

11 *ibid.*

12 African Union, 'Protocol Relating to the Establishment of the Peace and Security Council of the African Union', Addis Ababa, December 2003, p. 9.

being committed against minority groups or communities at risk within states. In other words, the AU has the right and the responsibility to protect.

The AU leadership has consistently said that the organisation would not sit idly while atrocities persisted in the region. To date the AU's interventions, for example in Burundi, Darfur, Somalia, Comoros, Mali and the Central African Republic (CAR), have been symbolic in terms of indicating the organisation's commitment towards upholding human protection across the continent. However, the AU continues to have capacity, financial and operational constraints when it comes to implementing an effective R2P. In particular, the AU remains spectacularly under-resourced which is squarely the responsibility of African governments and not of the donor community. Tax revenue from African citizens is financing huge domestic defence budgets, but the commitment to Pan-African security does not yet approximate the commitment shown to national defence.[13] In effect, AU member states have articulated their commitment to Pan-Africanism, collective security and human protection, but they have singularly failed to match this with the requisite funds to achieve their desired outcomes. This is a natural consequence of the over-emphasis of state sovereignty and an illusionary perception that individual states can secure their security without an adequate concern and financial commitment towards promoting the security of others. It is increasingly self-evident, through regional conflict systems such as the one in the Great Lakes region, that one nation-states' security is intricately bound up with the security of its neighbours. Therefore, there has to be a greater commitment from African governments to finance the operationalisation of the norms that they have explicitly articulated.

There is every indication that the AU, in line with Pillar Two of the R2P implementation framework, will continue to make an effort to respond to similar situations of mass atrocity if they arise in the future. Of course much pain and suffering could be prevented if the AU enhanced and strengthened its mechanism for preventive diplomacy and early response to potential conflicts before they escalate. Conflict prevention is without a doubt the most effective way to ensure human protection, as reiterated by the totality of Pillars One to Three of the R2P implementation framework. The AU has established an infrastructure to provide it with early warning, but it still falls short in terms of transforming this information into effective early response and conflict prevention processes. In particular, the AU PSC receives timely information from the AU Continental Early Warning System (CEWS), but often only reacts after tensions

13 M Mataboge, 'AU's dependence on cash from the West still rankles', *Mail and Guardian*, 11 June 2015, http://mg.co.za/article/2015-06-11-aus-dependence-on-cash-from-the-west-still-rankles, accessed 11 June 2015.

have escalated and crisis situations have precipitated human rights violations. The AU Panel of the Wise, which is supposed to be an autonomous body within the African Peace and Security Architecture, has become mired in bureaucratic constraints and restrictions which has undermined its preventive function. The situations which will be discussed below will illustrate how the AU has endeavoured to implement its human protection mandate, but significant constraints still affect its interventions. Furthermore, security-oriented interventions in isolation cannot achieve the stated objectives of sustaining human protection in isolation. Efforts to consolidate governance and achieve development are equally integral towards achieving the goal of preventing mass atrocities.

The AU's Pan-African Governance and Developmental Norms and the Quest for Socio-economic Rights

Human protection cannot be achieved or sustained without ensuring that governance and development processes are also strengthened and consolidated. Given the socio-economic vulnerability of Africa's citizens, there has been a parallel process of articulating governance and development norms at the level of the African Union. Specifically, on issues relating to governance the AU has sought to establish norms, notably through the African Union Charter on Democracy, Elections and Governance, to guide the behaviour of its member states. The challenge, however, in terms of this AU Charter is to ensure that these norms are actually adopted and implemented.

African countries have consistently expressed their desire to regain control of their economic development policies, in order to improve the access of their citizens to education and health care. So the external control of the economic policies of African countries is a situation that has to be addressed. The Structural Adjustment Programmes (SAPS) and so-called Poverty Reduction Strategy Papers (PRSPS) promoted and enforced by the International Monetary Fund (IMF) and World Bank have had a negative impact on Africa's development.[14] By the IMF and World Bank's own admission, these programmes did not achieve what they had intended.[15] The United Nations Conference on Trade

14 Fantu Cheru, *The Silent Revolution: Debt, Development and Democracy* (London: Zed Books, 1989); see also J Hawkins,, 'Understanding the Failure of IMF Reform: The Zambian Case', *World Development*, 19/7: 839–849 (1991).

15 Ruben Lamdany and Hali Edison (eds)., *Independent Evaluation at the IMF: The First Decade*, International Monetary Fund Independent Evaluation Office (Washington: IMF, 2012).

and Development (UNCTAD) estimates that IMF/World Bank policies dictated since 1980 have led to a ten per cent decline in economic growth in Africa.[16] The African Union has repeatedly voiced its commitment to bringing genuine development to its citizens. It is in this context that it adopted the New Partnership for Africa's Development (NEPAD) which the Group of Eight (G8) countries pledged to support at their meeting in Kananaskis, Canada, in June 2002.[17] NEPAD has however not illustrated any tangible and concrete outcomes in terms of contributing to human protection, in the context of the 3-Pillar R2P implementation framework.

The AU's Normative Approach to Civil Society Outreach

In line with Pillar Two of the R2P implementation framework, the Constitutive Act of the African Union states that one of the objectives of the Union is 'to build a partnership between governments and all segments of civil society' and to promote the 'participation of the African peoples in the activities of the Union'.[18] The AU has, from the outset, therefore articulated a normative commitment to engaging with civil society in the implementation of its objectives.[19] The Statutes of the AU Economic Social and Cultural Council (ECOSOCC) describe civil society as including social, professional groups, Non-Governmental Organisations (NGOs), Community-Based Organisations (CBOs), as well as voluntary and cultural organisations.

Despite the AU's stated commitment to civil society outreach and engagement the experience of African and international civil society organisations in engaging with the AU has been mixed.[20] Those civil society organisations that have experience with the continental body are able to regularly engage the AU. Some African and international NGO's have even taken the conscious decision to establish offices in Addis Ababa to engage with the AU directly, for

16 United Nations Conference on Trade and Development (UNCTAD), *Trade Performance and Commodity Dependence*,(Geneva: UNCTAD, 26 February 2004).

17 Nkhulu, Wiseman, *The New Partnership for Africa's Development: The Journey So Far* (Midrand: NEPAD Secretariat, June 2005).

18 African Union, *Constitutive Act of the African Union*, (Lome: African Union, 2000), preamble.

19 M. Muchie, A. Habib, and V. Panayachee, 'African Integration and Civil Society: The Case of the African Union', *Transformation: Critical Perspectives on Southern Africa*, Vol. 61, (2006), pp. 3–24.

20 African Union, *Economic Social and Cultural Council* (ECOSOCC), (Addis Ababa: African Union, 2002).

example the Oxfam International Liaison office to the AU. However, for civil society organisations not based in Addis Ababa, efforts to engage and interact with the AU have proven to be difficult and frustrating due to a lack of effective communication and coordination between them and the Union.[21] The African Citizens Directorate—the dedicated civil society unit within the Office of the Chairperson of the AU Commission—continues to strive to improve this outreach, albeit constrained by limited resources and personnel.

The AU's Engagement with Regional Economic Communities on Norm Promotion

According to the AU Constitutive Act, regional economic communities (RECs) are the building blocks of the Union. The AU recognises RECs such as the Economic Community of West African States (ECOWAS), the Intergovernmental Authority on Development (IGAD), the Southern African Development Community (SADC), the Economic Community of Central African States (ECASS), the East African Community (EAC), the Common Market of East and Southern Africa (COMESA) and the Arab Maghreb Union (AMU). In line with Pillar Two of the R2P implementation framework, the AU is supposed to leverage the regional capacity and relative local legitimacy of these RECs to enhance peace and security and also coordinate development initiatives.

To reinforce this provision the AU is working for the establishment of an African Standby Force (ASF) to cooperate where appropriate with the United Nations and sub-regional African organisations in conducting peace operations. In effect, the AU will continue to maintain a working relationship with the United Nations and other international organisations, namely the ECOWAS, IGAD, SADC, ECASS and AMU.

An African Standby Force is to be established comprised of five brigades from each of Africa's sub-regions, Southern, East, Central, West and North, which will effectively project the responsibility to react. The challenge has been that both the AU and the RECs have not yet operationalised effective communication channels and coordination platforms for norm building and promotion. There are ongoing efforts to remedy this situation through the institutionalisation of regular meetings between the heads of the organisations as well as regular exchanges and joint workplans at the level of technical

21 African Union, *Agenda 2063: The Africa we Want* (Addis Ababa: AU, February 2015), http://agenda2063.au.int/en/sites/default/files/agenda2063_popular_version_05092014_EN.pdf, accessed 1 June 2015, p. 24.

experts. The AU's normative responsibility to rebuild is currently being pursued through its Post-Conflict and Reconstruction Framework.

Currently, the AU is implicated in operationalising these norms with AU personnel supporting its peace operations in Somalia, through the African Union Mission in Somalia (AMISOM), launched in 2007; in Mali, through the African-led International Stabilization Mission in Mali (AFSIMA) launched in 2013 and subsequently transformed into the United National Multidimensional Integrated Stabilization Mission in Mali (MINUSMA); in the DRC through the African Intervention Brigade launched in 2014; the AU Electoral and Security Assistance Mission to the Comoros (AU-MAES), launched in 2008; and its contribution to the Joint AU-UN Hybrid Mission in Darfur (UNAMID), launched in 2007, taking over from the AU Mission in Sudan (AMIS). In addition, the Union personnel contributed towards stabilising the situation in Burundi, through the AU Mission in Burundi (AMIB) from 2003 to 2004.

The AU-UN Partnership on Human Protection

The United Nations (UN) was established with the noble objective of bringing about peace, security and development. Since its inception the organisation has had a relationship with Africa which has vacillated between paternalism and partnership. When the UN was established in 1945, very few African countries were independent members of the body. Therefore, in these early decades of the UN, African countries were effectively preached to rather than consulted as equals. At the inception of the UN there were only four African countries present as fully sovereign entities; Egypt, Ethiopia, Liberia and South Africa. South Africa was operating under the system of apartheid, internal colonialism, and institutionalised racism in favour of descendants of European heritage. So its status as an 'independent' African country can be disputed. This lack of adequate African representation at the creation of the UN meant that issues which typically would have been in the interests of African countries were not necessarily emphasised. As a result of this inadequate representation, at the outset, African voices were not sufficiently heard in the formulation of peace, security and development of policies at the UN. In fact, African countries, most of which were still under the yoke of colonialism were in fact still being treated in a paternalistic fashion by their former colonial powers who constitute, and continue to form, the axis-of-power in the UN. These paternalistic attitudes did not change significantly in the 1950s and the 1960s. From the late 1950's the UN's Special Political Committee presided over the decolonisation of African countries. Africa's insufficient representation in the first few decades of the UN set the tone for the interaction between the body and Africa. The newly independent African states had to effectively hit the ground running as far as catching up with the 'diplomatic game' that was playing itself out at the UN. The diplomatic 'rules of engagement', so to speak, had already been determined before the African countries joined the organisation. The effect of not having played a role in determining procedural issues means that the organisation adopted a posture of pushing through agendas, dictating and pronouncing on issues that related to Africa. This was done without adequate consultation or due diligence of the ramifications and consequences of such a top-down approach to dealing with Africa. This is especially true of the Security Council, where the Permanent Five (P5) can, and still do, prevent resolutions that are important to Africa particularly on issues of human protection, as was witnessed in the case with the genocide in Rwanda.

Paternalism can best be characterised as a top-down unidirectional relationship where one party establishes the framework and issues strictures for the development of a second party. Partnership on the other hand involves a mutually enriching relationship based on respect, collaboration established through dialogue. Given the asymmetrical relationship that the UN had with Africa, particularly in the early years, a culture of paternalism developed between the organisation and the continent. Since then Africa has been trying to challenge and dispense with paternalistic attitudes from, and within, the UN system. Today, Africa is attempting to forge an identity as a collective entity capable of functioning as an equal partner in the international sphere particularly on the issue of human protection. Close to fifteen years after the launch of the African Union (AU) it is appropriate to interrogate the relationship between Africa and the UN. One view is that we are witnessing the emergence of a UN-AU partnership particularly in human protection interventions.[22] As will be elaborated below, the AU's role in stabilising the situation in Burundi prior to the establishment of a UN peace operation to achieve human protection remains a key model of collaboration. In line with Pillar Two of the R2P implementation framework, the establishment of joint human protection interventions in the Darfur region of Sudan, has illustrated initiatives by the UN to forge a 'hybrid partnership' with Africa. This involved the establishment of a hybrid UN-AU force to stabilise the situation in the region.

22 Boutros Boutros-Ghali, *An Agenda for Peace: Preventive Diplomacy, Peacemaking and Peacekeeping*, (New York: United Nations, 1992).

AU and UN Human Protection in Burundi

Following decades of political tension and sporadic civil war, in 2003, the African Union Mission in Burundi (AMIB) was the AU's first peace and human protection operation wholly initiated, planned and executed by its members. In this regard, it represents a milestone for the AU in terms of self-reliance in operationalising and implementing a peace operation. AMIB was mandated to stabilise a fluid and dynamic situation in which the country could relapse back into violent conflict. In April 2003, the AU deployed AMIB with more than 3,000 troops from South Africa, Ethiopia, and Mozambique to monitor the peace process and provide security.[23] The AU appointed Mamadou Bah as its Special Representative to Burundi to oversee this peace operation. One of the tasks of the AU force was to protect returning politicians who would take part in the transitional government, which has subsequently become articulated in Pillar One of the R2P implementation framework. Other tasks included opening secure demobilisation centres and facilitating the reintegration former militia back into society. These centres supervised the demobilisation, disarmament and reintegration (DDR) process. AMIB was also involved in creating conditions that would allow Internally Displaced Persons (IDPs) and refugees, based in the eight Burundian provinces and three refugee camps in Tanzania, to return to their homes. Overall, AMIB had the task of establishing conditions to enable human protection, which would allow for a UN peace operation to come into the country. The UN was reluctant to enter into a situation in which there was the potential for a relapse into conflict. AMIB's role in this case was a vital and crucial one in creating conditions through which human protection could be pursued. In the absence of the AU Mission, Burundi would have been left to its own devices which probably would have led to an escalation of violent conflict and the outbreak of mass atrocities. AMIB was therefore engaging in preventing potential mass atrocity through violent conflict prevention and trying to lay the foundations for reconciliation and reconstruction.

Throughout its period of operation AMIB succeeded in de-escalating a potentially volatile situation and establishing conditions in which further human protection initiatives could be further developed. In February 2004 a UN evaluation team concluded that the conditions we appropriate to establish a UN peacekeeping operation in the country. Following the UN Security Council Resolution 1545, of 21 May 2004, to deploy a peacekeeping mission in Burundi, Kofi Annan, the UN Secretary-General appointed a Special Representative, Ambassador Berhanu Dinka, to head the mission on 1 June 2004. The former

23 Timothy Murithi, *The African Union: Pan-Africanism, Peacebuilding and Development* (Aldershot, England: Ashgate Publishing Ltd., 2005), pp. 91–95.

AMIB troops belonging to the African Union were incorporated into the UN Peace Operation in Burundi (ONUB). As of November 2006 some 20,000 military personnel have been demobilised, but many still lack economic opportunities and could pose a potential security threat.[24] Therefore, despite these initiatives, the constitutional crisis in Burundi in 2015, which precipitated political tension and violence suggests that it is too early to conclude whether the human protection foundations that were laid by both AMIB and ONUB will be sustained. Even though the UN took over from the AU, the case of Burundi demonstrates that the continental body can in fact make useful human protection interventions around the continent and does deserve to be treated with a modicum of respect. The AU's contribution to these developments is often forgotten and needs to be highlighted. As stipulated in Pillar Two of the R2P implementation framework, this AU-UN collaboration suggests that such a model might provide insights as to how both organisations might build upon their relationship in the future.

Joint AU-UN Human Protection Interventions in Darfur

The AU's fledgling institutions lack adequately trained personnel and the financial wherewithal to underwrite all the initiatives that it adopts. This has been exposed in the complex humanitarian situation in the Darfur region of Sudan, where the AU has faltered in delivering security to Darfurians. Ironically, as the tension and violence in Darfur unfolded in 2003, a lot of pressure was placed on the AU to do something to address the issue of human protection and resolve the dispute, with the proviso that the international community would follow-up with the political, diplomatic and financial support to enable it to successfully undertake the mission. Whether rightly or wrongly, the AU took the initiative and initially brokered the Humanitarian Ceasefire Agreement in N'djamena, Chad, on 8 April 2004, with the express objective of laying the foundations for human protection. The African Union Mission in Sudan (AMIS) deployed troops to oversee this ceasefire. More than a decade later it is clear that the AU force on the ground, of about 7,000 troops, had a weak mandate to effectively monitor the humanitarian crisis in the region and coordinate efforts to advance the cause of human protection, which remains elusive. This issue raises the question as to whether African leaders are genuinely serious about living up to the principles which they signed in the Constitutive Act of the AU and subsequently reiterated in the

24 Centre for Conflict Resolution (CCR) / Friedrich Ebert Stiftung (FES) seminar report on *African Perspectives on the UN Peacebuilding Commission*, Maputo, Mozambique, 3–4 August 2006, http://ccrweb.uct.ac.za.

R2P implementation framework. The Sudanese government, which is a co-signatory to the Act, could halt the atrocities being committed in Darfur if it genuinely wanted to do so, and alleviate the pressure placed on the AU to resolve this issue. The international support for the Khartoum government, notably from China, has complicated efforts to resolve this issue and perpetuated a situation that Gerald Prunier has described as the 'ambiguous genocide'.[25]

A Hybrid Partnership for Human Protection

UN Security Council Resolution 1706 requested 'the Secretary-General to take the necessary steps to strengthen AMIS through the use of existing and additional United Nations resources with a view to transition to a United Nations operation in Darfur.'[26] This led to the emergence of a 'hybrid UN-AU force' or a 'hybrid partnership' with the AU particularly on peacekeeping and human protection, and with reference to Sudan in particular. There are efforts to re-assure observers that this is not an effort to re-establish the asymmetrical relationship which prevailed in the early decades of the UN, but rather an effort to create something new – a hybrid partnership. The UN Department of Peacekeeping Operations (DPKO) is supporting AMIS through its UN Assistance Cell in Addis Ababa, Ethiopia, the AU headquarters. More specifically, DPKO and the AU's Peace Support Operations Division have signed an agreement to develop a joint action plan. In July 2006, the UN created a dedicated integrated capacity to oversee the implementation of this action plan. This integrated capacity will involve the 'collocation' of UN staff within the AU Commission in Addis Ababa. This innovative approach of embedding UN staff within the operational structures of a regional organisation represents a completely new form of partnership or a hybrid partnership. There is an emphasis on the fact that this is not an asymmetrical partnership, but an entirely new arrangement established through the mutual consent of both parties. Chapter VIII of the UN Charter is not explicit on the possibility of establishing such a hybrid partnership, therefore there is significant leeway to operationalise such a relationship if both the UN and the regional organisation are compliant. Article 52 in fact states that 'the Security Council shall encourage the development of pacific settlement of local disputes through such regional arrangements or by such regional agencies either on the initiative of the states concerned or by reference from the Security Council'. Therefore the legal basis for embedding UN staff within the AU, can be made.

---

25 Gerald Prunier, *Darfur: The Ambiguous Genocide* (Ithaca: Cornell University Press, 2005).

26 United Nations Security Council, Resolution 1706(2006), S/RES/1706(2006), 31 August 2006, paragraph 11.

Constraints and Limitations of the Joint UN-AU Partnership for Human Protection

Even though the nature of the UN-AU partnership on human protection is evolving, it is important to interrogate what this new relationship represents. Is the hybrid partnership in effect a hybrid form of paternalism - where AU troops and personnel do the basic and dangerous work on the ground in terms of human protection, guided by the all-wise and 'fatherly' coterie of UN advisors? Does this evolution in the UN-AU partnership for human protection represent a paradigm shift in relations between the AU and UN, or is it a case of old wine in new wine bottles? Certainly, it still remains an asymmetric relationship due to the fact that the UN is a much older institution, with more resources and experience compared to the AU. Therefore, in this relationship the advice and resources are more likely to be unidirectional – flowing from the UN to the AU. Naturally, as the regional organisation the AU has an important role to play in orienting efforts in a way that respects local sensibilities. However, it is not clear the extent to which it can declare total ownership of the conceptualisation, design, planning and implementation of its human protection interventions, when 'collocated' UN personnel maintain a dominant presence in its affairs. It is too early to pass definitive judgement on this emerging hybrid partnership. The AU has to remain vigilant to ensure that it does not descend into a form of hybrid paternalism. In particular, the AU should guard against allowing the UN's historical paternalism to re-manifest under a new guise, with UN brawn being used to direct African bodies on the ground.

Ultimately, African countries constitute a significant subset of the UN membership and the relationship should be based on a reciprocal respect, if the UN is to succeed in achieving the noble objectives which it set for itself at its inception. Given the confluence of mandates that the UN and the AU share on human protection, there is no question that there needs to be greater policy coherence and partnership between the two bodies. The bulk, more than 60 percent of the UN's peace, security and human protection issues, are focused on Africa, which suggests that it is vital to establish a genuine partnership based on equal respect, reciprocity and dialogue. African countries have an important role to play in the UN. Other countries and regional groupings recognise that they need to coordinate with the Africa Group and the AU to get support on substantive issues because of the number of votes that Africa can deliver, when it acts in unison. However, African countries have demonstrated that they can be divided by their own parochial interests as well as by coercion or co-optation by other more powerful actors. In the interests of achieving human protection it is important for African countries to maintain sufficient discipline so that they can act as a unified block at the UN. It is the only way that the AU can dispense with any paternalism towards Africa, which still lingers in the UN system.

The AU's Normative Dissonance with the International Actors

In the pursuit of its peace and security interventions the AU has not always seen eye-to-eye with the UN, the International Criminal Court (ICC) or the North Atlantic Treaty Organization (NATO). The UN Security Council's referral of the President of Sudan, Omar Al Bashir, to the ICC for alleged war crimes, crimes against humanity and genocide in the Darfur conflict in 2009, precipitated a tense stand-off between the AU and the ICC which is yet to be resolved amicably. This was subsequently exacerbated by the ICC summons and cases relating to the President of Kenya, Uhuru Kenyatta, and his Deputy President, William Ruto. Furthermore, NATO's intervention in Libya and the toppling of Muammar Gaddafi, through regime change, raised the spectre of an encroaching Western interventionism in Africa which has generated feverish debate among the AU's member states and placed the Union on the defensive. R2P is not just a recipe for 'military adventurism'; it should be the blueprint for securing Africa's future and the stability and prosperity of the continents citizens. The relationship between the AU, UN, ICC and NATO has to be transformed over the next ten years if effective peace and security systems are to be operationalised on the African continent.

The Limits of Norm Promotion in Africa

Those who are discontent with the AU acknowledge the formal existence of unity, but question the genuine Pan-African normative commitment of nation-states and African citizens. This critique is valid for several reasons. While the political and business elite, as well civil society actors, who work across borders are often supportive of Pan-African interaction and solidarity, the vast majority of citizens across the continent do not know that the AU exists. For this silent majority, Pan-Africanism is not yet a lived experience. Stringent visa restrictions, for example, remain in place, making a mockery of the notion of African unity as citizens from African countries are deported from fellow African countries. Among the positive aspects of the creation of the AU is its interventionist stance at the level of policy. The AU has embraced a policy of non-indifference to the suffering of African peoples. This is in stark contrast with the OAU's unspoken norm of 'non-intervention'. Another positive aspect is the AU's commitment to play a role in promoting peace across the continent and supporting the efforts of other inter-governmental organisations like the UN and the RECs.

While the AU is good at designing and proposing policy it still faces significant challenges in terms of its implementation due to a lack of political will. In terms of its limitations not all of Africa's heads of state and government are taking the African Union seriously. The norms and values that they have signed up to should be enough to encourage them to change behaviour. However, many leaders are behaving as though the AU does not exist. They continue to commit human rights atrocities, which form the basis for conflict escalation, with impunity. The AU has also faced criticism for being lethargic and slow in its response particularly to crisis and conflict situations across the continent.[27] This is due to the administrative bottlenecks which constrain the emergence of a culture of professionalism and efficiency particularly within the AU Commission. These administrative challenges also undermine the morale of AU staff in its various offices around the continent and it ultimately affects the AU's ability to effectively engage its member states, African citizens and partners. With Nkosazana Dlamini-Zuma's leadership as Chairperson of the AU Commission, from July 2012, it remains to be seen whether this change of regime at the AU marks a new departure for continental organisation. More than half-way through her first term, it remains to be seen whether Dlamini-Zuma will manage to lead the AU Commission out of its lethargic posture in terms of implementing its many important norms, treaties and protocols and upholding the 3-Pillar R2P implementation framework.

Global Politics and the Irresponsible Abuse of R2P

Some countries have misappropriated the term R2P and used it to justify the military confrontation with non-state actors. Some have gone as far as use R2P to justify the invasion and occupation of other countries. Specifically, in October 2002, George Bush is famously known to have deployed the rhetoric of R2P when the US and its coalition of the coerced states, in the lead up to the illegal war of aggression against Iraq, needed a convenient rationale by stating that 'there is no refuge from our responsibilities ... we will meet the responsibility

27 Sadiki Koko and Martha Bakwesegha-Osula, 'Assessing the African Union's Response to the Libyan Crisis', *Conflict Trends*, Issue 1 (2012), pp. 3–15.

of defending human liberty against violence and aggression.'[28] The subsequent invasion in 2003 only increased the number of human rights abuses and made Iraq's civilians more vulnerable. Kofi Annan, the former Secretary-General of the UN stated that he considered the US-led invasion to have been an illegal war waged under false pretences.[29] Currently, the legacy of the US-led invasion in Iraq has generated a quagmire of catastrophic proportions with the rampant violence that has been unleashed by a motley crew of fragmented militia forces, including the Islamic State in Iraq and Syria (ISIS), which has declared itsself a caliphate. When UN Member States signed up to the 2005 World Summit Outcome Document which legitimised R2P as an international doctrine, there was no inclination that it could be abused to in effect undermine human protection, which is the situation that currently prevails in Iraq.

Key Recommendations on Enhancing Human Protection

In order to avoid R2P becoming delegitimised and discredited as a norm for human protection, the international system needs to be transformed in order to prevent the propensity towards military adventurism, regime change, bringing or exporting freedom and democracy by force. This might require dismantling the United Nations Security Council, and replacing it with an institution that more adequately reflects the shifting balance of political and economic power in the 21st century. In effect, vigilance reinforced by institutional transformation is required in ensuring that the initial norms that animated the operationalisation of R2P are maintained.

Awareness raising on the importance of R2P to human protection should be achieved through policy development seminars, and civic education programmes at primary, secondary and tertiary levels. On this basis, it is vital to raise the global awareness of R2P. Citizens often feel powerless or disempowered in the face of repression, and therefore an awareness of the existence of R2P as a doctrine that speaks directly to their plight is necessary.

Concretely, in terms of key recommendations the AU needs to focus more effectively on norm implementation, in partnership with regional organisations, the UN and other international actors. This can be achieved by monitoring and evaluating where the challenges and obstacles to human protection are emanating from.

---

28 George W. Bush, 'Transcript: George Bush's Speech on Iraq', delivered in Cincinnati, 7 October 2002.

29 Kofi Annan, *Interventions: A Life in War and Peace* (London: Penguin, 2013), p. 364.

Conclusion

The AU remains, at its core, a disparate collection of nation-states who recognise the value of normative collective action and solidarity on a range of regional and international issues. In line with the 3-Pillar R2P implementation framework, the AU has the primary responsibility for establishing and operationalising the continent's peace and security architecture, and as such it has become the leading norm entrepreneur on issues pertaining to peace, human rights and civilian protection, security, democracy and development on the continent. However, this role is tempered by the fundamental primary character that continues to define the constituents of the Westphalian system, namely the self-interest of nation-states and the persistence of political realism in their day-to-day interactions. Almost fifteen years after its establishment, the AU is only beginning to assert its voice in the international system. Even though the AU is not always taken seriously by its interlocutors and the powerful countries in the global north, it is laying the foundation to empower its member states to play a more proactive role in international relations.

Ultimately, it is possible to make the case that the AU is committed to the R2P and human protection norms. The AU has taken an interventionist and active stance with regards to situations in Mali, CAR, Burundi, Darfur and Somalia and is actively involved in supporting other peace operations around the continent. Even though it has made a significant effort to conduct peace operations, the AU is far from operationalising an effective R2P regime. For example, the limitations of its fledgling institutions has been exposed in the complex humanitarian situation in the Darfur region of Sudan. Ultimately, it is too early to pass a definitive judgement on the AU's commitment to R2P and human protection since the paradigmatic shift in attitudes that the AU is attempting to bring about, and the institutions that it has developed to do so, have to be given an opportunity to work. The AU will need to seriously reorient the political leadership of the continent and take decisive and necessary action, without which the challenges of ensuring the implementation of R2P will not be achieved.

The ideals of Pan-Africanism and the objectives of the African Union as a normative framework for peace and security will only be achieved if there is the genuine political will to do so. More crucially they will only succeed if the ordinary people are empowered to contribute to this process. An uninformed population is easy to manipulate so a key strategy has to be to build the capacity of Africans to know how to address the challenges that confront them. This is the challenge of education, skills training on peace and security and raising awareness about the norms such as R2P, through Pan-African and international partnerships. These partnerships and exchanges could range from collaboration with other universities and educational institutions in Africa, collaboration with governments and civil society on peace and civic education, development management and so on.

The AU has emerged as a home-grown initiative to effectively take the destiny of the continent into the hands of the African people. However, there is a long way to go before the AU's role as a norm entrepreneur is actualised and its vision and mission realised. The injunction that the great Pan-Africanist Kwame Nkrumah bequeathed to subsequent generations continues to animate the AU and is still valid: 'Africa must Unite, or disintegrate individually'.[30]

---

30 Kwame Nkrumah, *Africa Must Unite* (London: Panaf, 1963), p. 4.

The Role of CSOs in Promoting Human Rights Protection, Mass Atrocities Prevention, and Civilian Protection in Armed Conflicts

Chukwuemeka B. Eze
West Africa Network for Peacebuilding (WANEP)
ceze@wanep.org

Abstract

The West Africa region is arguably the most turbulent region in Africa; from the civil wars of Liberia and Sierra Leone to the political disputes in Cote d'Ivoire, Guinea, Guinea Bissau and recently Mali; the region has hosted the highest numbers of the United Nations (UN) peacekeeping missions with mixed results. While the responsibility of peace, security and ensuring human protection resides with governments, Civil Society Organizations (CSOs) have demonstrated their capacity to complement government's efforts in peace and security; and political leadership across the world has come to realise the strength of CSOs in anticipating, preventing and resolving conflicts because of their in-depth knowledge of context and expertise in working closely with communities. This paper assesses the contributions of CSOs towards the promotion of human rights protection, mass atrocities prevention and civilian protection in conflict-affected areas in West Africa; and argues for continued involvement of CSOs in human protection.

Keywords

CSOs – conflict prevention – human rights – mass atrocities – partnerships and R2P

Within the last two decades, the Economic Community of West African States Commission and its member states have grappled with measures to ensure human protection occasioned by plethora of violent conflicts, which have sapped enormous energy and resources, meant for economic development and regional integration. Member States of the ECOWAS have come to the realisation that economic prosperity, cooperation and integration can only be achieved

 | DOI:10.1163/9789004363212_011

in an environment that is peaceful, stable and secure.[1] In other words, peace and security are prerequisites for sustainable economic development and human security advancement in the short term, whereas in the long term human-centred economic development that will eradicate extreme poverty is a pre-requisite for durable peace.

The protracted secessionist conflict in the Casamance region of Southern Senegal from 1982 to date, the prolonged civil wars in Liberia (1989–2003) and Sierra Leone (1990–2001), the armed violence and political instability in Guinea Bissau (1997–1998, 2004–2005 and currently), the armed rebellion in Cote d'Ivoire (2002–2006 and 2011 to 2012), the militant unrest in Nigeria especially in the Niger Delta and Jos, as well as the recent cases of violent extremism by members of the Islamic sect, Boko Haram, have catapulted CSOs in West Africa into the field of conflict resolution and peacebuilding to transform armed and destructive conflicts in order to support state efforts towards the protection of citizens from mass atrocities. The region has hosted the highest numbers of the United Nations peacekeeping missions with the mixed results of civilian casualties, human rights abuses and all forms of atrocities.

The 2014 UNDP Human Development Report, recognizes the current context of peace and security in West Africa as interwoven and complex especially as the region comprises of the poorest countries in the world with a large population living below the poverty line.[2] The economic potential of the region is undermined by instability and violent conflict. The region is still grappling with the devastating effects of these conflicts aforementioned coupled and further complicated by insecure borders, socio-economic problems, youth unemployment, systematic ethnic discrimination/exclusion, non-respect for human rights, and disputes over political participation, land and other natural resource allocation.

In addition to these, violent extremism has become manifest and spreading since the crisis that engulfed Libya in 2011 leading to the end of the Gadhafi regime. The violent implosion in Libya accelerated the proliferation of weapons with trained and well-equipped but illegally armed Tuareg rebels overrunning

1 Cheick Oumar Diarra, 'ECOWAS Protocol relating to the Mechanism on Conflict Prevention', Paper delivered at a Consultative Meeting organised on Human Security Mechanism for EAC and GIL, Nairobi, 24–28 February 2002.

2 United Nations Development Programme (UNDP), 'Human Development Report', 24 July 2014, http://hdr.undp.org/sites/default/files/hdr14-report-en-1.pdf, accessed 8 March 2016.

the northern half of Mali in early 2012.[3] Preceding these events, Boko Haram was already pillaging the northeastern region of Nigeria since 2009. The armed insurgency of the Tuareg rebels exposed the security vulnerability of the Sahelian region of West Africa. Extremist jihadists immediately exploited the security vacuum that was created, recruiting vulnerable youths, mostly the unemployed and former combatants. The attempts by these extremist insurgent groups to expand southwards and take hold of the whole of Mali with clear intentions to spread across the entire Sahel belt from the west in Mauritania and link up with Al Shabaab in the Horn of Africa exposed the real security nightmare and emerging threat confronting West Africa.[4]

Interconnected with the spread of violent extremism is the increase trade and trafficking of illicit drugs and money laundering. Across the region, the impact of climate change and the management and exploitation of natural resources is adding a strain to the peace and security environment of the region and on a daily basis raising questions about the capacities of the states in the region to protect their citizens against mass atrocities.

Democratic transitions remain a challenge to peace and stability across West Africa. It is estimated that more than 10,000 of its citizens have lost their lives in political crises in the last decade. Elections have been marred by spates of violence, with electoral periods often occasioning great fear for life and property among the populace. Regrettably, a few leaders as seen in Burkina Faso in 2014 still nurtured the possibility of long-term rule even if that means manipulating and influencing constitutional changes to extend their stay in power beyond the limited term mandates in constitutions.[5] Such practice is exacerbating the crisis of political stability, undermining good governance and breeding extremist groups.

To this end, ECOWAS has driven a paradigm shift from unilateral and state-centric action, to a multi-stakeholders participation of civil society. The role of CSOs in promoting human protection in conflict areas has become increasingly important as ECOWAS and governments in the sub region seek integrative approaches to address insecurity and instability under its vision 2020 – transitioning from ECOWAS of the states to ECOWAS of the people. The policy

3 Unpublished report on Countering Violent Extremism, Workshop organised by WANEP, Accra, Ghana May 2015.

4 Report on Workshop to Develop Early Warning Indicators to Monitor Violent Extremism in West Africa, Lagos - Nigeria, 21–23 October 2014.

5 West Africa Network for Peacebuilding, 'Transitions and Tensions in West Africa: Building on the Strength and Bridging the Gap in the ECOWAS Protocol on Democracy and Good Governance', *WANEP Policy Brief*, November 2014.

framework undergirding the operationalisation of the Responsibility to Protect (R2P), namely the protection responsibilities of the state, international assistance and capacity building to help states fulfil their national obligations and, thirdly, the commitment to timely and decisive collective action to cases of manifest failure in ways that are consistent with the UN charter all resonate very well with the regional experiences of ECOWAS.

For the purpose of this chapter, 'human protection refers to protection of civilians from human rights abuses, inside and outside of armed conflicts, with a particular focus on mass atrocity crimes – genocide, war crimes, crimes against humanity and ethnic cleansing.'[6] Against this background, this chapter attempts to provide insights on the role of CSOs in promoting human protection in West Africa in collaboration with ECOWAS and other state actors, the imperatives of collaboration for peace and security in a region enmeshed in violent conflicts, as well to proffer options for collaborative actions and engagement. Hence, this chapter contributes to the special issue of regional approaches to human protection by highlighting the role of CSOs via early warning systems that can enhance sub-regional frameworks to promote human protection.

The chapter is organised into four sections. Section one provides insights on the evolution of the ECOWAS Conflict Prevention Architecture, informed by the violent conflicts that plagued the region and the imperatives for R2P. Section two is on the operationalisation of ECOWAS' Early Warning System for Conflict Prevention. Section three highlights the role of the West Africa Network for Peacebuilding (WANEP) in the operationalisation and sustenance of the ECOWAS Early Warning and Response Mechanism (ECOWARN). Section four presents the challenges encountered by CSOs in the promotion of human protection as well as proffers strategic recommendations with a view to enhancing the role of CSOs in human protection. The chapter concludes by presenting key contributions of CSOs to the protection of civilian populations.

Evolution of the ECOWAS Conflict Prevention Architecture and the Imperatives for R2P

The ECOWAS mechanisms and protocols of 1978 on *Non-Aggression* and the 1981 protocol on *Mutual Assistance in Defence* aimed at defending national sovereignty and protecting member states from external aggression were found to be inadequate. There was therefore the need to develop a new legal framework,

6 See Charles T. Hunt, 'African Regionalism and Human Protection Norms: An Overview', in this volume.

the absence of which often caused disagreements among West African governments on how to intervene and manage crises in the sub-region. An important lesson for the sub-region was to prioritise conflict prevention in the same way as economic development and integration. This realisation provided the legal basis for the ECOWAS declaration of political principles of 1991 and the ECOWAS revised treaty of 1993. The ECOWAS protocol relating to the mechanism for Conflict Prevention, Management, Resolution, Peacekeeping and Security was signed in 1999. Following closely was the Supplementary Protocol on Democracy and Good Governance in 2001. Another important interrelated commitment was the declaration of a sub-regional approach to Peace and Security in 2003. Of significance to compliment these were the 2006 ECOWAS Convention on Small Arms and Light Weapons, their Ammunition and other related materials as well as the 2008 Conflict Prevention Framework.[7]

In December 1989, Liberia imploded into an internecine civil war marking the beginning of serious threats to peace and stability across West Africa. The Liberian civil war was vicious and prolonged (1989–1999), with a re-escalation in 2003. Sierra Leone was the next to implode with the most atrocious civil war of the sub-region from 1997 to 2000. From 1997 to 1999, both countries, close neighbours were engulfed in war.[8] In 1998 and again in 2003, Guinea Bissau was on the brink of total state collapse and since then continues to be a fragile state, experiencing a coup d'état in 2012. What started as an attempted coup d'état in Cote d'Ivoire in 2002 ended up as a rebellion. While fighting ended in 2004, the country remained divided between north and south and, despite an elaborate mediation process that was to culminate in a peaceful transition in 2008, violence and a semblance of an ethnic cleansing characterised the post-elections crisis, largely as a result of the refusal of the former President, Laurent Gbagbo, to step down from power after he lost the 28 November 2010 run-off elections.

In these armed conflicts, particularly in Liberia and Sierra Leone, the authority of Heads of State of ECOWAS deployed the ECOWAS Monitoring Group (ECOMOG) to intervene with military force and enforce peace. The ECOWAS interventions precipitated United Nations Peacekeeping interventions and the sub-region subsequently hosted three major Peacekeeping interventions.[9]

---

7 ECOWAS Protocols, http://www.ecowas.int/ecowas-law/find-legislation/, accessed 8 March 2016.

8 The Former President of Liberia, Charles Taylor, was sentenced to 50 years in prison in May 2012 by the Special Court for Sierra Leone for his role in atrocities committed during the civil war.

9 ECOWAS Monitoring Group (ECOMOG) Peacekeeping Missions in Guinea Bissau, Liberia and Sierra Leone.

West Africa's civil wars resulted in the weakening of the states directly consumed by the wars, while for the entire sub-region, the threats to regional peace and stability increased. Small and light weapons trafficking augmented dramatically due to the porous borders of the countries of the sub region while for the first time, children as young as eight years were recruited to fight in these wars. West African states caught in civil wars became vulnerable to the illicit trade in drugs and money laundering. In a very short period, West Africa became a major transit hub for drugs to Europe and North America. A sudden increase in human trafficking, refugees and internally displaced persons were all consequences of these wars. Another major consequence particularly for Liberia and Sierra Leone was the intensity of the wars around the control of natural resources such as diamonds and timber, which further exacerbated and fuelled the wars. By 2004, the UN human development report ranked 11 out of the 15 member states of ECOWAS in the category of the world's most poor countries - a trend that has continued with the 2014 report.[10]

In this setting of a West African political context in which armed and violent conflicts had become a direct threat to the overall vision of ECOWAS for sub-regional integration and enhancing development and promoting human security, a new political will emerged in 1999 via the Protocol Relating to the Mechanism for Conflict Prevention, Management, Resolution, Peacekeeping and Security, with a new sense of purpose for collective ownership of intervention in crises with an emphasis on prevention along the lines of the principles and three pillars of the responsibility to protect. The overall ECOWAS vision, which seeks to create an 'ECOWAS of Peoples - a borderless, prosperous and cohesive region where people have the capacity to access and harness its enormous resources through the creation of opportunities for sustainable development and environmental preservation',[11] could not be attained amidst political uncertainty, armed conflicts and the absence of a cohesive political framework to prevent conflicts. An emerging West African political will was informed by the challenges, experiences and lessons learnt from crisis intervention in the region. The principles of the R2P have been consciously harnessed in West Africa via the various ECOWAS normative frameworks as encapsulated in its Peace and Security Architecture. To this end, the conflict prevention mechanism of ECOWAS draws inspiration from the 2001 report of the UN Secretary General:

---

10 UNDP, 'Human Development Report'.

11 To reaffirm their commitment to improve the West Africa Integration process and enhance its effectiveness, the Authority of Heads of State and Government adopted a resolution in June 2007 and introduced the transformational ECOWAS Vision 2020.

> There is no higher goal, no deeper commitment and no greater ambition than preventing armed conflict. The prevention of conflict begins and ends with the promotion of human security and human development. Ensuring human Security is, in the broadest sense, the cardinal mission of the United Nations. Genuine and lasting prevention is the means to achieve that mission.[12]

The West African experience underscores the relevance of prevention to give meaning to the operationalisation of the responsibility to protect. Any intervention on the basis of the principles of the responsibility to protect that is reactive rather than preventive is bound to meet challenges in which new problems could be generated as a result of such reactive intervention. The North Atlantic Treaty Organization (NATO) intervention in Libya in 2011 provides a good example of a situation in which the African Union (AU) refrained from condemning the use of armed forces and weapons of the state disproportionately against the civilian population. The AU initiative to develop a road map for peace through a cessation of hostilities did not subsequently receive the support of the People's National Council based in Benghazi since they felt AU was not resolute with its stance during the crisis. On the other hand, there is an international concern by some member states of the United Nations as to whether NATO exceeded the terms of the mandate of Security Council Resolution 1973, which approved a no-fly zone over Libya authorising all necessary measures to protect civilians. The definition and application of 'all necessary measures' therefore became a subject of controversy in the protection of citizens, with each side of the divide defining it to suit their purpose and situation.

These on-going developments demonstrate very clearly that, although member states of the United Nations support the goals of the responsibility to protect, there is less support and unanimity on how to achieve its goals. Recent experiences of intervention such as in Cote d'Ivoire provide more than enough justification for a renewal of emphasis on preventive measures and on the ways to help states to meet their responsibility to protect obligations and responsibilities.

In the example of Cote d'Ivoire, ECOWAS was unambiguous in its intervention approach because what was needed was to refer to the relevant ECOWAS protocols and make decisions at the level of the Authority of Head of States and Governments. In this regard, the ECOWAS Extraordinary Session of the Authority of Heads of State and Government on Cote d'Ivoire of 7th December

12 Kofi Annan, 'Prevention of Armed Conflict', *Report of the Secretary General to the United Nations General Assembly*, A/55/985–S/2001/574, 7 June 2001.

2010 simply reaffirmed the ECOWAS commitment to the relevant provisions and principles of the ECOWAS Protocol on Democracy and Good Governance.[13] Though the decisions taken were an intervention in a post-election crisis, the guideline and legal basis for intervention had been earlier established in the relevant protocols minimising the ambiguity of approach to be taken. Whereas at the level of the African Union, at least two member states declared support for the incumbent President of Cote d'Ivoire at the time, such a scenario was not plausible at the ECOWAS level as member states were bound to the collective decisions of the Authority regardless of any remote affinity to the incumbent President who had refused to step down. In Cote d'Ivoire, despite the post-conflict reconstruction, there are still factors that raise concerns. For instance, the ex-rebels have not been brought to justice. While ECOWAS and indeed, WANEP, have a role to play in supporting countries in post-conflict era in reconciliation and justice, without the leadership of the UN and the international community, ECOWAS has, in some cases, been unable to take full control of responses to conflicts in the region. Although, this may fall outside the mandate of WANEP, it has implications for its work as a partner in executing conflict prevention and peacebuilding. In that, WANEP's work continues to be challenged as incomplete if violent conflicts persist.

The ECOWAS experience provides a useful lesson: that for the operationalisation of the responsibility to protect to be successful, a sub-regional response is required. In this regard, it has to be context specific and dependent on national and sub-regional ownership and capacities. International actors, including the UN system, should focus on strengthening such ownership, and be willing to let governments and regional economic communities in partnership with relevant CSOs take the lead in their own development process. Alongside the ECOWAS framework, many States have started the development of national architectures or infrastructures for peace. For instance, Ghana has an elaborate and well-respected National Peace Council, which is a state institution backed by an Act of Parliament with the mandate to provide dialogue and mediation services. During the contestation over the collation of results in the General Elections of 2008 and 2012, the National Peace Council with resource support from Civil Society facilitated an inter-party political dialogue that produced a very peaceful transition in which the winner of the Presidential elections won by a margin of only 0.46 %.[14]

---

13 ECOWAS, 'Final Communiqué of the Extraordinary Session of the Authority of Heads of State and Government on Cote d'Ivoire', Abuja, 7th December 2010.

14 Emmanuel Bombande, 'Building Peace through Inter-Party Political Dialogue and Strengthening the Democratic State: The Ghana Experience', WANEP, 2011.

Such institutional building of national capacities for political dialogue and peace is absolutely critical to the operationalisation of the responsibility to protect. Such institutional capacity building takes a long time and requires sustained commitment by the international community and the commitment of ECOWAS to such processes gave birth to the 2014 approval of the Authority of Heads of States and Government to the establishment of national early warning and response mechanisms for each of the member states. It is therefore important to move beyond the Centre at international level to focus on supporting local and regional governments. Building on national structures that already exist is more appropriate and adds more value than establishing entirely new structures at the national level on the responsibility to protect. The following section looks at the specific example of the ECOWAS Early Warning System (ECOWARN).

ECOWAS Early Warning System for Conflict Prevention

It is important to highlight that two of the protocols, the 1999 Protocol Relating to the Mechanism for Conflict Prevention, Management, Resolution, Peacekeeping and Security and 2001 Supplementary Protocol on Democracy and Good Governance, sought to address in a holistic manner the compelling nature, dynamics, and effects of conflicts in the sub region. While the 1999 protocol concentrated on how to deal with the immediate causes of conflicts, the 2001 protocol put the emphasis on addressing the structural causes of conflicts. They complimented one another and clearly set out the responsibilities of West African leaders to act collectively within the context of the legal obligations outlined in the protocols to protect populations whether citizens or non-residents in the member states of the sub-region from war crimes and crimes against humanity.[15]

The emphasis on prevention provided a focus on the ECOWAS Early Warning System under Chapter IV of the 1999 Mechanism on Conflict Prevention. The system comprises an Early Warning Directorate located in the ECOWAS Commission in Abuja with four Observation and Monitoring Zones. Established and now actively functioning with an interface and partnership with

15 These ECOWAS protocols have been elaborated in detail to cover all areas. Systematic violations of the basic rights and freedom of individuals or groups in a member state by either a regime or non-state actors with grave consequences and the potential of genocide and other crimes against humanity (Article 25d).

Civil Society Organisations,[16] the Early Warning System collects data and promotes the exchange of information on human security and collaboration among member states on early warning and response. The principles of timeliness, transparency, accessibility, cooperation and partnerships with other stakeholders undergird the operationalisation of ECOWARN. The reports generated provide qualitative and quantitative analysis informed by intuitive knowledge of the conflict terrain on the overall situation of the sub-region, country by country political, social and economic risks as well as thematic issues on a week-by-week basis.[17]

The partnership between WANEP and ECOWAS is embedded in normative and legal frameworks such as the 1993 Revised Treaty of ECOWAS, specifically Article 58, which provides for the establishment of a Peace and Security Architecture. These normative frameworks include the 1999 Protocol relating to the Mechanism for Conflict Prevention, Management, Resolution, Peacekeeping and Security, which establishes the framework for the setting up of a sub-regional peace and security observation system. The Early Warning System was definite in its provision for the role of CSOs within the peace architecture.[18]

The 2001 Supplementary Protocol on Democracy and Good Governance, the 2003 Declaration on a Sub-regional Approach to Peace and Security, which called for the operationalisation of the Early Warning Mechanism in view of growing intra-state conflicts, as well as the 2008 ECOWAS Conflict Prevention Frameworks, all gave credence to the partnership between ECOWAS and WANEP. The next section deals specially with the role of WANEP in the operationalisation of ECOWARN.

The West Africa Network for Peacebuilding (WANEP) is a leading regional peacebuilding organisation founded in 1998 in response to civil wars that plagued West Africa in the 1990s. Over the years, WANEP has succeeded in establishing strong national networks in every Member State of ECOWAS with over 500 member organisations across West Africa. WANEP places special focus on collaborative approaches to conflict prevention, and peacebuilding, working with diverse actors from civil society, governments, intergovernmental bodies, women groups and other partners in a bid to establish a platform for dialogue, experience sharing and learning, thereby complementing

16 The West Africa Network for Peacebuilding (WANEP) is lead agency and coordinates the Civil Society Interface for the collection and analysis of data in the operationalisation of ECOWARN.

17 The ECOWAS Early Warning and Response Mechanism (ECOWARN).

18 ECOWAS, 'Protocol Relating to the Mechanism of Conflict Prevention, Management, Resolution and Security, Lome, 10 December 1999, Chapter IV.

efforts at ensuring sustainable peace and development in West Africa and beyond.

At the continental level, WANEP is a member of the Peace and Security cluster of the African Union's (AU) Economic, Social and Cultural Council (ECOSOCC), representing West Africa. At international level, WANEP has a Special Consultative Status with the United Nations Economic and Social Council (ECOSOC) and is the West Africa Regional Representative of the Global Partnership for the Prevention of Armed Conflict (GPPAC). At these platforms, WANEP contributes to peace dialogues, and development agenda, and has become a key voice to advocate for the community at the regional and international levels. WANEP has also influenced peace and security policies and debates in an attempt to complement government efforts in ensuring state and human security and regional development.

In recent years, WANEP and its CSO member organisations have demonstrated their competence and dexterity in facilitating and negotiating peace in the region through the utilisation of early warning data. For instance, WANEP supported ECOWAS to broker peace deals in many West African countries as well as championed the ECOWAS policy on the establishment of peace education in West African schools, including developing resource materials to guide its implementation. Furthermore, WANEP helped in the design and establishment of a national architecture for peace through the Ghana National Peace Council and supported its election dispute agenda during its last elections in 2012. WANEP is also working with other ECOWAS member states, the UN, AU and ECOWAS to establish National Infrastructures for Peace in Benin, Cote d'Ivoire and Niger.

In this regard, WANEP recognises that the need for an effective multi-tiered, multi-national and multi-sectoral early warning platform that enhances human security, peace and development is critical to preventing violent conflicts and humanitarian crises. This appreciation is even more important in the context of globalisation and the need to prevent or mitigate the impact of violent conflicts on the socio-economic development of any nation. Central to this process is the need for adequate baseline information that captures the context specific causal factors and proximate conditions of conflicts to facilitate informed conflict prevention or mitigation interventions. To ensure the credibility and efficiency of this information, an organised platform for monitoring, reporting and analysis is key to strategic planning and response by relevant institutions and stakeholders in any given society or country.[19]

19 WANEP, 'National Early Warning Systems (NEWS) in West Africa', *WANEP Concept Paper*, July 2009.

The early warning system has been developed as a response to this challenge, providing for a broad participatory approach to conflict prevention and mitigation. Prevention and mitigation of destructive conflicts is the key objective of an effective early warning system. As countries and societies continually face new human security challenges and threats from conflicts, early warning and early response has gained wider appreciation and relevance as the core element for peace, security and long term social and economic development.[20]

Since 2000, WANEP has been committed to institutionalisation of the Early Warning system in West Africa through its program called WARN (West Africa Early Warning and Response Network). The role of civil society organisations in conflict prevention, management and transformation became increasingly important as member states sought integrated approaches to address insecurity and instability in the region. As a peacebuilding Network with over 500 members from grassroots to national levels WANEP has already recognised this importance and therefore developed the concept of 'proventive' Peacebuilding as a strategy for proactive response to destabilising conflicts through its WARN program.[21] Its emerging success and impact in this area through its Networks already established across West Africa positioned it as the obvious choice for partnership with ECOWAS.

Thus, in 2003, ECOWAS signed a Memorandum Of Understanding with WANEP to implement the ECOWAS Early Warning System otherwise referred as 'ECOWARN' to provide up to date reporting, analysis and communication to respective regional interveners in order to plan, prevent or mitigate the impact of violent conflicts in the sub-region.

ECOWARN is a regional initiative with the primary aim of monitoring incidents that are capable of inciting violence in West Africa via the collection and analysis of information. ECOWARN operates via an online database reporting system that is designed to capture data through a network of monitors. The monitors are representatives of governments in each of the member states and community-based monitors (CBM) managed by WANEP. In order to operationalise ECOWARN (see Figure 1), the region is divided into four zonal bureaus: Zone 1 (Cape Verde, Gambia, Guinea Bissau and Senegal with the headquarters in Banjul, Gambia); Zone 2 (Burkina Faso, Cote d'Ivoire, Mali and Niger with the capital in Ouagadougou, Burkina Faso); Zone 3 (Ghana, Guinea, Liberia and Sierra Leone with the headquarters in Monrovia, Liberia); and Zone 4 (Benin, Nigeria and Togo with the headquarters in Cotonou, Benin).

---

20 *ibid.*

21 *ibid.*

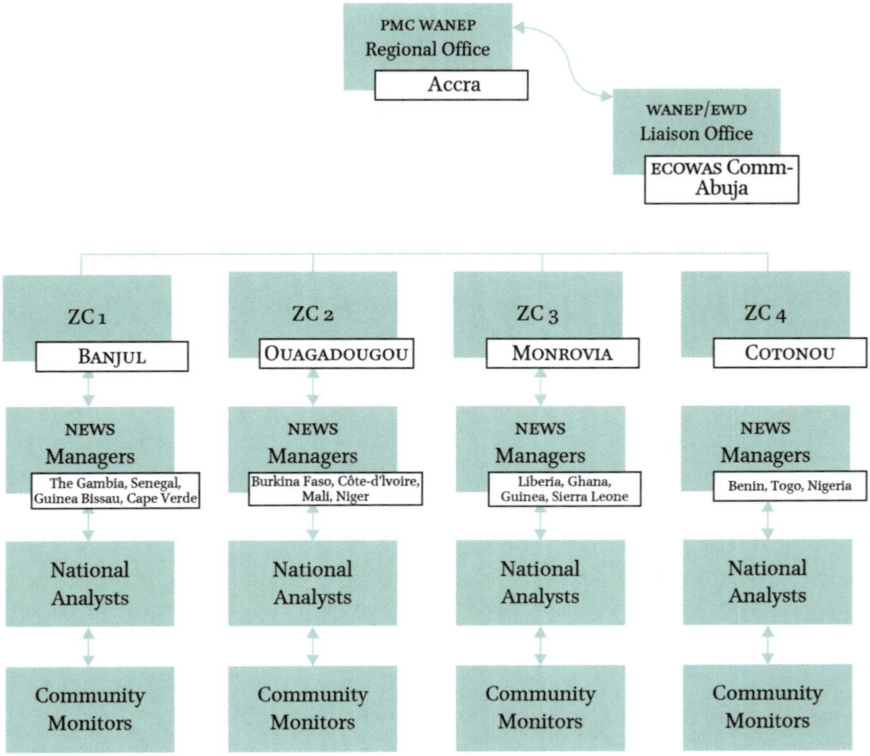

FIGURE 1 WANEP'S NEWS *Operating Structure in Support of* ECOWARN

The unique relationship between governments and civil society created through this partnership gave rise to the first platform that integrated the efforts of State and Non State Actors within a regional institution towards early reporting and response to proximate conditions in the sub region. ECOWARN has incrementally gained credibility and recognition through the pool of data, which is submitted into the system by reporters from WANEP National offices across the sub region as well as analysis provided by zonal coordinators in the four ECOWAS hubs of West Africa. Despite the giant strides already achieved in improving peace and security in the sub region, the system is still inhibited by the poor quality of the national platforms for Early Warning, which are critical to effective capture and input of the requisite data.

Though WANEP through its national networks already have local Peacebuilding organisations that constitute the core of the Network in each country, the lack of functional early warning systems at the national level limits the effectiveness of holistic data reported into the system and invariably the quality of analysis developed and utilised to formulate responses in the sub-region. In each country, a WANEP early warning reporter is burdened with the task of regular monitoring of entire regions and provinces in a country and therefore struggle to provide adequate coverage and report all issues within their country. This challenge has often been expressed by focal reporters. In realisation of this challenge, WANEP took steps to design and develop a National Early Warning System that captures the contextual issues in each of the ECOWAS member States that facilitates real time reporting and additional support for the focal point who feeds the relevant information into the ECOWARN system.

The novelty of the National Early Warning System (NEWS) is the improved reporting derived directly from emerging issues and proximate conditions from communities which are otherwise not reflected in media reports. It therefore provides focal points with a clearer understanding of the dimensions, trends, dynamics and connectors of conflicts in local communities towards a better national reporting of prevalent risk factors in each of the countries. The development and operations of the National Early Warning System has provided the mechanism for understanding and monitoring of local drivers of violent conflicts, especially as it relates to mass atrocities. The advantage of NEWS is that it is a step down from the broader ECOWARN system to the communities and forms a tripartite bridge for communication and response from the grassroots through to the national and up to the sub regional level.

The objectives of NEWS are to develop a pool of Conflict Monitors and Analysts across West Africa and link them to the ECOWAS Early Warning Mechanism at the various member states as well as the WANEP Peace Monitoring Centre in order to support the ECOWAS Commission's Situation Room at the Early Warning Directorate (EWD). It also seeks to build the capacity of civil society organisations to alert, mitigate, prevent and/or resolve violent conflicts at local levels and provide the state with the necessary support to do same.

Other objectives include consolidation of the institutional capacity of WANEP in conflict prevention and collaboration with other inter-governmental bodies such as the AU, UN (including the Office for the Coordination of Humanitarian Affairs (OCHA)), and other relevant partners to coordinate early warning and response efforts, as well as to foster collaborative relationships with/between civil society, think tanks, existing national, sub-regional/regional and international early warning, conflict prevention, and peacebuilding organisations. NEWS is also designed to share early warning reports, policy briefs, preventive instruments, mechanisms, tools, and strategies with partners, stakeholders, policy makers/actors, potential interveners, as well as promote pro-active/preemptive and integrated approaches to conflict prevention and peacebuilding.

Outputs of NEWS

Outputs of NEWS include *Weekly Highlights, Monthly Bulletin, Situation Tracking, Policy Brief* and *Annual Risk Index.* These publications are described in more detail below.

Weekly Highlights is a weekly report from the National Early Warning System that documents prioritised incidents critical to peace and security. It identifies and captures incidences that have further implications including threats to security or opportunities for peace across national networks of WANEP. The highlights are categorised under four basic thematic areas of Humanitarian, Political, Socio-economic and Environmental risks. It is generated from the incidence reports from data uploaded by early warning monitors. Additional information is derived from media reports and primary observation.

Monthly Bulletin publication presents a brief graphic analysis and description of highest proximate conditions emerging from its early warning reports. These reports are derived from the Network's online EW system, which facilitates the generation of data from monitors and reporters. The bulletin reflects data from incidence and situation reports of the EW system.

Policy Brief is a strong policy advocacy tool, which includes analyses of issues, identifies causes, accelerating and intervening factors, and envisages possible scenarios. The aim is to enhance the ability of decision makers to make strategic decisions on the basis of improved knowledge of the environment of operations, options available for response or action and finally, the implications of each decision or option made.

Situation Tracking tracks the government's and other actors' responses to conflicts or threats to human security in order to highlight the emerging issues and gaps in the response. It provides recommendations for better and more appropriate and effective intervention.

Annual Risk Index is comprised of data submitted into the NEWS platform for a period of one year which is interpreted with the help of a statistician into graphs and figures to clearly highlight the trends and progression of proximate condition of conflict and human security in the West Africa sub region. It also provides a comparative analysis of the situation in different ECOWAS member states with emphases on the underlying factors that make one state less prone to conflict and security threats.

The ECOWAS and WANEP partnership is arguably the first civil society and intergovernmental partnership not only in West Africa but Africa generally for the purposes of conceptualising, designing and operationalising a region-wide early warning network to collect and report human security threats. This culminated in the signing of a memorandum of understanding (MOU) with ECOWAS in 2003. Since then, the MOU have been consistently renewed and most recently for another 5 years, ending in 2019. Key issues in the MOU include mutual collaboration in the operationalisation of early warning systems (database of indicators for peace, conflict and human security in West Africa); joint trainings in data collection, collation and analyses; WANEP's establishment and maintenance of a functional Liaison Office at the Early Warning Department, EWD of the ECOWAS Commission; collaboration in production of strategic reports; and mutual exchange of technical support (views and studies) and joint mediation, research, analysis and other forms of intervention related to early warning and response. This experience of collaboration between WANEP and ECOWAS has been highlighted as the best practice of building alliances with CSOs in conflict prevention; and is a referral point currently being examined by other regional economic communities such as the Intergovernmental Authority on Development (IGAD).

Over the years, NEWS has proven to be viable, cost effective and real time and has continued to enhance information source, strength and potency of the ECOWARN system. In that way, a sub-regional system with various levels of response and impact is achieved for sustainable peace, security and development of the sub region. Therefore, the ultimate goal of ECOWARN and WARN is the development of an effective and efficient early warning and conflict management system that is capable of preventing and mitigating violent conflicts in West Africa.

The Dilemma and Challenges of CSOs

In practice, practitioners tend to sing their praises about the value and impact of their work, while academics and other researchers tend to magnify the shortcomings of CSOs. For example, in analysing the activities of CSO globally, Frerks noted eight sets of challenges that tend to undermine the value of the activities of CSOs especially in the field of peacebuilding, namely: i) the 'rotten apples' and the problem of staying impartial during or after conflict, ii) representation or the problem of the democratic deficit, iii) the issue of quality and the question of institutional strengthening and partnering, iv) the nature of peacebuilding, v) transparency and accountability, vi) measurability of impact, macro issues and power elites, vii) sustainability and viii) 'securitisation' of development.[22] In looking at the West African context of civil society's role

22 George Frerks, 'The Role of Civil Society in Peacebuilding' in Sol Iglesias (ed.), *The Role of Civil Society in Conflict Prevention and Peacebuilding* (Utrecht: European Centre for Conflict Prevention, 2006).

in conflict prevention, Ekiyor highlighted the many valuable contributions of West African CSOs yet zeroing on six areas of concerns: i) state-civil society relations, ii) narrow focus on NGOs, iii) weak and underfunded coordination mechanisms, iv) limited conflict prevention skills, v) lack of policy influence and vi) lack of documentation.[23]

It appears that the challenges and constraints of CSOs in conflict resolution and peacebuilding, especially in developing countries notably West African countries, are legion. The following sections argue that the causes are both endogenous and exogenous.

Endogenous Factors

In the 1990s, the civil wars in Liberia and Sierra Leone created complex political emergencies (CPE). The situation was characterised by gross human rights violations, violence against civilians and massive displacement of persons. CSOs in West Africa were largely ill-prepared to effectively and professionally address the emerging phenomenon of CPE, which presented national NGOs with new challenges and dilemmas regarding the effectiveness of the NGOs' work and their responsibility and mandate in terms of neutrality and addressing causes of violent conflict.

Weak coordination and collaboration among other CSOs often leads to duplication of efforts and lack of synergy for results. This is due to some extent the adversarial relationship between organisation over funding opportunities rather than collaboration for the collective promotion of human security and general tenets of responsibility to protect. The weak capacity and inadequate resources undermined the efforts of CSOs particularly CBOs to professionalise. International organisations had to source for funds, work and speak on behalf of CSOs in West Africa. Moreover, there was under-utilisation of Indigenous structures and institutions at both track I and track II levels as conflict resolution approaches. Because of these institutional weaknesses, CSOs are exposed to abuse and violent attacks. It renders the environment in which West African CSOs work very volatile and insecure.

Though much has been achieved in terms of improving coordination among CSOs, and while WANEP in the past 10 years has tried to coordinate peacebuilding activities in the sub region, there are still some gaps to be addressed.

23 Thelma Ekiyor, 'The Role of Civil Society in Conflict Prevention: West African experiences', *United Nations Institute for Disarmament Research* (UNIDIR) *Disarmament Forum: The complex dynamics of small arms in West Africa*, 4: 27–34 (2008), pp. 32–33.

Exogenous Factors

A large portion of funding for conflict resolution and peacebuilding comes from external partners such as the United States Agency for International Development (USAID), the Swedish International Development Agency (SIDA) etc. The funds are usually short-term in duration and limited in scope considering that foreign partners are suspicious of CSOs in West Africa. With limited funds, external partners demand results in very short and unrealistic timeframes especially given the complex nature of conflicts in the region.

On the other hand, there is little support for peacebuilding from the private and business sector in West Africa. Business operators and investors are hardly playing their contributing role to promote peacebuilding in West Africa. Their contributions in the peace process have not been significant towards the consolidation of peace and security in the region.[24]

Given the fragility of states in West Africa and porosity of their borders, cross-border crimes, banditry and violent conflicts pose a challenge to CSOs. Other challenges include:

Insufficient Funding: This has also inhibited the contributions of CSOs to the promotion of principles of responsibility to protect in the region, with emphasis on undertaking conflict prevention and management initiatives to ensure human protection.

Unskilled Workforce: While there is growth in the number of peacebuilding practitioners in the region, there is still a shortage of skilled personnel. To some extent, this leaves a gap and in some instances the situation can be exacerbated, especially when personnel intervene in conflict situations without requisite skills.

Relationship between State and CSOs: in comparison to other Regional Economic Communities in Africa, ECOWAS has demonstrated impeccable leadership through its well thought out normative frameworks and in its involvement of CSOs as stated in the 1999 Mechanism. However, some member states still perceive issues of security including R2P as the sole responsibility of the state. To this end, many governments are also suspicious of CSOs and see their activities as being tantamount to opposition.

Specifically the challenge of WANEP as a CSO network in the promotion of human protection is that many state institutions and security apparatuses in the region are unable or slow to confront emerging threats to peace, due to lack of resources and in some cases, lack of political will. This affects the

24 Chukwuemeka B Eze and Takwa Z. Sufion, 'Business for Peace: Developing Partnership Between Business Investment and Peacebuilding', *WANEP Concept note* (Accra: WANEP, June 2012).

effectiveness of WANEP. In addition, corrupt and ineffective governance mechanisms in some member states of the region undermine the gains of WANEP and ECOWAS in ensuring human security and development.

In addition, WANEP and ECOWAS as partners in peacebuilding have not been able to adequately act on early warning data. As in the case of Guinea and Cote d'Ivoire, (and most recently Mali) ECOWAS was unable to respond swiftly and precisely enough to avert violence in these countries even though early warning information and data was available. This weak link between early warning and early response continues to threaten the sustained effectiveness of WANEP, as collecting, analysing and reporting conflict early warning information is meaningless, unless it is properly connected to early response mechanisms. This has been the primary weakness of the Early Warning System since its inception.

Another limitation of WANEP and ECOWAS in the promotion of human protection is the concentration of response structures in ECOWAS hierarchy. This leads to bureaucracy and slow response to the early warning alerts and also limits the use of local peace and security structures as the immediate response agents.

Recommendations

In charting a path for civil society, the notion and practice of responsibility to protect has to be redefined. This would entail an expansion of the responsibility to protect concept beyond its current state-centric focus to embrace 'endogenous' insistence on good governance and a renewed international commitment to greater egalitarianism in global decision-making. In this regard, emphasis on multi-disciplinary approaches involving a range of governmental and non-governmental actors and on understanding their respective roles, and reliance on broad partnership (including local communities, civil society, media, the private sector, humanitarian organisations and others), is key. The need to foster confidence-building measures in relations between Governments, civil society organisations, law enforcement agencies and the general population in the implementation and adherence to the principles of R2P is very necessary in order to promote and ensure human protection.

Specifically, the under listed are recommended for ECOWAS, Member states and CSOs to prevent and mitigate violent conflicts:

1. ECOWAS Department of Political Affairs, Peace and Security (PAPS) should create joint situation rooms at PAPS to ensure that early warning responses are corroborated and delivered in a synergetic manner.

2. Ensure mechanisms for coordination and collaboration amongst directorates in PAPS; between PAPS and Peace Fund as well as PAPS and other Directorates such as Humanitarian Affairs and Gender.
3. Expansion of partnership with relevant CSOs to include other directorates of the ECOWAS Commission.
4. Annual contributions of ECOWAS from its Peace Funds and other sources to regional CSOs with formal partnership to fund conflict prevention and mitigation initiatives.
5. Organisation of an annual meeting between the ECOWAS Commission and CSOs and expansion of such meetings across the continent.
6. Review of the ECOWARN indicators to ensure it captures the current dynamics including violent extremism and mass atrocities, in particular.
7. Member States should engage their parliaments and CSOs to domesticate the ECPF as well as other strategic documents of ECOWAS. In this regard, CSOs should engage with relevant parliamentary sub committees and organise workshop to facilitate the ratification and operationalisation of the diverse ECOWAS protocols on peace and security.
8. Regional organisations should serve as an entry point for engaging national governments on R2P, to erase the perception that the international community could use R2P to effect regime change.
9. Ensure confidence building in the implementation of R2P that would involve carrying member states along through their focal points for data gathering and analysis; and preventive diplomacy.
10. CSOs should increase capacity building on responsibility to protect, all aspects of conflict prevention and popularise the principles of responsibility to protect.
11. CSOs should collaborate with relevant national and community stakeholders to ensure synergy and maximise results.
12. CSOs involved in conflict prevention, mediation and peacebuilding should intensify its advocacy and insistence on the preventive pillar of R2P since it is cheaper and less complex.
13. CSOs should be engaged in the development and operationalisation of the National Early Warning Mechanisms and the establishment of Peace Architectures as aptly couched in the policy document on the establishment of national early warning mechanisms and national peace architectures, which was adopted by Authority of Heads of State and Government in Abidjan and Accra in 2013 and 2014.[25]

---

25 Communiqués on adoption for the establishment of: (1) National Peace Architectures (see: 'Forty second ordinary session of the ECOWAS authority of heads of state and

Conclusion

Overall, there have been significant contributions of CSOs in promoting human rights, mass atrocities prevention and civilian protection in conflict areas in West Africa. Responses to conflict by ECOWAS in partnership with CSOs are increasing in speed and effectiveness, thereby reducing the risk of mass atrocities and civilian casualties. CSOs are increasingly involved in early warning and, because they are aware of events as they unfold, they can make important contributions. They can act swiftly and flexibly to respond to conditions as needed, often using innovative and non-coercive strategies and quality processes informed by their knowledge of context and conflict dynamics to address problems. CSOs can act when, for various reasons, official actors are immobilised (often related to mandates, lack of political will or the implications conveyed by their official status). Therefore, they have comparative advantages and can augment current institutional mechanisms/approaches.

The partnership between WANEP and ECOWAS examined in this chapter presents a great opportunity for learning and mutual understanding about partnership between CSOs and Inter-Governmental organisations. The unique arrangement has attracted a lot of attention from the international community and, more so, has become a catalyst for a paradigm shift in government-civil society relationship across the continent. It is an opportunity to invest in a unique relationship as an example of a solid foundation for future peacebuilding and peace support operations in Africa.

The challenges posed by the threat of violent and armed conflicts in West Africa remain a critical factor for regional stability, peace and economic development. However, WANEP and other Civil Society Groups continue to engage and support National Governments, ECOWAS, the African Union and other international partners in the search for sustainable peace and improved human protection. The ECOWAS experience and framework provides a good example of how to anchor the R2P around Regional Inter-Governmental Organisations with the participation of national governments and the civil society. Binding commitments and political principles on how to prevent armed conflicts and prevent mass atrocities are much more easily negotiated at regional levels.

---

government', *ECOWAS Communiqué*, Yamoussoukro, February 2013, http://www.ecowas.int/wp-content/uploads/2015/02/42nd-ECOWAS-Summit-Yamoussoukro-27-28-Feb-20131.pdf, accessed 8 March 2016; and (2) National Early Warning Mechanisms (see: 'Forty-fifth ordinary session of the authority of ECOWAS heads of state and government', *ECOWAS Communiqué*, Accra, July 2014, http://www.ecowas.int/wp-content/uploads/2015/02/45th-ECOWAS-Summit-Ghana-10-Dec-20141.pdf, accessed 8 March 2016.

A Regional Responsibility to Protect? Towards 'Enhancing Regional Action' in Africa

Obinna Franklin Ifediora
University of Queensland
obinna.ifediora@uq.net.au

Abstract

Ten years after its endorsement by the UN General Assembly, the operationalisation of the Responsibility to Protect (RtoP) concept faces challenges of consistency and capacity. Too often, global politics at the world's premier intergovernmental body, the UN, hampers effective action. Regional arrangements have a crucial role to play in this regard, however, questions of capacity to live up to this expectation remain. The Peace and Security Council (PSC) of the African Union (AU), mandated to implement the African Peace and Security Architecture (APSA) has primarily focused on developing the African Standby Force (ASF), which the AU succeeded in bringing to its 'Full Operational Capability' (FOC) in December 2015 for implementation. Deploying the ASF in deserving cases, for instance in Burundi in 2016, raises issues of sovereign consent, risks and costs. To avoid these complexities, this chapter argues that regional arrangements under Chapter VIII are primarily pacific tools of the Security Council; focusing on harnessing these peaceful mechanisms of conflict prevention offers potential for consistent and effective 'first responses' to crises, with fewer complications. Regional arrangements as mediation tools present great opportunity for peaceful settlement of local disputes. Support for mediation is typically by peace operations. This chapter proposes that mediation support by a 'preventive arbitration' tool through 'popular participation' under the African Governance Architecture (AGA) may have a pivotal role in this respect. Therefore, a regional responsibility to protect, through greater mediation, requires mediating challenges of governance in Africa.

1 For useful comments on earlier drafts of this article, I am grateful to Alex J. Bellamy and Charles T. Hunt. The responsibility for any errors of fact or interpretation remains with the author. I would also like to thank the reviewers and editors of the journal for their help during the revision and editing of this chapter.

 | DOI:10.1163/9789004363212_012

Keywords

mediation – governance – UN – AU – conflict prevention – R2P

Adopted at the October 2005 World Summit by the Heads of State and Government of the UN, the Responsibility to Protect (RtoP) concept addresses the prevention of genocide, ethnic cleansing, war crimes and crimes against humanity.[2] The RtoP concept reiterates the responsibility of states to protect its populations from atrocity crimes,[3] and imposes a moral duty on the international community,[4] represented by the UN, including regional organisations, to prevent atrocity crimes.[5] In many ways, the RtoP concept advances the 'collective security consensus'[6] system of the UN by seeking to mobilize 'multilateral solutions to problems' relating to human rights and rule of law.[7] Paragraph 139 of the Outcome Document stipulates, among other things, the international community's commitment to prevent atrocity crimes, in collaboration with relevant regional organisations. It calls for the deployment of diplomatic, humanitarian and other peaceful means consistent with Chapters VI and VIII of the UN Charter. In general terms, Chapter VI prescribes the peaceful policy instruments for conflict prevention. More so, Chapter VIII provides the role of regional and subregional arrangements in maintaining international peace and security, including by undertaking measures in assisting the international community in preventing local disputes. Consistent with these provisions, the UN Secretary-General, Ban Ki-moon, has issued several reports articulating the important role of regional organisations in implementing RtoP.[8] In his 2015 report, Ban Ki-moon stated the need for 'enhancing regional action' arguing

2 Hereinafter referred to as 'atrocity crimes'.

3 UNGA Res. 60/1, 16 September 2005, para. 138.

4 *Ibid.*, para. 139.

5 See also, Kofi Annan, 'Speech at the 54th Session of the United Nations General Assembly', SG/SM/7136-GA/9596, 20 September 1999; International Commission on Sovereignty and Intervention (ICISS), *The Responsibility to Protect* (Ottawa: IDRC, 2001).

6 See for instance, 'A More Secure World: Our Shared Responsibility', Report of the High Level Panel on Threats, Challenges and Change, A/59/565, 2 December 2004 and Kofi Annan, *In Larger Freedom: Towards Development, Security and Human Rights for All*, A/59/2005, 21 March 2005.

7 See the Preamble to UNGA Res. 60/1, para. 16.

8 See Ban Ki-moon, *Implementing the Responsibility to Protect*, A/63/677, 12 January 2009, para. 65. See also Ban Ki-moon, *The Role of Regional and Subregional Arrangements in Implementing the Responsibility to Protect*, A/65/877, 28 June 2011, paras. 8, 39.

that 'regional organizations – in partnership with the United Nations and other international actors – can assume even greater prominence in protecting populations from atrocity crimes'.[9]

Some have proposed that RtoP should be 'decentralized to the world's regions', emphasising that 'when the UN Security Council is unable to come to a decision to take definitive action when crises present themselves, decentralizing mobilization to alternative multilateral organizations would be encouraged when appropriate'.[10] Axworthy and Rock called for a debate on establishing concurrent powers whereby the UN Security Council and regional arrangements could pass enabling resolutions with regional powers taking direct action.[11] The pivotal contribution of regional arrangements in the maintenance of international peace and security was initially contextualised by Boutros-Ghali's famous report, 'An Agenda for Peace'.[12] In the Report, Boutros-Ghali took the view that:

> ...[R]egional action as a matter of decentralization, delegation and cooperation with United Nations efforts could not only lighten the burden of the Council but also contribute to a deeper sense of participation, consensus and democratisation in international affairs.[13]

Additionally, Boutros-Ghali argued that consultations between the UN and regional arrangements could do much to 'build international consensus on the nature of a problem and the measures required to address it'.[14] This requires that the relationship between the Security Council and regional organisations be governed by Chapter VIII of the UN Charter.[15] It is within this context that the African Union's (AU) Common African Position on the Reform of the UN, which addressed the RtoP concept, can better be understood.[16] In Part B of the

---

9 Ban Ki-moon, *A vital and Enduring Commitment: Implementing the Responsibility to Protect*, A/69/981, 13 July 2015, para. 68.

10 Lloyd Axworthy and Allan Rock , 'Making R2P work: now and in the future' in W. Andy Knight and Frazer Egerton (eds.), *The Routledge Handbook of the Responsibility to Protect* (Oxon: Routledge, 2012), p. 187.

11 Lloyd Axworthy and Allan Rock, 'R2P: A New and Unfinished Agenda', *Global Responsibility to Protect*, 1:54–69 (2009), p. 61.

12 Boutros Boutros-Ghali, 'An Agenda for Peace', A/47/277 – S/24111, 17 June 1992.

13 *Ibid.*, p. 64.

14 *Ibid.*, p. 65.

15 *Ibid.*, p. 63.

16 'The Ezulwini Consensus', Ext/EX.CL/2 (VII), 7–8 March 2005.

policy document known as the 'Ezulwini Consensus', the Executive Council of the AU noted that:

> Since the General Assembly and the Security Council are often far from the scenes of conflicts and may not be in a position to undertake effectively a proper appreciation of the nature and development of conflict situations, *it is imperative that Regional Organisations, in areas of proximity to conflicts, are empowered to take actions in this regard* (emphasis added).

In this context, the AU has established guiding principles for the interpretation and execution of peace operations in Africa under Chapter VIII. These include: mutual respect and adherence to the principle of comparative advantage based on political legitimacy and flexibility; support for African ownership and priority setting, partnership on the basis of [1] consultative decision-making; [2] division of labour; and [3] burden sharing; and division of labour underpinned by complementarity.[17] In endorsing the RtoP concept, the Report of the UN Secretary-General's High-level Panel on Threats, Challenges and Change entitled *A more secure world: our shared responsibility*,[18] emphasized regional cooperation and the promise of regional capacity to 'augment and not detract from the ability of the United Nations'. The challenge such cooperation poses to the Security Council and regional arrangements were noted.[19] This chapter argues that regional organisations have a responsibility to help resolve local disputes peacefully. Consequently, capacity-building policies in relation to atrocity crimes prevention should focus on developing pacific tools for effective 'first response'.[20] These include mediation, arbitration, and judicial settlement in line with *Article 33* of the UN Charter. There are other measures of humanitarian and diplomatic nature that are equally

17 'Common African Position on the UN Review of Peace Operations', AU Doc. PSC/PR/2(DII), 29 April 2015, para. 6(i–v). These principles have been recognised by the UN Department of Political Affairs (UN DPA), see UNDPA, *Multi-year Appeal* (2013): *UN/AU Mediation Work Plan, Update*, 2013.

18 See 'A more secure world', A/59/565.

19 *Ibid.*, paras. 220 and 270.

20 Alex J. Bellamy, 'The First Response: Peaceful Means in the Third Pillar of the Responsibility to Protect', Policy Analysis Brief, Stanley Foundation, December 2015, http://www.stanleyfoundation.org/publications/pab/Bellamy3rdPillarPAB116.pdf, accessed 7 Februry 2016.

peaceful, such as humanitarian access.[21] The focus of this chapter is on the African Union's mediation capacity, which could be supported by the proposed idea of 'preventive arbitration'.[22]

The idea of developing an African approach to conflict resolution and prevention on the continent was first mooted in the 'Kampala Document' of 1991 that established the Conference on Security, Stability, Cooperation and Development in Africa (CSSCDA), which stressed on the imperative to launch an effective process among African countries that would create a framework for preventing, containing, and eliminating pernicious intra and inter-African conflicts.[23] The CSSCDA process was designed to serve as an instrument for the management and resolution of disputes and conflicts in Africa. At the core of the CSSCDA process was the centrality of the African people in conflict prevention initiatives. In essence, the Process advanced conflict prevention mechanisms that not only put the peoples' concerns at the top of the agenda, but also sought to integrate the people in the negotiation processes. The Kampala Document recommended key policy measures that would meet these objectives, which included: [1] Mechanisms for mediation, conciliation and arbitration – these mechanisms re-emphasised the urgent requirement to prevent conflicts and disputes from escalating into armed hostilities, and therefore calls for strengthening of each tool at the governmental, political and diplomatic levels, within the framework of intervention; [2] Confidence building; [3] Africa's Elders Council for Peace; and [4] Lowering military expenditure. Gravitating from the CSSCDA towards actualising the above policy measures, the Heads of State and Government of the Organization of African Unity (OAU) (now the AU) adopted the Declaration on a Mechanism for Conflict Prevention, Management and Resolution (the 'Cairo Declaration') in June 1993. The Cairo Declaration called for the anticipation and prevention of conflicts and action on peace-making and peacebuilding. Critical to the argument and proposals submitted in this chapter, the CSSCDA focus on anticipation and prevention of conflict is rationalised by the conviction that such efforts will 'obviate the need to resort to the complex and resource-demanding

21 For a comprehensive list of peaceful means under 'pillar three', see Bellamy, 'The First Response'.

22 Obinna F. Ifediora, 'Preventive Arbitration: Towards Strengthening the African Union Mediation Capacity for Human Protection', *Australasian Review of African Studies* (Forthcoming).

23 Africa Leadership Forum, *The Kampala Document: Towards a Conference on Security, Stability, Development and Cooperation in Africa*, Kampala: OAU/United Nations Economic Commission for Africa (UNECA), 1991.

peacekeeping operations, our countries will find difficult to finance'.[24] Today, the Cairo Declaration has metamorphosed into the Protocol Establishing the Peace and Security Council (PSC) of the AU.[25] These approaches envisioned the peaceful resolution of local disputes. This focus was not lost by the creation of the AU. In fact, the AU restructured the CSSCDA as the African Citizens' Directorate. Even the establishment of the Pan African Parliament (PAP), now under the African Governance Architecture (AGA) is an advancement of the idea of promoting peoples involvement in dispute resolution and governance in Africa.

The use of pacific instruments has become critical aspects of the AU's responses to local disputes associated with atrocity crimes in the continent. In the case of Burundi (2015–16), for instance, the AU Assembly rejected the PSC's proposed African Prevention and Protection Mission in Burundi (MAPROBU). Instead, the Assembly preferred deploying pacific tools of mediation, in the context of promoting dialogue. Consequently, on 5 February 2016, the newly elected AU Chairman, President Idriss Déby Itno of Chad, appointed the AU High-level Delegation to Burundi to help promote dialogue between the government and the opposition. There are now questions whether the African Standby Force (ASF) that was declared to have attained 'Full Operational Capability' (FOC) on 15 January 2016, will ever be deployed in deserving situations, such as in Burundi.[26] This also raises questions about whether or not the millions of dollars already expended in developing ASF capacity were justified. Consequently, there is now pressing need for 'greater mediation' following the rejection by the AU Assembly to authorise the deployment of ASF in Burundi

24 See the OAU Declaration on a Mechanism for Conflict Prevention, Management and Resolution (Cairo Declaration) adopted at the OAU's 29th Ordinary Session in Cairo, Egypt, 28–30 June, 1993, para. 15.

25 For further perspectives on AU PSC, see particularly, Tim Murithi, 'The Role of the African Peace and Security Architecture in the Implementation of Article 4(h)' in Dan Kuwali and Frans Viljeon (eds.) *Africa and the Responsibility to Protect* (Oxon: Routledge, 2014), pp. 139–151, and Charles T. Hunt, 'The role of African Standby Force in Implementing Article 4(h)' in Kuwali and Viljeon, *Africa*, pp. 173–194. See also Emmanuel Kwesi Aning and Samuel Atuobi, 'Responsibility to Protect in Africa: An Analysis of the African Union's Peace and Security Architecture', *Global Responsibility to Protect*, 1(1): 90–113 (2009).

26 See the Statement of the Specialized Technical Committee on Defence, Safety and Security (STCDSS) at the African Union Peace and Security Council's 370th Meeting relating to PSC AMANI AFRICA-II and AFRIPOL, 21 January 2016, http://www.peaceau.org/en/article/press-statement-of-the-570th-psc-meeting-on-the-declaration-of-the-second-extraordinary-meeting-of-the-specialized-technical-committee-on-defence-safety-and-security-stcdss, accessed 12 February 2016.

without the government's consent, despite the informed recommendations of the PSC based on the African Commission on Human and Peoples Right's (ACHPR) report on Burundi. There are also cost issues, especially in relation to financial liability. Peace support operations are a capital-intensive venture and the AU relies heavily on external funding from donor nations to finance such missions. Moreover, there are further questions over the risks of militarising mediation processes in Africa. One concern held by some,[27] and rightly so, is the potential of state security services using military resources that are meant for human protection against civilian populations. For example in Nigeria, the US withheld lethal military assistance over concerns of the Nigeria's military abuses and atrocities against civilian populations in the fight against 'Boko Haram' insurgents. Indeed, given that the structure of the ASF requires that trained and equipped troops are to be stationed in the 'troop contributing countries' national militaries and police services, the potential for misuse, such as regime protection by host governments in the event of crisis, is real.

Even in cases of typical mediation support by peacekeeping missions or economic sanctions or targeted sanctions, mediating local disputes in Africa remains a challenge: from Sudan to Libya, to South Sudan, to Burundi – to mention a few – the AU's mediation efforts in these conflicts have proved unsuccessful. This calls for a rethink of AU mediation practices. Surely, a number of seminars, workshops and conferences have been convened by the AU Commission in conjunction with civil society organisations to find ways of strengthening AU's mediation capacity.[28] Besides the consensus to establish a Mediation Support Unit (MSU) within the AU Commission, it is not clear what support measures or additional institutional tools are being considered. In this regard, this chapter proposes for the institutionalisation of a 'preventive arbitration' tool within the AU Commission.

Accordingly, this chapter argues that focusing on building the pacific capacities of regional arrangements will make an important contribution to the prevention of mass atrocity crimes. Indeed, the apparent conflicting policy priorities of pacifism and interventionism has resulted in the AU not being

27 See for instance, Danielle Beswick, 'The Risks of African Military Capacity Building: Lessons from Rwanda', *African Affairs*, 113/451:212–231 (2014).

28 For example, the AU Peace and Security Department (PSD) convened Mediation Support Roundtable, held between 31 August and 2 September, 2015, which concluded with a consensus on establishing Mediation Support Unit (MSU) within the AU Commission. See also, the high-level seminar on 'Strengthening Mediation in Africa' jointly organised by the African Centre for the Constructive Resolution of Disputes (ACCORD) and the AU on May 4, 2015 in Addis Ababa, Ethiopia.

too efficient in undertaking both measures: with respect to the former, the AU simply lacks the technical know-how and necessary institutional support to be an effective pacifier; in relation to the latter, the AU lacks the courage, political will, and necessary resources, especially funding, to be an efficient enforcer – even with its enforcement arm, the ASF, attaining FOC. Consequently, the central aim of this paper is to stimulate the preventive focus of RtoP, through the 'second pillar',[29] which addresses questions of capacity-building in the context of 'international assistance'. The paper calls for the strengthening of the mediation capacities of regional and subregional arrangements for 'first response' measures under 'pillar three'.[30] Moreover, a 'regional responsibility to protect' is advanced in the context of undertaking peaceful initiatives in relation to conflict prevention, consistent with Chapters VI and VIII as called for in paragraph 139 of *Resolution 60/1*. Indeed, developing peaceful capacities of national and regional authorities have been endorsed as the surest, sustainable means of preventing atrocity crimes.[31] Although there are a plethora of peaceful measures under 'pillar three', the focus of this chapter is on mediation tools to prevent conflicts from escalating.[32] With the challenges facing the AU in successfully deploying mediation tools in theatres of conflicts in Africa, this chapter considers ways the AU's mediation capacity can be strengthened, such as by 'preventive arbitration'; and the potential role of the facilities under the African Governance Architecture (AGA). Moreover, 'regional responsibility to protect' informs that the AU is an instrument of 'first response' of the Security Council, and therefore requires 'international assistance' in the context of 'pillar two'. Indeed, there are growing views in favour of support for peace operations in Africa to be directed through multilateral organisations, such as the AU.[33] To advance the notion of a 'regional responsibility to protect', the first part of this chapter proceeds by examining its legal basis.

---

29 UNGA Res. 60/1, paras. 138.

30 UNGA Res. 60/1, para. 139. See also Bellamy, 'The First Response'.

31 See especially Ban Ki-moon, *Fulfilling Our Collective Responsibility: International Assistance and the Responsibility to Protect*, A/68/947, 11 July 2014; and Kofi Annan, *Interventions: A Life in War and Peace*, (London: Penguin Books, 2012).

32 For instance, ECOWAS accepted this responsibility regarding conflict prevention, management and resolution in West Africa in relation to the recent coup d'état in Burkina Faso, see ECOWAS Authority, 'Extraordinary Session of the Authority of Heads of State and Government on the Political Crisis in Burkina Faso', Final Communiqué, 16–17 September 2015, para. 23.

33 See for example Paul D. Williams, 'Enhancing U.S. Support for Peace Operations in Africa', Centre for Preventive Action, Council on Foreign Relations, Council Special Report, No.73, May 2015.

Regional Responsibility to Protect by Resolving Local Disputes through Peaceful Means

This section examines the legal foundation of a 'regional responsibility to protect'. It argues that regional organisations can support human protection in a variety of ways. As noted above, peaceful means under 'pillar three' encompasses multifaceted approaches, including diplomatic and humanitarian responses, as well as the specific policy tools provided for in *Article 33* of the UN Charter, all of which have been so eloquently articulated elsewhere.[34] To be clear, the focus of this chapter is on the role of regional organisations within the purview of Chapters VI and VIII of the UN Charter in preventing atrocity crimes through 'greater mediation'. Accordingly, Chapter VI deals with 'pacific settlement' of local disputes that may endanger international peace and security. Specifically, *Article 33(1)* provides, thus:

> The parties to any dispute, the continuance of which is likely to endanger the maintenance of international peace and security, shall, first of all, seek a solution by negotiation, enquiry, *mediation, conciliation, arbitration, judicial settlement*, resort to *regional agencies or arrangements*, or other peaceful means of their own choice (emphasis added).

There is sufficient clarity with regard to the legislative intent of the policy instruments enumerated above – that is, mutual dialogue or third-party assisted dialogue or authoritative decision-making-institution assisted resolution of disputes. The intent, it appears, was to promote party-driven systems of dispute resolution. The only unclear aspect of the provision is the direction it gave to parties to disputes to engage with the conflict prevention mechanisms of relevant 'regional agencies or arrangements'.[35] In this respect, Chapter VIII of the UN Charter elaborates the provision of *Article 33(1)*, and provides:

[1]. Nothing in the present Charter precludes the existence of regional arrangements or agencies for dealing with such matters relating to the maintenance of international peace and security as are appropriate for regional action, provided that such arrangements or agencies and their

---

34 See Bellamy, 'The First Response'.

35 The term 'Parties' refer to both Member and non-Member States of the UN. However, I will argue that, in the context and nature of contemporary conflicts non-state actors should be given access to formal regional and subregional institutional mechanisms - either existing or yet to be created - for dispute resolution.

activities are consistent with the Purposes and Principles of the United Nations.

[2]. The Members of the United Nations entering into such arrangements or constituting such agencies *shall make every effort to achieve pacific settlement of local disputes through such regional arrangements or by such regional agencies before referring them to the Security Council* (emphasis added).

[3]. *The Security Council shall encourage the development of pacific settlement of local disputes through such regional arrangements or by such regional agencies* either on the initiative of the states concerned or by reference from the Security Council (emphasis added).

These provisions permit regional organisations to employ peaceful initiatives to resolve local disputes. The only proviso contained in *Article 52(1)* is that any peaceful measure adopted by regional arrangements must conform to the principles and purposes of the UN.[36] The inability of regional organisations to resolve local disputes by peaceful means creates the opportunity for the Security Council's intervention. In this regard, *Article 53(1)* states:

> The Security Council shall, where appropriate, utilize such regional arrangements or agencies for enforcement action under its authority. But no enforcement action shall be taken under regional arrangements or by regional agencies without the authorization of the Security Council…

Conversely, the possibility of inaction by the Security Council when required to intervene in fulfilment of its Charter obligation of maintaining international peace and security does not provide regional organisations the dispensation to initiate enforcement measures.

Regional instruments also confer the AU with additional constitutional powers to deal with issues relating to continental peace, security and stability. This authority resides with the AU Assembly, which is the supreme decision-making organ of the Union by virtue of *Article 9* of the Constitutive Act of the AU. In this context, the Assembly's decisions or policies on peace, security and stability of the continent has direct implications to fulfilling the mandate given to it under *Article 4(h)* of the AU Constitutive Act – *Article 4(h)* deals with

---

36 Note that *Article 53 (1&2)* create further provisos to the effect that regional organisations can take enforcement action with the authorisation of the Security Council, except in measures against enemy states, where prior authorisation is not necessary. Though in practice, the view is widely held that Security Council consent can be sort *ex post facto*.

the Union's right to intervene in Member States in grave circumstances, including genocide, war crimes, and crimes against humanity. It should be noted that this provision does not contradict the stipulations in Chapter VII of the UN Charter in relation to the sole authority of the UN Security Council to use force or to authorise the use force in maintaining international peace and security, including the prevention of atrocity crimes contained in *Article 4(h)* of the AU Constitutive Act. Essentially, the AU still defers to the Security Council on use of force. Additionally, *Articles 5(2)* and *9(2)* provide the Assembly a dispensation to delegate its powers to any organ of its choice. In line with this system, the Assembly established the PSC, and mandated it to implement the Union's pacific policy instruments relating to conflict and atrocity crimes prevention, among others.[37] In this respect, the PSC is guided by the principles of peaceful settlement of disputes by virtue of *Article 4(a)*. Moreover, *Article 6(c)*, states the primary functions of the PSC, which includes anticipation and prevention of conflicts through preventive diplomacy and peace-making, specifically 'the use of good offices, mediation, conciliation and enquiry'. To further the aims of the above functions, the PSC is supported by the AU's Continental Early Warning System (CEWS), the Panel of the Wise (PoW) and the Peace Fund. Consistent with *Article 2(1)* of the Constitutive Act and in the context of pacific orientation of Chapter VI, and the injunction given under Chapter VIII – that is, that every effort shall be made to 'achieve pacific settlement of local disputes' through regional arrangements – and the relevant clauses in Paragraph 139 of *Resolution 60/1*, it is supported that the PSC should be used as the collective security and early warning arrangement of the AU and the international community. This will facilitate the fulfilment of the overall objective of Chapter VIII and help buttress the role of regional arrangements in implementing RtoP by providing timely and efficient peaceful responses to conflicts in Africa.

Accordingly, the combined effect of the foregoing provisions was to establish a regional capacity for conflict prevention, as well as the prevention of atrocity crimes. This consists of, firstly, the use of pacific mechanisms of mediation, arbitration, to mention two. The AU has made extensive use of its mediation mechanisms in various conflicts in Africa, including in Kenya's post-election violence from 2007–8, which led the constitutional reforms that enabled the country to remain progressively in the part of sustainable democratisation through peaceful, fair, transparent and credible elections. The AU's intervention was initiated by its Chairman, John Kufuor, who helped to mediate the initial peace agreement towards a power-sharing deal between the

37 See the Protocol Relating to the Establishment of Peace and Security Council of the African Union, 2002, *Article 7(1)(e–g)*.

Party of National Unity-led (PNU) government and the Orange Democratic Movement (ODM) opposition party, before the Panel of Eminent African Personalities, led by former UN Secretary-General, Kofi Annan, took over the mediation process. It took Kofi Annan 41 days to successfully mediate the Kenyan conflict. This happened because of several notable reasons: the international community supported the process in line with Chapter VIII principles; there was 'popular participation' by Kenyan people, especially by involving the parliamentarians. This type of mediation is what is being referred to in this chapter as 'greater mediation'.[38]

In Central African Republic (CAR), the resumption of hostilities by the Séléka rebel coalition (this group had been agitating for inclusion in the political life of CAR) in December 2012, which resulted in the coup d'état in March 2013 that deposed the democratically elected president, François Bozizé, momentarily undermined the peacebuilding efforts in the country by the UN – in 2010, the United Nations Integrated Peacebuilding Office in the Central African Republic (BINUCA) was established to assist the country in the democratisation process, consisting of disarmament, demobilisation, and reintegration processes, and conducting free and fair elections. In the aftermath of the failed mediation by the Economic Community of Central African States (ECCAS) in March 2013 – ECCAS had assisted in negotiating a peace deal between the Muslim Séléka and the government of François Bozizé in January 2013 – the AU intervened by establishing the African-led International Support Mission in Central Africa (MISCA), backed by Security Council *Resolution 2127*, in December 2013. One of the key objectives of MISCA was to mediate the conflict, which by then had turned into a sectarian conflict between the Séléka rebel coalition (mostly Muslims) and the anti-Balaka vigilante group (mostly Christians). In July 2014, MISCA, through the ECCAS mediator, President Denis Sassou Nguesso of the Republic of the Congo, negotiated the first significant peace agreements between the CAR parties. MISCA was re-hatted to the United Nations Multidimensional Integrated Stabilization Mission in Central African Republic (MINUSCA) in September 2014 following Security Council *Resolution 2149* in April 2014. Subsequent peace agreements in 2015 led to the successful national elections in January 2016. What these two cases demonstrate is that 'greater mediation', as observed in Kenya, by regional arrangements can effectively obviate the extraordinarily expensive and complex

38 Some have proposed 'stronger mediation' that will involve use of military force and economic sanctions, see for example Helen Scanlon, Ahunna Eziakonwa, and Elizabeth Myburgh, 'Africa's Responsibility to Protect', Policy Advisory Group Seminar Report, Somerset South Africa: Centre for conflict Resolution, University of Cape Town, 2007, p. 9.

peace operations deployed in CAR ('stronger mediation'), where the situation remains fragile.

Similarly, other subregional arrangements, such as the Intergovernmental Authority on Development-led (IGAD), (later reconstituted as IGAD-Plus) mediation in South Sudan in 2015, the ECOWAS mediation in Burkina Faso in 2015 and the ECOWAS-led mediation effort in Mali since 2012, have also contributed to the maintenance of international peace and security by employing peaceful measures. In these cases, although the mediation was initially successful, the current situation in these countries indicates that conflict is not yet over. What these processes lacked was 'greater mediation' – that is 'popular participation'. Additionally, the intervention in Mali, such as in Burundi, and initially in the Darfur crisis in Sudan, shows that regional organisations in Africa rarely intervene militarily in member states without consent. This practice is ingrained in the dictum 'African solutions to African problems', a tenaciously held position of the AU, which privileges political solutions to African conflicts or what has been referred to as 'African tradition' – that is, mutual dialogue between parties to conflicts. However, in many cases, this approach to conflict resolution in Africa has proved ineffective, owing to the underdeveloped mediation capacities of regional organisations in managing African conflicts. In many ways, this inadequacy propelled the move to develop coercive capacities of the AU, and wrongly so, as the case of Burundi demonstrates; just as similar lapses in ECOWAS mediation in West Africa galvanised the Commission to establish the ECOWAS Monitoring Group (ECOMOG) in the 1990s. This uncharacteristic move by ECOWAS (the Revised Treaty of ECOWAS of 1993 in *Article 4(f)* reemphasised 'peaceful settlement of disputes') was later aptly referred to as 'a bold attempt at regional peace keeping'.[39] Although the ECOMOG, deployed without consent of the authorities in Liberia and Sierra Leone, was largely successful, recent conflicts in West Africa, particularly in Mali in 2012, did not receive the same response from ECOWAS. Apart from logistics and associated costs of financing such missions, ECOWAS waited for the invitation of the Malian government before deploying the African-led International Support Mission to Mali (AFISMA), which was mostly underwritten by the UN and donor partners. The implications of such delays could be serious for populations at risk of atrocity. What is required is 'greater mediation'.

There is evident practice of reluctance on the part of African regional organisations to deploy military interventions for human protection purpose in Member States without their consent, such as in Burundi in January 2016,

39 Margaret A. Vogt, (eds.) *The Liberian Crisis and ECOMOG: A Bold Attempt at Regional Peace keeping* (Lagos, Nigeria: Gabumo Publishing, 1992).

regardless of the existence of grave circumstances as envisaged by *Article 4(h)* of the Constitutive Act of the AU. Besides the cases of Burundi and Mali, this scenario played out in Libya in 2011, and in Darfur, Sudan in the 2000s before a deal was reached with the government to establish a Joint AU-UN mission. This attitude is characteristic of African governments and the intergovernmental bodies they helped to set up for the development, peace and security of the African people. As noted above, this position has long history in Africa, but has been institutionalised. For instance, the AU Common African Position in response to the UN Review of Peace Operations states:

> The Constitutive Act of the African Union and the established practice of African solutions to African problems places a priority on political responses to imminent crises and actually occurring armed conflicts. The absolute priority of the African Union and APSA is to ensure a rapid and effective political response. This is also where the comparative advantage of the AU lies, relative to all external actors. The AU remains fundamentally committed to the principle that political solutions are necessary and preferable and that the dispatch of an armed peace support operation is a last resort, to be undertaken solely and exclusively in support of a political process. To that end, the AU underlines the primacy of the political and will maintain, at all times, the supremacy of political guidance over military peace operations.[40]

In light of this clearly stated policy statement, it would have been propitious for the AU, the UN and donor partners to develop mediation tools prior to the ASF. The latter should have been considered only if mediation instruments, operating at optimum capacity, were still ineffective. As noted earlier, these contradicting policies of capacity development have had (and could still have) serious consequences for populations at risk of atrocity crimes (if priorities remain misplaced). The UN and donor agencies and governments should refocus on harnessing the primary role of regional arrangements in Africa for 'greater mediation'. The AU's reluctance to use force in member states without the consent of the relevant government is an opportunity to deemphasise the mainstream peace operations model; rather, additional funding should be channelled towards redeveloping mediation capacities and operationalising 'preventive arbitration' for 'greater mediation'.

Moreover, the focus on the ASF raises important questions regarding how it should be put to best use in the current conflict situations in Africa. Indeed,

40 AU Doc. PSC /PR/2(DII), 2015, para. 17.

if military intervention for human protection purposes is based on mutually consented political processes (a conspicuously missing element in the Burundi case), then the scope for its use would be very limited. In other respects, it could be that the AU's ASF mechanism is merely a deterrent tool; if so, then it is proposed that the AU needs to find efficient ways of maximizing its potential. This can be fostered by pursuing agreements with the target state whereby the AU agrees not to deploy ASF on the condition that the state concerned complies with AU's demands. These conditions may include protection of civilians, conducting free, fair and transparent elections, good governance and executing institutional reforms, with a clearly set timeline of implementation. The Panel of the Wise is better placed to handle such negotiations and such agreements could be supervised by the AU Commission (AUC) through the Department of Political Affairs (AU DPA). The overarching normative principle that would govern the negotiations and implementation processes will be the AU Charter on Democracy, Elections and Governance. In order that these objectives are realized, the international community, donor partners and African nations, including the AU and other regional arrangements should refocus on the primary role of regional organisations as stipulated in Chapter VIII of the UN Charter – that is, peaceful settlement of local disputes through 'greater mediation'. This will be fostered by powerful governance institutions at the continental, regional and national levels, under the auspices of the African Governance Architecture (AGA).[41] This is already embedded in the AU's shared values and reflects in the notions of 'African solution to African problems' and 'African tradition'.

Challenges of Building Pacific Capacities of Regional Arrangements for Peaceful Resolution of Local Disputes in Africa

This section addresses issues of capacity-building and implementing a 'regional responsibility to protect'. It highlights potential impediments to operationalising and practising 'greater mediation' and proffers some solutions.

In responding to the coup d'état in Burkina Faso in September 2015, ECOWAS noted its responsibility, as well as its role, in conflict prevention, management

41 For a detailed analysis of the role of AGA in implementing RtoP in Africa, see Obinna F. Ifediora, 'The Structural Bases of Implementing the Responsibility to Protect in Africa: Towards Advancing the African Governance Architecture', *African Conflict and Peacebuilding Review* (Indiana University Press, Forthcoming).

and resolution in West Africa.[42] Similarly, the AU had noted the 'African ownership and priority-setting' in relation to responses to conflict in Africa, especially in the use of mediation tools.[43] Acknowledging responsibility to prevent conflicts or accepting ownership of measures and policies for conflict prevention in Africa is commendable, but the ways in which these efforts are contextualised in the atrocity prevention work by Africa's regional and subregional organisations needs to be addressed. This gap was recently highlighted in a study on conflict prevention initiated by some regional arrangements in Africa. The study observed that in pursuing peaceful means to resolving local disputes efforts were often focused on short-term political solutions or preventing election-related violence, and do not usually extend to addressing the deeper divisions that contribute to conflicts.[44] Perhaps, what is required, in addition, is to initiate action and policy towards embedding RtoP principles into regional and subregional mediation efforts aimed at resolving local disputes. Adopting an 'atrocity prevention lens' approach to peacefully resolving local disputes in Africa may require redeveloping the AU's, and other regional arrangements', mediation tools, and most importantly, practices. This will invariably contribute to 'enhancing regional action' in implementing RtoP by peaceful means in Africa. The crucial question is: how can the international community, including regional arrangements, redevelop mediation capacities of regional and subregional organisations to be able to operationalise 'greater mediation'?

It is safe to say that the AU's capacity to successfully mediate local conflicts in the continent is undermined by a range of factors, including the number of actors involved and lack of resources – both material and human. For instance, the AU Peace and Security Department (PSD) convened a Mediation Support Roundtable, in 2015 to 'advance strategic thinking' within the AUC about ways of strengthening mediation support. The Roundtable concluded with a consensus on establishing a Mediation Support Unit (MSU) within the AUC. In this respect, the concept of 'preventive arbitration' has been proposed towards supporting the AU's mediation tools.[45] Similarly, the high-level seminar on 'Strengthening Mediation in Africa' jointly organised by the African Centre for the Constructive Resolution of Disputes (ACCORD) and the AU on 4 May, 2015 in Addis Ababa, Ethiopia, highlighted some critical gaps in the AU's mediation capacity. One of the major challenges acknowledged as an impediment to the

42 See ECOWAS Authority, Final Communiqué.

43 See, AU Doc. PSC /PR/2(DII), para. 6(i–v). See also, the UN DPA, *Multi-year Appeal*, p. 20.

44 Jaclyn D. Streithfeld-Hall, 'Preventing Mass Atrocities in West Africa', Global Centre for the Responsibility to Protect, *Occasional Paper Series*, No.6, September 2015, p. 21.

45 Ifediora, 'Preventive Arbitration'.

AU's mediation in Africa is lack of coordination of responses and approaches by multiple-stakeholders.[46]

Although international support for the AU's capacity development has been ongoing since the adoption of the Ten-Year Capacity Building Programme for Africa in 2006, the need to further strengthen the Union's capacity for mediation, especially in the areas of resources, and technical skills, was underscored at the Roundtable in 2015. An important practical question over how best to use Chapter VIII for greater impact on resolving conflicts peacefully remains unaddressed. Perhaps, it has to be reiterated that Chapter VIII operates on the principles of 'collaboration and partnership'. The UN DPA has acknowledged the AU's principles of engagement in mediation in what it called 'productive DPA collaboration with regional organizations on mediation, conflict prevention and peacebuilding responses'.[47] Furthermore, the UN High-level Panel on Threats, Challenges and Change had argued that the ability of the Security Council to become more 'proactive in preventing and responding to threats will be strengthened by making fuller and more productive use of the Chapter VIII provisions of the Charter of the United Nations than has hitherto been the case'.[48] This envisaged partnership has not been entirely productive.[49] Ban Ki-moon highlighted the difficulties facing the UN and the AU in this respect, and stressed that without a truly 'strategic relationship and clear guidance, our efforts to work together will continue to be short-term, *ad hoc*, more complicated and often more costly'.[50]

This lack of strategic relationship and collaboration between the UN and the AU has reflected in the poor management of conflicts in Africa, in several instances. It has also affected the capacity of the AU to mediate conflicts in

46 See, Laurie Nathan, 'Plan of action to build the AU's mediation capacity', paper presented at seminar on 'Towards Enhancing the Capacity of the AU in Mediation', AU Commission, Addis Ababa, October 2009. See also Ibrahim Gambari, 'Multilateralism: Challenges of International Mediation in Regional Conflicts', *African Conflict & Peacebuilding Review* 1(1): 133–138 (2011); Annan, *Interventions*, p. 187.

47 See the UNDPA, 'Multi-year Appeal', p. 20. See also AU Doc. PSC/PR/2(DII), para. 6(i–v).

48 See Annan, 'A more secure world', para. 270.

49 On the partnership between the AU and the UN in peace operations in Africa, see especially Arthur Boutellis and Paul D. Williams, *Peace Operations, the African Union, and the United Nations: Toward More Effective Partnerships*, (New York: International Peace Institute, April 2013) and Paul D. Williams and Solomon A. Dersso, *Saving Strangers and Neighbors: Advancing UN-AU Cooperation on Peace Operations*, (New York: International Peace Institute, February 2015).

50 'Support to African Union Peacekeeping Operations Authorized by the United Nations', A/65/510–S/2010/514, 14 October, 2010, para. 55.

the region. One striking example was the situation in Libya in 2011. Initially promoted as a triumph of RtoP authorisation and implementation in Africa, the UN Security Council *Resolution 1973*, while noting the AU's decision to send its 'ad hoc High Level Committee to Libya with the aim of facilitating dialogue [African solution] to lead to the political reforms necessary to find a peaceful and sustainable solution', it 'recognized [only] the role of the League of Arab States (LAS) in matters relating to the maintenance of international peace and security in the region'.[51] Today, with the current situation in Libya, and its reverberating effects on the migration crisis in Europe, the international community, in acknowledging its mistakes in Libya can do better by recommitting to larger productive use of Chapter VIII. The point can be clearly put forward by arguing that capacity-building for the AU under the auspices of the Ten-Year Capacity Building Programme will be fruitless if the AU's efforts at mediating African conflicts are unwittingly undermined by conflicting approaches and priorities for peaceful resolution of conflicts and conflict prevention in Africa.

Additionally, the conflict in Darfur, Sudan, is another good example of lack of 'strategic' collaboration between the UN and the AU in conflict management in Africa, consistent with Chapter VIII protocol and in line with the proposed 'effective use of comparative advantage' principle. The indictment of the Sudanese President, Omar al-Bashir, by the International Criminal Court (ICC) against the AU's preferred mediation responses, and the neglect of repeated calls by the AU to the UN Security Council to exercise its power under *Article 16* of the Rome Statute to ask the ICC Prosecutor to withdraw the charges, in order to allow for a peaceful dialogue and resolution of the conflict, show the differences in approach between the two institutions against the spirit of Chapter VIII. Because of this gulf, the AU has started a parallel programme of developing a criminal jurisdiction within its own court. Moreover, there were propositions for a continent-wide withdrawal from the ICC jurisdiction and some initiatives toward signing of bilateral agreements to the effect that state signatories will not adhere to request from the ICC in relation to arrest warrants issued against senior government officials of African descent.[52] These conflicting approaches to interventions in African conflicts not only adversely affect the AU's performance in mediating peace in Africa; it amounts to a waste

51 See UNSC Res. 1973, 17 March 2011, paras. 2, 5. See also Alex de Waal, 'African Roles in the Libyan Conflict of 2011', *International Affairs* 89/2: 365–379 (2013), p. 368.

52 See the AU Assembly Res. AU/Dec. 547(XXIV), (Assembly/AU/18(XXIV) January 2015, para. 18.

of resources expended by the international community.[53] In general, in such situations where there is lack of coordination of responses by the UN and the AU, the most likely affected are civilian populations whose expectations to be protected from atrocity crimes by the international community will remain unrealised. In order to 'enhance regional action' in Africa through 'greater mediation', the UN and the AU should respect the provisions of Chapter VIII and the principles agreed to by the two organisations for implementation.

Similarly, the question over collaboration between the UN and the AU was raised in the intervention in Mali in 2012 following the collapse of the Malian government, brought about by actions of the rebels from the Azawad region of Mali, and the attempted take-over of power in Bamako. Multilateral intervention began as an African-led International Support Mission to Mali (AFISMA) in January 2013, pursuant to UN Security Council *Resolution 2085* (2012). AFISMA was later re-hatted to United Nations Multidimensional Integrated Stabilization Mission in Mali (MINUSMA) in April 2013, in line with UN Security Council *Resolution 2100* (2013) resulting to changes to the Concept of Operations (CONOPS) – essentially, CONOPS typically details the objectives and means of achieving those objectives of UN missions. The issue raised by the AU was the lack of consultation during the drawing up of the CONOPS, thus further straining its partnership with the UN[54] in the ongoing peacebuilding efforts in the country.

Given that the UN and the AU (and this will apply to other regional agencies in Africa) often adopt different policy approaches and objectives in peace operations in Africa, as the above cases demonstrate, adopting a 'regional responsibility to protect' approach, which entails redeveloping pacific tools of regional organisations in order to consistently deliver on the 'greater mediation' method, thus obviating the need for multidimensional peace operations, will surely promote the much required 'greater strategic coherence' within the purview of Chapter VIII. Successful 'first response' through regional mediation tools, such as 'preventive arbitration', proposed herein, can also help reduce the Security Council's role in meeting 'regional responsibility to protect'

53 Clearly, the situation in Darfur has polarised the international community, regional organisations and national governments, especially in relation to developing a common approach to the crisis: however, there are aspects of the responses where consensus was reached, such the Joint UN-AU Hybrid Mission in Darfur; in other areas, such as accountability, huge gaps in approach created deep division. For further perspectives on UN-AU operations in Africa, see Boutellis and Williams, *Peace Operations*.

54 See 'The Need for Greater Coherence', AU Doc. PSC/AHG/3. (CCCXCVII), 23 September 2013, para. 16.

objectives; reduce global-regional tension; engender clarity of conflict prevention aims and goals; and ultimately assist in 'enhancing regional action'.[55]

Towards Greater Use of Chapter VIII of the UN Charter

This section looks at ways in which the pacific roles of regional organisations can be systematised in crises responses through global-regional recommitment to promoting the provisions of Chapter VIII. It argues that due to Africa's unique[56] security challenges, tailor-made approaches will be crucial.

In ideational terms, the principal underlying precept of the RtoP concept is to 'build a broader understanding of the problem of reconciling intervention for human protection purposes and sovereignty', and to 'develop a global political consensus on how to ... move towards action within the international system'.[57] This thrust was ratcheted up in the Secretary-General's High-level Panel report, 'A more secure world: our shared responsibility', in what the Panel described as 'common security consensus'. More so, *Resolution 60/1* declared in clear terms the need for 'multilateral solution to the problems' it identified, including human protection and preventing RtoP related crimes. In this regard, paragraph 139 of *Resolution 60/1* emphasised the overriding principles of Chapter VIII measures in coalescing a common front in the global effort to end mass atrocities. Therefore, the bedrock axiomatic principle governing Chapter VIII deployments – that is, 'comparative advantage', especially the 'local knowledge' component, should be promoted, respected, and strictly adhered to by the international community, in pursuing the goals of RtoP.

The AU, in particular, has demonstrated its commitment to end conflicts in Africa through peaceful means, specifically by mediation.[58] This commitment can be gleaned from the programmes it has initiated in the past years,

---

55 Indeed, regional-subregional approaches to peace processes in Africa also militate against the AU's mediation practices. For instance, in the Côte d'Ivoire election crisis from 2010 to 2011 the AU and ECOWAS had disagreements over the course of resolving the conflict: the AU, characteristically, preferred a political solution and pushed for an exit route for the embattled president, Laurent Gbagbo; ECOWAS backed the president-elect, Alassane Ouattara, and welcomed French intervention that effectively brought the crisis to an end.

56 See for example Cedric De Coning, John Karlsrud, and Linnea Gelot, (eds.) *The Future of African Peace Operations: From the Janjaweed to Boko Haram*, (Zed Books, 2016).

57 ICISS, *The Responsibility to Protect*, pp. 1 and 7.

58 See for example the 'Windhoek Declaration: Silencing the Guns – Terrorism, Mediation, and Armed Groups', following the 6th Annual Retreat of Special Envoys and Mediators on the Promotion of Peace, Security, and Stability in Africa, Windhoek, Namibia, 21–22 October 2015.

including the 'Silencing the Guns by 2020', 'Women, Peace and Conflict', and 'Agenda 2063'. These programmes have galvanised a pivotal dimension of conflict prevention in Africa that is consistent with the proposed 'regional responsibility to protect' through 'greater mediation' – that is, mediating conflicts of governance.[59] For instance, 'Agenda 2063', an AU Commission's project under the auspices of AGA seeks to mobilise regional resources, synergies, ideas, conflict responses, and norms towards Africa's development, security, peace and good governance. 'Agenda 2063' effectively adopts a governance approach to conflict prevention that puts the African peoples on the agenda of the regional and national policies as called for in the Continental Structural Conflict Prevention Framework (CSCPF) of the AU, which emphasises 'mainstreaming conflict prevention into the activities and programs of the Commission'.[60] Similarly, 'Silencing the Guns by 2020' implies governance up-front in a context of conflict management and resolution.[61] In addition, the special needs of Africa necessitates that Africa's development, through sustainable governance initiatives, should be prioritised, 'if the "responsibility to protect" is to make a difference'.[62] Moreover, the Common African Position on the Review of UN Peace Operations recognised the changing nature of conflicts in Africa that is linked to 'governance challenges', and argued that this 'gives the AU and its Regional Mechanisms a comparative advantage in the area of conflict prevention'.[63] Therefore, this chapter proposes that in order to enhance regional action, the region's responsibility to protect ought to be prioritised.

Regional responsibility to protect should prioritise mediating conflicts of governance as a 'first response' action. Mediating conflicts of governance entails that the AU, for instance, should pre-eminently integrate institution-building agenda, for concerned member states, in its mediation response framework. Additionally, mediating conflicts of governance requires 'popular participation' in any negotiation processes. One of the means of ensuring popular participation is to establish a system that provides would-be insurgents or rebels the opportunity of taking their grievances directly to the AU

59 See Ifediora, 'The Structural Bases of Implementing the Responsibility to Protect in Africa'.

60 See 'Structural Conflict Prevention', AU Doc. PSC/PR/2(D), 29 April 2015.

61 See for instance, Gilbert M. Khadragala, *Silencing the Guns: Strengthening Governance to Prevent, Manage, and Resolve Conflicts in Africa* (New York: International Peace Institute, 2015).

62 See Helen Scanlon, 'Conclusion', in Adekeye Adebajo and Helen Scanlon , (eds.) *A dialogue of the deaf: essays on Africa and the United Nations* (Auckland, South Africa: The Centre for Conflict Resolution, 2006), p. 281.

63 AU Doc. PSC /PR/2(DII), para. 14.

Commission for resolution.[64] Moreover, the AU-led mediation in Kenya's post-election conflict in 2007–8, mediated by the former UN Secretary-General, Kofi Annan, offers some practical lessons. Annan employed 'popular participation' and governance strategy by ensuring that the people of Kenya were included in the process, through: media transparency; inclusion of long-term issues and solutions, such as inequality, constitutional reform, land rights reform and consolidation of national cohesion and transparency in the mediation agenda; and the involvement of the *Kamukunji* – that is, the parliamentarians. Most importantly, the principle of 'comparative advantage' in Chapter VIII was respected, which fostered a common understanding of the issues and unity of approach to addressing those issues; the international community spoke with one voice, thus avoiding challenges of 'coordination'[65] and 'mediation shopping';[66] this method – 'greater mediation' – inexorably led to a resounding success.[67] Kenya was the archetypical case of Chapter VIII in greater use. Furthermore, 'regional responsibility to protect' implies international support in order to make 'peace operations' truly 'a last resort' by ensuring that governance crises are mediated successfully, through 'greater mediation', just as the AU PSC is now beginning to mainstream 'governance challenges'[68] into its conflict prevention strategies.

The current situation in Burundi also offers some practical lessons relating to redeveloping and supporting peaceful capacities of regional organisations for peaceful resolution of local disputes. On 17 December 2015 the AU PSC adopted a Communiqué on the situation in Burundi, which authorised use of force to protect civilians. The PSC, relying on the report of the fact-finding mission of the African Commission on Human and Peoples' Rights (ACHPR) that detailed ongoing abuses including acts of torture, arbitrary killings and targeted assassinations, arbitrary arrests and detention, decided to deploy an African Prevention and Protection Mission (MAPROBU). The Mission was authorised with initial troop strength of 5,000. The mandate included provision to: (a) prevent any deterioration of the security situation, monitor its evolution and report developments on the ground; (b) contribute, within its capacity and in its areas of deployment, to the protection of civilian populations under imminent threat; (c) contribute to the creation of the necessary conditions for

64 On this, see Ifediora, 'Preventive Arbitration'.

65 Gambari, 'Multilateralism', p. 135.

66 Annan, *Interventions*, p. 187.

67 For a detailed account of the AU-led mediation in Kenya, see Elizabeth Lindenmayer and Josie Lianna Kaye, *A Choice for Peace? The Story of Forty-One Days Mediation in Kenya* (New York: International Peace Institute, August 2009).

68 AU Doc. PSC /PR/2(DII), para. 14.

the successful holding of the inter-Burundian dialogue and to the preservation of the gains made through the Arusha Agreement for Peace and Reconciliation in Burundi; (d) facilitate, in collaboration, as appropriate, with other international actors, the implementation of any agreement the Burundian parties would reach, including, but not limited to, the disarmament of militias and other illegal groups, as well as the protection of political personalities and other actors whose security would be threatened; and (e) protect AU personnel, assets and installations.[69] Although the mission mandate was comprehensive, especially in the context of protection of civilians, the AU Assembly did not authorise its deployment; rather, the Assembly preferred the traditional African solution, often implemented by mutual dialogue that are facilitated by the Panel of the Wise (PoW). Invariably, the AU by adopting a pacific stance to the human rights concerns in Burundi emblemize its pacifist orientation – that is, preference to political processes, intervention with consent and peace operations as a last resort.[70] What is worrying in this preferred approach, though, is that the Union's capacity for 'first response' by mediation is still under development. This approach failed in 2015, and without additional support, there are concerns relating to how similar initiatives will fare in 2016, and perhaps, beyond. In many ways, adopting a 'regional responsibility to protect' approach outlined above can make a tremendous difference on the ground for civilian populations under risks of atrocity crimes. Institutionalising the experience in Kenya offers the potential for consistent greater use of Chapter VIII.

Conclusion

Understanding that the RtoP concept seeks to galvanise multilateral action towards helping states to fulfil their primary RtoP, the proposed reframing of the notion of a 'regional responsibility to protect' advances the prospects of 'enhancing regional action' and regional organisations assuming 'greater prominence' in protecting populations from atrocity crimes. Moreover, focusing on the unique roles of regional organisations in realising RtoP can help foster concerted policy for mediation capacity-building for regional organisations towards effective peaceful preventive action for human protection and the prevention of atrocity crimes. Indeed, Ban Ki-moon had noted the importance of strengthened mediation capacity of the UN Department

69 AU Doc. PSC/PR/COMM.(DLXV), 17 December 2015, para. 13.

70 Of course, there are other unspoken considerations, such as interests and political and diplomatic choices of regional powers.

of Political Affairs to deploy mediators within 72 hours to any corner of the globe,[71] in order to help prevent conflicts from escalating. Thus, 'enhancing regional action' also requires strengthening mediation capacity at the regional level. This will enable regional arrangements to become 'ready partners' of the UN in the preventive aspects of 'human protection' operations. Additionally, such an enabling capacity will provide the necessary facility for regional organisations to assume greater roles in protecting populations from atrocity crimes.

Above all, effective regional action must be anchored on a healthy global-regional partnership, based on greater use of Chapter VIII, as the AU-led mediation in Kenya informs, and the framework widely adopted for enunciating its provisions. As the cases examined demonstrate, the AU strived to remain and maintain its pacific role by insisting on deploying its mediation tools in those conflicts, but was unwittingly undermined by differences in approach adopted by the UN, other regional arrangements and donor partners. In hindsight, especially in the cases of Libya and Sudan, the AU's approach to the conflicts through mutual dialogue may have fared better, and this is nonetheless, informed by the AU's local knowledge and comparative advantage principle. But to be certain, the AU's instruments of self-pacification, such as political dialogue by mediation, should be developed, strengthened, and supported in operational contexts. On one occasion that easily comes to mind where the UN unequivocally supported the AU's mediation effort – that is in Kenya – the outcome was strikingly good. Now the AU has started a process in order to develop and establish a Mediation Support Unit within the AUC, it is hoped that this will not amount to another parallel venture; rather, it is envisaged that the UN and other development partners should support the drive to strengthen Africa's mediation tools – the AU's best hope of creating a more peaceful, prosperous, and democratic African continent; the basis upon which atrocity crimes can be peacefully and sustainably prevented in Africa – that is through 'greater mediation'. In searching for ideas for implementing mediation support in Africa, the AU and the international community should be reminded that mediation tools are inherently pacific instruments. Therefore, support measures should consist of similar pacific oriented mechanisms, such as the proposed 'preventive arbitration' framework. Complex peace operations African nations cannot finance can be shelved if a 'regional responsibility to protect', operationalized through 'greater mediation', becomes a reality.

---

71 See Ban Ki-moon, 'Human Protection and the 21st Century United Nations', Speech at the Cyril Foster Lecture at Oxford University, Oxford, United Kingdom, 2 February 2011.

Regionalizing Protection: AU and ASEAN Responses to Mass Atrocity Crimes against Internally Displaced Persons

Phil Orchard
University of Wollongong
orchardp@uow.edu.au

Abstract

Forcible displacement can constitute a mass atrocity crime. This is something that is considered within the non-binding Guiding Principles on Internal Displacement. Efforts to implement the Guiding Principles at the regional level suggest one path to implement stronger legal protections for internally displaced persons (IDPs), in particular, against mass atrocity crimes. These regional processes, however, can vary in remarkable ways. In the African Union, the Kampala Convention has brought the Guiding Principles and protections against mass atrocity crimes directed at IDPs into regional hard law; it also includes robust implementation and enforcement mechanisms. At this stage, however, these mechanisms remain anticipatory rather than effective; consequently international assistance will be vital to entrench the rights anchored in the Convention. By contrast, ASEAN has introduced no overt protections for IDPs. However, its developing legal human rights framework through the ASEAN Declaration of Human Rights, coupled with the Association's response to the Rohingya IDP crisis in Myanmar, suggests that a policy-focused change, while incremental, may be happening.

Keywords

Internally Displaced Persons (IDPs) – Responsibility to Protect (RtoP) – Guiding Principles on Internal Displacement – Kampala Convention – mass atrocity crimes

1 My thanks to Vickie Frater and Rebekkah Markey-Towler for research assistance, and to Sara Davies, Charles Hunt, and Noel Morada for comments. A portion of this work has been supported by an Australian Research Council Discovery Award (DP150102453).

 | DOI:10.1163/9789004363212_013

Introduction[1]

In his 2011 Cyril Foster Lecture at the University of Oxford, UN Secretary-General Ban Ki-Moon argued that human protection was an essential component of the global agenda.[2] As Hunt notes in his chapter, human protection refers to the 'protection of civilians from human rights abuses, inside and outside of armed conflicts, with a particular focus on mass atrocity crimes – genocide, war crimes, crimes against humanity and ethnic cleansing.' A critical issue for human protection, however, is how the international community should respond to people who are forcibly displaced due to mass atrocity crimes.

Three points with respect to forcible displacement are critical. The first is that the overall growth in forced migrants over the past decade has been substantial. At the end of 2017, the United Nations High Commission for Refugees (UNHCR) found that globally there were 68.5 million forcibly displaced people, including 25.4 million refugees and 40 million internally displaced persons.[3] Second, many of the crises producing forced migrants are clearly linked with mass atrocity crimes. The Syrian conflict, in which the civilian population face mass atrocity crimes committed both by state security forces and affiliated militias, and by some armed opposition groups, has created 5.6 million refugees and over 6.7 million IDPs.[4] At the same time, Eritrea had produced 486,200 refugees by the end of 2017.[5] There, a UN Human Rights Council Commission of Inquiry on Human Rights found that 'systematic, widespread and gross human rights violations have been and are being committed in Eritrea under

2 Ban Ki-moon, 'Human Protection and the 21st Century United Nations', Cyril Foster Lecture at Oxford University 2 February 2011, http://www.un.org/apps/news/infocus/sgspeeches/search_full.asp?statID=1064.

3 This includes 19.9 million refugees under UNHCR's mandate, and 5.4 million Palestinian refugees under the mandate of the United Nations Relief Works Agency (UNRWA). See UNHCR, 'Global Trends: Forced Displacement in 2017', (Geneva: UNHCR, 2018), p. 2.

4 Global Centre for the Responsibility to Protect, 'Populations at Risk: Syria', 2018, http://www.globalr2p.org/regions/syria. The Internal Displacement Monitoring Centre (IDMC), 'Syria', December 2017, http://www.internal-displacement.org/countries/syria.

5 UNHCR, 'UNHCR Global Trends, Forced Displacement in 2017', p. 15.

the authority of the Government. Some of these violations may constitute crimes against humanity.'[6]

The third is that forced displacement can directly qualify as a mass atrocity crime given two factors: the deliberate intent of the perpetrators, and the widespread or systematic nature of their acts. Thus, the Responsibility to Protect (RtoP) doctrine provides one potential form of response. It establishes that each state as well as the international community as a whole has the responsibility to protect populations from genocide, war crimes, ethnic cleansing, and crimes against humanity.[7] As I argue below, ethnic cleansing has the clearest linkage to forced displacement but is the only mass atrocity crime adopted within the World Summit Outcome Declaration (WSOD) which does not have explicit grounding in current international treaty law. Forced deportation or transfers can qualify as either as a war crime or crime against humanity, while forcible transfer of children can qualify as an act of genocide. Further, the Secretary-General's 2009 Report[8] directly drew linkages between forced displacement and the RtoP, not only noting that asylum could provide one route for protection from mass atrocity crimes, but that the protection of refugees and internally displaced person was a direct goal of the RtoP.[9]

But how do we ensure that such protections are not just words on paper? Much of the current focus of the UN is on Pillars One and Two – how states can protect their own populations from mass atrocities, and how the international community can assist states to uphold that responsibility. Therefore, providing practical, on the ground protection to the displaced and to civilians who may fall victim to mass atrocity crimes is an important area of focus.

Historically, asylum was a critical way for civilians to flee mass atrocities, to leave the state where the atrocities were being committed.[10] And yet the 1951 Refugee Convention is an inadequate tool to respond to mass atrocities. It is focused on individualized state-based persecution, not on persecution by non-state actors, on flight caused by generalized violence, or flight created

---

6 UN Human Rights Council 'Report of the Commission of Inquiry on Human Rights in Eritrea', A/HRC/29/42, 4 Jun 2015, http://daccess-dds-ny.un.org/doc/UNDOC/GEN/G15/114/50/PDF/G1511450 .pdf?OpenElement, p. 1.

7 United Nations '2005 World Summit Outcome', UNGA Res. 60/1, 16 September 2005; Ban Ki-Moon, *Implementing the Responsibility to Protect*, A/63/677, 12 January 2009, p. 17.

8 Ki-Moon, 'Implementing the Responsibility to Protect', p. 17.

9 *ibid.*, p. 29.

10 Brian Barbour and Brian Gorlick, 'Embracing the "Responsibility to Protect": A Repertoire of Measures Including Asylum for Potential Victims', *International Journal of Refugee Law* 20/4 (2008).

through mass atrocities. Further, while IDPs find themselves in situations analogous to those of refugees – coercively displaced from their own homes – unlike refugees they do not have clear international protections since they have not left their own state. Instead, they remain under the responsibility of their own state, a state which may be unable or unwilling to protect them.

Responding to IDPs required a shift in contemporary understandings of sovereignty, a shift which has been integral to the emergence of the RtoP. Francis Deng, the first Representative of the UN Secretary-General for Internally Displaced Persons, coined the term 'sovereignty as responsibility' to justify international action in such circumstances. As he argued, for a government to be legitimate it must provide a certain level of protection for its population. Most governments do so, and if unable, they call upon the international community to assist. However:

> Under exceptional circumstances when governments fail to discharge this responsibility and masses of their citizens become threatened with severe suffering and death, the international community should step in to provide the needed protection and assistance, even if the government of a state has not requested aid.[11]

This formulation, Evans notes, became 'a central conceptual underpinning of the responsibility to protect norm as it finally emerged.'[12]

Critically, the issue of IDP protection has been recognized through the 1998 Guiding Principles on International Displacement.[13] While non-binding, the Guiding Principles use as their foundation existing international human rights law, humanitarian law, and refugee law.[14] They introduce a clear right against arbitrary displacement, one that draws on the right against forcible transfers anchored in crimes against humanity and war crimes. The Guiding

11 Francis Mading Deng, 'Promoting Responsible Sovereignty in Africa', in Francis Mading Deng and Terrence Lyons (eds.), *African Reckoning: A Quest for Good Governance*, (Washington: The Brookings Institution, 1998), p. 3.

12 Gareth Evans, *The Responsibility to Protect: Ending Mass Atrocity Crimes Once and for All* (Washington: Brookings Institution Press, 2008), p. 37; see also Luke Glanville, *Sovereignty and the Responsibility to Protect: A New History* (Chicago: University of Chicago Press, 2014), pp. 174–76.

13 Office for the Coordination of Humanitarian Affairs, 'Guiding Principles on Internal Displacement', (New York: UNOCHA, 1999).

14 Walter Kälin, 'The Guiding Principles on Internal Displacement as International Minimum Standard and Protection Tool', *Refugee Survey Quarterly* 24/3 (2005): 29–30.

Principles have been brought into domestic legislation and policies by a range of states with current IDP situations, including in both Africa and the Asia-Pacific.

More notable, however, have been recent developments in IDP protection at the regional level through both the African Union (AU) and the Association of South East Asian Nations (ASEAN). Here, the AU appears to have a much stronger pattern of practice, including through the ratification of the Kampala Convention, which has strong protections for IDPs and rights against arbitrary displacement. Introducing such provisions into regional law provide an important safeguard on domestic standards along with clear implementation and enforcement standards.

This appears to represent a significant variation in practice across regions; while the Asia-Pacific has similar numbers of IDP situations and a similar record of introducing domestic protections, there has been no recognition of IDP issues at the regional level or sub-regional level. This is misleading in two ways, however. First, while the Kampala Convention introduces clear standards on paper, its actual implementation continues to lag. Second, while neither ASEAN nor other sub-regional organizations have taken steps to legalize IDP protections, ASEAN does appear to be entrenching a clear policy response towards IDPs, driven by the Rohingya situation in Myanmar. This suggests that regional protections for IDPs – and against mass atrocity crimes more generally – are an important step forward. As they develop, however, they can take much different forms.

Forced Displacement as an International Crime

There are specific forms of forced displacement which cross the line into mass atrocity crimes and hence fall within the RtoP doctrine. Ethnic cleansing is included as a specific form of mass atrocity within the WSOD but is the least clearly elaborated crime in international law. By contrast, most forms of forced displacement which would qualify as international crimes would be considered as either war crimes or crimes against humanity.

This reflects the historical origins of these crimes. The Charter for the Nuremberg Trials, in defining both war crimes and crimes against humanity,[15]

15 There is debate as to whether the Nuremberg Charter created a new crime, or articulated one already established in customary international law. Darryl Robinson, 'Defining "Crimes against Humanity" at the Rome Conference', *American Journal of International Law*, 93/1: 43–57 (1999), p. 44.

specifically established that 'deportation to slave labour' constituted a violation of the laws or customs of war, and hence a war crime. Deportation committed against any civilian population, either before or during the war, and persecutions on political, racial or religious grounds in execution or connected to any other crime constituted crimes against humanity.[16]

Further, the Genocide Convention explicitly includes the forcible transfer of children from one group to another as well as acts which are 'deliberately inflicting on the groups conditions of life calculated to bring about its physical destruction in whole or in part.'[17] From this, we could infer that forcible displacement more broadly, particularly if used in such a way, can also constitute genocide. [18] How wide this category is, however, is unclear.[19]

The Geneva Conventions also 'expressly forbid the forced displacement of civilians and subsequent resettlement of the occupying power's own population in occupied territory.'[20] Here, too, there are questions of what specific protections are warranted, and as Jacques notes, 'diverging interpretations abound.'[21] The International Committee of the Red Cross (ICRC) has also concluded that there are customary international legal protections due to civilian populations of occupied territory, including that they cannot be deported or forcibly transferred in either international or non-international armed

16 Charter of the International Military Tribunal, Art. 6.

17 Convention on the Prevention and Punishment of the Crime of Genocide, Art 2(e).

18 Grant Dawson and Sonia Farber, *Forcible Displacement Throughout the Ages: Towards an International Convention for the Prevention and Punishment of the Crime of Forcible Displacement* (Martinus Nijhoff Publishers, 2012), p. 57.

19 Machteld Boot, *Genocide, Crimes against Humanity, War Crimes: Nullum Crimen Sine Lege and the Subject Matter Jurisdiction of the International Criminal Court*, vol. 12 (Intersentia nv, 2002), p. 451.

20 Mélanie Jacques, *Armed Conflict and Displacement: The Protection of Refugees and Displaced Persons under International Humanitarian Law* (Cambridge University Press, 2012), p. 79. The Geneva Convention IV, Art. 49 notes 'Individual or mass forcible transfers, as well as deportations of protected persons from occupied territory to the territory of the Occupying Power or to that of any other country, occupied or not, are prohibited, regardless of their motive' and Art. 85 precludes an Occupying Power from transferring parts of its own civilian population into the territory it occupies. Art. 17 of the Additional Protocol II, which deals with non-international armed conflicts, provides that: 'Civilians shall not be compelled to leave their own territory for reasons connected with the conflict.' See Jean-Marie Henckaerts, Louise Doswald-Beck, and Carolin Alvermann, *Customary International Humanitarian Law: Volume 1, Rules*, vol. 1 (Cambridge University Press, 2005), pp. 458–50.

21 Jacques, *Armed Conflict and Displacement*, p. 79.

conflicts unless 'the security of the civilians involved or imperative military reasons so demand.'[22]

The 1951 Convention Relating to the Status of Refugees establishes that a refugee is a person who has fled 'owing to a well-founded fear of being persecuted for reasons of race, religion, nationality, membership of a particular social group or political opinion' and is both outside their country of nationality and unable or, owing to such fear, unwilling to avail themselves of the protection of that country.[23] But while the Convention provides rights for refugees, it does not place any obligation on governments to refrain from engaging in actions that would create refugees.[24]

The 1990s saw the new term 'ethnic cleansing' introduced into the lexicon in which significant violence was used to drive people of a specific ethnic group from a particular territory. As Jackson Preece notes, while this may have been a new term, it had a long history in practice.[25] But what form of crime was ethnic cleansing? At least initially, it was equated with genocide, such as in a 1992 UN General Assembly resolution.[26] That same year, the UN Special Rapporteur on the Situation of Human Rights in the Territory of the Former Yugoslavia, Tadeusz Mazowiecki, provided a clearer definition of as 'the elimination by the ethnic group exerting control over a given territory of members of other ethnic groups.'[27] Given the conflict situation, he suggested that practices of ethnic cleansing constituted both war crimes as well as human rights violations.[28] A Commission of Experts established by the Security Council subsequently

22 Henckaerts et al, *Customary International Humanitarian Law*, p. 457.

23 *Convention Relating to the Status of Refugees*, Art. 1 A.(2).

24 Dawson and Farber, *Forcible Displacement Throughout the Ages*, p. 59.

25 Jennifer Jackson Preece, 'Ethnic Cleansing as an Instrument of Nation-State Creation: Changing State Practices and Evolving Legal Norms', *Human Rights Quarterly* 20/4 (1998), p. 818.

26 'The Situation in Bosnia and Herzegovina', UN General Assembly Res. 121, adopted on Dec. 18 1992, UN General Assembly *Official Records*, 47th Sess., UN Doc. A/RES/47/121 (1993); William A Schabas, 'Problems of International Codification-Were the Atrocities in Cambodia and Kosovo Genocide', *New England Law Review*, 35 (2000), p. 294. Boot suggests that the term may have been used in this case precisely because it was not legally defined, whereas the use of Genocide 'would trigger states' obligations deriving from the Genocide Convention.' Boot, *Genocide, Crimes against Humanity, War Crimes*, p. 447.

27 Tadeusz Mazowiecki, 'Report on the Situation in the Territory of the Former Yugoslavia to the 47th Session of the Security Council and the General Assembly', A/47/666, 17 Nov 1992, p.6. See also Preece, 'Ethnic Cleansing as an Instrument of Nation-State Creation'.

28 Mazowiecki, 'Report on the Situation in the Territory of the Former Yugoslavia', p. 16.

defined ethnic cleansing as 'a purposeful policy designed by one ethnic or religious group to remove by violent and terror-inspiring means the civilian population of another ethnic or religious group from certain geographic areas.'[29]

Ethnic cleansing has not been recognized as an international crime in law in its own right.[30] However, the term has led to important shifts in how other mass atrocities are understood. Thus, it was not explicitly included as a crime within the Statute of the International Criminal Tribunal for the former Yugoslavia. Instead, the Statute provided that the International Tribunal:

> shall have the power to prosecute persons responsible for the following crimes when committed in armed conflict, whether international or internal in character, and directed against any civilian population: ...(d) deportation (h) persecutions on political, racial and religious grounds (i) other inhumane acts.[31]

Thus, the 1999 indictment against Slobodan Milosevic included:

> the unlawful deportation and forcible transfer of thousands of Kosovo Albanians from their homes in Kosovo involved well-planned and coordinated efforts by the leaders of the FRY and Serbia, and forces of the FRY and Serbia, all acting in concert.[32]

As Schabas notes, the allusion to ethnic cleansing here 'implies that this too was a crime against humanity and not genocide.'[33] He adds that the 'principal act of genocide listed in the Convention is killing... Herein lies the fundamental difference with ethnic cleansing, which generally involves killing, but with the intent to effect forced migration from a territory.'[34]

29 UN Security Council 'Letter dated 24 May 1994 from the Secretary-General to the President of the Security Council' (S/1994/674), 27 May 1994, p. 33.

30 Erin D Mooney, 'Something Old, Something New, Something Borrowed... Something Blue? The Protection Potential of a Marriage of Concepts between R2P and IDP Protection', *Global Responsibility to Protect*, 2/1:60–85 (2010), p. 65.

31 United Nations, 'Updated Statute of the International Criminal Tribunal for the Former Yugoslavia' September 2009, http://www.icty.org/x/file/Legal%20Library/Statute/statute_sept09_en.pdf, accessed 18 May 2015.

32 National Criminal Tribunal for Former Yugoslavia (Prosecutor v. Milosevic), May 22, 1999 (Indictment No. IT-99-37-I).

33 Schabas, 'Problems of International Codification', p. 294.

34 *ibid.*, p. 295.

The International Court of Justice has taken a similar view. The Court established that acts described as 'ethnic cleansing' may constitute genocide:

> if they are such as to be characterized as, for example, deliberately inflicting on the group conditions of life calculated to bring about its physical destruction in whole or in part… [and] provided such action is carried out with the necessary specific intent.[35]

However, the Court noted that in the context of the Genocide Convention:

> the term 'ethnic cleansing' has no legal significance of its own. Thus, not surprisingly perhaps, the International Committee of the Red Cross has determined ethnic cleansing to be a 'composite war crime' as it includes a range of acts which are prohibited under the Geneva Conventions, their Protocols, and in customary international law.[36]

Finally, the Rome Statute of the International Criminal Court (ICC) provides the clearest statement on this issue. While not including ethnic cleansing, it includes 'deportation or forcible transfer of population' as a crime against humanity 'when committed as part of a widespread or systematic attack directed against any civilian population, with knowledge of the attack.'[37] There is no requirement that armed conflict needs to be present, nor, except with respect to the crime of persecution, that the crime requires a discriminatory motive. For it to be widespread requires it to be a large-scale action involving a substantial number of victims, while for it to be systematic requires a high degree of orchestration and planning.[38]

The Rome Statute defines deportation or forcible transfer as 'forced displacement of the persons concerned by expulsion or other coercive acts from the area in which they are lawfully present, without grounds permitted under international law.'[39] However, the distinction between deportation and forcible transfer is not necessarily clear. Bassiouni notes that 'deportation is

---

35 International Court of Justice, Application of the Convention on the Prevention and Punishment of the Crime of Genocide case (Bosnia and Herzegovina v. Serbia and Montenegro), Merits, Judgement, 26 February 2007, p. 123.

36 Henckaerts et al, *Customary International Humanitarian Law*, p. 603; Mooney, 'Something Old, Something New', p. 65.

37 Rome Statute of the International Criminal Court Art. 7(1).

38 Robinson, 'Defining "Crimes against Humanity" at the Rome Conference', pp. 45–6.

39 Rome Statute of the International Criminal Court Art. 7(1).

the forced removal of people from one country to another while population transfer applies to compulsory movement of people from one area to another within the same state.'[40] By contrast, Meindersma suggests population transfers should be viewed as any:

> deliberate policy, with the direct or indirect involvement of the government, to move people – currently under its jurisdiction – into or away from a certain area, having the purpose or effect of compelling people to leave their territory or accept the implantation of (alien) settlers into that territory, aimed at transforming the demographic composition or political status of the territory concerned... this description does not create the distinction between movement across international borders or within the State...[41]

Jurisprudence at the International Criminal Tribunal for the former Yugoslavia (ICTY), in the Stakid Appeal, supports the former interpretation, but only with respect to clear borders. In that case, the Appeals Chamber noted that deportation can include being forced to cross either *de jure* or *de facto* borders, which does not include 'constantly changing frontlines.'[42] For other cases where neither *de jure* nor *de facto* borders were crossed, the Appeals Chamber concluded that 'punishment for such forcible transfers may be assured by the adoption of proper pleading practices in the Prosecution's indictments.'[43]

From this, it is clear that engaging in either widespread or systematic acts with the goal to deliberately displace a civilian population, irrespective of their status as nationals, qualifies as a crime against humanity under the Rome Statute. Deliberately displacing them across *de jure* or *de facto* borders qualifies as deportation, while deliberately displacing them within a state's territory qualifies as forcible transfer. Such a reading subsumes ethnic cleansing as a

40 M. Cherif Bassiouni, *Crimes against Humanity in International Criminal Law*, (Dordrecht, Boston-London, 1999), p. 312.

41 Christa Meindersma, 'Legal Issues Surrounding Population Transfers in Conflict Situations', *Netherlands International Law Review* 41/1 (1994), p. 33.

42 In the case of Milomir Stakid, the Appeals Chamber noted that 'the *actus reus* of deportation is the forced displacement of persons by expulsion or other forms of coercion from the area in which they are lawfully present, across a de jure state border or, in certain circumstances, a de facto border, without grounds permitted under international law.' The Appeals judgement was specifically challenging an argument made by the Trial Chamber that deportation could encompass displacements across 'constantly changing frontlines.' Stakid (Case No. IT-97-24-A, Appeal Judgement 22 March 2006), pp. 92, 99.

43 Stakid (Case No. IT-97-24-A, Appeal Judgement), p. 99.

crime against humanity, but this reflects practice, if not law, since the conflict in the former Yugoslavia. The Rome Statute, therefore, also provides one route for the international community to ensure protections for the displaced and would-be displaced against these crimes: through the mechanism of individual prosecution by the International Criminal Court.

Implementing Protections Against Deportation and Forced Transfer

The ICC, however, represents a limited tool, one which can only prosecute a small number of cases and one in which prosecutions may occur years after violations occur. As noted in the introduction, advocates for the RtoP doctrine are increasingly focused on how Pillars One and Two can be used to provide robust protections using regional and domestic mechanisms. As the Secretary-General noted in his 2011 Report, 'the development of regional and sub-regional arrangements has varied markedly from region to region, whether measured in terms of their scope, capacity, or authority.'[44] He suggests that 'regional and sub-regional arrangements can encourage governments to recognize their obligations under relevant international conventions and to identify and resolve sources of friction within their societies before they lead to violence or atrocity crimes.'[45]

In ensuring the protection of the displaced from mass atrocities, the Guiding Principles on Internal Displacement can play a key role. As noted in the introduction, while the Principles are non-binding, they are based on international human rights law, international humanitarian law, and analogous refugee law.[46] The principles define who IDPs are, establish that they continue to possess legal rights in spite of being displaced, and acknowledge that the state and international community both hold responsibilities towards IDPs. There is substantial evidence that the Principles are widely accepted at the international, regional, and state levels, where a number of states have sought to implement domestic policies or legislation to protect their own internally displaced populations in line with the principles.[47]

44 United Nations, 'The Role of Regional and Sub-Regional Arrangements in Implementing the Responsibility to Protect: Report of the Secretary-General', (New York: United Nations, 2011), p. 3.

45 *ibid.*, p. 5

46 Kälin, 'The Guiding Principles on Internal Displacement', pp. 29–30.

47 Phil Orchard, 'Protection of Internally Displaced Persons: Soft Law as a Norm-Generating Mechanism' *Review of International Studies* 36/2 (2010), p. 294; Phil Orchard, 'Implementing

Notably, in Principle 6, the Guiding Principles note:

> Every human being shall have the right to be protected against being arbitrarily displaced from his or her home or place of habitual residence.
>
> 2. The prohibition of arbitrary displacement includes displacement:

(a) When it is based on policies of apartheid, 'ethnic cleansing' or similar practices aimed at or resulting in alteration of the ethnic, religious or racial composition of the affected population;
(b) In situations of armed conflict, unless the security of the civilians involved or imperative military reasons so demand;
(c) In cases of large-scale development projects that are not justified by compelling and over-riding public interests;
(d) In cases of disasters, unless the safety and health of those affected requires their evacuation; and
(e) When it is used as a collective punishment.[48]

Kälin recognizes that 'an explicit prohibition of "ethnic cleansing" has not yet been adopted…' but that this principle reflects existing international law, including that 'ethnic cleansing' may constitute genocide.[49] Further, he notes 'forced population transfers for the purpose of "ethnic cleansing" and similar purposes can never be justified under international law and, therefore, always have to be considered arbitrary.'[50] Hence, the right against arbitrary displacement established in Principle 6, and particularly in elements 6 (2) (a), (b), and (e), clearly reflects existing legal prohibitions against mass atrocities. Further, it applies protection against these prohibitions not only to the internally displaced, but to all persons who may become internally displaced, whether through these crimes or through other acts.[51]

a Global Internally Displaced Persons Protection Regime', in Alexander Betts and Phil Orchard (eds.), *Implementation and World Politics: How International Norms Change Practice*, (Oxford: Oxford University Press, 2014), p. 107.

48 Office for the Coordination of Humanitarian Affairs, 'Guiding Principles on Internal Displacement', Principle 6.

49 Walter Kälin, *Guiding Principles on Internal Displacement: Annotations*, 2nd ed. (Washington D.C.: The American Society of Internationa Law, 2008), pp. 30–31.

50 *ibid.*, p. 31; See also Brookings-Bern Project on Internal Displacement, 'Protecting Internally Displaced Persons: A Manual for Law and Policymakers', (Washington, D.C.: Brookings Institution, 2008), p. 45.

51 Other soft law instruments for IDPs offer similar protections. The International Law Association's 'Draft Declaration of International Law Principles on Internally Displaced

The Guiding Principles, like the RtoP doctrine itself, is soft law and, while it has a strong basis in international law, it is unlikely to lead to an international convention. How, then, can we implement such measures? In other work, I have defined implementation as 'a parallel process to institutionalization which draws attention to the steps necessary to introduce the new international norm's precepts into formal legal and policy mechanisms within a state or organization in order to routinize compliance.'[52] The RtoP doctrine reflects a bundle of different norms, or a regime, in which a range of existing international norms around mass atrocities have been linked together by a new norm requiring the United Nations Security Council to consider its response to mass atrocity on a case by case basis. Welsh notes that RtoP does not require a particular type of action be taken upon its invocation. The response, rather, 'will depend on a host of factors, *including* other important international norms.'[53] Instead, she suggests the R2P demands 'a duty of conduct' by members of the international community: 'to identify when atrocity crimes are being committed (or when there is threat of commission) and to deliberate on how the three-pillar framework might apply.'[54]

Both Africa and the Asia-Pacific have similar numbers of countries with IDP situations as of 2014 – twenty-one African states and twenty-five Asia-Pacific states. A range of these states have introduced or are in the process of adopting their own domestic policies, which frequently include direct references to the illegality of arbitrary displacement under international law. To give two recent examples, Kenya's 2012 Act[55] establishes that, while subject to the Kenyan Constitution, the provisions of the Great Lakes Protocol and of the Guiding Principles 'shall apply to all internally displaced persons in Kenya.'[56]

Persons' (2000), p. 11, notes in Article 4(3) that 'Measures aimed at deliberate alteration of the demographic composition of a given region (e.g., "ethnic cleansing") or at genocide are strictly prohibited.'

52 Alexander Betts and Phil Orchard, 'Introduction: The Normative Institutionalization-Implementation Gap', in Alexander Betts and Phil Orchard (eds.), *Implementation and World Politics: How International Norms Change Practice*, (Oxford: Oxford University Press, 2014), p. 2.

53 Jennifer Welsh, 'Implementing the "Responsibility to Protect": Catalyzing Debate and Building Capacity', in Alexander Betts and Phil Orchard (eds.), *Implementation and World Politics: How International Norms Change Practice*, (Oxford: Oxford University Press, 2014), p. 136.

54 *ibid.*, p. 136.

55 Republic of Kenya, 'The Prevention, Protection and Assistance to Internally Displaced Persons and Affected Communities Act, 2012', 31 Dec 2012.

56 *ibid.*, II. 3.

The government accepts a duty to both prevent internal displacement, and to 'protect every human being against arbitrary displacement.'[57] Further, the Act establishes that 'no person shall cause, aid or abet arbitrary displacement through acts that amount to genocide, a crime against humanity or a war crime in accordance with international law and shall be punished in accordance with the International Crimes Act, 2008.'[58]

In 2013, the Congress of the Philippines passed an Act to protect IDPs;[59] however, it was vetoed by President Benigno Aquino III over concerns that powers accorded to the Commission on Human Rights to determine damages incurred against IDPs violated the Commission's powers under the Constitution.[60] The draft Act included clear language that arbitrary internal displacement was prohibited, including acts:

> (a) based on policies of apartheid, 'ethnic cleansing' or similar practices aimed at or resulting in altering the ethnic, religious or racial composition of the affected population; (b) in situations of armed conflict, unless the security of civilians is involved;... (e) when used as a form of collective punishment.[61]

But have these policies been adequately implemented? This is an important question - as UNHCR has argued, 'international, regional and national

57 *ibid.*, II. 5(2), 6(1).

58 *ibid.*, VI 23(1). The International Crimes Act brings into force in Kenya the Rome Statute. See International Committee of the Red Cross 'IHL National Implementation- International Crimes Act, 2008', https://www.icrc.org/applic/ihl/ihl-nat.nsf/6fa4d35e5e30253941 25673e00508143/57d55469fc1bd9 c9c12576ce003cd1f2?openDocument.

59 Republic of the Philippines, Congress of the Philippines 'An Act Protecting the Rights of Internally Displaced Persons, Providing Penalties for Violations Thereof and for Other Purposes', 5 Feb 2013.

60 IDMC, 'A Bend in the Road is Not the End of the Road- The Veto of the IDP Act in the Philippines'. 13 Jun 2013, http://www.internal-displacement.org/assets/library/Asia/Philippines/pdf/IDMC-NRC-public-statement-Philippines-13-june-2013.pdf. A revised version was approved by the Philippines House of Representatives in 2014, but has not been passed by the Senate. Republic of the Philippines House of Representatives, 'Proposed Internal Displacement Act of 2014 approved on 2nd Reading', http://www.congress.gov.ph/press/details.php?pressid=8085, accessed 14 May 2015; Llanesca Panti, 'Bill on Displaced Persons Gathers Dust in Congress', *The Manila Times*, 14 March 2015 http://www.manilatimes.net/bill-on-displaced-persons-gathers-dust-in-congress/169395/.

61 Republic of the Philippines, Congress of the Philippines, 'An Act Protecting the Rights of Internally Displaced Persons', Section 6.

standards for IDPs are meaningful only if effectively implemented in practice.'[62] And yet, in both regions the passage of such laws or policies has slowed down. As I detail in Table 1 below, in Africa, only eight countries have created IDP laws or policies at the domestic level, and only one new policy has been introduced in the last five years. In Asia, by contrast, a greater number of states have adopted laws or policies – eleven states currently have policies, and one more has a policy in preparation. Further, I have noted elsewhere that as documents, these laws and policies actually do a relatively poor job of reflecting the Guiding Principles. Across twenty-nine domestic policies introduced globally:

> Only seventeen explicitly mention the guiding principles, and only seven explicitly endorse its IDP definition. In fact, most of these laws and policies either do not provide a definition or introduce a more restrictive definition than that of the principles.[63]

Similarly, Beyani notes that these domestic frameworks 'vary in scope, the guarantees of protection and assistance to internally displaced persons, and the coverage of relevant issues.'[64] Weaknesses in these frameworks can be balanced by regional and international law. While the Guiding Principles as soft law have no formal enforcement provisions, Africa as a region has taken two important steps forward to bring the Guiding Principles into regional hard law, first through the 2006 Great Lakes Protocol on Protection and Assistance to Internally Displaced Persons, and more recently through the African Union's 2009 Convention for the Protection and Assistance of Internally Displaced Persons in Africa (the Kampala Convention), which entered into force in 2012. Thus, Africa appears to have taken a leadership position in introducing clear rights against arbitrary displacement and other rights for the internally displaced.

By contrast, in the Asia-Pacific there have been few moves at the regional level, either in formal multilateral regional organizations such as the Association of South East Asian Nations (ASEAN), or less formal multilateral initiatives. UNHCR has noted that with respect to IDP protection in the Asia-Pacific, regional processes have significantly lagged behind domestic legislative and

62 UNHCR, 'Commitments for Protection and Solution in OSCE Region', (Geneva: UNHCR, 2013), p. 7.

63 Phil Orchard, 'Implementing a Global Internally Displaced Persons Protection Regime', p. 112; see also Susan Carr, 'From Theory to Practice: National and Regional Application of the Guiding Principles', *International Journal of Refugee Law* 21/1 (2009), p. 39.

64 Human Rights Council, 'Report of the Special Rapporteur on the Human Rights of Internally Displaced Persons, Chaloka Beyani', 4 April 2014, A/HRC/26/33, p. 16.

policy initiatives.[65] Prior to 2015 ASEAN, for example, had only made a commitment to IDPs in relation to a narrow commitment to strengthen ASEAN humanitarian assistance through the 'orderly repatriation of refugees/displaced persons and resettlement of internally displaced persons.'[66]

Other Asia-Pacific regional processes have also neglected IDPs. The Central Asian Almaty Process for Refugee Protection and International Migration does not explicitly address IDP protection, even though a number of its members have current IDP situations and they have committed to the importance of 'establishing appropriate national legal frameworks' to ensure the human rights of migrants.[67] The South Asian Association for Regional Cooperation (SAARC), which includes a number of states with IDP problems, has a Social Charter that notes that state parties shall endeavor to ensure that 'internal migration resulting in excessive population concentration' should be 'carefully, diligently and effectively managed.'[68] However, 'the region, with its strong emphasis on state sovereignty and territorial integrity, considers IDPs to be a domestic matter'[69] and the issue is simply not on SAARC's agenda.

However, neither the African nor the South East Asian cases are as clear cut as they appear. While I argue below that the Kampala Convention has introduced strong legal rights for IDPs, its implementation has lagged. ASEAN has introduced no overt protections for IDPs. However, its developing legal human rights framework through the ASEAN Declaration of Human Rights, coupled with the Association's response to the Rohingya IDP crisis in Myanmar, suggests that a regional change, while incremental, may be happening.

The Role of Regional IDP Protection in Africa

It should not be surprising that the African Union (AU) has taken the lead in developing new regional law on this issue. The AU and its predecessor, the

65 UNHCR, *Overview of UNHCR's Operational Strategies in the Asia-Pacific Region*, (Geneva: UNHCR, 2013), p. 1.

66 ASEAN, *ASEAN Security Community Plan of Action*, (Vientiane, Laos: ASEAN, 2004).

67 Ministry of Foreign Affairs of the Republic of Kazakstan, *Ministerial Conference on Refugee Protection and International Migration: The Almaty Process*, (Almaty Ministry of Foreign Affairs of the Republic of Kazakstan, 2013), p. 12.

68 SAARC, 'Social Charter of the South Asian Association for Regional Cooperation', SAARC/SUMMIT.12/SC.29/27, 2004, p. 9.

69 Menaka Lecamwasam, 'The Internally Displaced in South Asia: Lessons from Kampala', *Asia Pacific Journal on Human Rights and Law*, 15/1-2 (2014), p. 172; Paula Banerjee, 'IDP Protection at the National Level in South Asia', *Forced Migration Review* 18 (2006).

TABLE 1 *IDP Regional or National Legislation and Policies in Africa and the Asia-Pacific.*[70]

State	Number of IDPs (2014)*	Nairobi Protocol	Kampala Convention **	National Legislation or Policy***	Explicitly cites Guiding Principles Definition	Bureaucratic Role Assigned
Africa						
Algeria	No recent figure					
Angola	No recent figure		R	2001/2	Yes	Yes- New
Burundi	77,600	S	S	2001	Yes	Yes- New
Central African Republic	436,300	S	R			
Chad	8,500		R			
Congo	7,800		R			
Cote d'Ivoire	300,000		R			
Democratic Republic of the Congo	2,857,400	S	S			
Eritrea	10,000 (2008 figure)		S			
Ethiopia	396,100		S			
Kenya	309,200	S		2012	Yes	Yes- New

Liberia	23,000 (2013 figure)		S	2004	Yes	Yes- New
Libya	400,000					
Mali	86,026		R			
Niger	11,000 (2013 figure)		R			
Nigeria	1,235,300		R	In preparation		
Rwanda	0	S	R			
Senegal	24,000 (2013 figure)		S			
Sierra Leone	0		R	2001	Yes	Yes
Somalia	1,107,000		S	2014	Yes	Yes
South Sudan	1,520,300		S			
Sudan	3,100,000	S		2009		
Togo	1,500 (2006 figure)		R			
Uganda	29,800	S	R	2004	Yes	Yes
Zimbabwe	36,000 (2013 figure)		R			

TABLE 1 *IDP Regional or National Legislation and Policies in Africa and the Asia-Pacific.*[70] (cont.)

State	Number of IDPs (2014)*	Nairobi Protocol	Kampala Convention **	National Legislation or Policy***	Explicitly cites Guiding Principles Definition	Bureaucratic Role Assigned
Total: 21 states	**11,871,326**		21 (13 Ratifications)	8 laws or policies (1 in preparation)		
Asia-Pacific						
Afghanistan	829,300			2005	Yes	Yes
Bangladesh	431,000					
India	616,140			2003		Yes-New
Indonesia	81,740			2001	No	No
Laos	4,500					
Myanmar	662,400					
Nepal	50,000			2007	Yes	Yes-New
Pakistan	274,800			2009	No	No
Papua New Guinea	7,500			In preparation		
Philippines	127,000			2013 (vetoed)	Yes	
Russia	41,000			1993		Yes
Sri Lanka	90,000			2002		Yes- New
Tajikistan	0			1994		Yes
Timor-Leste	900					

Turkmenistan	4,000	
Uzbekistan	3,400	
Yemen	334,100	
Total: 17 states	**3,557,780**	8 laws or policies (2 in preparation)

70 Source: Adapted from Author. Notes: In cases where more than one piece of legislation or policy has been passed, year of adoption of the first policy is used. Sources: *IDMC, 'Latest IDP numbers by country' (http://www.internal-displacement.org/global-figures, accessed 30 Apr 2015). All figures rounded to the nearest thousand. Where IDP figures are represented by a range, I have used the low estimate. Some cases where either no recent figure exists or where a prior IDP situation has ceased are included to reflect policy adoption. **Internal Displacement Monitoring Centre (IDMC) 'The Kampala Convention' (Available at: http://www.internal-displacement.org/sub-saharan-africa/kampala-convention/) and Elizabeth Ferris and Chareen Stark, 'Internal Displacement in West Africa: A Snapshot', (Washington D.C.: Brookings-LSE Project on Internal Displacement 2012), p. 22–3. This list includes only countries with IDP current or recent IDP situations; a total of 25 states have ratified and 43 states have signed the Convention. IDMC 'IDP Laws and Policies: A Mapping Tool.' Available at: http://www.internal-displacement.org/law-and-policy, accessed 4 March 2016. *** Brookings Institution-London School of Economics Project on Internal Displacement, 'National and Regional Laws and Policies on Internal Displacement Database'. Available at: http://www.brookings.edu /projects/idp/Laws-andPolicies/idp_policies_ index.aspx.; IDMC 'IDP Laws and Policies: A Mapping Tool.' Available at: http://www.internal-displacement.org/law-and-policy.

Organization for African Union (OAU), have taken steps to introduce both refugee law and a right of intervention beyond international standards. The OAU's 1969 Convention Governing the Specific Aspects of Refugee Problems in Africa provided a wider definition for refugees than either the UN Refugee Convention or Protocol, adding that:

> The term 'refugee' shall also apply to every person who, owing to external aggression, occupation, foreign domination or events seriously disturbing public order in either part or the whole of his country of origin or nationality, is compelled to leave his place of habitual residence in order to seek refuge in another place outside his country of origin or nationality.[71]

The African Union's Constitutive Act enshrines a right of intervention to the organization, noting 'the right of the Union to intervene in a Member State pursuant to a decision of the Assembly in respect of grave circumstances, namely: war crimes, genocide and crimes against humanity.'[72]

The first regional law reflecting the Guiding Principles was the Great Lakes Protocol,[73] which applies to the eleven member states of the International Conference on the Great Lakes Region. The Protocol uses the IDP definition from the Guiding Principles and 'member states undertake to prevent arbitrary displacement and to eliminate the root causes of displacement.'[74] The signatories further accepted that 'they bear the primary responsibility for the protection of the physical and material safety of internally displaced persons during flight, in places of displacement, and upon return, or resettlement elsewhere within the territory of the State.' They also commit to establishing and designating government organs to coordinate protection and assistance for IDPs and 'enact national legislation to domesticate the Guiding Principles fully.'[75]

The Kampala Convention reflects a similar expansion of regional rights to the internally displaced. The Convention acknowledges explicitly the inherent rights of the internally displaced as laid out in the Guiding Principles, and introduces a range of obligations on its State parties to refrain from arbitrary displacement and to abide by their responsibilities under human rights and

---

71 Organization for African Unity, *Convention Governing the Specific Aspects of Refugee Problems in Africa*, Article II.

72 African Union, 'Constitutive Act of the African Union', 11 July 2000, Art 4(h).

73 International Conference on the Great Lakes Region, 'Protocol on the Protection and Assistance to Internally Displaced Persons', 30 November 2006.

74 *ibid.*, Art 3(1).

75 *ibid.*, Art 3(5), 6(1).

humanitarian law. This is an important step, as the Kampala Convention adopts wholesale the definition of internal displacement first provided in the Guiding Principles as:

> persons or groups of persons who have been forced or obliged to flee or to leave their homes or places of habitual residence, in particular as a result of or in order to avoid the effects of armed conflict, situations of generalized violence, violations of human rights or natural or human-made disasters, and who have not crossed an internationally recognized State border.[76]

Further, it is also applied to non-state armed groups, and notes that 'Members of Armed groups shall be held criminally responsible for their acts which violate the rights of internally displaced persons under international law and national law.'[77]

But the Kampala Convention also enshrines elements of the Responsibility to Protect. It only notes the RtoP explicitly in its preamble, with state parties 'affirming our primary responsibility and commitment to respect, protect and fulfil the rights to which internally displaced persons are entitled, without discrimination of any kind.'[78] However, the Convention does include three clear clauses with respect to mass atrocity crimes.

The first reflects the illegality of arbitrary displacement. The Convention establishes that 'all persons have a right to be protected against arbitrary displacement' which is defined as including eight prohibited categories. The first is displacement based on policies of racial discrimination or other similar practices. The second is displacement in 'situations of armed conflict unless the security of the civilians involved or imperative military reasons so demand, in accordance with international humanitarian law.'[79] Similar prohibitions are established against intentional displacement as a method of warfare;

76 African Union, 'African Union Convention for the Protection and Assistance of Internally Displaced Persons in Africa (Kampala Convention), 22 October 2009, Art. 1(k).

77 *ibid.*, Art. 7(4).

78 *ibid.*, Preamble. Abebe suggests that 'the Convention avoided making explicit references to concepts such as "humanitarian intervention", "responsibility to protect", and others mainly out of fear that these references will "radicalise" the text making any future adoption of the Convention extremely difficult.' Allehone Mulugeta Abebe, 'The African Union Convention on Internally Displaced Persons: Its Codification Background, Scope, and Enforcement Challenges', *Refugee Survey Quarterly* 29/3 (2010) p. 57.

79 Kampala Convention, Art. 4(b).

displacement caused by generalized violence; as a result of harmful practices; non-required forced evacuations during natural or human made disasters; displacement as collective punishment; and any act of comparable gravity.[80] A separate clause reinforces that 'State Parties shall declare as offences punishable by law acts of arbitrary displacement that amount to genocide, war crimes or crimes against humanity.'[81] The Convention also establishes that state parties have an obligation to protect the rights of IDPs by refraining from and prevention 'genocide, crimes against humanity, war crimes and other violations of international humanitarian law against internally displaced persons.'[82] And the Convention introduces a remedies clause, establishing that 'State Parties shall provide persons affected by displacement with effective remedies' including compensation and reparations frameworks at the domestic level 'in accordance with international standards.'[83]

Finally, the Convention 'confirms that the AU's powers of intervention apply to internally displaced persons.'[84] It reiterates Article 4(h) of the African Union's Constitutive Act, noting the 'African Union shall have the right to intervene in a Member State… in respect of grave circumstances, namely: war crimes, genocide, and crimes again humanity.'[85] As Omorogbe notes;

> it follows that where there are internally displaced persons, Article 8 of the Kampala Convention provides the AU with a right to intervene across the range of circumstances covered by the 'responsibility to protect', including cases of armed conflict and gross violations of international criminal law.[86]

Measuring Implementation

And yet, how can we measure the Convention's implementation? Has it been effective in ensuring that IDPs have access to the rights embodied within it? Its rapid entry into force is one important marker of its success. Introduced in 2009, it came into force in 2012. Twenty-five countries have now ratified it, and

---

80 *ibid.*, Art. 4(c-h).

81 *ibid.*, Art. 4(6).

82 *ibid.*, Art. 9 1(b).

83 *ibid.*, Art. 12 (1) and (2). It also includes a further clause that 'State Party shall be liable to make reparation… when such a State Party refrains from protecting and assisting internally displaced persons in the event of natural disasters.' Art. 12 (3).

84 Eki Yemisi Omorogbe, 'The African Union, Responsibility to Protect and the Libyan Crisis', *Netherlands International Law Review* 59/2 (2012), p. 151.

85 The Kampala Convention, Article 8(1).

86 Omorogbe, 'The African Union, Responsibility to Protect and the Libyan Crisis', pp. 151–2.

another eighteen states have signed it.[87] The AU's Executive Council has also promoted the convention, urging member states initially to move forward with the implementation of the Convention.[88] With its entry into force, the Executive Council has continued to urge the member states 'that have not yet done so to expedite signing and ratification of the Kampala Convention...'[89]

On paper, at least, the Convention introduces strong mechanisms to monitor implementation and compliance. The first of these is an agreement to establish a Conference of State Parties which will 'enhance their capacity for cooperation and mutual support' and 'shall be convened regularly and facilitated by the African Union.'[90] As Kidane notes, the Convention 'does not properly define the mandate of the "Conference"... [it] does not give any meaningful guidance as to how the Conference of States may carry out its mission of monitoring compliance.'[91] Based on this, he concludes the 'contracting states obviously did not want to create a robust enforcement mechanism' suggesting that they could have created an independent agency to monitor the Convention had they wished to do so.[92] But creating such an agency would have entailed significant costs, and it would also be variant from both international practice – where there is no single-purpose IDP body – and also with past African practice such as around the OAU Convention. So far, this issue has been moot. As the then-United Nations' Special Rapporteur on the Human Rights of Internally Displaced Persons, Dr. Chaloka Beyani, noted in 2014: 'the Conference of States Parties has never convened despite the provision in article 14 (2). The Special Rapporteur has repeatedly expressed his wish for the Conference of States Parties to be established in the near future.'[93] Since then, the Conference has met only once, in 2017.

Further, this does not take into account the other potential enforcement mechanisms within the Kampala Convention. It also requires that state parties

87 IDMC, 'IDP Laws and Policies: A Mapping Tool', http://www.internal-displacement.org/law-and-policy.

88 African Union Executive Council, 'Decision on the Humanitarian Situation in Africa', Doc. EX.CL/668(XIX), 23–28 June 2011.

89 African Union Executive Council, 'Decision on the Report of the Sub-Committee on Refugees, Returnees, and Internally Displaced Persons in Africa', EX.CL/802(XXIV), V, 21–28 Jan 2014.

90 Kampala Convention, Art. 14 (1–3).

91 Won Kidane, 'Managing Forced Displacement by Law in Africa: The Role of the New African Union IDPs Convention', *Vanderbilt Journal of Transnational Law*, 44 (2011), pp. 76–7.

92 *ibid.*, p. 77.

93 Human Rights Council, 'Report of the Special Rapporteur on the Human Rights of Internally Displaced Persons, Chaloka Beyani', 4 April 2014, A/HRC/26/33, p. 15.

will indicate any legislative and other measures when presenting their reports under the Article 62 process of the African Charter on Human and Peoples' Rights. As Goodman and Jinks have noted in a general context, 'the significance of periodic state reports can help states and other interested actors to assess actual practices under the terms of the treaty.'[94]

At present, however, this process is poorly upheld. A number of countries have either never submitted a report, or are decades behind on their reporting responsibilities. Of the 23 periodic reports submitted since the Kampala Convention came into force, less than half even mention IDPs, and only nine point to concrete legislative and policy changes towards IDPs.[95] As an example, the government of Kenya, which is only a signatory to the Great Lakes Protocol, not the Kampala Convention, notes that they have adopted a policy to prevent future displacement and to fulfil its responsibilities in line with regional and international law, and have drafted an IDP bill.[96]

The Convention also establishes that 'any dispute or differences arising between the States Parties with regard to the interpretation or application of this Convention' shall be settled amicably, but in the event of a failure to settle 'either State may refer the dispute to the African Court of Justice and Human Rights' or to the Conference of States Parties 'which will decide by consensus or, failing which, by a two-third (2/3) majority...'[97] Hence, it is entirely possible (if unlikely) for a State Party to refer another State Party for a failure to either implement or abide by the Convention.

Finally, as noted above, the Convention establishes a clear responsibility on its signatories to introduce domestic legislation. And yet, there has been no domestic acceleration of implementation efforts – in fact, these processes seem to have almost stopped in Africa since the Convention was negotiated, with only one new piece of national legislation (that of Kenya) introduced since 2009. The Convention should provide an opening to domestic and international actors to pressure governments to conform to the legislation; thus it is surprising that – as of yet at least – there has been no clear regional shift at the domestic level.

---

94 Ryan Goodman and Derek Jinks, 'How to Influence States: Socialization and International Human Rights Law', *Duke Law Journal*, 54/3: 621–703 (2004), pp. 694.

95 Article 62 Process Reports are available at: http://www.achpr.org/states/reports-and-concluding-observations/. Since 2012, 23 reports have been submitted, including from four states which have ratified and two states which have signed the Convention.

96 Republic of Kenya, 'Combined 8th-11th Periodic Report on the African Charter on Human & Peoples' Rights', November 2014, p. 27.

97 Kampala Convention, Art. 22 (1–2).

At this stage, therefore, it is easier to discuss the Convention as having anticipatory enforcement mechanisms, rather than effective mechanisms. But it is important to note that these do reflect clear obligations that state parties have agreed to: to implement domestic legislation, to report periodically on that implementation, and to meet regularly to monitor and review implementation. The AU Commission played an important role in getting the Convention ratified, including formulating a clear Plan of Action and a subsequent Ministerial-level meeting.[98] Beyond the AU itself, a range of actors – including UNHCR and the Internal Displacement Monitoring Centre (IDMC) – have welcomed the Convention, and IDMC has begun training programs on it.[99] However, it is also important that the international community encourage the state parties to implement these monitoring and enforcement mechanisms.

ASEAN: Limited Protections for IDPs

In contrast to the AU, ASEAN has taken few formal steps towards providing protections to IDPs.[100] This was in spite of a number of recent large scale IDP situations within its member states. These included up to 1.4 million internally displaced Indonesians between 1999 and 2001 as a result of religious-based conflicts including local ethnic cleansing, of whom some 80,000 remain displaced;[101] up to a hundred and twenty thousand displaced Filipinos as a result of violence in Mindanao driven by Muslim separatist non-state armed groups;[102] and the long term displacement of over 600,000 people in

98 Marina Sharpe, 'Engaging with Refugee Protection? The Organization of African Unity and African Union since 1963', in *New Issues in Refugee Research* (Geneva: UNHCR, 2011), p. 31.

99 See IDMC, 'Workshop Report - Domesticating the Kampala Convention: Law and Policy Making', 30 June -2 July 2014, Monrovia, Liberia, http://www.internal-displacement.org/publications/2014/domesticating-the-kampala-convention-law-and-policy-making, accessed 19 May 2015.

100 Eva-Lotta E Hedman, 'Refugees, IDPs, and Regional Security in the Asia-Pacific', in ed. Brian L. Job and E. E. Williams (eds.), *CSCAP Regional Security Outlook 2009–2010: Security through Co-Operation*, (Kuala Lumpur: Council for Security Cooperation in the Asia Pacific, 2009).

101 Eva-Lotta E Hedman 'Introduction: Dynamics of Displacement in Indonesia', in Eva-Lotta E Hedman (ed.), *Conflict, Violence, and Displacement in Indonesia*, (Ithaca: Cornell Souteast Studies Program Publications, 2008), pp. 4–6.

102 IDMC, 'Philippines IDP Figures Analysis', May 2015, http://www.internal-displacement.org/south-and-south-east-asia/philippines/figures-analysis.

Myanmar as a result of protracted conflict between the government and a range of ethnic separatist non-state armed groups.[103] As of 2014, there were some 870,000 people internally displaced within ASEAN (see Table 1 above). Further, the international response to internal displacement tends to follow the wider precepts of the Association. As Kälin notes, 'by virtue of state sovereignty, the international community is not entitled to substitute for national authorities but plays a subsidiary role of supporting or complementing governmental action.'[104] Thus as ASEAN has begun to develop human rights and migrant policies at the regional level, this has also begun to affect how the Association responds to internally displaced persons.

Human rights were not initially a concern of the Association, and were not mentioned in its constitutive Declaration.[105] This also reflects a lack of engagement with other multilateral human rights Conventions. ASEAN, for example, is only one of two regions globally (the other being the Middle East) with virtually no signatories to the 1951 Refugee Convention - only Cambodia has ratified it.[106] Instead, the majority of states are signatories to the 1966 Bangkok Principles which, while establishing an expectation to provide refugees with asylum and protection against refoulement, are non-binding and 'do not create reciprocal regional expectations about how refugees should be treated.'[107] There is also a mixed record of ratifications across ASEAN member states with respect to core international human rights instruments.[108]

In the past decade, however, there has been a steady shift within the Association towards entrenching human rights. The ASEAN Charter, which was adopted in 2007, continued to respect the independence of its members. However, it also noted that one of the Association's purposes was to 'promote and protect human rights and fundamental freedoms, with due regard to the rights

---

103 IDMC, 'Myanmar: Internal Displacement in Brief', Dec 2013, http://www.internal-displacement.org/south-and-south-east-asia/myanmar/summary.

104 Walter Kälin, 'Internal Displacement', in Elena Fiddi an-Qasmiyeh, et al. (eds.), *The Oxford Handbook of Refugee and Forced Migration Studies*, (Oxford: Oxford University Press, 2014), p. 166.

105 Yuval Ginbar, 'Human Rights in ASEAN - Setting Sail or Treading Water?', *Human Rights Law Review* 10/3 (2010), pp. 505–6.

106 UNHCR, 'State Parties to the 1951 Convention Relating to the Status of Refugees and the 1967 Protocol', April 2015, http://www.unhcr.org/protect/PROTECTION/3b73b0d63.pdf.

107 Sara E Davies, 'The Asian Rejection? International Refugee Law in Asia', *Australian Journal of Politics & History* 52/4 (2006), p. 563.

108 Theodor Rathgeber, 'Human Rights and the Institutionalisation of ASEAN: An Ambiguous Relationship', *Journal of Current Southeast Asian Affairs* 33/3 (2014).

and responsibilities of the Member States of ASEAN.'[109] As Ginbar argues, 'the sheer generality of the Charter's human rights provisions would make it difficult… to consider them as more than declaratory, or as creating specific obligations on member states.'[110]

Even so, the Charter represented a shift to a 'binding regional pact' for the ASEAN member states, one which did include a provision to establish a new human rights body.[111] This led to the ASEAN Intergovernmental Commission on Human Rights in 2009 and the subsequent creation of the 2012 ASEAN Human Rights Declaration. The Declaration lays out a human rights framework for the region, one that recognizes the civil and political rights in the United Nations' Universal Declaration of Human Rights, including an inherent right to life, to personal liberty and security, 'to freedom of movement and residence within the borders of each State,' and 'the right to seek and receive asylum in another State in accordance with the laws of such State and applicable international agreements.'[112]

The Declaration has been subject to wide-ranging critiques. The language in the Declaration is limiting – the United States government has criticized it for 'stipulating that domestic laws can trump universal human rights, incomplete descriptions of rights that are memorialized elsewhere; introducing novel limits to rights; and language that could be read to suggest that individual rights are subject to group veto.'[113] It is also non-binding: through it 'the commission has no power to investigate governments or impose sanctions. It is strictly a consultative mechanism accountable to the foreign ministers of ASEAN.'[114] At the same time, it reflects a process of incremental institutionalization of human rights within ASEAN.

The 2015 Rohingya Crisis

The 2015 Rohingya crisis in Myanmar challenged these processes. While the Rohingya population in Rakhine State dates tc the 16th century, they were not

109 ASEAN, 'ASEAN Charter', http://www.asean.org/archive/publications/ASEAN-Charter.pdf, p. 4.

110 Ginbar, 'Human Rights in ASEAN – Setting Sail or Treading Water?', p. 512.

111 Hsien-Li Tan, *The ASEAN Intergovernmental Commission on Human Rights: Institutionalising Human Rights in Southeast Asia* (Cambridge University Press, 2011), p. 4; ASEAN, 'ASEAN Charter', p. 19.

112 ASEAN Human Rights Declaration, 2012, Art. 10,11,14,15.

113 U.S. Department of State, 'ASEAN Declaration on Human Rights', 20 Nov 2012, http://www.state.gov/r/pa/prs/ps/2012/11/200915.htm.

114 Rathgeber, 'Human Rights and the Institutionalisation of ASEAN', p. 161.

recognized as citizens in the 1982 Burma Citizenship Law. Widespread violence since 2012 saw 150,000 Rohingya Muslims internally displaced, while more than 100,000 fled the country.[115] The UN Special Rapporteur on the Situation of Human Rights in Myanmar noted that 'discriminatory restrictions on freedom of movement for internally displaced Muslims remain in place' and that the Rohingya have a right 'to self-identification according to international law.'[116] These are both issues which violate the ASEAN Human Rights Declaration. Combined, these IDP and refugee movements have challenged the limited nature of the ASEAN framework, and driven a policy, if not a legal, solution by the Association.

It was the growing refugee numbers, particular those escaping by boat who were frequently being pushed back to sea, coupled with the discovery of mass graves of refugees in Thailand, which triggered this shift.[117] By May 2015, individual ASEAN states were arguing for a change in policy. Following his countries rejection of a number of boats, Malaysian Prime Minister Datuk Seri Najib Tun Razak, ASEAN's chairman at the time, argued that while ASEAN respected non-interference, 'when a certain problem has spread and affects the leadership of other ASEAN nations and possibly outside ASEAN, then we need to find solutions through an ASEAN forum and cooperate with other parties.'[118] Former Malaysian Prime Minister Mahathir Mohamad was less cautious in his criticism, noting that what was happening to the Rohingya 'is so terrible that nothing can describe it… If Myanmar wants to commit genocide, then leave ASEAN.'[119]

115 ASEAN Parliamentarians for Human Rights, 'The Rohingya Crisis and the Risk of Atrocities in Myanmar: An ASEAN Challenge and Call to Action', (APHR, 2015), p. 3; Human Rights Watch, 'Burma: New Violence in Araken State', (New York: Human Rights Watch, 2012).

116 UN General Assembly, 'Report of the Special Rapporteur on the situation of Human Rights in Myanmar, Yanghee Lee', A/HRC/28/72, 23 Mar 2015, pp. 12, 14.

117 Thomas Fuller and Joe Cochrane, 'Rohingya Migrants From Myanmar, Shunned by Malaysia, are Spotted Adrift in Andaman Sea', *The New York Times*, 14 May 2015, http://www.nytimes.com/2015/05/15/world/asia/burmese-rohingya-bangladeshi-migrants-andaman-sea.html; Emanuel Stoakes, 'Thailand human trafficking death toll far greater than feared, claims rights group', *The Guardian*, 6 May 2015, http://www.theguardian.com/global-development/2015/may/06/thailand-human-trafficking-mass-grave-burma-rohingya-people.

118 'ASEAN needs to jointly address Rohingya refugee issue, says Najib', *The Star* (Malaysia), 16 May 2015, http://www.thestar.com.my/News/Nation/2015/05/16/Najib-Asean-Rohingya-issue/.

119 Quoted in Luke Hunt, 'ASEAN Move on Rohingya, Slow but Forward', *The Diplomat*, 22 Jun 2015, http://thediplomat.com/2015/06/asean-move-on-rohingya-slow-but-forward/.

This triggered a special meeting on irregular migration in the Indian Ocean hosted by the Thai government on 29 May 2015 and included seventeen governments, including all the ASEAN member states. While the Myanmar government was initially unwilling to participate, they relented following bilateral meetings with the Foreign Ministers of Indonesia and Malaysia and following a commitment that the word 'Rohingya' would not be used during the meeting.[120] As part of the outcome of that meeting, Indonesia and Malaysia both agreed to provide temporary shelter to the Rohingya trapped at sea, but also agreed to address root causes, including 'addressing factors in the areas of origin including... enhancing a sense of security and belonging, promoting full respect for human rights...'[121]

This crisis may have lasting effects in two ways. First, it directly affected ASEAN's reputation. Xiong notes that 'the failure to tackle the refugee crisis could have cast skepticism on the credibility of the ASEAN Community...'[122] The Bangkok meeting was able to maintain the norms of consensus and non-interference that are pivotal to the Association. However, the meeting created an informal mechanism to end the plight of the Rohingya boat people in the region. In addition, there appears to have been some pressure put on Myanmar to attend. This suggests that the ASEAN member states are prepared to push Myanmar not just on the Rohingya issue generally, but also on how it is treating the Rohingya within its territory, albeit in limited ways.

Second, the Rohingya crisis provided an opportunity to civil society for renewed engagement to frame how the Association should respond to human rights violations. The ASEAN Parliamentarians for Human Rights, for example, issued a report noting that 'denied citizenship, Rohingya are considered stateless and lack the protections and rights afforded to citizens.'[123] But the report also argued that the crisis represented a problem for all of ASEAN and called on its leaders to both:

120 Sampa Kundu, 'The Rohingyas: Security Implications for ASEAN and Beyond', IDSA Issue Brief, 2015, http://www.idsa.in/issuebrief/TheRohingyas_skundu_280515.html.

121 Ministry of Foreign Affairs of The Kingdom of Thailand, 'Summary: Special Meeting on Irregular Migration in the Indian Ocean, 29 May 2015, Bangkok, Thailand' 29 May 2015, http://www.mfa.go.th/main/en/media-center/14/56880-Summary-Special-Meeting-on-Irregular-Migration-in.html.

122 David Han Guo Xiong, 'Rohingya Refugee Crisis: Testing Malaysia's ASEAN Chairmanship', *RSIS Commentary*, No. 128 (2015), p. 2.

123 ASEAN Parliamentarians for Human Rights, 'The Rohingya Crisis and the Risk of Atrocities in Myanmar: An Asean Challenge and Call to Action', p. 4.

> Expand the mandate of the ASEAN Intergovernmental Commission on Human Rights (AICHR) to include country visits, inquiries, complaints, and emergency protection mechanisms, and ensure adequate independence and staffing support for its members… Call upon the Myanmar government to adhere to regional and international human rights and humanitarian standards.[124]

This suggests that policy solutions are not enough, and that the ASEAN Intergovernmental Commission on Human Rights and the ASEAN Human Rights Declaration mechanisms can be used to further entrench human rights in the region. This may provide an opening, too, to entrench specific rights for the internally displaced, anchored in the Guiding Principles on Internal Displacement. Here, the Kampala Convention may provide a model worthy of emulation.

Conclusions

Instances of forcible displacement – particularly forced deportation across a state's borders and forcible transfer within a state – can qualify either as crimes against humanity or war crimes, and hence fall within the remit of the Responsibility to Protect (RtoP) doctrine. But how to ensure the rights of the displaced against such mass atrocity crimes are upheld? One important step is ensuring these international rights are brought into practice at the regional and domestic levels.

The Guiding Principles on Internal Displacement, while soft law, reflect these mass atrocity crimes, particularly with respect to a clear right against arbitrary displacement. In both the Asia-Pacific and Africa, a range of states have introduced domestic legislation and policies which reflect the Guiding Principles and this right against arbitrary displacement. However, there is a clear disparity with how these issues are dealt with at the regional level. In Africa there has been a move to introduce the Guiding Principles into binding regional law, first through the Great Lakes Protocol, and now through the African Union's Kampala Convention. By contrast, in the Asia-Pacific, there has been little formal or even informal regional cooperation on the issue. As ASEAN builds its human rights architecture, however, anchored in the ASEAN Intergovernmental Commission on Human Rights and the ASEAN Human Rights Declaration, there may be space for change in the region.

---

124 *ibid.*, pp. 15–16.

The Kampala Convention introduces not only a legal model for how IDP rights can be brought into international law for other regional organizations like ASEAN, but also how other aspects of the RtoP doctrine can be introduced in a more binding manner. The Convention notes the illegality of mass atrocity crimes against IDPs and establishes the right of the AU to intervene in such circumstances. Further, the Convention introduces a range of mechanisms to monitor and enforce its implementation. As I have argued, at this time these mechanisms remain anticipatory. But this is a clear example of Pillar Two of the RtoP doctrine at work; here, international assistance to help states effectively implement the Kampala Convention is not only warranted, but will provide IDPs with a clear and comprehensive set of rights to protect them against mass atrocity crimes.

Conclusion

Learning Lessons across and between Regions: Norm Promotion and Capacity Building for Human Protection

Charles T. Hunt and Noel M. Morada

Regional organisations and sub-regional arrangements play a critical role in norm promotion and capacity building for human rights protection and atrocities prevention. This was clearly articulated by former UN Secretary General Ban Ki-moon in his annual report on the Responsibility to Protect in 2011.[1] The examinations and analyses in this book contribute to building policy-relevant knowledge on the role of regionalism and its importance to human protection. They do so in the context of South-South dialogue and the potential it holds for sharing experiences and facilitating exchange.[2] The chapters herein have reflected on the progress, challenges, and prospects for pursuing human protection through the regional organisations in Southeast Asia and across Africa. They have provided a detailed examination of how norms concerning human rights, civilian protection and prevention of mass atrocities have fared, explored the different experiences of the two regions, and investigated the expression of human protection norms in regional organisations and thematic policy agendas as well as the role of civil society processes.

Although these two regions and their inter-governmental organisations display many differences in their respective contexts and experiences in promoting human rights protection and atrocities prevention, it is important to also identify and examine some of the common normative and institutional challenges they face. Specifically, the foregoing analyses offer a range of insights that provide rich opportunities for south-south exchange when it comes to promoting and building capacity for human protection at the regional level. Therefore, in the spirit of pushing beyond the Bandung Asian-African conference of 1955,[3] the organisations in both regions could learn from each other's experiences in overcoming some common challenges in implementing

1 *The Role of Regional and Sub-regional Arrangements in Implementing the Responsibility to Protect.* Report of the Secretary-General, S/2011/393, 27 July 2011.

2 Gosovic, Branislav. 'The resurgence of South–South cooperation', *Third World Quarterly*, 37/4:733–743 (2016).

3 Andrew Phillips, 'Beyond Bandung: the 1955 Asian-African Conference and its legacies for international order', *Australian Journal of International Affairs*, 70/4: 329–341 (2016).

 | DOI:10.1163/9789004363212_014

universal norms and supporting the efforts of the United Nations in promoting human rights protection and the Responsibility to Protect.

To reiterate, the contributions to this volume shared three main objectives. The first is to create a space for dialogue and exchange of ideas among scholars, civil society representatives, and practitioners on the current state, dynamics, and challenges in norm promotion and capacity building in human rights, mass atrocities prevention, and civilian protection in Southeast Asia and Africa. The second is to identify the challenges and opportunities confronting regional institutions or frameworks such as the ASEAN and the AU or subregional arrangements in implementing human protection norms. The third is to highlight the roles played by various stakeholders in building the capacity of states and regional arrangements in these regions to prevent and respond to human protection issues.

This conclusion proceeds in four sections. The first reflects on the lessons emerging from the chapters investigating elements of human protection regime in Southeast Asian region. The second section draws together similar insights from the chapters focused on regional experiences in Africa. The third part identifies a number of areas where there are opportunities for inter-regional learning across regions of the global south and the final section discusses of the aspects of south-south dialogue and exchange on human protection that warrant further research and engagement.

Reflections from Southeast Asia

Based on the discussions presented in this volume that focused on Southeast Asian regionalism and human protection, a number of key lessons are in order. First, the promotion of human rights protection and atrocities prevention still face a number of challenges in the region. For one, the strong adherence of many ASEAN member states to traditional norms of sovereignty and non-interference constrains the mainstreaming of human rights and Responsibility to Protect in the agenda of ASEAN, specifically in its existing mechanisms such as AICHR. This particularly makes it difficult for all member states to reach a consensus on giving priority to implementing human protection norms, even though many of ASEAN's documents and treaties fundamentally reflect agreement with universal norms on human rights protection and various elements of R2P. This fact was highlighted especially in the contributions of Morada and Sripapha. Notwithstanding this constraint, however, both authors argued that conducting regional and national dialogues on R2P and human rights protection are important in overcoming these challenges. Specifically, holding public seminars and engaging critical stakeholders in the region could contribute to a better understanding of international norms on human protection and to what extent they can be adopted in ASEAN's regional and national contexts. Even so, ASEAN members continue to struggle in striking a balance between its state- and people-centred principles—i.e., state sovereignty vs. human security—especially when internal conflicts spill over into other member states or the region. Morada's contribution on Myanmar, which examines the non-interference principle in the context of political developments in that country since it became a member of ASEAN in 1997, shows the constraints and limitations of ASEAN in preventing and responding to human rights violations and atrocities obtaining in a member state, including the protection of the stateless Rohingya population.

Secondly, there are opportunities for advancing human protection and atrocities prevention in ASEAN especially in the area of protecting women from violence and in the context of sexual violence in armed conflicts, which is a major concern in the region. As argued by Veneracion-Rallonza, some ASEAN member states can play the role of vertical, horizontal, and intersectional norm entrepreneurs in promoting and deepening the commitment of states in the protection of women. For example, some states like Cambodia, Myanmar, Indonesia, and the Philippines could be vertical norm entrepreneurs who could elevate their respective best practices at home (through national action plans on women, peace and security or WPS) to the regional and international levels. Other states like Vietnam have the potential for horizontal entrepreneurship and encourage other member states of ASEAN to work towards a common cause, such as promoting and implementing a regional plan of action on WPS and CEDAW, for example, in the context of AICHR's and ACWC's agenda and activities. Complementing Veneracion-Rallonza's point, Tanyag's feminist approach in examining the prospects for advancing WPS and R2P in the larger context of ASEAN's three community pillars argues for the progressive inclusion of gender in both the political-security and economic pillars, and not just in the socio-cultural pillar. A good starting point is the set of goals identified in the regional plan of action on eliminating violence against women, which to her is consistent with the ASEAN Community's Post-2015 Vision statement.

Finally, it is important to underscore the fact that, as Bellamy pointed out, there has been a significant progress in the Asia Pacific region in both reducing the frequency and scale of mass atrocities as well as in building a regional consensus on R2P, especially with regard to the primary role of states in protecting vulnerable populations from atrocity crimes. It is however imperative that, in order for this progress to be sustained, states and regional organisations such as ASEAN must take steps to translate their commitments into practical realities. This includes building national architectures, creating early warning systems, and developing capacity-building for atrocities prevention. As well, it is important for regional mechanisms such as AICHR to mainstream R2P and atrocities prevention in its agenda and the ARF to prioritize capacity building in monitoring and managing risk factors through technical assistance to build the capacity of states in the region to respond to crisis situations, civilian protection, conflict prevention, and election monitoring, among others.

Reflections from Africa

The chapters in this collection that focused on regions and regional capacities across Africa identify a number of areas in which lessons can be drawn and addressed within the continent's human protection architecture.

First, incremental institutionalisation of a human protection agenda points to the potential to advance human rights and atrocities prevention in Africa. As Murithi highlighted, the AU has acted as a norm entrepreneur in this regard. For example, human protection values and objectives have been enshrined in the organisation's normative, legal, and institutional frameworks across the region's arrangements for peace and security. Furthermore, the rise of protection norms has been met with recognition of mutually reinforcing elements of the good governance and development agendas at the AU. Further still, sub-regional arrangements such as ECOWAS have begun to acknowledge and harness the important role Civil Society Organisations (CSOs) can play at the regional level. As emphasised in Eze's chapter, ECOWAS has leveraged the comparative advantages of the CSO sector in contributing to the prevention and resolution of conflicts due of their in-depth knowledge of the local context and expertise in working closely with communities.

Second, as with Southeast Asia, a number of hurdles will need to be overcome and capacities developed if human protection is to flourish in the practices of regional arrangements across Africa. Notwithstanding some impressive achievements in the development of a regional architecture with human protection a priority, challenges remain when it comes to arriving at a joined up approach by the multiplicity of regional bodies and capacities on the continent. For example, clarifying questions of subsidiarity, enhancing interoperability, and addressing tensions between the AU and the many Regional Economic Communities (RECs) raise questions about the relative benefits of further localising versus regionalising protection obligations and responses (see Ifedoria chapter). Furthermore, building consensus on an African vision for human protection remains a challenge. Renaissance rhetoric around 'African solutions to African problems' does not really reflect reality. Current solutions to major human protection crises on the continent are rarely conceived of, mounted or financed by African actors. Resisting the external diagnoses and solutions proffered from outside is difficult to sustain in this context. Clarifying global-regional collaboration and elaborating on the relationship between regional arrangements and the UN through Chapter VIII of the Charter is also critical in this regard.

Third, notwithstanding these challenges, at the regional level across Africa a range of principles and policy frameworks that privilege human protection have now been promulgated. The next steps must focus on operationalising the associated practical tools and mechanisms in order for them to be brought to life. For example, committing to the finalisation of the long overdue African Standby Force (ASF) will be an important step. However, this must be complemented by commensurate progress on the African Peace and Security Architecture (APSA) as a whole and importantly how this relates to the African Governance Architecture (AGA) if there is to be a systemic approach to promoting and building capacities for human protection on the continent.

Areas and Opportunities for Inter-Regional Learning

The experiences elaborated and lessons identified in the contexts of Southeast Asia and Africa show that there is great potential for inter-regional learning through south-south dialogue and exchange.

First, based on the foregoing it evident that ASEAN member states could reflect on a number of significant lessons from the AU's evolution and experiences in promoting human protection. The transformation of its norm of non-interference (under the Organisation of African Unity) to the principle of non-indifference, especially in the context of preventing and responding to massive human rights violations and atrocity crimes is an obvious example. Given the continent's past and continuing challenges in dealing with humanitarian crisis brought about by so many internal conflicts of member states in Africa, ASEAN can look to the AU as a template if not a model for developing collective political will in pursuing and giving priority to shared values and regional identity, especially with regard to promoting human protection. There is no question that the AU is more advanced than ASEAN with regard to having more robust normative, legal, and institutional frameworks for cooperation at the regional level even as the latter relies mainly on the ASEAN Way of consensus-decision making, in which agreements are based on least common denominator. ASEAN could also learn from the AU's progress in building regional institutions and frameworks that enable the organisation to prevent and respond to humanitarian protection issues, extending capacity building assistance to member states, as well as enhancing mechanisms for engaging and promoting partnerships with non-state actors and civil society groups in advancing human rights protection, atrocities prevention, and civilian protection in conflict areas. ASEAN would also do well to reflect on the AU's experience in developing critical support for UN peace missions not just outside the region but more importantly within Southeast Asia. While the issue of having an ASEAN standby force is still a politically sensitive issue at this time, there is much that the AU can share with ASEAN in mainstreaming civilian protection in the latter's agenda under its Political-Security Community pillar and in the context of defense and security sector cooperation in the region. Indeed, there is already a consensus in ASEAN on the importance of civilian protection as some members have voluntarily contributed police and military troops for UN-led peacekeeping operations in the region, specifically in Cambodia in the early 1990s and in Timor L'este in the late 1990s.

Second, there are a number areas where African countries and regional bodies can benefit from the experiences of the ASEAN region. Notwithstanding a good deal of progress on establishing a human protection architecture across Africa, consensus amongst member states on how and when to utilise the institutions and implement policies that have been created remains fragile. ASEAN's highly consultative and consensus-based decision-making process offers food for thought to African counter-parts. This is particularly true given the tendency for regional hegemons to set and dominate the agenda when it comes to questions of peace, stability and humanitarian crises in Africa. Drawing lessons on building constituencies for effective action is an area that Africa could learn from the ASEAN way. Furthermore, African regional bodies such as the AU and the various RECs, stand to benefit from the experiences of ASEAN in having member states embedding key human protection frameworks within domestic legislation, institutions and human rights instruments, as a means to strengthening regional norms. See for example Veneracion-Rallonza's chapter and argument regarding the implementation of Women, Peace and Security (WPS) framework through national action plans and the 'trickle-up' effects at the regional level. More generally, the reduction of mass atrocities in Southeast Asia and its neighbourhood, documented by Bellamy, represents an opportunity for African countries and regional bodies to: (i) examine the processes of development, state formation and governance reform undertaken across ASEAN member states; and, (ii) assess what might work in their own context.

Third, these two regions could learn from and assist each other on contemporary issues germane to the global south as a whole. For instance, the emerging and important role for civil society organisations – as highlighted by Eze in west Africa, Murithi at the African continental level and Veneracion-Rallonza in Southeast Asia – provides an opportunity to exchange ideas on how to be more people-oriented and how CSOs can complement the work of government actors and state-based organisations in meeting human protection objectives. Another example relates to the idea of 'regional approaches to regional problems'. Here there is potential for constructive dialogue about what this means in different contexts and how to overcome the difficulties and dilemmas associated with reconciling autochthonous, indigenous forms of governance and conflict resolution with international norms and frameworks for action on human protection. Lastly, different regions of the global south have much to share with and learn from each other when it comes to shaping engagement with outside interveners and offers of support. For example, how can those in the global south articulate what assistance is required to enhance structural and operational prevention against atrocities and rights abuses. Doing so would facilitate the development of modalities that enable regional actors to request and/or influence capacity-building initiatives in line with their own demands rather than according to what is supplied as standard by the international community writ large.

Avenues for Future Research and Engagement

From the foregoing reflections on Southeast Asian and African regionalism and human protection, it evident that future research could focus on the following areas, to wit:

Promoting South-South Dialogue and Inter-Regional Learning

Thus far, it is apparent that opportunities for exchange of best practices and inter-regional learning among global South states are severely limited. This is particularly true in the area of human protection. However, such South-South cooperation, as with its antecedents in the Bandung Conference of 1955, is an important platform for developing countries in Asia and Africa to exchange knowledge as well as other resources. The UN and donor countries should encourage and support activities that would contribute to building more opportunities for South-South dialogue on human rights and atrocities prevention among relevant stakeholders from Africa, Asia, Latin America, and the Middle East.

Specifically with regard to Southeast Asian and African experiences of building capacities for human protection, more exchanges between the two regions on their best practices could focus on enhancing the capacity of regional institutions and mechanisms to provide assistance to member states in addressing root causes of internal conflicts, managing risk factors, building national resilience, and responding to humanitarian crisis situations. Other areas of exchange could include the role of parliaments and parliamentarians in promoting human rights protection and atrocities prevention; strengthening the rule of law and good governance; and promoting accountability in the security sector.

The Southeast Asian and African regions could also benefit and learn from tripartite exchange with the Latin American region. In particular this could focus on their experiences in addressing past atrocities especially under military rule; protection of indigenous peoples; and promoting accountability among member states when they fail to fulfil their regional treaty obligations on peaceful transfer of power and human rights protection.

Broadening the Knowledge Base and Diversifying the Knowledge Production Community

The knowledge pool on regional experiences in promoting human protection norms is limited and would benefit from additional contributions. The range of interests and experiences across the global south speaks to the value of cross-regional dialogue and research.

First, there should be a greater focus on questions of capacity-building at the regional level. There is some interest and scholarship on the formation of regional security communities as well as the relationship between security actors (e.g. peace operations mounted by regional organisations subsequently re-hatted and replace by UN missions). However, there is much less analysis of what capacities and regional arrangements at the regional level are effective in promoting and embedding human protection norms in their everyday policies and practices. To that end, dedicated studies of particular (sub-)regions are warranted. These could include: evaluations of thematic issues and patterns over time; good practices and individual case studies looking at where human protection capacities have been established; and, in-depth analyses of the salient regional bodies' peace, security, governance and development architectures. Furthermore, additional and elaborated accounts of effective norm entrepreneurship and promotion at the regional level would also support more constructive exchange and inter-regional translation.

Second, this research should be more inclusive of scholars and practitioners from the global south. Notwithstanding efforts such as this volume to include researchers from the regions in question, this area of research still tends to be dominated by those from the global north. This is to the detriment of the field. Research into the opportunities and challenges of south-south dialogue would benefit from a greater involvement of researchers (scholars and practitioners) from global south. The insights from those who are familiar with regional mechanisms and have experience both studying and working with these institutions are much-needed to bring precision and regional voices to this challenge.

Third, regardless of who produces the research, it is imperative that the findings and recommendations of these exchanges are disseminated in a way that increases accessibility and visibility in the global south. A research agenda in this area therefore needs to incorporate a plan to publish in open access journals where possible. In addition it is also necessary to produce a series of research products – such as policy briefs and working papers – that are more freely available and readily accessible (both physically and intellectually) than traditional academic outputs.

Integrated Africa and Southeast Asia Bibliographic Entries

Abad Jr., M. C. 'The Challenge of Balancing State Security with Human Security', Paper presented at the 9th Harvard Project for Asian and International Affairs Conference, Beijing, 27–30 August 2000.

Abebe, Allehone Mulugeta. 'The African Union Convention on Internally Displaced Persons: Its Codification Background, Scope, and Enforcement Challenges,' Refugee Survey Quarterly 29/3 (2010).

Acharya, Amitav. 'Democratisation and the Prospects of Participatory Regionalism in Southeast Asia', Third World Quarterly 24/2 (2003), pp. 375–390.

Acharya, Amitav. 'How Ideas Spread: Whose Norms Matter? Norm Localization and Institutional Change in Asian Regionalism', International Organization 58/2 (2004), pp. 239–275.

Acharya, Amitav. 'The Emerging Regional Architecture of World Politics', World Politics, 59/4: 629–652 (2007).

Acharya, Amitav. *Whose Ideas Matter? Agency and Power in Asian Regionalism* (Ithaca: Cornell University Press, 2009).

Acharya, Amitav. 'The R2P and Norm Diffusion: Towards A Framework of Norm Circulation', Global Responsibility to Protect, 5/4: 466–479 (2013).

Acharya, Amitav. 'Studying the Bandung conference from a Global IR perspective', Australian Journal of International Affairs 70/4: 342–357 (2016).

Adedeji, Adebayo. 'NEPAD's African Peer Review Mechanism: Progress and Prospects', in John Akokpari, Angela Ndinga-Muvumba and Timothy Murithi (eds.) *The African Union and Its Institutions* (Cape Town: Jacana Media, 2008): 241–70.

Adler, Emanuel and Michael Barnett (eds.) *Security Communities* (Cambridge: Cambridge University Press, 1998).

Africa Leadership Forum, *The Kampala Document: Towards a Conference on Security, Stability, Development and Cooperation in Africa,* Kampala: OAU/United Nations Economic Commission for Africa (UNECA), 1991.

African Development Bank, Addressing Fragility and Building Resilience in Africa: The AfDB Group Strategy 2014–2019, 30 June 2015.

African Union, *Constitutive Act of the African Union,* (Lome: African Union, 2000).

African Union, *Protocol Establishing the Peace and Security Council of the African Union,* (Addis Ababa: African Union, 2002).

African Union, *Economic Social and Cultural Council* (ECOSOCC), (Addis Ababa: African Union, 2002).

African Union, 'The common African position on the proposed reform of the United Nations: The Ezulwini Consensus', Executive Council 7th Extraordinary Session, 7–8 March 2005, Addis Ababa, Ethiopia, Ext/EX.CL/2 (vii).

African Union, Agenda 2063: The Africa we Want,(Addis Ababa: AU, February 2015), http://agenda2063.au.int/en/sites/default/files/agenda2063_popular_version_05092014_EN.pdf, accessed 1 June 2015.

African Union, 'AU Policy on Post-Conflict Reconstruction and Development (PCRD)' (Addis Ababa: African Union), http://www.peaceau.org/uploads/pcrd-policy-framwowork-eng.pdf.

Agence France Press, "Malaysia hails Myanmar's move to push ahead with democracy," 25 September 2001, Burma Related News, from http://www.burmalibrary.org/TinKyi/archives/2001–09/msg00020.html, accessed on 6 February 2017.

Agence France Presse, "6,700 Rohingya killed in first month of Myanmar violence: Doctors Without Borders," Channel News Asia, 14 December 2017, from https://www.channelnewsasia.com/news/asiapacific/6–700-rohingya-killed-in-first-month-of-myanmar-violence-doctors-9498880, accessed on 14 December 2014.

John Akokpari, Angela Ndinga-Muvumba and Timothy Murithi (eds.) *The African Union and Its Institutions* (Cape Town: Jacana Media, 2008).

Alagappa, Muthiah. (ed.), *Asian Security Order: Instrumental and Normative Features* (Stanford, CA: Stanford University Press, 2003).

Alexandra, Lina. 'Indonesia and the Responsibility to Protect,' The Pacific Review 25/1 (2012), pp. 51–74.

Alison, Miranda. 'Wartime Sexual Violence: Women's Human Rights and Questions of Masculinity' Review of International Studies, 33:75–90 (2007).

Almonte, Jose T. "ASEAN 10: Implications for the Asia-Pacific", 11th Asia Pacific Roundtable, ASEAN-ISIS, Istana Hotel, Kuala Lumpur, Malaysia, 7 June 1997.

Amate, C.O.C. *Inside the OAU: Pan-Africanism in Practice* (London: Macmillan Publishers, 1986).

Aning, Emmanuel Kwesi and Samuel Atuobi. 'Responsibility to Protect in Africa: An Analysis of the African Union's Peace and Security Architecture', Global Responsibility to Protect, 1/1: 90–113, (2009).

Ankomah, Baffour. 'African Union: From Non-Interference to Non-Indifference', New African, no. 460 (2007).

Annan, Kofi. 'Prevention of Armed Conflict', Report of the Secretary General to the United Nations General Assembly, A/55/985–S/2001/574, 7 June 2001.

Annan, Kofi. Speech at the 54th Session of the United Nations General Assembly, SG/SM/7136-GA/9596, 20 September 1999.

Annan, Kofi. In Larger Freedom: Towards Development, Security and Human Rights for All, A/59/2005, 21 March 2005.

Annan, Kofi. *Interventions: A Life in War and Peace*, (London: Penguin Books, 2012).

APF (2015) 'African-led Peace Support Operations', (African Peace Facility, European Union), https://www.africa-eu-partnership.org/sites/default/files/documents/african-led-psos-v2.pdf.

Arendshorst, John. "The Dilemma of Non-Interference: Myanmar, Human Rights, and the ASEAN Charter," Northwestern Journal of International Human Rights, 8 (1) Fall 2009.

Arnold, Wayne. "Rift over Myanmar emerges at ASEAN summit," The New York Times online, 19 November 2007, from http://www.nytimes.com/2007/11/19/world/asia/19iht-asean.3.8393052.html, accessed on 12 February 2017.

Asante, Samuel KB and Kingsley Y Amoako. *Regionalism and Africa's Development: Expectations, Reality and Challenges* (Basingstoke: Macmillan, 1997).

Asante, Samuel KB. *The Political Economy of Regionalism in Africa: A Decade of the Economic Community of West African States (ECOWAS)* (Praeger New York, 1986).

Associated Press, "Bush imposes economic sanctions on key officials from Myanmar government," Fox News online, 27 September 2007, from http://www.foxnews.com/story/2007/09/27/bush-imposes-economic-sanctions-on-key-officials-from-myanmar-government.html, accessed on 12 February 2017.

Associated Press, "Cyclone Nargis embodied the perfect storm," NBCNews.com, 8 May 2008, from http://www.nbcnews.com/id/24526960/ns/world_news-asia_pacific/t/cyclone-nargis-embodied-perfect-storm/#.WKEEtBirlBw, accessed on 13 February 2017.

Association of Southeast Asian Nations (ASEAN), "A Bridge to Recovery: ASEAN's Response to Cyclone Nargis," Jakarta: ASEAN Secretariat, July 2009.

ASEAN, 'ASEAN Charter.' Available at: http://www.asean.org/archive/publications/ASEAN-Charter.pdf

ASEAN, Chairman's Statement of the 13th ASEAN Summit, "One ASEAN at the Heart of Dynamic Asia" Singapore, 20 November 2007, from http://asean.org/?static_post=chairman-s-statement-of-the-13th-asean-summit-one-asean-at-the-heart-of-dynamic-asia-singapore-20-november-2007, accessed on 13 February 2017.

ASEAN, Chairman's Statement of the 14th ASEAN Summit, "ASEAN Charter for ASEAN Peoples", Cha-am, 28 February – 1 March 2009, from http://asean.org/chairman-s-statement-of-the-14th-asean-summit-asean-charter-for-asean-peoples-cha-am-28-february-1-march-2009/, accessed on 14 February 2017.

ASEAN, Chairman's Statement of the 25th ASEAN Summit: "Moving Forward in Unity to a Peaceful and Prosperous Community", Nay Pyi Taw, 12 November 2014, http://www.asean.org/wp-content/uploads/images/pdf/2014_upload/Chairman%20Statement%20of%20the%2025th%20ASEAN%20Summit.pdf, accessed 6 April 2017.

ASEAN Commission on the Promotion and Protection of Women and Children Terms of Reference (ACWC TOR), http://www.asean.org/storage/images/archive/documents/TOR-ACWC.pdf accessed 31 August 2016.

ASEAN, 'ASEAN Political and Security Community Blueprint', 2009, http://www.asean.org/archive/5187–18.pdf, accessed 24 April 2015.

ASEAN, 'ASEAN Social and Cultural Community Blueprint'.

ASEAN, ASEAN Human Rights Declaration 2012.

ASEAN, The ASEAN Charter, 2008.

ASEAN Humanitarian Assistance Centre (AHA), "AHA Centre Delivers 80 Tons of Relief Materials to Rakhine State, Myanmar," AHACentre.org, 26 October 2017, from http://ahacentre.org/news/aha-centre-delivers-80-tons-of-relief-materials-to-rakhine-state-myanmar/, accessed on 2 November 2017.

ASEAN, "Statement of ASEAN Foreign Ministers on the Recent Developments in the Rakhine State, Myanmar" Phnom Penh, Cambodia, 17 August 2012, from http://www.asean.org/wp-content/uploads/images/archive/documents/Statement%20of%20ASEAN%20FM%20on%20Recent%20Developments%20in%20the%20Rakhine%20State.pdf, accessed on 23 March 2017.

ASEAN Parliamentarians for Human Rights (APHR), "Parliamentarians call on ASEAN leaders to address the Rohingya crisis and the growing risk of atrocity crimes in Myanmar," ASEAN Parliamentarians for Human Rights (APHR) online, 22 April 2015, from http://aseanmp.org/2015/04/22/parliamentarians-call-on-asean-leaders-to-address-the-rohingya-crisis-and-the-escalating-risk-of-atrocity-crimes-in-myanmar/, accessed on 17 April 2017.

APHR, 'The Rohingya Crisis and the Risk of Atrocities in Myanmar: An ASEAN Challenge and Call to Action,' (APHR, 2015).

ASEAN Regional Plan of Action on the Elimination of Violence against Women (ASEAN RPA on EVAW) (Jakarta: ASEAN Secretariat, February 2016), http://www.asean.org/wp-content/uploads/2012/05/Final-ASEAN-RPA-on-EVAW-IJP-11.02.2016-as-input-ASEC.pdf accessed 31 August 2016.

Axworthy, Lloyd and Allan Rock, 'R2P: A New and Unfinished Agenda', Global Responsibility to Protect, 1/1:54–69 (2009).

Axworthy, Lloyd and Allan Rock , 'Making R2P work: now and in the future', In W. Andy Knight and Frazer Egerton (eds.), *The Routledge Handbook of the Responsibility to Protect* (Oxon: Routledge, 2012).

Ayangafac, Chrysantus and Jakkie Cilliers, 'African Solutions to African Problems: Assessing the Capacity of African Peace and Security Architecture', in Chester A. Crocker, Fen Osler Hampson and Pamela R Aall (eds.) *Rewiring Regional Security in a Fragmented World* (Washington, DC: US Institute of Peace Press, 2011): 115–48.

Baaz, Maria Eriksson and Maria Stern, 'Why Do Soldiers Rape? Masculinity, Violence, and Sexuality in the Armed Forces in the Congo (DRC)', International Studies Quarterly, 53/2 (2009), pp. 495–518.

Bach, Daniel C. 'Regionalism Versus Regional Integration: The Emergence of a New Paradigm in Africa', in Jean Grugel and Wil Hout (eds.) *Regionalism across the*

North-South Divide. State Strategies and Globalization (Oxford: Routledge, 1999): 152–66.

Bach, Daniel C. *Regionalisation in Africa: Integration & Disintegration* (Indiana University Press, 1999).

Bachmann, Olaf. 'The African Standby Force: An Element of Prospective Multilevel Security Governance', IDS Bulletin 43/4: 14–19 (2012).

Ban, Ki-moon, Implementing the Responsibility to Protect, A/63/677, 12 January 2009.

Ban, Ki-moon, 'Human Protection and the 21st Century United Nations', Speech at the Cyril Foster Lecture at Oxford University, Oxford, United Kingdom, 2 February 2011.

Ban, Ki-moon, The Role of Regional and Subregional Arrangements in Implementing the Responsibility to Protect, A/65/877, 28 June 2011.

Ban, Ki-moon, Fulfilling Our Collective Responsibility: International Assistance and the Responsibility to Protect, A/68/947, 11 July 2014.

Ban, Ki-moon, A vital and Enduring Commitment: Implementing the Responsibility to Protect, A/69/981, 13 July 2015.

Banerjee, Paula. 'IDP Protection at the National Level in South Asia,' Forced Migration Review 18 (2006).

Bangura, Abdul Karim. *Toyin Falola and African Epistemologies* (London: Palgrave Macmillan, 2015).

Barbour, Brian and Brian Gorlick, 'Embracing the "Responsibility to Protect": A Repertoire of Measures Including Asylum for Potential Victims', International Journal of Refugee Law 20/4 (2008).

Barnett, Michael and Thomas G. Weiss, *Humanitarianism Contested: Where Angels Fear to Tread* (London: Routledge, 2011).

Baron, Laignee. 'Regional MPS warn of Rohingya "crisis'"ahead of asean meeting', Myanmar Times, 23 April 2015, http://www.mmtimes.com/index.php/national-news/14085-regional-mps-warn-of-rohingya-crisis-ahead-of-asean-meeting.html, accessed 15 December 2015.

Bassiouni, M. Cherif. *'Crimes against Humanity in International Criminal Law,'* (Dordrecht, Boston-London, 1999).

Bellamy, Alex J. 'Introduction: International Society and the English School' in Alex J. Bellamy (ed.) *International Society and Its Critiques* (New York, New York: Oxford University Press, 2005), pp. 9–10.

Bellamy, Alex J. 'Mass Atrocities and Armed Conflict: Links, Distinctions and Implications for the Responsibility to Protect', Policy Analysis Brief for the Stanley Foundation, February 2011.

Bellamy, Alex J. 'To Build Regional Community, Southeast Asian Leaders Advocate for "Responsibility to Protect"', 5 September 2014, http://theglobalobservatory.org/2014/09/southeast-asia-responsibility-to-protect-r2p/ accessed 20 February 2015.

Bellamy, Alex J. 'The First Response: Peaceful Means in the Third Pillar of the Responsibility to Protect', Policy Analysis Brief, Stanley Foundation, December 2015. Available at: http://www.stanleyfoundation.org/publications/pab/Bellamy3rdPillar PAB116.pdf, accessed 7 February 2016.

Bellamy, Alex J. 'The humanisation of security? Towards an International Human Protection Regime', European Journal of International Security, 1/1: 112–133 (2016) doi: doi:10.1017/eis.2015.5.

Bellamy, Alex J. 'Atrocity Prevention: From Promise to Practice in the Asia Pacific,' Global Responsibility to Protect 8: 180–199 (2016).

Bellamy, Alex J. *East Asia's Other Miracle: Explaining the Decline of Mass Atrocities* (Oxford University Press, 2017).

Bellamy, Alex J. and Jon Western (eds.), 'The Politics and Practice of Estimating Civilian Casualties', special issue of Global Responsibility to Protect, 2017 forthcoming.

Beswick, Danielle. 'The Risks of African Military Capacity Building: Lessons from Rwanda', African Affairs, 113/451: v212–231 (2014).

Betts, Alexander and Phil Orchard, 'Introduction: The Normative Institutionalization-Implementation Gap,' in *Implementation and World Politics: How International Norms Change Practice,* ed. Alexander Betts and Phil Orchard (Oxford: Oxford University Press, 2014).

Boege, Volker, Anne Brown, and Kevin Clements, 'Hybrid Political Orders, Not Fragile States', Peace Review, 21/1: 13–21 (2009).

Boege, Volker, Anne Brown, Kevin Clements, and Anna Nolan, 'On Hybrid Political Orders and Emerging States: State Formation in the Context of 'Fragility'', Berghof Handbook Dialogue No. 8 (2008).

Bombande, Emmanuel. 'Building Peace through Inter-Party Political Dialogue and Strengthening the Democratic State: The Ghana Experience', WANEP, 2011.

Bond, Jennifer and Laurel Sherret 'Mapping Gender and the Responsibility to Protect: Seeking Intersections, Finding Parallels,' Global Responsibility to Protect, 4/2: 133–153 (2012).

Boot, Machteld. Genocide, Crimes against Humanity, War Crimes: Nullum Crimen Sine Lege and the Subject Matter Jurisdiction of the International Criminal Court, vol. 12 (Intersentia nv, 2002).

Boutellis, Arthur and Paul D. Williams, *Peace Operations, the African Union, and the United Nations: Toward More Effective Partnerships,* (New York: International Peace Institute, April 2013).

Boutros-Ghali, *Boutros An Agenda for Peace: Preventive Diplomacy, Peacemaking and Peacekeeping,* (New York: United Nations, 1992).

British Broadcasting Corporation (BBC), "Nuns in Burma anti-junta rallies," BBC News, 23 September 2007, from http://news.bbc.co.uk/2/hi/asia-pacific/7009005.stm, accessed on 12 February 2017.

BBC, "Burmese military threatens monks," BBC News, 24 September 2007, from http://news.bbc.co.uk/2/hi/asia-pacific/7010839.stm, accessed on 12 February 2017.

BBC, "Overview of Burma sanctions," BBC News online, 18 December 2009, from http://news.bbc.co.uk/2/hi/asia-pacific/8195956.stm, accessed 12 February 2017.

BBC, "France angered by Burmese delays," BBC News online, 17 May 2008, from http://news.bbc.co.uk/2/hi/asia-pacific/7405998.stm, accessed on 13 February 2017.

BBC, "Burma 'approves new constitution'," BBC news online, 15 May 2008, from http://news.bbc.co.uk/2/hi/asia-pacific/7402105.stm, accessed on 20 February 2017.

Brookings-Bern Project on Internal Displacement, '*Protecting Internally Displaced Persons: A Manual for Law and Policymakers*,' (Washington, D.C.: Brookings Institution, 2008).

Brownmiller, Susan *Against Our Will: Men, Women and Rape* (New York: Fawcett Columbine, 1975).

Bull, Hedley *The Anarchical Society: A Study of Order and International Politics* (Houndmills: McMillan, 1977).

Bunwaree, Sheila 'NEPAD and Its Discontents', in John Akokpari, Angela Ndinga-Muvumba and Timothy Murithi (eds.) *The African Union and Its Institutions* (Cape Town: Jacana Media, 2008): 227–40.

Bush, George W. 'Transcript: George Bush's Speech on Iraq, delivered in Cincinnati, 7 October 2002.

Buzan, Barry and Ole Waever, *Regions and Powers: The Structure of International Security* (Cambridge: Cambridge University Press, 2003).

Caballero-Anthony, Mely 'The Responsibility to Protect: opening up spaces for advancing human security,' The Pacific Review 25/1: 113–124 (2012).

Carr, Susan 'From Theory to Practice: National and Regional Application of the Guiding Principles,' International Journal of Refugee Law 21/1 (2009).

Centre for Conflict Resolution (CCR)/ Friedrich Ebert Stiftung (FES) seminar report on African Perspectives on the UN Peacebuilding Commission, Maputo, Mozambique, 3–4 August 2006, available at: http://ccrweb.uct.ac.za.

Convention on the Elimination of Discrimination Against Women (CEDAW) 'Concluding Observations on the Combined Fifth and Sixth Periodic Reports of the Philippines', adopted by the CEDAW Committee during its 36th session, 7–25 August 2006, http://docstore.ohchr.org/SelfServices/FilesHandler.ashx?enc=6QkG1d%2fPPRiCAqhKb7yhss1YTnoqfX85YJz37paIgUBv4vlgYcYcx0pgO%2fMtF1URO4inWo8Kmt7ON5Vqrd1zgkBFouIs1Z%2fIb51RmktHrSGwqkd7QdsDpcuWrDnFMuNh, accessed 30 November 2014.

CEDAW, 'Concluding Observations on the Combined Second and Third Periodic Reports of Myanmar', adopted by the cedaw Committee during its 42nd Session, 20 October to 7 November 2008, http://docstore.ohchr.org/SelfServices/FilesHandler.ashx?enc=6QkG1d%2fPPRiCAqhKb7yhsGOTxO5cLIZoCwAvhyns%2byL9QoGtuF exI9MoVz2%2fFKXwVzM4d2ozv%2faAMUIZuUK1iPEK9lebyTJrbNMftwlO48K6MgdfRBGdcKaMKazTc%2foP, accessed 30 November 2014.

CEDAW, 'Concluding Observations on the Combined Sixth and Seventh Period Reports of Indonesia', adopted by the Committee during its 52nd Session, 9–27 July 2012, available at http://daccess-dds-ny.un.org/doc/UNDOC/GEN/N12/455/72/PDF/N1245572.pdf? OpenElement, accessed 30 November 2014.

CEDAW, 'Concluding Observations on the Fourth and Fifth Periodic Report of Cambodia' adopted by the Committee at its fifty-sixth session (30 September–18 October 2013), http://docstore.ohchr.org/SelfServices/FilesHandler.ashx?enc=6QkG1d%2fPPRiCAqhKb7yhsglff%2fiazrVw%2bcyfdY9GxZ62YXIcKp9qTzonRzgoWWfPCWuduIoAQDgIdC71U7lPYiIffLoiBHKqR9Sh2Vo3nWax969tKGbDUkflPsXeZyF8sAhoDtowkyo5T8krCgqvhQ%3d%3d, accessed 30 November 2014.

Chabal, Patrick and Jean-Pascal Daloz, *Africa Works: Disorder as a political instrument* (Oxford: James Currey, 1999).

Channel New Asia, "ASEAN's non-interference policy must be reviewed: Former Malaysian minister," Channel News Asia, 24 April 2015, from http://www.channelnewsasia.com/news/business/asean-s-non-interference/1804054.html, accessed on 24 March 2017.

Charlesworth, Hilary 'Feminist Reflections on the Responsibility to Protect', Global Responsibility to Protect, 2/3: 232–249 (2010).

Checkel, Jeffrey T. 'The Constructivist Turn in International Relations Theory', World Politics 50/2: 324–48 (1998).

Cheru, Fantu *The Silent Revolution: Debt, Development and Democracy*, (London: Zed Books, 1989).

Chirot, Daniel and Clark McCauley, *Why Not Kill Them All? The Logic and Prevention of Mass Political Murder* (Princeton, NJ: Princeton University Press, 2006).

Chowdhury, Anwarul 'Women and Conflict: A Frontline Issue?', nato Review (2010), http://www.nato.int/docu/Review/2010/Women-Security/Women-resolution-1325/EN/index.htm, accessed 2 June 2015.

Eze, Chukwuemeka B and Takwa Z. Sufion, 'Business for Peace: Developing Partnership Between Business Investment and Peacebuilding', WANEP Concept note (Accra: WANEP, June 2012).

Cilliers, Jakkie and Johann Pottgieter, 'The African Standby Force' in Ulf Engel and J. Gomes Porto (eds.) *Africa's New Peace and Security Architecture: Promoting Norms, Institutionalizing Solutions, Global Security in a Changing World* (Ashgate, 2010): 111–142.

Ciorciari, John 'Institutionalizing Human Rights in Southeast Asia', Human Rights Quarterly 34:3 (2012).

Clark, Ian *Legitimacy in International Society* (Oxford: Oxford University Press, 2005).

Cochrane, Joe "Indonesia and Malaysia agree to care for stranded migrants," The New York Times online, 20 May 2015, from https://www.nytimes.com/2015/05/21/world/asia/indonesia-malaysia-rohingya-bangladeshi-migrants-agreement.html?action=click&contentCollection=Asia%20Pacific&module=RelatedCoverage&region=Marginalia&pgtype=article, accessed on 24 March 2017.

Cochrane, Joey "In reversal, Myanmar agrees to attend meeting on migrant crisis," The New York Times online, 21 May 2015, from https://www.nytimes.com/2015/05/22/world/asia/myanmar-rohingya-migrant-crisis-malaysia-thailand-indonesia.html?_r=0, accessed on 24 March 2017.

Cockburn, Cynthia 'Gender Relations as Causal in Militarization and War,' International Feminist Journal of Politics 12/2 (2010).

Cohen, Roberta "Reconciling R2P with IDP Protection," in Sara E. Davies and Luke Glanville (eds.), *Protecting the Displaced: Deepening the Responsibility to Protect* (Leiden: Martinus Nijhoff Publishers, 2010), pp. 35–58.

Coomaraswamy, Radhika 'Of Kali Born: Violence and the Law in Sri Lanka' in Margaret Schuler (ed.), *Freedom from Violence: Women's Strategies from Around the World*, (New York: Widbooks, 1992).

Council for Security Cooperation in the Asia Pacific (CSCAP) Study Group on the Responsibility to Protect, Final Report, 2011.

Davies, Matthew 'Women and Development, Not Gender and Politics: Explaining ASEAN's Failure to Engage with the Women, Peace and Security Agenda,' Contemporary Southeast Asia 38/1: 106–127 (2016).

Davies, Sara E. 'The Asian Rejection? International Refugee Law in Asia,' Australian Journal of Politics & History 52/4 (2006).

Davies, Sara and Sarah Teitt, 'Engendering the Responsibility to Protect: Women and the Prevention of Mass Atrocities', Global Responsibility to Protect 4/2:198–222 (2012).

Davies, Sara, Zim Nwokora, Eli Stamnes, and Sara Teitt (eds), *Responsibility to Protect and Women, Peace and Security: Aligning the Protection Agendas* (Leiden: Martinus Nijhoff, 2013).

Davies, Sara E., Kimberly Nackers and Sarah Teitt, 'Women, Peace and Security as an ASEAN priority,' Australian Journal of International Affairs 68/3: 333–355 (2014).

Davies, Sara and Jacqui True, 'Reframing conflict-related sexual and gender-based violence: Bringing gender analysis back in,' Security Dialogue 46/6: 495–512 (2015).

Davies, Sara, Sarah Teitt, and Zim Nwokora, 'Bridging the Gap: Early Warning, Gender, and the Responsibility to Protect', Cooperation and Conflict, 50/2: 228–249 (2015).

Davies, Sara, Jacqui True and Maria Tanyag, 'How women's silence secures the peace: analysing sexual and gender-based violence in a low-intensity conflict,' Gender and Development (forthcoming).

Dawson, Grant and Sonia Farber, *Forcible Displacement Throughout the Ages: Towards an International Convention for the Prevention and Punishment of the Crime of Forcible Displacement* (Martinus Nijhoff Publishers, 2012).

De Coning, Cedric, John Karlsrud, and Linnea Gelot, (eds.) *The Future of African Peace Operations: From the Janjaweed to Boko Haram*, (Zed Books, 2016).

de Waal, Alex 'African Roles in the Libyan Conflict of 2011', International Affairs 89/2 (2013).

Dembinski, Matthias and Berenike Schott, 'Converging around Global Norms? Protection of Civilians in African Union and European Union Peacekeeping in Africa', African Security, 6/3–4: 276–96 (2013).

Demick, Barbara Nothing to Envy: Real Lives in North Korea (London: Granta, 2010).

Deng, Francis Mading 'Promoting Responsible Sovereignty in Africa', in Francis Mading Deng and Terrence Lyons (eds.), *African Reckoning: A Quest for Good Governance*, (Washington: The Brookings Institution, 1998).

Deng, Francis M. and Roberta Cohen, *Masses in Flight* (Washington, DC: Brookings Institution Press, 1998).

Dersso, Solomon A. 'The Role of the African Human Rights System in the Operationalisation of Article 4(H).' in D. Kuwali and F. Viljoen (eds.) *Africa and the Responsibility to Protect: Article 4(H) of the African Union Constitutive Act* (Oxford: Routledge, 2013): 195–206.

Deutsche Welle, "EU imposes fresh sanctions on Myanmar," DW online, 19 November 2007, from http://www.dw.com/en/eu-imposes-fresh-sanctions-on-myanmar/a-2934373, accessed on 12 February 2017.

Diarra, Cheick Oumar 'ECOWAS Protocol relating to the Mechanism on Conflict Prevention', Paper delivered at a Consultative Meeting organised on Human Security Mechanism for EAC and GIL, Nairobi, 24–28 February 2002.

Downes, Alexander B. *Targeting Civilians in War* (Ithaca: Cornell University Press, 2008).

Draft National Plan of Action for the Advancement of Women, 2011–2015, http://www.burmalibrary.org/docs09/UNCT_unCountryTeam_Annex2-Plan%20of%20Action_eng.pdf, accessed 15 June 2015.

Drummond, Catherine 'Non-interference and the Responsibility to Protect: Canvassing the Relationship between Sovereignty and Humanity in Southeast Asia', no date, p. 1,http://www.polsis.uq.edu.au/dialogue/articledrummond2.pdf, accessed 20 February 2015.

Dunne, Tim *Inventing International Society: A History of the English School* (London: Macmillan, 1998).

Dunne, Tim 'The New Agenda' in Alex J. Bellamy (ed.), *International Society and Its Critics* (Oxford: Oxford University Press, 2004), pp. 65–79.

ECOWAS, 'Protocol Relating to the Mechanism for Conflict Prevention, Management, Resolution, Peace-Keeping and Security', 10 December 1999 http://www.comm.ecowas.int/sec/?id=ap101299.

ECOWAS, 'Protocol Relating to the Mechanism of Conflict Prevention, Management, Resolution and Security, Lome, 10 December 1999.

ECOWAS Protocols, http://www.ecowas.int/ecowas-law/find-legislation/, accessed 8 March 2016.

ECOWAS, 'Final Communiqué of the Extraordinary Session of the Authority of Heads of State and Government on Cote d'Ivoire', Abuja, 7th December 2010.

ECOWAS, 'Forty second ordinary session of the ECOWAS authority of heads of state and government', ECOWAS Communiqué, Yamoussoukro, February 2013, <http://www.ecowas.int/wp-content/uploads/2015/02/42nd-ECOWAS-Summit-Yamoussoukro-27–28-Feb-20131.pdf>, accessed 8 March 2016).

ECOWAS, 'Forty-fifth ordinary session of the authority of ECOWAS heads of state and government', ECOWAS Communiqué, Accra, July 2014, <http://www.ecowas.int/wp-content/uploads/2015/02/45th-ECOWAS-Summit-Ghana-10-Dec-20141.pdf>, accessed 8 March 2016).

Thelma Ekiyor, 'The Role of Civil Society in Conflict Prevention: West African experiences', United Nations Institute for Disarmament Research (UNIDIR) Disarmament Forum: The complex dynamics of small arms in West Africa, 4: 27–34 (2008).

El Abdellaoui, Jamila 'The Panel of the Wise: A Comprehensive Introduction to a Critical Pillar of the African Peace and Security Architecture' ISS Paper, no.193 (2009).

El-Ayouty, Yassin and I. William Zartman *The OAU after Twenty Years* (Praeger, 1984).

Elson, Diane (ed), *Male bias in the Development Process,* 2nd ed (Manchester; New York: Manchester University Press, 1995).

Emmerson, Donald K. 'What do the blind-sided see? Reapproaching regionalism in Southeast Asia', The Pacific Review, 18/1 (2005).

Enloe, Cynthia Bananas, *Beaches and Bases: Making Feminist Sense of International Politics* (Berkeley, CA; London: University of California Press, 2014/1989).

Epstein, Charlotte 'Stop Telling Us How to Behave: Socialization or Infantilization?', International Studies Perspectives, 13/2: 135–45 (2012).

European Parliament (EU), European Parliament recommendation to the Council of 18 April 2013 on the UN principle of the 'Responsibility to Protect', 18 April 2013, http://www.europarl.europa.eu/sides/getDoc.do?type=TA&reference=P7-TA-2013–0180&language=EN, accessed 1 March 2015.

Evans, Gareth *The Responsibility to Protect: Ending Mass Atrocity Crimes Once and for All* (Washington: Brookings Institution Press, 2008).

Fan, Lilian and Hanna B. Krebs, 'Regional organisations and humanitarian action: the case of ASEAN', September 2014, http://www.odi.org/sites/odi.org.uk/files/odi-assets/publications-opinion-files/9207.pdf, accessed 1 August 2015.

Farrell, Mary, Björn Hettne and Luk Van Langenhove, *Global Politics of Regionalism: Theory and Practice* (Pluto Press, 2005).

Fawcett, Louise L'Estrange and Andrew Hurrell, *Regionalism in World Politics: Regional Organization and International Order* (Oxford: Oxford University Press, 1995).

Fawcett, Louise 'Exploring Regional Domains: A Comparative History of Regionalism', International Affairs, 80/3: 429–46 (2004).

Fawcett, Louise 'Regionalism from a historical perspective', in M. Farrell et al (eds.) *Global Politics of Regionalism: Theory and Practice* (London: Pluto Press, 2005).

Fawole, W Alade *Crisis of the State and Regionalism in West Africa* (Codesria, 2005).

Ferris, Elizabeth and Chareen Stark, 'Internal Displacement in West Africa: A Snapshot,' (Washington D.C.: Brookings-LSE Project on Internal Displacement 2012).

Financial Times (FT), "Fears of mounting death toll in Burma," Financial Times online, 29 September 2007, from http://www.ft.com/cms/s/0/32f71724–6e62–11dc-b818–0000779fd2ac.html?ft_site=falcon&desktop=true accessed on 12 February 2017.

Financial Times, "UN envoy Gambari in Burma crisis talks," Financial Times online, 30 September 2007, from https://www.ft.com/content/0d0623bc-6de4–11dc-b8ab-0000779fd2ac, accessed on 12 February 2017.

Finnemore Martha and Kathryn Sikkink, 'International Norm Dynamics and Political Change', International Organization, 52/4: 887–917 (1998).

Frerks, George 'The Role of Civil Society in Peacebuilding' in Sol Iglesias (ed.), *The Role of Civil Society in Conflict Prevention and Peacebuilding* (Utrecht: European Centre for Conflict Prevention, 2006).

Fuller, Thomas and Joe Cochrane, 'Rohingya Migrants From Myanmar, Shunned by Malaysia, are Spotted Adrift in Andaman Sea' The New York Times, 14 May 2015. Available at: http://www.nytimes.com/2015/05/15/world/asia/burmese-rohingya-bangladeshi-migrants-andaman-sea.html.

Galtung, Johann 'Violence, Peace, and Peace Research," Journal of Peace Research 6/3 (1969).

Gambari, Ibrahim 'Multilateralism: Challenges of International Mediation in Regional Conflicts', African Conflict & Peacebuilding Review 1/1: 133–138 (2011).

Ginbar, Yuval 'Human Rights in ASEAN—Setting Sail or Treading Water?,' Human Rights Law Review 10/3 (2010).

Glanville, Luke *Sovereignty and the Responsibility to Protect: A New History* (Chicago: University of Chicago Press, 2014).

Global Centre for the Responsibility to Protect, 'Populations at Risk: Syria', 2015, from http://www.globalr2p.org/regions/syria.

Goodman, Ryan and Derek Jinks, 'How to Influence States: Socialization and International Human Rights Law,' Duke Law Journal (2004).

Gosovic, Branislav 'The resurgence of South–South cooperation', Third World Quarterly, 37/4: 733–743 (2016).

Gray, Kevin and Barry K. Gills, 'South–South cooperation and the rise of the Global South', Third World Quarterly, 37/4: 557–574 (2016).

Haacke, Jürgen and Paul D. Williams, 'Regional arrangements and security challenges: a comparative analysis', Crisis States Research Centre working papers series, 2/52 (London, UK: Crisis States Research Centre, London School of Economics and Political Science, 2009).

Hall, Lucy and Laura J. Shepherd, 'WPS and R2P: Theorising Responsibility and Protection' in Davies et al., *Responsibility to Protect and Women, Peace and Security* (Leiden: BRILL, 2013).

Hawkins, Jeffrey 'Understanding the Failure of IMF Reform: The Zambian Case', World Development, 19/7: 839–849 (1991).

Hedman, Eva-Lotta E 'Introduction: Dynamics of Displacement in Indonesia,' in *Conflict, Violence, and Displacement in Indonesia,* ed. Eva-Lotta E Hedman (Ithaca: Cornell Souteast Studies Program Publications, 2008).

Hedman, Eva-Lotta E 'Refugees, IDPs, and Regional Security in the Asia-Pacific,' in *Cscap Regional Security Outlook 2009–2010: Security through Co-Operation,* ed. Brian L. Job and E. E. Williams (Kuala Lumpur: Council for Security Cooperation in the Asia Pacific, 2009).

Henckaerts, Jean-Marie, Louise Doswald-Beck, and Carolin Alvermann, *Customary International Humanitarian Law: Volume 1, Rules,* vol. 1 (Cambridge University Press, 2005): 458–50.

Hettne, Björn, Andras Inotai and Osvaldo Sunkel, *Globalism and the New Regionalism* (London: Palgrave Macmillan, 1999).

Hettne, Björn and Fredrik Söderbaum, 'Theorising the Rise of Regionness', New Political Economy, 5/3: 457–472 (2000).

Hewitt, Sarah 'Overcoming the Gender Gap: The Possibilities of Alignment between the Responsibility to Protect and the Women, Peace and Security Agenda,' Global Responsibility to Protect 8: 3–28 (2016).

High Level Advisory Panel's Report, 'Mainstreaming Responsibility to Protect in Southeast Asia: Pathway Towards a Caring ASEAN Community', 9 September 2014.

Hill, Feicity, Mikele Aboitiz and Sara Poehlman-Doumbouya, 'Nongovernmental Organizations' Role in the Build-up and Implementation of Security Council Resolution 1325', Signs 28/4 (2003).

Hoge, Warren "UN report finds 31 killed in Myanmar crackdown," The New York Times online, 7 December 2007, from http://www.nytimes.com/2007/12/07/world/asia/07iht-07nations.8645448.html, accessed on 12 February 2017.

Hook, Glenn and Ian Kearns (eds.) *Sub Regionalism and World Order* (London: Macmillan, 1999).

Humaniti, 'Former ASEAN Leaders Issue Letter on Myanmar Intolerance,' 22 April 2015, http://www.burmapartnership.org/2015/04/former-asean-leaders-issue-letter-on-myanmar-intolerance/, accessed on 15 December 2015.

Human Rights Watch (HRW), 'Burma: New Violence in Araken State,' (New York: Human Rights Watch, 2012).

HRW, 'All you can do is pray: Crimes against Humanity and Ethnic cleansing of Rohingya Muslims in Burma's Arakan State', Human Rights Watch online, 2013, https://www.hrw.org/report/2013/04/22/all-you-can-do-pray/crimes-against-humanity-and-ethnic-cleansing-rohingya-muslims.

HRW, "Thailand mass graves found in Rohingya trafficking camp," Human Rights Watch online, 1 May 2015, from https://www.hrw.org/news/2015/05/01/thailand-mass-graves-rohingya-found-trafficking-camp, accessed on 23 March 2017.

Hun, Sen Address at the International Conference on Responsibility to Protect: Progress, Challenges and Opportunities in the Asia-Pacific: Cambodia Takes Leading Role in the Prevention of Genocide in asean, 26 February 2015, http://cnv.org.kh/address-at-the-international-conference-on-the-responsibility-to-protect-progress-challenges-and-opportunity-in-asia-pacific-cambodia-takes-the-leading-role-in-the-prevention-of-genocide-i/ accessed 1 April 2015.

Hunt, Charles T. 'The role of African Standby Force in Implementing Article 4(h)', In Dan Kuwali and Frans Viljeon (eds.) *Africa and the Responsibility to Protect*, (Oxon: Routledge, 2014): 173–194.

Hunt, Charles T. 'Cote d'Ivoire', in Alex Bellamy and Tim Dunne (eds.) *Oxford Handbook on the Responsibility to Protect* (Oxford: Oxford University Press, 2016): 693–716.

Hunt, 'Charles T. Emerging Powers and the Responsibility to Protect: Non-linear Norm Dynamics in Complex International Society', Cambridge Review of International Affairs 29/2: 761–781 (2016).

Hunt, Luke 'ASEAN Move on Rohingya, Slow but Forward' The Diplomat, 22 Jun 2015. Available at: http://thediplomat.com/2015/06/asean-move-on-rohingya-slow-but-forward/.

Hurrell, Andrew 'One World? Many Worlds? The Place of Regions in the Study of International Society', International Affairs, 83/1: 127–46 (2007).

Hutchful, Eboe 'From Military Security to Human Security', in in John Akokpari, Angela Ndinga-Muvumba and Timothy Murithi (eds.), *The African Union and Its Institutions* (Cape Town: Jacana Media, 2008): 63–84.

Huth, Paul and Benjamin Valentino Mass Killing of Civilians in Times of War, 1945–2000 in Hewitt, Wilkenfield and Gurr (eds.), *Peace and Conflict 2008* (Boulder: Paradigm 2008), pp. 79–92.

Ifediora, Obinna F. 'Preventive Arbitration: Towards Strengthening the African Union Mediation Capacity for Human Protection', Australasian Review of African Studies, 37/1: 21–51 (2016).

Ifediora, Obinna F. 'The Structural Bases of Implementing the Responsibility to Protect in Africa: Towards Advancing the African Governance Architecture', African Conflict and Peacebuilding Review, 6/2: 94–111 (2016).

Ikenberry, John and Charles Kupchan., 'Socialization and Hegemonic Power', International Organization, 44:3 (1990).

Internal Displacement Monitoring Centre (IDMC) "IDP Laws and Policies: A Mapping Tool', http://www.internal-displacement.org/law-and-policy, accessed 4 March 2016.

IDMC, 'The Kampala Convention--Two years on: time to turn theory into practice' December 2014 from http://www.internal-displacement.org/sub-saharan-africa/kampala-convention/.

IDMC, 'A Bend in the Road is Not the End of the Road- The Veto of the IDP Act in the Philippines' 13 June 2013 http://www.internal-displacement.org/assets/library/Asia/Philippines/pdf/IDMC-NRC-public-statement-Philippines-13-june-2013.pdf (Accessed 14 May 2013).

IDMC *Disaster-related Displacement Risk: Measuring the Risk and Addressing the Drivers* (Geneva: Internal Displacement Monitoring Centre and the Norwegian Refugee Council, 2015).

IDMC, Disaster-related Displacement Risk. UNHCR, 'Asia and the Pacific' in Global Reports 2013, 2014–2015, http://www.unhcr.org/asia-and-the-pacific.html accessed 31 August 2016.

IDMC, 'Syria IDP Figures Analysis', December 2015, http://www.internal-displacement.org/middle-east-and-north-africa/syria/figures-analysis.

International Commission on Sovereignty and Intervention (ICISS), *The Responsibility to Protect* (Ottawa: IDRC, 2001).

International Committee of the Red Cross 'IHL National Implementation- International Crimes Act, 2008' https://www.icrc.org/applic/ihl/ihl-nat.nsf/6fa4d35e5e3025394125673e00508143/57d55469fc1bd9 c9c12576ce003cd1f2?openDocument, accessed 5 May 2015.

International Federation of Red Cross and Red Crescent Societies (IFRC), "Myanmar: Cyclone Nargis 2008 Facts and Figures," IFRC online, 3 May 2011, from http://www.ifrc.org/en/news-and-media/news-stories/asia-pacific/myanmar/myanmar-cyclone-nargis-2008-facts-and-figures/, accessed on 13 February 2017.

International Monetary Fund, *Independent Evaluation at the IMF: The First Decade, edited by Ruben Lamdany and Hali Edison, Independent Evaluation Office,* (Washington: IMF, 2012).

Interim Recommendations, Advisory Commission on Rakhine State, March 2017.

Intervention by H.E. Mr. Kyaw Tin, Permanent Representative of the Republic of the Union of Myanmar to the United Nations at the General Assembly Informal Interactive Dialogue on the Report of the Secretary-General on the Responsibility to Protect, New York, 8 September 2014.

Jacques, Mélanie *Armed Conflict and Displacement: The Protection of Refugees and Displaced Persons under International Humanitarian Law* (Cambridge University Press, 2012).

Jakarta Globe, "Indonesia ready to help Myanmar achieve political stability," Jakarta Globe online, 29 April 2017, from http://jakartaglobe.id/news/indonesia-ready-help-myanmar-achieve-political-stability-jokowi/, accessed on 1 May 2017.

Jaye, Thomas, Dauda Garuba, and Stella Amadi, *ECOWAS and the Dynamics of Conflict and Peace-Building* (African Books Collective, 2011).

Jenkins, Carolyn and Lynne Thomas, 'African Regionalism and the SADC' in Mario Telò (ed.) *European Union and New Regionalism. Regional Actors and Global Governance in a Post-Hegemonic Era.* (Aldershot: Ashgate, 2001).

Joint statement: Ministerial meeting on irregular movement of people in Southeast Asia," Reliefweb, 21 May 2015, from http://reliefweb.int/report/myanmar/joint-statement-ministerial-meeting-irregular-movement-people-southeast-asia, accessed on 24 March 2017.

Jones, Lee "ASEAN's Albatross: ASEAN's Burma Policy from Critical Engagement to Critical Disengagement," Asian Security, 4 (3): 271–293 (September 2008).

Jones, Lee 'Democratization and foreign policy in Southeast Asia: the case of the ASEAN InterParliamentary Myanmar Caucus', Cambridge Review of International Affairs, 22/3: 387–406 (2009).

Kälin, Walter 'The Guiding Principles on Internal Displacement as International Minimum Standard and Protection Tool,' Refugee Survey Quarterly 24/3: 29–30 (2005).

Kälin, Walter 'Internal Displacement,' in *The Oxford Handbook of Refugee and Forced Migration Studies*, ed. Elena Fiddi an-Qasmiyeh, et al. (Oxford: Oxford University Press, 2014).

Kassim, Yang Razali and Nur Azha Putra, 'Responsibility to Protect: How Should Southeast Asia Respond?', rsis Commentaries, 25 April 2010, http://www.rsis.edu.sg/rsis-publication/nts/1333-responsibility-to-protect-how/#.VS96tfAp02E, accessed 1 April 2015.

Khadragala, Gilbert M. *Silencing the Guns: Strengthening Governance to Prevent, Manage, and Resolve Conflicts in Africa* (New York: International Peace Institute, 2015).

Kholifa, Dwi Rubiyanti 'Indonesian Implementation of UNSCR 1325: Adapting to the National Context', 8 April 2014, https://www.womenpeacemakersprogram.org/

news/indonesian-implementation-of-unscr-1325-adapting-to-the-national-context/, accessed 13 November 2014.

Kidane, Won 'Managing Forced Displacement by Law in Africa: The Role of the New African Union IDPs Convention,' Vanderbilt Journal of Transnational Law 44 (2011).

Kioko, Ben 'The Right of Intervention under the African Union's Constitutive Act: From Non-Interference to Non-Intervention', Revue Internationale de la Croix-Rouge/International Review of the Red Cross, 85/852: 807–26 (2003).

Kivimaki, Timo *The Long Peace of East Asia* (Aldershot: Ashgate Press, 2014).

Koko, Sadiki and Martha Bakwesegha-Osula, 'Assessing the African Union's Response to the Libyan Crisis', Conflict Trends, Issue 1, (2012), pp.3–15.

Kraft, Herman J. 'RtoP by increments: the aichr and localizing the Responsibility to Protect in Southeast Asia,' The Pacific Review 25/1: 27–49 (2012).

Kreft, Sönke, David Eckstein and Inga Melchior, *Global Climate Risk Index 2017* (Bonn; Berlin: Germanwatch, 2016).

Krook, Mona Leena and Jacqui True, 'Rethinking the Life Cycles of International Norms: The United Nations and the Global Promotion of Gender Equality', European Journal of International Relations 18/1: 103–27 (2012).

Kundu, Sampa 'The Rohingyas: Security Implications for ASEAN and Beyond,' IDSA Issue Brief (2015), http://www.idsa.in/issuebrief/TheRohingyas_skundu_280515.html.

Kuwali, Dan and Frans Viljoen, eds. *Africa and the Responsibility to Protect: Article 4(h) of the African Union Constitutive Act.* (Oxford: Routledge, 2013).

Lancaster, Carol 'The Lagos Three: Economic Regionalism in Sub-Saharan Africa' in John Willis Harbeson and Donald S. Rothchild (ed.) *Africa in World Politics: Post-Cold War Challenges* (Boulder: Westview Press Inc., 1995).

Landsberg, Chris 'The Birth and Evolution of NEPAD', in John Akokpari, Angela Ndinga-Muvumba and Timothy Murithi (eds.) *The African Union and Its Institutions* (Cape Town: Jacana Media, 2008): 207–26.

Lecamwasam, Menaka 'The Internally Displaced in South Asia: Lessons from Kampala,' Asia Pacific Journal on Human Rights and Law, 15 nos. 1&2 (2014).

Lee-Koo, Katrina 'Translating UNSCR 1325 into Practice: Lessons Learned and Obstacles Ahead', in Davies et al., *Responsibility to Protect and Women, Peace and Security*, pp. 35–52.

Lewa, Chris "Unregistered Rohingya Refugees in Bangladesh: Crackdown, Forced Displacement, and Hunger," The Arakan Project, 11 February 2010.

Lindenmayer, Elizabeth and Josie Lianna Kaye, '*A Choice for Peace? The Story of Forty-One Days Mediation in Kenya*' (New York: International Peace Institute, August 2009).

MacKinnon, Ian and James Sturcke, "After 20 days adrift, Burmese boat people land with tales of abuse and starvation," The Guardian online, 4 February 2009, from https://www.theguardian.com/world/2009/feb/04/burmese-boat-survivors, accessed on 20 March 2017.

Malaysiakini, "Mahathir warns rapid Burma reforms would risk sparking anarchy," 19 August 2002, Malaysiakini.com, from http://www.malaysiakini.com/news/12626, accessed on 6 February 2017.

Malaysiakini, "Burmese junta vetoed plans for meeting with Suu Kyi," 21 August 2002, Malaysiakini.com, from http://www.malaysiakini.com/news/12648, accessed on 6 February 201.

Mamdani, Mahmood *Citizen and Subject: Contemporary Africa and the Legacy of Late Colonialism* (Princeton University Press, 1996).

Mataboge, Mmanaledi 'AU's dependence on cash from the West still rankles', Mail and Guardian, 11 June 2015, http://mg.co.za/article/2015–06–11-aus-dependence-on-cash-from-the-west-still-rankles , accessed 11 June 2015.

Mathews, Kay 'Renaissance of Pan-Africanism: The AU and the New Pan-Africanists', in John Akokpari, Angela Ndinga-Muvumba and Timothy Murithi (eds.), *The African Union and Its Institutions* (Cape Town: Jacana Media, 2008): 25–40.

Mayersen, Deborah and Annie Pohlman. *Genocide and Mass Atrocities in Asia: Legacies and Prevention* (Abingdon: Routledge, 2013).

Mazowiecki, Taddeus Report on the Situation in the Territory of the Former Yugoslavia to the 47th Session of the Security Council and the General Assembly, A/47/666, 17 Nov 1992, 6.

Mbeki, Thabo 'The African Renaissance Statement' (Office of the Executive Deputy President, 13 August 1998), <http://www.anc.org.za/ancdocs/history/mbeki/1998/tm0813.htm>.

Mbaku, John Mukum *Africa at the Crossroads: Between Regionalism and Globalization* (Praeger Publishers, 2004).

Mclaughlin, T. and Nyan Lynn Aung, 'Govt succeeds in keeping Rohingya off asean Summit agenda', The Myanmar Times, 12 May 2014, http://www.mmtimes.com/index.php/national-news/nay-pyi-taw/10324-govt-succeeds-in-keeping-rohingya-off-asean-summit-agenda.html, accessed 30 April 2015.

McLoughlin, S. *The Structural Prevention of Mass Atrocities: Understanding Risk and Resilience* (London: Routledge, 2014)\.

Meindersma, Christa 'Legal Issues Surrounding Population Transfers in Conflict Situations,' Netherlands International Law Review 41/1: 33 (1994).

Meyer, Angela 'Peace and Security Cooperation in Central Africa: Challenges and Prospects', Discussion Paper 56 (Uppsala: Nordiska Afrikainstitutet, 2011).

Ministry of Women Affairs of the Royal Government of Cambodia, National Action Plan to Prevent Violence against Women, December 2014, Unofficial English translation.

Ministry of Foreign Affairs of the Republic of Kazakstan, 'Ministerial Conference on Refugee Protection and International Migration: The Almaty Process,' (Almaty Ministry of Foreign Affairs of the Republic of Kazakstan, 2013).

Ministry of Foreign Affairs of the Kingdom of Thailand, 'Summary of Special Meeting on Irregular Migration in the Indian Ocean, 29 May 2015, http://www.mfa.go.th/main/en/media-center/14/56880-Summary-Special-Meeting-on-Irregular-Migration-in.html, accessed 1 August 2015.

Ministry of Foreign Affairs of The Kingdom of Thailand, 'Summary: Special Meeting on Irregular Migration in the Indian Ocean, 29 May 2015, Bangkok, Thailand' 29 May 2015. Available at: http://www.mfa.go.th/main/en/media-center/14/56880-Summary-Special-Meeting-on-Irregular-Migration-in.html.

Mon, Ye and Shoon Naing, "ASEAN FMs pledge support on Rakhine," Myanmar Times online, 20 December 2016, from http://www.mmtimes.com/index.php/national-news/24298-asean-fms-pledge-support-on-rakhine.html, accessed on 20 December 2016.

Mooney, Erin D 'Something Old, Something New, Something Borrowed... Something Blue? The Protection Potential of a Marriage of Concepts between R2P and IDP Protection,' Global Responsibility to Protect 2/1: 65 (2010).

Morada, Noel M. 'ASEAN at 40: Prospects for Community Building in Southeast Asia', Asia Pacific Review 15/1: 36–55 (2008).

Morada, Noel M. "The ASEAN Charter and the Promotion of R2P in Southeast Asia: Challenges and Consttraints," Global Responsibility to Protect, 1: 198–199 (2009).

Morada, Noel M. 'Europe and Southeast Asia: ASEAN-EU Interregionalism between Pluralist and Solidarist Societies', Review of European Studies, 4/3 (July 2012).

Morada, Noel M. "The Rohingya Crisis: High on Outrage, Short on Action," The Global Observatory, 13 October 2017, from https://theglobalobservatory.org/2017/10/rohingya-crisis-high-on-outrage-short-on-action/, accessed on 13 October 2017.

Motala, Ahmed 'The African Court on Human and Peoples' Rights: Origins and Prospects', in John Akokpari, Angela Ndinga-Muvumba and Timothy Murithi (eds.) *The African Union and Its Institutions* (Cape Town: Jacana Media, 2008): 271–90.

Muchie, Mammo, Adam Habib, and Vishnu Panayachee, 'African Integration and Civil Society: The Case of the African Union', Transformation: Critical Perspectives on Southern Africa: 3–24 (2006).

Murithi, Tim *The African Union: Pan-Africanism, Peace Building and Development* (Aldershot: Ashgate, 2005).

Murithi, Tim 'The African Union at ten: An appraisal', African Affairs, 111/445: 662–669 (2012).

Murithi, Tim 'African indigenous and endogenous approaches to peace and conflict resolution' in David J. Francis (ed.), *Peace and Conflict in Africa* (London: Zed, 2008): 16–30.

Murithi, Tim and Charles Mwaura, 'The Panel of the Wise' in Ulf Engel and J. Gomes Porto (eds.) *Africa's New Peace and Security Architecture: Promoting Norms, Institutionalizing Solutions, Global Security in a Changing World* (Ashgate, 2010): 79–90.

Murithi, Tim 'The Role of the African Peace and Security Architecture in the Implementation of Article 4(H).', in D. Kuwali and F. Viljoen (eds.) *Africa and the Responsibility to Protect: Article 4(H) of the African Union Constitutive Act* (Oxford: Routledge, 2013): 139–51.

Murray, Rachel *Human Rights in Africa: From the OAU to the African Union* (Cambridge: Cambridge University Press, 2004).

Mutasa, Charles 'A Critical Appraisal of the African Union–ECOSOCC Civil Society Interface', in John Akokpari, Angela Ndinga-Muvumba and Timothy Murithi (eds.) *The African Union and Its Institutions* (Cape Town: Jacana Media, 2008): 291–306.

Muyangw, Monde and Margaret Vogt, *An Assessment of the OAU Mechanism for Conflict Prevention, Management, and Resolution, 1993–2000* (New York: International Peace Academy, 2000).

Mwanasali, Musifiky 'From Non-Interference to Non-Indifference: The Emerging Doctrine of Confl Ict Prevention in Africa', in John Akokpari, Angela Ndinga-Muvumba and Timothy Murithi (eds.) *The African Union and Its Institutions* (Cape Town: Jacana Media, 2008): 41–62.

Mydans, Seth "Monks silenced, and for now, the internet is, too," The New York Times online, 4 October 2007, from http://www.nytimes.com/2007/10/04/world/asia/04info.html, accessed on 12 February 2017.

Mydans, Seth "Myanmar faces pressure to allow major aid effort," New York Times online, 8 May 2008, from http://www.nytimes.com/2008/05/08/world/asia/08myanmar.html, accessed on 13 February 2017.

Nair, Tamara 'Women, Peace and Security in the ASEAN: Need for a Distinct Ac¬tion Plan,' RSIS Commentary, 23 December 2015, https://www.rsis.edu.sg/wp-content/uploads/2016/03/Women-Peace-and-Security-in-the-Asia-Pacific.pdf accessed 31 August 2016.

Nathan, Laurie 'Plan of action to build the AU's mediation capacity', paper presented at seminar on 'Towards Enhancing the Capacity of the AU in Mediation', AU Commission, Addis Ababa, October 2009.

Nathan, Laurie *Community of Insecurity: SADC's Struggle for Peace and Security in Southern Africa* (Ashgate Publishing Limited, 2013).

Ndugulile, Gabriel S. *The Organization of African Unity (OAU): Its Successes and Failures in the Liberation Struggle* (Centre for Foreign Relations, 1981).

Nkrumah, Kwame *Africa Must Unite* (London: PANAF, 1963).

Nkhulu, Wiseman *The New Partnership for Africa's Development: The Journey So Far*, (Midrand: NEPAD Secretariat, June 2005).

Office for the Coordination of Humanitarian Affairs (OCHA), '*Guiding Principles on Internal Displacement*,' (New York: UNOCHA, 1999).

Okumu, Washington A.J. *The African Renaissance: History, Significance and Strategy* (Trenton, NJ: Africa World Press, 2002).

Omorogbe, Eki Yemisi 'The African Union, Responsibility to Protect and the Libyan Crisis,' Netherlands International Law Review 59/02 (2012).

Onwuka, Ralph I. and Amadu Sesay, *The Future of Regionalism in Africa* (St. Martin's Press, 1985).

Organization of African Unity (OAU) Declaration on a Mechanism for Conflict Prevention, Management and Resolution (Cairo Declaration) adopted at the OAU's 29th Ordinary Session in Cairo, Egypt, 28–30 June, 1993.

Organisation for Economic Co-operation and Development (OECD), States of Fragility 2015: Meeting Post-2015 Ambitions, 2015, http://www.oecd.org/dac/governance-peace/publications/documentuploads/SOF2015.pdf.

Panti, Llanesca 'Bill on Displaced Persons Gathers Dust in Congress', The Manila Times, 14 March 2015 http://www.manilatimes.net/bill-on-displaced-persons-gathers-dust-in-congress/169395/, accessed 14 May 2015.

Peou, Sorpong 'Diplomatic Pragmatism: ASEAN's response to the July 1997 Coup' in Dylan Hendrickson (ed.) *Safeguarding peace: Cambodia's constitutional challenge, Accord No. 5* (1998).

Petcharamesree, Sriprapha 'The Human Rights Body: A Test for Democracy Building of asean', (IDEA, 2009), http://www.idea.int/resources/analysis/upload/Sriprapha_low_2.pdf.

Philippine Country Statement by Secretary Teresita Quintos Deles during the High-Level Review on the United Nations Security Council Resolution (UNSCR) 1325 on Women, Peace and Security, http://opapp.gov.ph/news/philippine-country-statement-secretary-teresita-quintos-deles-during-high-level-review-united.

Philippines Statement, UN General Assembly Informal Interactive Dialogue on the Responsibility to Protect: "Fulfilling our collective responsibility: International assistance and the responsibility to protect," 6th annual informal, interactive dialogue on the Responsibility to Protect, New York City, 8 September 2014.

Phillips, Andrew 'Beyond Bandung: the 1955 Asian-African Conference and its legacies for international order', Australian Journal of International Affairs, 70/4: 329–341 (2016).

Pisanò, Attilio 'Towards an ASEAN human rights mechanism: the ASEAN Commission on the Promotion and Protection of the Rights of Women and Children,' The International Journal of Human Rights, 20/3 (2016).

Preece, Jennifer Jackson 'Ethnic Cleansing as an Instrument of Nation-State Creation: Changing State Practices and Evolving Legal Norms,' Human Rights Quarterly 20/4: (1998).

'Press Release: Special Meeting on Irregular Migration in the Indian Ocean', http://www.europarl.europa.eu/meetdocs/2014_2019/documents/dase/dv/dase0610_4_pressrelease1_/dase0610_4_pressrelease1_en.pdf, accessed 20 February 2016.

Pollard, Vincent K. 'ASA and ASEAN, 1961–1967: Southeast Asian Regionalism', Asian Survey 10/30: 244–255 (1970).

Prunier, Gerald *Darfur: The Ambiguous Genocide*, (Ithaca: Cornell University Press, 2005).

Pruitt-Hamm, Bruce 'Humanitarian Intervention in Southeast Asia in the Post Cold War World: Dilemmas in the Definition and Design of International Law', Pacific Rim Law & Policy Journal, 3/1 (1994).

Rathgeber, Theodor 'Human Rights and the Institutionalisation of ASEAN: An Ambiguous Relationship,' Journal of Current Southeast Asian Affairs 33/3 (2014).

Report of the Commission of Inquiry on Human Rights in the Democratic Peoples' Republic of Korea, A/hrc/25/63, 7 February 2014.

Report on Workshop to Develop Early Warning Indicators to Monitor Violent Extremism in West Africa, Lagos - Nigeria, 21–23 October 2014.

Republic of Kenya, 'The Prevention, Protection and Assistance to Internally Displaced Persons and Affected Communities Act, 2012', 31 Dec 2012.

Republic of the Philippines, Congress of the Philippines 'An Act Protecting the Rights of Internally Displaced Persons, Providing Penalties for Violations Thereof and for Other Purposes' 5 Feb 2013.

Republic of the Philippines House of Representatives 'Proposed Internal Displacement Act of 2014 approved on 2nd Reading' http://www.congress.gov.ph/press/details.php?pressid=8085 Accessed 14 May 2015.

Reuters, "Japan mourns video journalist killed in Yangon," Reuters, 8 October 2007, from http://www.reuters.com/article/us-myanmar-japan-funeral-idUST23546620071009.

Reuters, "OIC envoy calls for UN intervention in Arakan state," The Irrawady, 18 January 2017, from http://www.irrawaddy.com/news/asia/oic-envoy-calls-for-un-intervention-in-arakan-state.html, accessed on 20 January 2017.

Reuters, "Malaysian PM sends off aid ship bound for Burma," The Irrawady Online, 3 February 2017, from http://www.irrawaddy.com/news/burma/malaysian-pm-sends-off-aid-ship-bound-burma.html, accessed on 4 February 2017.

Reuters, "Burma, EU At Odds Over UN Fact-Finding Mission," The Irrawady Online, 3 May 2017, from https://www.irrawaddy.com/news/burma/burma-eu-odds-un-fact-finding-mission.html, accessed on 26 June 2017.

Radio Free Asia (RFA), "Rohingya raised at ASEAN meeting," Radio Free Asia.com, 13 July 2012, from http://www.rfa.org/english/news/myanmar/rohingya-07132012163418.html, accessed on 23 March 2017.

Robinson, Darryl 'Defining "Crimes against Humanity" at the Rome Conference,' American Journal of International Law (1999): 44.

Roughneen, Simon "Plight of Rohingya strains ASEAN unity," Nikkei Asian Review online, 9 February 2017, from http://asia.nikkei.com/magazine/20170209/On-the-Cover/Plight-of-the-Rohingya-strains-ASEAN-unity, accessed on 9 February 2017.

South Asian Association for Regional Cooperation (SAARC) 'Social Charter of the South Asian Association for Regional Cooperation,' SAARC/SUMMIT.12/SC.29/27, 2004.

Sandholtz, Wayne 'Dynamics of International Norm Change: Rules against Wartime Plunder', European Journal of International Relations, 14/1: 101–31 (2008).

Salzman, Todd 'Rape Camps as a Means of Ethnic Cleansing: Religious, Cultural and Ethical Responses To Rape Victims in Former Yugoslavia', Human Right Quarterly 20:348–78 (1998).

Scanlon, Helen, Ahunna Eziakonwa, and Elizabeth Myburgh, 'Africa's Responsibility to Protect', Policy Advisory Group Seminar Report, Somerset South Africa: Centre for conflict Resolution, University of Cape Town, 2007.

Scanlon, Helen 'Conclusion', in Adekeye Adebajo and Helen Scanlon, (eds.) *A dialogue of the deaf: essays on Africa and the United Nations* (Auckland, South Africa: The Centre for Conflict Resolution, 2006): 275–281.

Schabas, William A 'Problems of International Codification-Were the Atrocities in Cambodia and Kosovo Genocide,' New England Law Review. 35/2: 287–302 (2000).

Sharer, Robert 'Africa, Regionalism and Globalisation', Paper presented at the Regional economic integration and the globalisation process, Report on the proceedings of a Southern African conference, (Windhoek, 1998).

Sharpe, Marina 'Engaging with Refugee Protection? The Organization of African Unity and African Union since 1963,' in New Issues in Refugee Research (Geneva: UNHCR, 2011).

Shaw, Martin *War and Genocide: Organised Killing in Modern Society* (Cambridge: Polity, 2003).

Secretary-General's remarks at open debate of the Security Council on Myanmar [as delivered]", 28 September 2017, from https://www.un.org/sg/en/content/sg/statement/2017-09-28/secretary-generals-remarks-open-debate-security-council-myanmar, accessed on 29 September 2017.

Seybolt, Taylor (ed.), *Counting Civilian Casualties: An Introduction to Recording and Estimating Non-Military Deaths in Conflict* (Oxford: Oxford University Press, 2013).

Shepherd, Laura 'Advancing the Women, Peace and Security agenda: 2015 and beyond,' Norwegian Peacebuilding Resource Centre Expert Analysis¬, 28 August 2014, http://www.peacebuilding.no/Themes/Inclusivity-and-gender/Publications/Advancing-the-Women-Peace-and-Security-agenda-2015-and-beyond.

Shepherd, Laura and Jacqui True, 'The Women, Peace and Security Agenda and Australian Leadership in the World: From Rhetoric to Commitment?' Australian Journal of International Affairs, 68/3: 257–284 (2014).

Schulz, Michael, Fredrik Söderbaum and Joakim Öjendal, 'Key Issues in the New Regionalism: Comparisons from Asia, Africa and the Middle East' in B. Hettne, A. Inotai, O. Sunkel (eds.), *Comparing regionalisms: Implications for global development* (Basingstoke: Palgrave-Macmillan, 2001).

Sikkink, Kathryn 'Human Rights, Principled-Issue Networks and Sovereignty in Latin America', International Organization 47/3 (1993).

Skehan, Craig "PM launches sanctions against junta," The Sydney Morning Herald online, 27 September 2007, from http://www.smh.com.au/news/world/pm-launches-sanctions-against-junta/2007/09/27/1190486462513.html.

Skjelsbæk, Inger 'Responsibility to Protect or Prevent? Victims and Perpetrators of Sexual Violence Crimes in Armed Conflict', in Davies et al., *Responsibility to Protect and Women, Peace and Security*, pp. 81–100.

Söderbaum, Fredrik 'African Regionalism and EU-African Interregionalism', in M. Teló (ed.) *European Union and New Regionalism: Regional Actors and Global Governance in a Post-Hegemonic Era* (Ashgate, 2007): 269–85.

Söderbaum, Fredrik and Ian Taylor, *Afro-Regions: The Dynamics of Cross-Border Micro-Regionalism in Africa* (Nordiska Afrikainstitutet, 2008).

Soderbaum, Fredrik 'Comparative Regional Integration and Regionalism', in Todd Landman and Neill Robinson (eds), *The Sage Handbook of Comparative Politics* (London: SAGE Publications Ltd, 2009).

S. Rajaratnam School of International Studies, 'Plight of the Rohingya: ASEAN Credibility Again at Stake', 19 November 2012, http://www.fairobserver.com/region/central_south_asia/plight-rohingya-asean-credibility-again-stake/, accessed 25 April 2015.

Stamnes, Eli 'The Responsibility to Protect: Integrating Gender Perspectives in Policies and Practices', Global Responsibility to Protect 4/2: 172–197 (2012).

Stapleton, Timothy J. *A History of Genocide in Africa* (Santa Barbara, CA: Praeger, 2017).

Stoakes Emanuel 'Thailand human trafficking death toll far greater than feared, claims rights group,' The Guardian, 6 May 2015. Available at: http://www.theguardian.com/global-development/2015/may/06/thailand-human-trafficking-mass-grave-burma-rohingya-people.

Straus, Scott *Making and Unmaking Nations: The Origins and Dynamics of Genocide in Con¬temporary Africa* (Ithaca: Cornell University Press, 2015).

Streithfeld-Hall, Jaclyn D. 'Preventing Mass Atrocities in West Africa', Global Centre for the Responsibility to Protect, Occasional Paper Series, No.6, September 2015.

Sturman, Kathryn and Aïssatou Hayatou, 'The Peace and Security Council of the African Union: From Design to Reality' in Ulf Engel and J. Gomes Porto (eds.) *Africa's New Peace and Security Architecture: Promoting Norms, Institutionalizing Solutions, Global Security in a Changing World* (Ashgate, 2010): 57–76.

Sukma, Rizal 'The ASEAN Political Security Community (APSC): opportunities and constraints for R2P in Southeast Asia,' 25/1: 135–152 (2012).

Summary: Special Meeting on Irregular Migration in the Indian Ocean, 29 May 2015, Bangkok, Thailand, Reliefweb, 29 May 2015, from http://reliefweb.int/report/myanmar/summary-special-meeting-irregular-migration-indian-ocean-29-may-2015-bangkok-thailand, accessed on 24 March 2017.

Sun, Yun 'Myanmar's ASEAN Chairmanship: An Early Assessment', 23 September 2014, http://www.isn.ethz.ch/Digital-Library/Articles/Detail/?lng=en&id=183736, accessed 1 August 2015.

Sunstein, Cass R. 'Social norms and social roles.' Columbia law review (1996), pp. 903–968.

Sutthisunsanee, Sutthisunsanee Response of ASEAN to Human Rights Violations in Southeast Asia: Case studies of Cambodia and East Timor, Unpublished ma Thesis for the fulfillment of ma in Human Rights, Mahidol University, October 2006.

Statement by the Deputy Permanent Representative of the Republic of Indonesia to the United Nations at the Informal Interactive Dialogue on the Report of the Secretary General on 'Fulfilling our collective responsibility: international assistance and the responsibility to protect', New York, 8 September 2014.

Statement by Ambassador Karen Tan, Permanent Representative of Singapore to the United Nations, at the Informal Interactive Dialogue of the General Assembly on Responsibility to Protect, New York, 11 September 2013.

Statement by H.E. Ambassador Hussein Haniff, Permanent Representative of Malaysia to United Nations on 'Fulfilling our responsibility: international assistance and the responsibility to protect' New York, 8 September 2014.

Statement by H.E. Mr. Norachit Sinhaseni, Ambassador and Permanent Representative of Thailand to the United Nations, Intervention of Thailand at the unga informal interactive dialogue on the report of the Secretary General on R2P, 'Fulfilling our collective responsibility: International assistance and the r2p', New York, 8 September 2014.

Statement by H.E. Ambassador Le Hoai Trung Permanent Representative of the Socialist Republic of Viet Nam on behalf of Member States of the Association of Southeast Asian Nations at the Security Council Open Debate on Women, Peace and Security, 17 April 2013, http://www.vietnam-un.org/en/vnun.php?id=243&cid=20, 30 May 2015.

Statement of by Ms. Nguyen Phuong Nga, Permanent Mission of Viet Nam to the un, October 2014, http://peacewomen.org/sites/default/files/scwps2014_statement_vietnam_0.pdf, accessed 5 June 2015.

Tan, Hsien-Li *The ASEAN Intergovernmental Commission on Human Rights: Institutionalising Human Rights in Southeast Asia* (Cambridge University Press, 2011).

Tanyag, Maria 'Peace, Sex and Violence in Mindanao,' 15 August 2016, http://www.internationalaffairs.org.au/australian_outlook/peace-sex-and-violence-in-mindanao/ accessed 31 August 2016.

Tanyag, Maria 'Sexual & Gender based violence: Regional Consultation of the ASEAN Commission on Women and Children with Civil Society Organisations on the Implementation of Regional Plans of Actions on the Elimination of Violence against Women and Children,' Asia Pacific Outlook, April 2016, Issue 2 (Asia-Pacific Centre for the Responsibility to Protect).

Tay, Simon SC and Jesus Estanislao, 'The Relevance of asean : Crisis and Change' in Simon sc Tay, Jesus Estanislao and Hadi Soesastro (eds.), *A New asean in a New Millennium*, (Jakarta, csis, 2000).

Taylor, Ian 'Globalization and Regionalization in Africa: Reactions to Attempts at Neo-Liberal Regionalism', Review of International Political Economy, 10/2: 310–330 (2003).

Teitt, Sarah 'Women's Empowerment and Atrocities Prevention', 2014, http://www.e-ir.info/2014/11/11/womens-empowerment-and-atrocities-prevention/, accessed 21 June 2015.

Tetreault, Mary Ann 'Justice for All: Wartime Rape and Women's Human Rights', Global Governance 3/2:197–212 (1997).

The Star, 'Rohingya refugee issue now for Asean to solve, says Anifah', The Star Online, 25 April 2015, http://www.thestar.com.my/News/Nation/2015/04/25/Rohingya-refugee-issue-now-for-Asean-to-solve-says-Anifah/, accessed 5May 2015.

The Star, 'Asean needs to jointly address Rohingya refugee issue, says Najib,' The Star (Malaysia), 16 May 2015. Available at: http://www.thestar.com.my/News/Nation/2015/05/16/Najib-Asean-Rohingya-issue/.

Tonkin, Derek "The 2008 Constitution in the Context of Myanmar Reality," in Li Chenyang and Wilhelm Hofmeister (eds.) *Myanmar: Prospect for Change* (Singapore and Kunming: Select Publishing, Konrad Adenauer Stiftung and Yunnan University, 2009.

True, Jacqui 'The Political Economy of Gender in UN Peacekeeping,' in Dianne Otto and Gina Heathcote (eds), *Rethinking Peacekeeping, Gender Equality and Collective Security* (Palgrave Macmillan, 2014), pp. 243–262.

True, Jacqui *The Political Economy of Violence Against Women* (New York: Oxford University Press, 2012).

True, Jacqui 'Winning the Battle but Losing the War on Violence,' International Feminist Journal of Politics, 17/4: 554–572 (2015).

True, Jacqui 'Post-conflict economic reform is a Women, Peace and Security Issue,' 31 July 2016, http://wilpf.org/post-conflict-economic-reform-is-a-women-peace-and-security-issue/ accessed 31 August 2016.

True, Jacqui 'Explaining the global diffusion of the Women, Peace and Security agenda,' International Political Science Review 37/3: 307–323 (2016).

True, Jacqui and Maria Tanyag "Global Violence and Security from a Gendered Perspective," in Anthony Burke and Rita Parker (eds.), *Global Insecurity: Futures of Global Chaos and Governance* (Palgrave, 2017), pp. 43–63.

United Nations (UN), 'An Agenda for Peace', A/47/277 - S/24111, 17 June 1992.

UN, 'A More Secure World: Our Shared Responsibility', Report of the High Level Panel on Threats, Challenges and Change, A/59/565, 2 December 2004.

UN '2005 World Summit Outcome', UNGA Res. 60/1, 16 September 2005.

UN, *Framework of Analysis For Atrocity Crimes: A Tool for Prevention* (New York: United Nations 2014).

UN, 'Updated Statute of the International Criminal Tribunal for the Former Yugoslavia' September 2009, http://www.icty.org/x/file/Legal%20Library/Statute/statute_sept09_en.pdf, accessed 18 May 2015.

United Nations Conference on Trade and Development (UNCTAD), 2004, Trade Performance and Commodity Dependence,(Geneva: UNCTAD, 26 February).

United Nations Development Programme (UNDP) 'Human Development Report', 24 July 2014, http://hdr.undp.org/sites/default/files/hdr14-report-en-1.pdf, accessed 8 March 2016.

United Nations General Assembly (UNGA) 'World Summit Outcome Document,' Res. 60/1, 16 September 2005.

United Nations General Assembly (UNGA), 'Report of the Special Rapporteur on the situation of Human Rights in Myanmar, Yanghee Lee,' A/HRC/28/72, 23 Mar 2015.

United Nations High Commission for Refugees (UNHCR) 'State Parties to the 1951 Convention Relating to the Status of Refugees and the 1967 Protocol,' April 2015. Available at: http://www.unhcr.org/protect/PROTECTION/3b73b0d63.pdf.

UNHCR, 'Commitments for Protection and Solution in Osce Region,' (Geneva: UNHCR, 2013).

UNHCR, 'Overview of UNHCR's Operational Strategies in the Asia-Pacific Region,' (Geneva: UNHCR, 2013).

UNHCR, 'World at War: UNCHR Global Trends, Forced Displacement in 2014', http://unhcr.org/556725e69.html, p. 50.

UNHCR, '*Global Trends: Forced Displacement in 2014*', (Geneva: UNHCR, 2015).

UN Human Rights Council (UNHRC) 'Report of the Commission of Inquiry on Human Rights in Eritrea', A/hrc/29/42, 4 June 2015, http://daccess-dds-ny.un.org/doc/UNDOC/GEN/G15/114/50/PDF/G1511450.pdf?OpenElement.

UNHRC, 'Report of the Special Rapporteur on the Human Rights of Internally Displaced Persons, Chaloka Beyani', 4 April 2014, A/HRC/26/33, 16.

United Nations Population Fund (UNFPA), *Shelter from the Storm: State of the World Population 2015* (New York: UNFPA, 2015).

Unpublished report on Countering Violent Extremism - A Workshop organised by WANEP, Accra - Ghana May 2015.

United Nations Security Council (UNSC), S/Res/2171 2014, Preambular Clause 9, http://www.un.org/ga/search/view_doc.asp?symbol=S/RES/2171(2014), accessed 23 June 2015.

UNSC, Resolution 1706 (2006), S/RES/1706 (2006), 31 August 2006.

UNSC, 'Letter dated 24 May 1994 from the Secretary-General to the President of the Security Council' (S/1994/674), 27 May 1994.

UN Women, 'Indonesia Fact Sheet', http://www.unwomen-eseasia.org/docs/factsheets/03%20INDONESIA%20factsheet.pdf, accessed 13 November 2014

UN Women, Peace and Security: In Brief, 2013, http://www.unwomen.org/en/what-we-do/peace-and-security accessed 31 August 2016.

UN Women, Preventing Conflict, Transforming Justice, Securing the Peace: A Global Study on the Implementation of United Nations Security Council Resolution 1325, 2015, http://wps.unwomen.org/en accessed 31 August 2016.

Veneracion-Rallonza, Maria Lourdes 'Grounding the International Norm on Women, Peace and Security: The Role of Domestic Norm Entrepreneurs and the Challenges Ahead', Femina Politica 22/2: 67–85 (2013).

Veneracion-Rallonza, Maria Lourdes 'Building the Women, Peace and Security Agenda in the ASEAN through Multi-Focal Norm Entrepreneurship,' Global Responsibility to Protect 8: 158–179 (2016).

Veneracion-Rallonza, Maria Lourdes and Miguel Niccolo Rallonza, 'Women Count: Security Council Resolution 1325– Civil Society Monitoring Report, Philippines', WE Act 1325 and gnwp report, 9 January 2015, http://weact1325.org/wp-content/uploads/2012/04/Women-Count-2014_Phil-Report_COMPLETE-VERSION.02.13.15.pdf, accessed 30 May 2015.

Vienna Declaration and Plan of Action para. 5, http://www.ohchr.org/EN/ProfessionalInterest/Pages/Vienna.aspx, accessed 13 April 2015.

Vogt, Margaret A. (ed) *The Liberian Crisis and ECOMOG: A Bold Attempt at Regional Peace keeping* (Lagos, Nigeria: Gabumo Publishing, 1992).

Wane, El-Ghassim, Charles Mwaura, Shewit Hailu, Simone Kopfmüller, Doug Bond, Ulf Engel and João Gomes Porto, 'The Continental Early Warning System: Methodology and Approach' in Ulf Engel and J. Gomes Porto (eds.) *Africa's New Peace and Security Architecture: Promoting Norms, Institutionalizing Solutions, Global Security in a Changing World* (Ashgate, 2010): 91–110.

West Africa Network for Peacebuyildig (WANEP), 'National Early Warning Systems (NEWS) in West Africa', WANEP Concept Paper, July 2009.

WANEP, 'Transitions and Tensions in West Africa: Building on the Strength and Bridging the Gap in the ECOWAS Protocol on Democracy and Good Governance', WANEP Policy Brief, November 2014.

Weiss, Thomas *Humanitarian Intervention*, (Cambridge : Polity Press, Second Edition, 2013).

Welsh, Jennifer 'Norm Contestation and the Responsibility to Protect', Global Responsibility to Protect, 5/4: 365–396 (2013).

Wendt, Alexander *Social Theory and International Politics* (Cambridge: Cambridge University Press, 1999).

Wiener, Antje *A Theory of Contestation* (Heidelberg: Springer, 2014).

Williams, Paul D. 'From non-intervention to non-indifference: the origins and development of the African Union's security culture' African Affairs 106/423: 253–279 (2007).

Williams, Paul D. 'The "Responsibility to Protect", Norm Localisation, and African International Society', Global Responsibility to Protect 1/3: 392–416 (2009).

Williams, Paul D. and Jürgen Haacke, 'Regional Approaches to Conflict Management', in Chester A. Crocker, Fen Osler Hampson and Pamela R Aall (eds.) *Rewiring Regional Security in a Fragmented World* (Washington, DC: US Institute of Peace Press, 2011): 49–74.

Williams, Paul D. 'Enhancing U.S. Support for Peace Operations in Africa', Centre for Preventive Action, Council on Foreign Relations, Council Special Report, No.73, May 2015.

Williams, Paul D. and Solomon A. Dersso, *Saving Strangers and Neighbors: Advancing UN-AU Cooperation on Peace Operations*, (New York: International Peace Institute, February 2015).

Win, U Khin Maung Deputy Minister for Foreign Affairs of the Union of Myanmar, "Myanmar Roadmap to Democracy: The Way Forward," Seminar on Understanding Myanmar, 27–28 January 2004, MICT Park, Yangon, Myanmar Institute of Strategic and International Studies, from http://www.ibiblio.org/obl/docs/KMWroadmap104.htm, accessed on 6 February 2017.

Xiong, David Han Guo 'Rohingya Refugee Crisis: Testing Malaysia's Asean Chairmanship,' RSIS Commentary, no. 128 (2015).

Yih, Ben Lih "Malaysia migrant mass graves: police reveal 139 sites, some with multiple corpses." The Guardian.com, 25 May 2015, from https://www.theguardian.com/world/2015/may/25/malaysia-migrant-mass-graves-police-reveal-139-sites-some-with-multiple-corpses, accessed on 23 March 2017.

Young, Marion I. "The Logic of Masculinist Protection: Reflections on the Current Security State," Signs 29/1: 1–25 (2003).

Yuval-Davis, *Nira Gender and Nation* (London: Sage Publications, 1997).

Index

Note: Page numbers followed by '*n*' refer to notes.